Card Games for Everyone

By the same author

KNOW THE GAME PATIENCE
ORIGINAL CARD GAMES
TEACH YOURSELF CARD GAMES FOR THREE
TEACH YOURSELF CARD GAMES FOR FOUR
TEACH YOURSELF CARD GAMES FOR TWO
ALL THE BEST CARD GAMES
TEACH YOURSELF POKER AND BRAG
THE PENGUIN BOOK OF PATIENCE
THE PENGUIN BOOK OF CARD GAMES
THE PENGUIN BOOK OF WORD GAMES

Card Games for Everyone

David Parlett

HODDER AND STOUGHTON
LONDON SYDNEY AUCKLAND TORONTO

Note: Much of the material in this book was first published in the Teach Yourself series under these titles: *Card Games for Two, Card Games for Three, Card Games for Four, Poker and Brag.* Some chapters have been rewritten and a considerable amount of new material has been added especially for this edition.

Playing cards used in illustrations are reproduced by courtesy of Waddingtons Playing Card Co. Ltd.

British Library Cataloguing in Publication Data

Parlett, David
    Card games for everyone.
    1. Cards
    I. Title
    795.4   GV1243

ISBN 0–340–32007–9

To
Andrew and Fiona Parlett
a latish wedding present

CONTENTS

INTRODUCTION

AN INVITATION TO CARDS

Cards are much older than most people think, though still young by comparison with games of the Ludo, Backgammon and Chess families. Younger than dice, of course; but older than dominoes. They have indeed been popular in the west for over 500 years, and presumably popular some time before that in the 'mysterious East', from which they seem first to have reached the mainland of Europe – via Italy – in the 1370s.

(Some charlatans pretend that ordinary playing cards derive from fortune-telling tarot cards, whose history is supposedly even more ancient, if not more mysterious and oriental. Have none of this. Tarots were invented in the 15th century and subsequently added to the standard pack. They have always been used primarily for playing games – still are, in many parts of Europe – and only became favoured tools of the occultists several hundred years later.)

Several different reasons have been suggested for their early popularity and the way in which card games spread over the continent like wildfire – or perhaps rather like the Black Death which had preceded them by barely a decade. One reason is that they appealed more to women, unlike dice and most board games which had hitherto been the only table games in general use. Another is that most games previously available were restricted to two players, whereas card games are generally playable by any small group of people. Yet another is that, with the growth of paper supplies and development of printing, cards became easy to produce and cheap to come by – true heralds of today's throw-away consumer society.

No doubt their early popularity was a combination of several such reasons, but I think the most important of all was the rich variety of different games, and different types of game, to which these ingenious and pretty little bits of pasteboard can be turned. One-player games alone range from the idiocy of Auld Lang Syne to the elegance of Belle Lucie. Two may play

Cribbage over a pint of bitter, or Bézique over a glass of crème de menthe (or eight-pack Bézique over a pint of crème de menthe). Three may be carried away by Black Maria, or don their *lederhosen* and experiment with Skat. Four may remain tight lipped at Bridge or declare wild cards with abandon at Canasta. Five parents can get as much fun out of Poker as five children out of Snap, provided they approach it the right way. Yes, the extraordinary and distinctive feature of cards is that they are not one game, suited to one type of mind as are Chess and Backgammon, but a whole world of games offering something to every age, taste and temperament.

Small wonder, then, that a recent national survey carried out on behalf of Waddingtons Playing Card Co. Ltd. showed that no less than 60 per cent of the adult population say that they do play cards, with varying degrees of frequency, and that up to 75 per cent own a pack of cards even though they may not count themselves as players. More than one quarter of the 20 million acknowledged card players play at least once a week, every week.

To discover what the most popular card games were, respondents were asked what game or games they had played within the last twelve months. In descending order of popularity, the results were: Rummy (7·25 million played); Whist – other than Solo, but possibly including Knockout (6·4 m); Pontoon (6 m); Brag (5 m); Cribbage (3·8 m); Newmarket (3·4 m); Solo (2 m); Poker (2 m); Contract Bridge (1·7 m); Canasta (0·85 m). Some 5 m mentioned various other games, which I would expect to include Nap quite prominently.

Bridge lovers and Bridge haters alike may be surprised by the game's low turnout in view of its high status. More books are published each year on Bridge than on any other card game – indeed than on all other card games put together, and probably more than on any other indoor game except Chess – while every serious newspaper and magazine runs a regular Bridge column, and even television producers have essayed its presentation on the small screen. (Thus demonstrating to non-addicts exactly what is meant by the word 'dummy'. For glamour and excitement the result is not a patch on Test Card C.)

One reason for this anomaly is that Bridge lends itself to deeper analysis and technique development than many other card games. Of those listed above, for example, only Whist, Solo, Poker and possibly Canasta would be capable of responding well to such attention. The other is that for most of its players Bridge is not 'a' card game, or their favourite of several card games: it is *the* fashionable activity of a particular class of people who have no interest in games generally but regard the playing of Bridge as a social accomplishment, like seducing chambermaids or knowing when asparagus is in season. In other words, Bridge is not popular; it is merely prominent. Similar comments might be made about Canasta and Poker, also prominent games but with comparatively little numerical support. Canasta was a craze of the 1950s, and lingers on as second string to the Bridge player's bow. Poker, although one of the most popular games in America, is chiefly played in Britain by people whose occupation or temperament renders them most vulnerable to American culture, such as media men and aspiring gangsters. (The equivalent folk game in Britain is Brag, just as Whist or Solo is the equivalent of Bridge, and Rummy is of Canasta.)

Apart from Nap, a surprising omission from the list is Patience or Solitaire in any of its hundreds of forms. Presumably it would have been included in the five million 'other' responses. It does figure, however, in the only other comparable survey that I know of, which was made of card players in America in 1940 or thereabouts. (My source, Ostrow's *The Complete Card Player*, is somewhat vague in its reportage.) The best *known* card games of the time were, from highest to lowest, Rummy, Solitaire, Contract Bridge, Poker, Auction Bridge, Pinochle, Hearts, and Five Hundred, but the most frequently *played* arranged themselves in the following descending order: Contract, Pinochle, Auction, Poker, Rummy, Five Hundred, Whist, Solitaire, Hearts. Contract Bridge probably still remains high on the list, since it is an essentially American game, though the proportion may have dropped. At the time the survey was made, less than ten years had elapsed since Contract Bridge had been made a national craze, largely through a brilliantly engineered publicity exercise on the part of Ely Culbertson. Auction Bridge had evidently then not been entirely displaced by Contract, but I doubt if anyone plays it any more except as a curiosity. Poker, Five Hundred and Rummy also originated in America. Five Hundred has probably disappeared by now, though it has had the strange good fortune to have become virtually the national card game of Australia. Pinochle, brought with them by German immigrants in the middle to late 19th century, retains a following which I should say is paralleled by that of Cribbage in Britain. The reason why Whist comes high on the British list and low on the American is the reverse of that for the discrepancy between Bridge and Poker on opposite sides of the Atlantic, namely, that Whist, like Brag and Cribbage, is of English origin.

All of which goes to show that card games exhibit variety and flexibility not only according to age and temperament, but also according to nationality and the passage of historical time. The aim of this book is to present a wide selection of games that have been popular with various groups of people at various times – to demonstrate the variety of cards rather than emphasise one or two favoured games at the expense of others. They are arranged in sections, chiefly according to the number of players for which each game is best suited. This should not be taken too literally, however. Several games, though designed for a given number of players, can readily be adapted for other numbers. In most cases, however, it would be advisable to play with the recommended number first, as many games only release their full flavour when the most suitable number is adhered to. Games which are not expressly designed for two, three or four players used to be known as 'round games', a term which I reintroduce in the appropriate section following games for four. A final section is devoted to round games which are essentially gambling games, in the sense that they are usually played for money, or are designed for those curious people who play cards for no other reason than the redistribution of wealth.

BEGINNER'S GUIDE AND TECHNICAL TERMS

We have already seen that the greatest virtue of cards as playing equipment is the tremendous variety of games for which they can be used. But there is a bonus to that – a complementary virtue of equal value. It is that the thousands of games that have been devised for them are mostly variations on a few basic themes, so that they can all be grouped together into a quite manageable number of distinctive *families* of games. How many families there are depends on what standards you use for relating them, but 'about twenty' will give some idea of the range involved. And even these families are not entirely dissimilar from one another, most of them making use of a few basic features which might be described as logical consequences of the way a pack of cards is constituted. Just as every substance in the universe is made up of a few basic elements in various combinations, so every card game is a unique mixture of a few basic gaming elements. This makes it easy to pick up new card games once you have met one or two of each distinguishable type. The following 'beginner's guide' introduces most of the features common to traditional card games and the technical terms used to refer to them.

The pack (or *deck*, an older English word still used in America). There are 52 cards in a standard or full pack, divided into four *suits* of 13 cards each. The suits are distinguished by red or black symbols, black suits being *spades* (♠) and *clubs* (♣), red ones *hearts* (♡) and *diamonds* (♢).

Each suit contains 13 *ranks*. These consist of the *numerals* (or *spot cards*) from 1 to 10, followed by three *court* cards: Jack, Queen, King. The 'one' is called 'Ace' and has the letter 'A' in the corner. In most games it is not the lowest card but the highest, outranking even the King. The Jack was formerly called the Knave, and still is by more ancient players; but this begins with the same letter as King, which is inconvenient in writing about cards and also useless as an *index* (the sign in the top left corner of a card telling you its rank and suit), so Jack it is.

In writing about cards it is also inconvenient to type or print two characters for the '10' of each suit where all the other ranks need only one. In this book, therefore, I use the initial 'T' for 'Ten' – but don't look for it on the cards themselves.

To summarise, the normal ranking order in each suit is, from highest to lowest:

A K Q J T 9 8 7 6 5 4 3 2

This order is changed in some card games, but for the time being it may be regarded as standard.

The Joker. Most packs contain two easily distinguishable Jokers. Very few games make any use of them, though they can, for fun, be introduced into almost any game provided you invent the rules to go with them. (Any resemblance between the modern Joker and the card known as The Fool in tarot packs is purely coincidental. The Joker does not derive from the Fool.)

Length of pack. Although all games use four suits, they do not necessarily use all 13 cards of a suit, but may be stripped to produce short packs. The commonest short pack is one of 32 cards, with Ace high and Seven low in each suit. This may be made by stripping out all numerals from Two to Six, but 32-card packs are widely sold on the Continent and are readily available from specialist game shops in Britain. Other commonly used short packs are those of:

40 cards   A K Q J 7 6 5 4 3 2 in each suit
36 cards   A K Q J T 9 8 7 6 in each suit
24 cards   A K Q J T 9 in each suit

Sometimes games make use of lengthened packs, made by shuffling two or more packs together. Canasta, for instance, uses two full packs each with its two Jokers, making 2 × 54 or

108 cards in all. Short packs may also be doubled up. Pinochle uses a 2 × 24 pack (48 cards), and there are versions of Bézique for two, four, six and even eight 32-card packs shuffled together – up to 216 cards in all!

Tricks and trumps. Most card games involve the playing and winning of *tricks.* One player *leads* to the trick by playing any card he likes. Each player in turn then contributes one card to the trick, usually being obliged by the rules of the game to *follow suit* if possible – that is, play one of the same suit as the card led. All the cards so played constitute the trick, which is won by the person who played the highest ranking card of the suit led. The winner of the trick squares the cards up into a neat pile and places the trick face down on the table before him. He then has the privilege of leading to the next trick.

If a player cannot follow suit because he has none left (he is said to *be void* or *have a void* in that suit), he may play any card, but cannot thereby win the trick no matter how high ranking it may be. Thus even the lowest card of a suit can win a trick, if it is led to the trick and no one can follow suit.

Unless, however, there is a *trump* suit. *Trump* is a corruption of *triumph*: it means a suit which by previous agreement beats all the others. In this event, if a non-trump or *plain* suit is led, a player who is void in that suit may (if he wishes) play a card from the trump suit. This beats the led card, regardless of rank, and will win the trick, unless a later player plays a higher ranking trump. If trumps are led, of course, the trick can only be won by the highest card of the suit led. Thus the highest trump is usually the one unbeatable card of the pack.

Whether or not there is a trump suit, and how it is chosen if so, depends on the game being played. A common method of choosing it is by the process of *bidding* in an *auction.* This means that the trump suit is selected by the player or partnership who undertakes to win the greatest number of tricks in return for the privilege of choosing trumps. Whoever makes the highest bid is called the *bidder* or *declarer,* and his undertaking is a *contract.*

The mechanics of trick play described above are what I refer

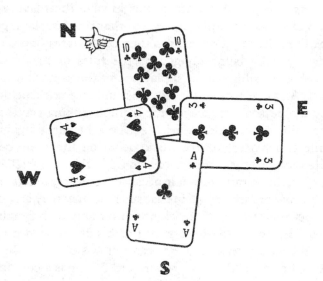

FIGURE I

How tricks are played, illustrating 'the usual rules of trick-taking'. Hearts are trumps. North, to start, decides to open a round of clubs and leads the Ten. East, obliged to follow suit but unable to beat the Ten, discards the lowest club he has. South has the Ace, and expects it to win the tricks. But West has no clubs at all, and is therefore entitled to play any trump (hearts) and so win the trick, regardless of rank. He would have been permitted by the rules to discard from any other suit, but could not then have won the trick. West takes the trick, and it is now his turn to lead.

to in this book as 'normal rules of trick play', but these are varied in some games. In some, for example, it is obligatory to trump if you cannot follow suit; in others it is merely optional.

Melds. A meld is a group of cards which go together in some way to form a distinctive combination. The commonest melds are the *sequence* and the *group* or *set*. A sequence is three or more cards of the same suit which are consecutive in rank, such as A–2–3 or T–J–Q–K–A. (Ace often counts high or low as preferred.) A group is three or more cards of the same rank, e.g. Aces, Tens or whatever. Games of the Rummy family, of which Canasta is the most complex example, involve collecting cards together so as to form melds, the object being to get rid of all the cards from your hand by melding them in related groups on the table.

Some games involve melds *and* tricks, the most noteworthy examples being Piquet, Bézique and Pinochle. Others, particularly Poker, involve more complex combinations of related cards, which are not called melds although they work on exactly the same principle.

Values. Many games involving neither tricks nor melds are concerned only with the numerical or arithmetical value of cards. In Pontoon or Blackjack, for example, the object is to get cards totalling as close to 21 as possible, counting courts as 10 each. Other games with a strong arithmetical element include Cribbage and Cassino.

Values may be attached to cards in trick taking games, so that the object is not just to win tricks but to capture valuable cards in them. Such games, sometimes known as complex trick taking games (as opposed to simple ones, in which only the number of tricks counts), are not native to Britain but are widespread on the Continent. Notable examples are the German national card game, Skat, and Pinochle, an American game of German and French origins.

PRACTICE AND PROCEDURE

A *deal* or *round* or *hand* of cards means all the play that takes place between one deal and the next. Sometimes a deal can be a game in itself; more usually, a game consists of a number of deals. This may be either a specific number of deals, or as many deals as it takes for one player to reach a predetermined target score.

Questions of seating and partnerships do not normally arise in domestic play, but may be determined, if desired, as follows. To choose partners, players draw cards from a shuffled pack, those drawing the two highest cards being partners. The player drawing the highest card has first choice of seating, and his partner sits opposite. In non-partnership games, the drawer of the highest card has first choice of seats, second highest has second choice, and so on. For these purposes Ace usually counts low, with King the highest card. In case of a tie, draw again.

Drawing may also be carried out to determine who has the first deal. Everything that goes in turns – the responsibility of dealing, the turn to bid or to play a card etc. – passes to the left in British and American play, that is, in a clockwise direction as viewed from the top.

Before every deal the cards must be shuffled, unless the rules of the game specifically state otherwise. (There are some players who think it clever or fun to play with a 'stacked' or unshuffled pack, but this silly practice subordinates skill to memory and is chiefly followed by players more interested in gambling than card playing.) Anybody who wishes may shuffle, but the dealer has the right to shuffle last.

Before dealing, the dealer should offer the pack to be 'cut' by the player on his right. The purpose of this practice is to prevent the bottom card from being known, as it may be seen during the shuffle. The pack is placed face down on the table. Dealer's right hand neighbour lifts off the top half (approximately) and places it face down beside the bottom. Dealer completes the cut by placing the bottom half on what was formerly the top. At least half a dozen cards should remain in each half during the cut.

Whether cards are dealt singly or in batches of two or more at a time depends on the rules of the particular game being played – if it is not specified, deal singly. The first card or batch goes to the player at dealer's left; the next to the player at his left; and so on around the table, so that the dealer receives the last card or batch himself. Cards are always dealt face down unless otherwise specified.

A misdeal may be claimed if cards are dealt in the wrong order or if any card is exposed during the course of the deal. If at least one player insists on a redeal, the dealer must gather the cards, shuffle, cut, and deal again.

In domestic or otherwise informal play, as is assumed to apply throughout this book, there is no need to follow elaborate rules and rituals to cover irregularities of play, such as playing out of turn. If the players cannot come to some amicable agreement as to sorting the irregularity out, they should not be playing together in the first place! On the assumption that the irregularity was a genuine mistake, it is reasonable to try and restore the position before it occurred and to continue play from that point.

A common irregularity is the *revoke*, which occurs in trick taking games when a player fails to follow suit even though able to do so. If this is discovered before the trick has been quitted and the next one led, two cards may be taken back and replayed up to the point of error. The revoker should then leave his wrongly played card face up on the table and play it on demand from an opponent when legally able to do so.

In a game where one player is playing solo against the combined forces of the others, it is reasonable to decree that an irregularity on his part loses him the game or bid in question, while an error on the part of his opponent results in his winning it by default.

It is bad manners to take one's cards up before all have been dealt; to speak during play other than when required to do so or to draw attention to procedures or irregularities; to look at another player's cards even if he has finished playing with them; to criticise another person's play, especially one's partner's; and to bore everyone with post mortems when the play is over!

1. CARD GAMES FOR CHILDREN

Stationers and toyshops today are full of specially designed card games for children, most of which, when you come to look at them closely, are merely prettified rehashes of traditional children's card games such as Snap, Donkey, Old Maid, and their relatives. There's no harm in that, of course, except that they don't really lead anywhere. By letting children play the same games with *real* cards you give them an earlier start in the manipulation of numbers and symbols, and enable them to graduate to adult card games at their own speed. By the time children's hands are big enough to handle playing cards, their minds are sufficiently developed to get as much pleasure out of the abstract patterns in which cards abound as they did out of the cartoon donkeys and so on which were necessary to them at an earlier stage of development.

We hear much about the educational value of games these days – manufacturers tend to talk about it as if it were a special ingredient of their own invention. In fact there is not a great deal of difference between playing and learning as far as children are concerned, and it is unnecessary to point out those aspects of formal education which may be brought out by individual card games, especially the overtly numerical ones. Of equal importance, but less frequently mentioned, is the early training offered by card games in social behaviour. A game of cards is an organised pattern of behaviour with rules designed to ensure that it works properly to everyone's mutual satisfaction. There are few better ways of helping children to mature into law abiding citizens than by accustoming them early to the pleasures of abiding by the laws and rules of games. And there are few cheaper or more enjoyable ways of achieving this than by putting cards into their hands at an early age.

Authors

From four to eight players can play Authors, using a full 52-card pack. Authors is so called because when first invented it was played with special cards labelled with the names of famous authors and their works. This was reckoned to be 'educational' and therefore A Good Thing.

The cards are shuffled and dealt round one at a time as far as they will go. It doesn't matter if some people get more than others. The object of play is to get rid of all your cards in sets of four, e.g. all four Aces, or Jacks, or Sixes, and so on.

The player at dealer's left starts by choosing any other player (by name or by pointing) and asking them for all the cards they have of a particular rank. The asker cannot choose any old rank, but only one that he has at least one of in his own hand. For example, if he has one or more Tens he may say 'Tens, please'. The person asked must then hand over all the Tens he has, if any. If successful, the asker then gets another turn and does the same thing, asking the same or another player for cards of any rank of which he holds at least one. This continues until somebody who is asked for a particular rank does not have any. In this event he replies 'None', and takes over the turn to ask somebody else for cards.

Each time a player manages to get all four of a given rank in his hand, he shows them to the others and lays them in a neat pile on the table before him. The winner is the first person to get rid of all his cards, partly by giving them away and partly by discarding them in groups of four.

Beggar-my-Neighbour

Also known as 'Beat your Neighbour out of Doors', this must be the second card game I ever learnt after Snap. It may be played by any number from two upwards. A full pack of 52 cards is used, though with a smaller number of players you may prefer to speed the game up by removing the lower cards, e.g. all the Twos, Threes, Fours and so on until you have a size of pack that seems to work best for the number of players. Since players drop out one by one until only the winner is left, it may be useful to start with a 52-card pack and finish with (say) one of 32 cards, with nothing lower than the Sevens.

Deal all the cards around, face down, as far as they will go. It doesn't matter if some get more than others. Each player holds his pile of cards face down in one hand and plays from the top at each turn, or leaves his pile on the table if his hand is not big enough to hold it.

The object of the game is to win all the cards.

Starting at dealer's left, each player in turn takes the top card of his pile and plays it face up to the centre of the table to form a waste pile. This continues, one card at a time, until someone plays a Jack, Queen, King or Ace, which calls for the next player in turn to 'pay' him. Thus if your card is a Jack, the player on your left must pay you one card by turning his next card face up on the pile. If his card is not a payment card, you win the whole pile. Similarly, if you play a Queen he must pay you two cards, while a King calls for three and an Ace for four. If the next player's two, three or four cards are not themselves payment cards, you win the whole pile and are the next to play.

If, however, your neighbour in paying you turns up a Jack, Queen, King or Ace, then your turn ends, he stops paying, and the player on his left has to pay the appropriate number of cards.

Each time you win a pile of cards, you turn it face down and put it at the bottom of your own pile. Anyone who plays his last card drops out of play. Eventually all players will drop out, leaving a winner.

Cheat

This is a good game to find out who is the best at cheating, because he is bound to win and you can avoid playing anything else with him for the rest of the day. It works best with four or five players and a single 52-card pack. If more take part, it may be better to use two packs shuffled together. (Another version, called *I Doubt It*, is on p. 19.)

Deal all the cards out as far as they will go: it doesn't matter if some have more than others. Hold your cards up so that you can see them but nobody else can. The object of play is to be the first to get rid of all your cards. (Warning: this may take a long time, so if you have anything important to do, do it before you start.)

The player at dealer's left starts by playing any card face *down* to the table, and announcing what rank it may or may not be. For example, he may say 'Seven', or 'King', or anything else like that, and the card he played may or may not actually be a Seven or a King. The only way of finding out is to call 'Cheat!'. In this case he turns his card up. If he was not cheating, and the card is what he said, then the person who accused him of cheating must add that card to his hand, and the one who was challenged then plays another card in the same way. If the challenge was correct, and the card was different from what he said, then the challenged player must take it back, and the turn to play passes to his left. However, it is not much fun to accuse anyone of cheating when there is only one card on the table. The real object is to get someone to take a whole pile.

So let us assume that the first player played a card, said 'Seven', and was not challenged. Then the player on his left is next in turn. He must say 'Eight', and play a card face down on top of the first one. The player on his left then says 'Nine' while adding to the face down pile, and so on – Ten, Jack, Queen, King, Ace, Two, etc.

At any time, of course, you can shout 'Cheat!' if you think the player is putting out a card different from what he says it is. He then turns it up, and if you are right, he takes the pile; if you are wrong, you take it.

Simple, isn't it?

Donkey

This game is also known as Pig, the difference being in the shape of the tail, or the noise it makes, or possibly the smell. But as all this is completely unimportant it might as well be called Aardvark, Bandicoot, Carcharodontosaurus or any other animal you take a particular fancy to.

From three to thirteen may play, but five or six is about right. From one pack, select as many groups of four as there are players. For example, with five players you might use all four Aces, Fives, Tens, Queens and Kings, and so on.

Shuffle these cards together and deal them all round one at a time, so that each player receives exactly four. Hold your cards up so that only you can see what you've got.

Each player now takes one card from his hand and passes it face down to the player at his left. Everyone does this together, not one by one round the table. The same thing is then done again, and again, and again, until . . .

Until one player gets all four cards of the same rank in his hand. He then, as slyly and quietly as possible, lays his hand of cards face down on the table and rests one finger wisely against his nose. Anyone who notices him doing so also puts his cards down and rubs his nose, even if he hasn't got four of a kind. Eventually, everybody will notice what's going on and do the same thing. One player, however, will be the last to do so, and he is the donkey (pig, aardvark, bandicoot, carcharodonto-saurus, etc.) for that round.

There are various ways of celebrating the result. The donkey may have to pay a forfeit, or pay a certain number of counters to the player who got four of a kind. Another good way is as follows: write everyone's name down on a piece of paper. The first time a player is a donkey the letter D is written by his name, followed by an O the second time, and so on until he has lost six times and is the ultimate donkey for the whole game.

Or carcharodontosaurus, if you want the game to go on all day and all night.

Fish

Fish is like Authors, only more nourishing!

From three to six may play, using a 52-card pack, and the object is to collect matching groups of four – e.g. four Aces, four Jacks, etc. Deal five cards to each player and leave the rest face down in the middle as a stockpile.

The player at dealer's left starts by choosing another player

and asking him for a particular card – ♡6, for example, or
♠Q, but only if he already holds a Six or a Queen. He may not
ask for any rank of which he does not hold at least one already.
If the chosen person has the required card he surrenders it to
the asker, who then gets another turn and may ask any player
for any other card. If not, the chosen person says 'Fish', or
'Go and fish'. It then becomes his turn to choose someone and
ask for a card, and the disappointed asker must draw the top
card of the stock and add it to his hand.

Play continues in this way (except that, when the stock is
exhausted, it continues without fishing) until one player gets
rid of all his cards. There are two ways of getting rid of cards.
One is giving them away when asked for them. The other is by
placing four of the same kind in a pile in front of you whenever
you complete such a set, after showing it to the other players
to prove you have it. If more than one go out at the same time,
the one with more groups of four in front of him wins.

Go Boom

Any number may play from two to twelve, using an ordinary
pack of cards or two packs shuffled together if there are more
than six taking part. Once again the object is to be the first to
get rid of all your cards.

Seven cards are dealt to each player and the rest laid face
down in the middle of the table as a stockpile. The player at
dealer's left starts by playing any card face up to the table. Each
in turn after that must play a card on top of it, and it must, if
possible, be a card of the same suit. A player who has no cards
of that suit may instead play a card of the same rank as the
first card – e.g. if the first card was ♡6 and you have no hearts,
you may instead play a Six of any suit. What happens if you
have no Six either? Well, in that case you must keep drawing
cards from the top of the stockpile and adding them to your
hand until you draw a card which you *can* play – any heart or
any Six – whereupon you thankfully do so, and it is the turn of
the next player to follow suit or play a card of the same rank
as the first.

When everybody has played, the trick (meaning the pile of cards made by each person playing one) is taken and laid aside face down by the person who won it – that is, whoever played the highest card of the suit which was first led – and he continues the game by leading any card to the next trick. If two packs are used, and identical highest cards are played, the first one played beats the second.

When there are no cards left in the stockpile, anyone who cannot follow suit or match the first rank merely knocks on the table and misses his turn.

As soon as one player plays the last card from his hand he calls 'Boom' and wins. He scores the total value of all cards left in the other players' hands, for which purpose Jacks, Queens and Kings count 10 each, Ace counts 1 and the others follow according to their numbers.

The overall winner is the first to reach 250 points.

I Doubt It

This is a variation on the game of Cheat described earlier. The cards are dealt as far as they will go and the player at dealer's left starts by placing one, two, three or four cards face *down* on the table and saying 'Aces'. The next in turn does the same, saying 'Twos', the next 'Threes' and so on. The object is to get rid of all your cards first, for which purpose you are allowed to 'cheat' by not actually putting out all the cards you say. For instance, if you say 'Aces', and put out three cards of which one or more is *not* an Ace, then you are cheating. This is fine if you can get away with it. However, anyone who thinks another player is cheating may say 'I doubt it'. The challenged player must then show all the cards he has just laid down. If he cheated, he must add the whole pile of cards so far played to his hand. If he was telling the truth, it is the challenger who has to take them up. The next person to play is the one who won the challenge, and the eventual winner is the first to get rid of all his cards.

Memini

The fact that I do not like memory games (though I can't remember why) has not stopped me from inventing them, and here's one that has not been published before.

It needs at least three players and up to six, but I wouldn't advise a greater number. It also requires two packs of cards, which should be of different back designs or colours so as not to get mixed up. If only three or four are taking part both packs should be stripped to 24 cards by removing all ranks lower than Nine, unless you really want to play it the hard way.

A game consists of as many rounds as there are players, since each one must take turns to be the dealer, who does not take part in the memorising. The dealer shuffles one pack and deals them all out evenly amongst the other players, receiving none for himself. If six play, so that there are five 'other players', they receive only ten cards each and the other two are left face down out of play.

Each player now takes his hand of cards, holds them so that only he can see them, and tries to memorise them all. While this is going on, the dealer shuffles the other pack and keeps an eye on the clock. After a suitable amount of time – say half a minute, but you can vary this – the dealer says 'Time up', at which everyone must lay his hand of cards face down in a pile in front of him.

Now the dealer turns cards face up one by one from the second pack, announces what each one is and lays it face up on the table before him. Anyone who thinks such a card matches one in his original hand says 'Mine!' and takes it. If nobody claims a card, the dealer waits a second or two and then turns the next, after which the unclaimed card can no longer be called for. If more than one person claims a card, the dealer adds it face up to a separate pile of duplicate claims.

When the last card has been turned and either claimed or not, each player compares his original hand of cards with those he has claimed and scores as follows. For each perfect match, 1 point. For a non-match (a wrongly claimed card), minus 1 point. For a card in his original hand matching a card in the duplicate pile, 2 points.

The scores are carried forward to the next deal and the winner is the player with the highest total when everybody has had a turn as dealer.

My Ship Sails

This is a collecting game for three to seven players, using an ordinary pack of 52 cards. The object is to be the first to collect seven cards of the same suit – spades, hearts, clubs or diamonds.

Deal seven cards each and place the rest face down in a pile to one side (they have no further part in the game). Everybody looks at their cards and places one of them face down on the table at their left. The one they get rid of in this way will be of a suit they are not planning to collect. When everyone is ready, they each pick up the card lying at their right and add it to their hand. If anyone now has seven of the same suit he says 'My ship sails' and lays his cards face up on the table, thereby winning the game. If not, there is another round of discarding, and as many more rounds as may be necessary to produce a winner.

If two fill their hands at the same time, the winner is the first to call 'My ship sails' – or, if you prefer, whichever of them has the highest ranking card, or second highest if a tie, and so on.

Old Maid

A famous old Victorian game suitable for three or more players. If more than six take part, use two packs shuffled together. Before shuffling all the cards together, remove the Queen of hearts from the pack. Deal all the cards round as far as they will go – it doesn't matter if some receive more than others. The object is to avoid being the loser (there is no single winner). The loser is the player who finishes up with an odd Queen in his hand.

As soon as everyone is ready they all examine their cards looking for pairs of the same rank, e.g. two Aces, or Jacks, or

Threes, etc. Any and all such pairs are placed face down on the table in front of them. If, at this point or any later time in the game, a player manages to get rid of all his cards by pairing, he drops out of play, safe in the knowledge that he will not finish up as the Old Maid (with the odd Queen).

When no more pairing can be done, the player at dealer's left holds his hand of cards out, face down, to the player at his own left, who takes one and adds it to his hand. He then offers his cards to his left, and so on round the table, until the player who started the round receives one from the player on his right. Everyone now examines their cards and discards a pair if possible.

Play continues in this way, with people gradually dropping out as they get rid of their cards in pairs. Eventually they will all be out except the Old Maid.

Parliament

Also known as Card Dominoes, Sevens, Fan Tan and probably other things as well, Parliament calls for a little bit of thinking to be played successfully – rather like the real thing, which is why I prefer this particular title.

It is for two or more players and uses an ordinary 52-card pack, which is dealt round as far as it will go – it doesn't matter if some players have more than others. The object is to get rid of all your cards before anyone else.

The player at dealer's left starts by placing any Seven face up in the middle of the table. (If he has none, the turn passes to the left until someone can start with a Seven.) This starts off a display which will eventually consist of four rows of cards, each row being all of one suit and running in sequence from Ace at one end to King at the other. After the first card has been played, each player in turn adds a card to the display if possible. A card may only be added to the display alongside a card already in position, which means it must either be of the same suit and next in sequence, or of the same rank as an existing card and in the row next to it. For example, suppose the first card played is ♣7. Then the next to play may add ♣8 to its right or ♣6 to its left, or any other Seven to start a row next to it.

Anyone who cannot legally play a card when it is his turn simply loses that opportunity of lessening his hand. The game ends when one player plays his last card, and wins.

Pelmanism

Pelmanism is a memory game also known as Concentration. Two or more may take part, using a standard 52-card pack. If it is desired to make the game easier (with smaller children, for example), you may strip out all four cards of several ranks, e.g. all the pictures, or all cards lower than Seven. But make sure there remain in the pack exactly four each of whatever ranks are left.

The cards are thoroughly shuffled and spread out face down on the table, preferably not touching one another, but not necessarily in neat rows. (It is a good idea to use Patience cards.)

The object is to win cards. Each player in turn chooses any two cards and peeps at them to see what they are, without showing them to anyone else. If they are both of the same rank, he shows them and wins them, and the turn passes to the left. If not, he leaves them face down in the same positions.

Ranter-Go-Round

I believe this ancient game is widely known in Europe – or at least in northern Europe, where it is known as Cuckoo. Three or more may take part – preferably more, indeed as many as you like – using a full 52-card pack. Each player starts with three 'lives', represented by counters or marks on a bit of paper, and the game ends when all but one player have lost all three, the survivor being the winner.

One card is dealt to each player face down. Aces are lowest, Kings are highest, and the object is to avoid being left with the lowest card in play after a certain amount of exchanging and general skulduggery. (I'm not quite sure what skulduggery is, but it sounds like a good place for archaeologists.)

Starting at dealer's left, each player in turn looks at his card and decides whether it is high enough to keep, or whether he wishes to exchange in hope of getting a better one. If he keeps, the turn passes to his left. If not, he confronts the player at his left and says 'Change!' or words to that effect. The player thus addressed *must* then exchange cards with him (keeping them both face down so that no one else knows who has what) – unless, however, he has a King, in which case he declares that fact and keeps it, much to the annoyance of the first player, who is stuck with his original card.

The turn then passes to the player who may or may not have been ordered to exchange, and he may or may not do likewise to the player at his own left.

This continues all the way round the table until the dealer is reached. He may not order the first player to exchange, but if he thinks his card dangerously low he may cut the pack of undealt cards and take the top card of the bottom half. If it is a King he loses a life; otherwise he keeps what he gets and hopes for the best.

All players then reveal their cards, and the one with the lowest rank loses a life. If there is a tie for lowest, the tied players all lose one.

The deal then passes to the left and another round is played. This continues, and as each loses his third life he drops out (or, more usually, dies a highly theatrical death). When only one player is left in, he is declared the winner, in default of having anyone to exchange cards with.

Slapjack

This has been described as 'an exciting game that does not need any understanding of cards except the ability to recognise the Jacks'.

Two or more may play and the object is to win all the cards for yourself while leaving none for anybody else.

Deal all the cards round as far as they will go. Without looking at their cards, everybody arranges them in a neat pile face down on the table. Starting at dealer's left, each in turn quickly

takes the top card of his pile and places it face up in the middle
of the table. Whenever a Jack appears, the first person to 'slap'
it – by covering it with his hand – wins the whole pile of cards
in the middle. He then picks them up, shuffles them in with the
rest of his original pile, and starts the next round by playing to
the middle.

If anyone slaps a card which is not a Jack, he must 'pay' one
card from his pile to the person who played the card he slapped
by mistake.

When a player runs out of cards he is entitled to one opportunity to get back into the game by slapping a Jack and winning
a new pile. If he fails to get there first, he drops out of the game.

Snap

One of many games which I prefer to Russian Roulette, Snap
is probably the best known and first learnt of all children's card
games, not to say least in need of description. (But you'll get
one, just the same.)

Two or more may play, and the object is either to win all the
cards or to be the last to flake out from sheer exhaustion.

Deal all the cards round. Everybody makes a neat pile of their
cards, without looking at them, and either places it face down
on the table or holds it face down in one hand. Starting at
dealer's left, each in turn rapidly takes the top card of his pile
and plays it face up to the middle of the table. Whenever a
card is played which exactly matches the rank of the previous
one – e.g. an Ace on an Ace or a Six on a Six — the first player
to yell 'Snap!' wins the pile in the middle. He turns the pile
upside down and places it at the bottom of his own pile, and
play continues from the left of the person who played the last
card.

A player who gets rid of all his cards drops out of play: he
may not snap his way back in again. A player who 'snaps' by
mistake must 'pay' one card from his pile to each other player.

As with all classic games, Snap boasts variations, additions
and alternative rules.

One good idea is the introduction of a pool. If two or more

players shout 'Snap!' simultaneously, the central pile is placed to one side as a pool and play continues with the start of a new pile. Whenever a card played to the new pile matches the top card of the pool, the first player to call 'Snap pool' wins the pool (not the main pile) and adds it to his cards.

A more advanced version of the game works as follows. Each in turn plays his next card, not to a single pile in the middle of the table, but to a face-up waste pile in front of himself. 'Snap' may be called whenever such a card is played which matches the top card of any other player's face-up pile, the caller winning both piles and adding them to his playing stock.

If this version is played, it may be agreed that if two call simultaneously, or if one calls mistakenly, their pile of face-up cards is placed in a pool, which is later won by a player calling 'Snap pool' when a card is played matching the top card of the pool.

It may also be agreed that when a player runs out of face-down cards, he takes his pile of face-up cards and turns them down to use as a new stock.

Spock

This is a variation on a previously published game of mine called Spec. It is rather like Concentration, or Pelmanism, but I think more interesting.

The game is best for two to five players, and requires a pack of 52 cards plus a Joker, which must be of the same back design and colour as the rest. (But I will give you a variation on the game which does without one.) The cards should be clean, or at least unmarked on their backs.

The cards are thoroughly shuffled and spread face down all over the table. It doesn't really matter if some are covered up, though it isn't a bad idea to use small cards such as those specially made for playing Patience.

The object of play is to win cards: the more, the better.

Each player in turn points to a face-down card and announces by rank and suit what he thinks it is – for example 'Ace of hearts', 'Queen of clubs', etc. He may not say 'Joker'. He then turns the card up so that everyone can see it.

If it is completely different from what he said, being neither the same suit nor the same rank, he leaves it face up on the table and the turn passes to the left.

If it is the same *suit* as the one he said, he wins that card together with any other face-up cards there may be of the same suit, and has another turn.

If it is the same *rank* as the one he said, he wins that card plus all other face-up cards there may be on the table, and has another turn.

If it is exactly the card he said, he wins it and all the cards left on the table, face up or down, and the game ends.

If it is the Joker, he wins the Joker and the game is at an end.

The winner is the player who has won most cards. Or you can play several games, noting how many cards each player wins in each one and adding them together. In this case the final winner is the first player to score, say, fifty or one hundred.

There should, of course, be a penalty for announcing a card that has already gone, either lying face up on the table or having been won by a previous player. If one player thinks another has called a card which has already gone, he shouts 'Spock!'. An examination is made to see if the challenge is correct, for which purpose players must look through their won cards as well as those lying face up. If the challenge is correct (i.e. the 'spocker' is right), the challenged player (the 'spockee') must hand over to him all the cards he has so far won, if any. If the challenge is wrong, and the said card has not in fact already been turned, then the spocker must give up his won cards to the spockee.

If two or more players correctly call 'Spock!' simultaneously, the spockee does not give his cards to either of them but adds them face up to those on the table, where they may be won by a correct guess later in the game.

If you have no Joker, or if you prefer the following variation, play it this way: any time that a Jack is turned up, whether it is won or left on the table, it is left face up in a prominent position (e.g. on top of a player's pile of won cards). As soon as the fourth Jack is turned the game ends. The last Jack is not won by the player who turned it unless he previously guessed that it would be a Jack.

2. CARD GAMES FOR ONE

The Americans call Patience 'Solitaire', emphasising the most distinctive feature of it: that it is a game, or family of games, for one player. It is true that there are some two-or-more player so-called 'competitive' patiences, but once the solitaire element is lost the exercise takes on a wholly different aspect – playing against another player is quite different from, as patience buffs put it, 'playing against the pack'. (Which does not mean that competitive games based on Patience principles are not play-worthy. A really excellent version for two players is Spite and Malice – see p. 91.)

Of all the card games, Patience ranks only with Poker in terms of being misunderstood by those who do not themselves indulge in it, and even by some who do. Patience is generally regarded as a mindless way of passing or wasting time for invalids or elderly widows who have nothing more constructive to do. Many people who do play a little know only one sort of Patience, and not the best at that. Yet the fact of the matter is that there are hundreds of Patience games of varying degrees of skill and ingenuity, and that the best of them exhibit that form of intellectual elegance which knowledgeable people usually associate with Chess problemism. It is a constant source of puzzlement to me that Patience has not seen a revival in recent years as a result of the boom in puzzle magazines and manipulative puzzles such as Rubik's Cube.

Let's get our bearings first, before plunging into a small selection of the games themselves.

In nearly all Patience games the object of play is to start with a shuffled pack and finish with all the cards in order, typically built up into four piles (or eight, if using a double pack) corresponding to the four suits, with all the cards in each suit running in sequence from the Ace (usually the lowest card in Patience) up to the King. Because the mechanism by which this object is achieved may involve many subsidiary piles of cards being formed on the way, I use a special word for the finished, ordered piles which you are aiming for, namely *suites* (pronounced 'sweets'. A suite just means a sequence, as for example in the phrase 'a suite of dances', and its spelling also suggests the idea of being built up in cards of the same *suit*).

Auld Lang Syne

A simple game requiring no skill at all – but curiously compulsive – Auld Lang Syne is the toughest way I can think of to get across the real meaning of the word 'patience'.

Take out the four Aces and lay them in a row at the top of the table. The object is to build each one up to the King, always following suit. Deal the next four cards face up immediately below them, then pause and build what you can – i.e. if they include a Two, build it on the Ace of the same suit. If they also include the Three, that can go on the Two; but the chances against it are so great that you could not have shuffled the pack properly and ought by rights to start again.

Having built, or (more probably) not, deal the next four cards face up on the previous ones, overlapping slightly so that all are visible. Again, pause and build what you can. As you continue in the same way, building if possible and then dealing four more, you will gradually form four columns of overlapping cards coming towards you. Only the exposed card of each column is available for building on the four main suites, but, of course, as each one is taken it releases the one beneath it.

A harder version of the game is known as Tam O'Shanter. In this, you do not pick the Aces out first but start dealing four at a time, only putting the Aces out as each one turns up in the deal.

Either of these games can be made more likely to succeed by increasing the number of columns, for example by dealing five or six at a time instead of four. An interesting challenge is to start with four columns, then try five on the second game, six on the third, and so on until you succeed. The number of columns used on your eventual success becomes, as it were, your handicap for the game as a whole.

Quadrille

Skill is not everything in life, and although it plays no part in this game I find Quadrille enjoyable to play for its marriage of decorative layout and apposite title.

Take out all the Queens, Sixes and Fives. Arrange the four Queens at the centre of the table in the form of a cross, or in some such way as to suggest the nucleus of a square dance. Around them, in a circle, arrange the Fives and Sixes alternately. The Queens are not built on during the course of play, but the Fives and Sixes form the base cards of eight suites which are to be built in suit – the Sixes in ascending numerical order to the Jacks, the Fives in numerical order down to the Kings (5, 4, 3, 2, A, K).

Deal cards one at a time face up to the table to form a waste pile. If you turn a card which can be built on a suite, do so. You may also add to a suite the top card of the waste pile if it fits as a result of building one from the main stock.

Having, as is usual, reached the end of the stock without being able to finish the suites, pick up the waste pile, turn it upside down, and use it as the new stock for another deal.

Traditionally, you are allowed to turn the waste pile three times, making four deals in all. But the end result of Queens surrounded by alternating Kings and Jacks is so worthy of consummation that you have my express permission to go on redealing until you bring it to a successful conclusion. You may then regard the number of deals it took as your handicap for the game, and seek to improve it in subsequent playings.

Golf

A classic game, also known as One Foundation (and as Fan Tan, though this title applies to several quite unrelated games), Golf displays the unusual though not unheard-of feature that cards are built on to a single suite regardless of suit. Hence its title, the object being to 'putt' as many cards as possible into the single 'hole'.

After thorough shuffling, deal seven cards face up in a row at the top of the table. Deal seven more across them, overlapping but not concealing the first row, and do this five times, until you have a layout consisting of seven columns of five cards each. Deal the 36th card face up to one side as a base for the single suite which is to be built, or the hole into which the rest are to be putted.

The object of the game is to build all 35 cards of the layout on to the single suite. Upon the base card of the suite, and thereafter upon whatever happens to be its topmost card at the time, may be built any available card which is immediately consecutive to it, either one rank higher or one lower, regardless of suit.

The sequence of cards on the suite may change direction, up or down, as often as necessary; but Ace and King are not consecutive: only a Two may go on an Ace, only a Queen on a King.

The exposed card at the bottom of each column is 'available' for building on the suite, and, as each one is so used, it releases the one below it for the same purpose when possible.

When stuck, with no available card consecutive with the top of the suite, set the game going again by dealing the next card from the stock face up on the suite, and continuing as before.

If you use up all sixteen cards of the stock in this way before clearing all the cards off the layout, you have lost, the number of cards remaining in the layout being your 'handicap' for the game.

Otherwise, you have won. There is no redeal.

Klondike (or Canfield)

This is one of the best known solitaires, being known simply as 'Patience' to so many players blissfully unaware of how many different patience games there are. Its very popularity has led to some confusion in title. The game is traditionally known as Canfield in Britain and as Klondike in America, but Canfield in America denotes the game traditionally known as Demon in Britain. Obviously, the best way of avoiding confusion is to drop the name Canfield altogether so as to emphasise that Klondike and Demon are two quite different games. Older

English books also describe this game under the title Triangle. It rarely comes out, unless you bend the rules.

Deal seven cards in a row, face down. Deal a second card face down on top of the first six of them, a third face down on the first five, a fourth on the first four, and so on until you have dealt a seventh on the first pile only. This results in 28 cards dealt face down in seven 'packets' whose contents range from one card to seven at the opposite end. Turn the last card of each packet face up. Hold the remaining 24 cards face down as a stock.

The object is to set out the four Aces as and when they appear, and to build each one up in suit and sequence to its King.

Turn cards from the stock one by one (see below for alternative dealing in fans of three), and either build, pack or discard them face up to a single waste pile. 'Build' means start a suite if the turned card is an Ace, or add it to a suite if it is the next higher one of the appropriate suit. 'Pack' means place it on one of the upturned cards of the layout, partly but not entirely covering it, so as to start a series of columns of face-up cards which grow towards you as more cards are subsequently packed. Packing is to take place in descending sequence and alternating colour, i.e. a card may only be packed on one which is immediately higher in rank and opposite in colour (red Five on black Six, black Four on red Five, etc.).

At any point in the game, the exposed card (the one nearest you) of such a packed sequence may be built on a suite if it fits, or it may be transferred to another packed column if it follows the descending/alternating rule. A whole sequence of packed cards may be so transferred so long as the join follows the same rule.

When a face-down card of one of the original packets is cleared, it is turned face up to start a new column for packing. When the last card of such a packet has been turned face up and built, leaving a gap in the columns, its space may be filled only with a King, or with a sequence of properly packed cards from another column starting with a King.

The top card of the waste pile is always available for building or packing if it will fit. But the waste pile may not be turned and used for a redeal when the stock has run out: if the game does not then come out, you have lost. Unless, of course, on mature consideration, you change the rules.

There is an alternative method of play as to the turning of cards from the stock. Under it, three are turned at a time and faced up in the form of a fan, overlapping slightly so as to preserve the sequence. If the exposed one (the one not over-lapped) can be built or packed it may be, and this releases the second for the same purpose, and this (if possible) the third. If not, it and the one(s) below it are discarded to the waste pile in a batch. If this method of play is followed, the waste pile may be turned twice so that you have three deals altogether.

Klondike rarely comes out, but a more frequently successful variation known as Thumb and Pouch introduces the following rather unusual rule: cards may be packed on the layout not necessarily in alternating colour but merely in differing suit. For example, on the six of hearts may be packed any Five except the heart.

Sir Tommy

This is said to be one of the ancestral Patience games, as its alternative title – Old Patience – suggests.

The object is to set out the four Aces at the top of the table, as and when they turn up, and to build each one up in sequence to the King but regardless of suit.

Turn cards from the stock one by one and build them on the four suites if possible. If not, discard each one to any of four waste piles, face up. The top card of a waste pile is always available for building on a suite if it fits, thereby releasing the one beneath it for the same purpose. If in doubt as to whether or not it is wise to build a particular card from a waste pile, you may peek at the next card to come from the stock provided that you have already placed the previous one.

Cards may not be transferred from one waste-pile to another and there is no redeal, so the chances of bringing it to a successful conclusion are rather slim.

Strategy

One of my favourite patiences, and the invention of Albert Morehead and Geoffrey Mott-Smith, Strategy is a variation on Sir Tommy which, though more skill demanding, comes out far more frequently with careful play.

The object is to set the Aces out at the top of the table as and when they appear, and to build each one up in suit and sequence to its King. Apart from the Aces, however, no cards may be built until they have all been dealt from the stock on to the display, as follows.

Turn cards from stock one by one and (apart from Aces) place each one on any of four waste piles. The cards of each 'pile' should be spread towards you so that they form four columns of overlapping cards. At this stage, any card may be played on any exposed card regardless of suit or sequence, though considerable thought is needed to make the right choices.

When the 48 cards have been dealt to the layout, the Aces must be built upon in suit and sequence up to the Kings. For this purpose only the exposed card of each column is available for building, its removal releasing the one beneath it for the same purpose. If all the best choices have been made in attaching the right cards to the right columns, it should be possible (more often than not, I believe) to bring the game to a successful conclusion.

If you fail, play again, this time dealing cards to five piles or columns, and so on, increasing the number of columns each time you fail and decreasing it each time you succeed. If you manage to do it in three columns, consider yourself a genius – but a lucky one.

Bristol

A pretty little game, and another invention of Morehead and Mott-Smith. Once again, the object is to set out the four Aces as and when they appear, and build them up in suit and sequence to their respective Kings.

Deal eight fans of three cards each face up to the table (or, if you prefer, eight columns of three cards each, overlapping the three of each column so that only one is exposed). If there are any Kings visible, shift them to the bottom of their fans or columns. If there are any Aces, move them to the top of the table as bases, but do not replace them from stock.

The exposed card of each fan is available for building on a suite if it fits. They may also be packed on one another in descending sequence regardless of suit – e.g. an exposed Five may be placed on the exposed Six of another fan, and so on.

Having done as much building and packing as may be possible to start with, turn the next three cards from the stock and place them face up at the bottom of the table to form three waste piles. These are available for building on suites or packing on the original fans if possible. Again, having done what you can, deal three more on the waste piles in order from left to right. (Or right to left, if you are left-handed.) Continue the game in this way, dealing three at a time to the waste piles, and packing and building as and when you can.

If a fan is emptied, it is not restarted. If a waste pile is emptied, it is only restarted by the next deal of three cards. There is no redeal of the waste piles. The inventors estimate chances of success as one game in three.

Belle Lucie

If I admit to not knowing who the original 'Fair Lucy' might be, I hope I may be inundated with explanatory letters from knowledgeable readers. The game is another one involving fans, like Bristol, and that it is something of a classic is suggested by its numerous alternative titles, including Clover Leaf, Alexander the Great, and Midnight Oil.

Deal all the cards face up into seventeen fans of three each – ideally, and if you have room enough, in such a way as to represent a large fan on the table, with the solus 52nd card forming its handle. Treat the whole layout as eighteen fans, even though one of them has only one card to start with.

The object is to release the Aces when possible, set them to one side and build them up in suit and sequence to their respective Kings.

The exposed cards of each fan are available for building on the suites and for packing on each other, packing to take place in descending sequence, strictly in suit (e.g. on ♡6 may be packed only ♡5), and only one at a time. A space made by emptying a fan is not refilled, and there may never be more than eighteen fans in all.

When you cannot build or pack any further, the game continues in a rather unusual way. Gather up all the cards of the display, shuffle them well, and deal them out again in as many fans of three as they will make (one or two odd cards forming a 'fan' of their own). Two such redeals are allowed.

The only variation worth mentioning is Trefoil, in which the Aces are taken out to start with and the remaining cards dealt out in sixteen fans of three. This marginally increases the chances of success.

Scorpion

There is a small but distinctive sub-group of Patience games in which the building of the suites takes place within the display itself, instead of on separate piles at one end of the table. The chief member of this family is called Spider. Scorpion, the best of the one-pack versions, is once again the invention of the indefatigable Morehead and Mott-Smith.

Deal seven cards in a row, the first three face down and the rest face up. Deal another row of seven overlapping the first row, again three down and four up, and repeat the process twice more. Finish the layout by dealing three more rows of seven, but this time all face up. You will finish with 49 cards arranged in seven columns of seven each, all face up except the top four cards of the first three columns. (These down-cards often prove to be the sting in the tail of the game.) The three undealt cards go face down to one side as a reserve.

The object of play is to build complete suit sequences from Ace to King within the columns of the display, removing each of the four as it is completed.

The exposed card at the bottom of each column may be packed upon in suit and descending sequence. For example, if ♡6 is at the bottom of a column, ♡5 (and nothing else) may be packed upon it. However, any face-up card within the display may be taken for packing on its next higher neighbour, even if it is not itself at the end of a column: if so removed, all the cards covering it lower down in the same column are shifted *en bloc* with it to the new column. Sequences may not 'turn the corner' – that is, a King may not be packed on its Ace.

Whenever a face-down card is uncovered, turn it face up. When a whole column is emptied, it may be filled again only with a King, but together with any cards lying below it in the same column. When stuck, or at any other desired point in the game, deal the three reserve cards face up to the bottom of the first three columns and continue play.

Whenever a complete suit sequence is formed in the columns, with the Ace at the bottom of a column (the inventors do not specify this detail, but it seems logical) remove it from the game. The game is won if you succeed in eliminating four such suites, which is more difficult than it sounds.

Black Hole

A game of my own invention, Black Hole is similar to Golf in that the object is to build a single suite of cards. It differs in being a completely 'open' game – that is, you can see the positions of all 52 cards at the start of play and do a considerable amount of working out in advance. A black hole, by the way, is a sort of dead star which swallows up everything unfortunate enough to fall in its gravitational path.

Place the Ace of spades in the centre of the table, representing the black hole of the title. Deal the remaining 51 cards in seventeen fans of three each, face up, in a circle or ellipse around the Ace so as to look like objects orbiting around it. In each fan all three cards should be visible, but overlapping so that only one is exposed.

The object of the game is to build all the cards up into a single suite based on the central Ace. For this purpose only the exposed card of each fan is available for building, its removal releasing the one immediately below it. When a fan is emptied it is not replaced.

An available card may only be built on the central pile if it is consecutive in rank, whether higher or lower, with the topmost card. Ace and King are consecutive for this purpose, and you may change direction as often as you like during the course of play. Thus the game might start like this: A, K, Q, K, A, 2, 3, 2, 3, 4 . . . etc. Suit is irrelevant.

You win if you get all 51 of the orbiting cards sucked into the black hole. If not, the number left in orbit may be counted as your handicap for the game, a record to be beaten next time.

With perfect play, this game should come out more often than not. A word of warning: do not change direction in the central suite more often than necessary. Many games can be brought out without changing direction at all, whereas excessive changes tend to make it impossible.

Monte Carlo

This is the first of several games in which, unlike most patiences, the object is not just to build cards up in suites. Here, for example, the object is to eliminate cards in pairs until none are left.

Deal 25 cards face up in five rows of five, without overlapping. Remove from the display any two which are of the same rank and lying next to each other, whether edge to edge or corner to corner. After removing a pair, close the cards up so as to fill the gaps, by moving any card into an empty space at its left. If there is a space at the extreme right of a row, fill it with the first card to the left of the row beneath and move up again. This brings all the gaps down to the bottom right. Fill them with cards face up from the stock, and repeat the process. You win if you manage to eliminate all cards in pairs by this method.

Poker Patience

Shuffle the cards and turn them one by one from the pack. As they come, play them face up on the table in such a way as to build up a square consisting of five rows and five columns. Once a card has been placed in position it may not be moved in relation to its neighbours.

The object of the game is to make as many and as high Poker hands as possible, counting each row and each column of five cards as such a hand, making ten hands in all. Give yourself a score for each hand as indicated in the table below:

one pair	1
two pair	3
triplets	6
straight	12
flush	5
full house	10
four of a kind	16
straight flush	30

A good target is 75: count the game as 'won' if you reach that total. Poker hands are explained on p. 538. The apparent discrepancy in the scoring given above is due to the fact that the probabilities of making the various hands differ in this game from those of Poker itself. A flush, for instance, is easily made if you choose to go for it, whereas a straight is harder to make than a full house. Incidentally, it does not matter in what order the cards appear in any given line – 3, 5, A, 4, 2 is a straight, no less than A, 2, 3, 4, 5.

Striptease

A game of my own invention, Striptease really is as tantalising as its title suggests. Theoretically it should be easy to bring to a successful conclusion since virtually all cards are visible from the outset and can therefore be worked out in advance. In practice, however . . . Well, see for yourself.

Lay the four Queens in a row at the top of the table. Shuffle the pack, and deal the next four cards face down across the Queens, covering all except their faces, so as to form the start of four columns descending towards you. Deal the rest of the cards face up, also in fours across the rows, until you finish with four columns of thirteen cards each. The object is to strip all four Queens of their covering cards in accordance with the following rules.

The exposed (bottom) card of each column is available for discarding, its discard releasing the one above it for the same purpose. Discard all available exposed cards one at a time to any of four waste piles, but in such a way that the cards on each waste pile are in sequence, up or down and regardless of suit. For this purpose, Jacks are consecutive with Kings, and Kings with Aces. A waste pile started with a Ten, for instance, may continue J, K, A, 2, 3, 2, A, etc.

The down-cards covering the four Queens may not be turned until all four of them have been cleared. They are then turned face up together, and, if they can be discarded to the waste piles – still following the rule of sequence – the Queens are exposed and you have won the game.

So far, I haven't.

Spaces and Aces

Card wizard Robert Harbin devised this improved version of a game otherwise known as Maze. It is rather like a sliding block puzzle.

Deal all the cards face up in four rows of thirteen cards each. No card overlaps any other. Remove the Aces and place one at the leftmost end of each row. This changes the layout into four rows of fourteen positions each, four of the positions being blanks or 'spaces' as in the title. The object is to move cards into spaces one at a time in such a way as to finish with four complete suit sequences, one in each row, from Ace at the extreme left to King at the right.

At each move, take up any card (other than an Ace) and reposition it in a space. It may not go in any old space, however: it can only be positioned to the immediate right of a card of the same suit and lower in rank. For example, you could move ♡5 into a space to the immediate right of ♡4 or 3 or 2 or A, but not to the right of a higher heart or any card of another suit.

This game should come out more often than not with correct

play, but be careful of the Kings. No card may be placed to the immediate right of a King, so until a King is transferred to its ultimate position at the end of a row any space to the right of one is dead and unfillable, thus reducing by one quarter the number of moves open to you.

Quilt (2 packs)

Also known as Indian Carpet and Japanese Rug, Quilt takes up a fair amount of space, as its titles may suggest. It is a very attractive game, and comes out more often than not with proper play.

Remove one Ace of each suit and one King of each suit. Shuffle the other cards thoroughly and deal 64 of them face up on the table (or floor) in eight rows of eight cards each, making a large square. Not only are the cards not to overlap one another, but also they are to be arranged in a distinctive way, as follows: the first card of the first row is positioned vertically, i.e. with its short sides at top and bottom; the second goes horizontally next to it, i.e. with its short sides at left and right; the third goes vertically, the fourth horizontally, and so in in alternation to the end of the row. In the second row the same alternation follows, except that the first one goes horizontally. Follow the same alternation throughout the deal. In the final display, each short side of every card will be lying adjacent to the long side of another, except for those exposed at the edges of the square. This forms the quilt.

Next, arrange the four Aces in a row or column, and the four Kings likewise. The object is to build these into eight suit-sequences, the Aces being built in ascending sequence to their Kings, the Kings in descending sequences to their Aces. The undealt cards form a stock from which cards may be taken one by one as they are needed for building. You may hold the stock face up so that you can always see what the next card is, but you must keep it squared up so as not to see what will be coming up after it.

The top card of the stock is always 'available', and so is any card in the quilt which has at least one short edge free. At the start of play only sixteen cards of the quilt are available, namely, those which have a short edge projecting from the side of the quilt. As each one is taken, it unblocks the short edge of an adjacent card, thus releasing it for play in its turn. Gradually, therefore, throughout the game, the quilt disappears as if being eaten up by moths.

An available card may be built on one of the Ace or King suites if it is of the right suit and next in sequence (upwards on Ace suites, downwards on Kings). Or it may be discarded face up to a single waste pile. The waste pile may be started with any available card, but thereafter each card added to it must be next in sequence – up or down, and regardless of suit – with the top card of the pile. (Aces and Kings do not count as consecutive for this purpose.) The top card of the waste pile is also available for building on a suite if and when it fits.

Suite-to-suite reversal is permitted. For example, if the top card of the suite built on ♡A is (say) ♡6, and the top card of that built on ♡K is ♡7, then either the Six may be taken and placed on the Seven, or vice versa. However, Aces and Kings themselves may not be reversed in this way.

If the stock runs out before the game is finished, you may turn the waste pile upside down and use it as a new stock, always keeping its top card faced so that you know which card is available. Only one such redeal is allowed.

Terrace (2 packs)

One of my favourite games, Terrace combines some distinctive and elegant rules of play and makes the ideal call on skill, in that careful play usually brings it to a successful conclusion, but there are many opportunities for making irrevocable mistakes. The game is also known as Queen of Italy, or Signora.

After thorough shuffling, deal eleven cards face up in a row, overlapping one another, at the top of the table. This forms a reserve known as the terrace.

Beneath the terrace, imagine a row of eight cards which are not overlapping one another, and deal four cards face up into the first four positions of this row. Choose one of these four to act as the base card of a pile of cards in suit and ascending sequence, move it to the left of its row, and transfer the other three to the first three positions of yet another row beneath the second. If one of those three is of the same rank as the base card, however, leave it in the second row as the base of another suite. To complete the opening display, deal more cards face up to the third row until there are nine altogether. If they include a card of the same rank as the first base, put it into the second row and deal a replacement.

The object of the game is to build eight suit sequences in the second row. As each card of the same rank as the first base becomes available it is placed in position in the second row. Cards in these suites must follow in ascending sequence, passing from King to Ace if necessary, until they total thirteen, the topmost card being one rank lower than the bases. For example, if the base card is a Jack, the sequence continues Q, K, A, 2 and so on up to Ten.

Cards available for building on these suites are: the exposed card of the terrace (its removal releasing the one it overlaps), any exposed card in the third row, the top card of the stock, and the top card of the waste pile which will grow during the course of play.

Turn cards from the stock one by one, and either build them on appropriate suites, or pack them on the tableau, or discard them face up to a single waste pile. The top card of the waste pile is always available for building or packing. The exposed card of the terrace, however, may only be built on a suite, not packed in the tableau.

The nine cards in the third row start the tableau. Upon them may be placed, overlapping, cards in descending sequence and alternating colour (e.g. red Ten on black Jack, black Nine on red Ten, etc.), so as to form nine columns of overlapping cards descending towards you. The exposed card of each column is always available for building, or may be transferred to another column if it fits in accordance with the rule. Whenever the last card of a column is taken, the gap it leaves must be immediately filled with the top card of the stock or the waste pile – not from the terrace or the tableau.

No redeal of the waste pile is allowed, but the following variation seems perfectly acceptable. If the stock is exhausted before the game comes out, you may take up the waste pile, turn it upside down and use it as a new stock to continue play. This time, however, you may not form another waste pile: each card as it comes must be either built on a suite or packed on the tableau, and if this is impossible then the game is finally lost.

The skill of the game lies, first, in choosing a suitable rank to act as the base, for which purpose you must examine the terrace carefully to see which chosen rank will most rapidly enable the terrace cards to be taken. It would be self-defeating, for example, to choose as the base a card of the same rank as the one buried at the far end of the terrace. Even then, the game does not play itself. Much skill is required in the correct management of the terrace so that you never reach a position in which a card buried in the terrace is vital to the continuance of the game.

Similar games to Terrace are General's Patience, Thirteen, Falling Star, and Blondes and Brunettes.

Interregnum (2 packs)

Another great patience, with some elements of similarity to Terrace and calling for no less skill.

Deal eight cards in a row at the top of the table, not over-lapping one another. These are the 'indicators'.

Imagine a second row of eight cards beneath the first, but leave it blank for the moment.

Immediately below the (empty) second row, deal a third row of eight, also non-overlapping. These form the top row of a tableau, which during play will be built into columns of over-lapping cards descending towards you.

The object of the game is to build eight piles of thirteen cards in the second row, each pile to consist of cards in ascending numerical sequence but regardless of suit. The sequence is circular – that is, it may turn the corner from King to Ace where necessary. The base card of each sequence is to be one rank higher than the card lying immediately above it in the top row, the upper card itself – the 'indicator' – being used as the thirteenth and crowning card of the suite to indicate that it has been completed. No more cards may be added to a sequence that has been completed and crowned with its indicator.

Any card in the third row may be taken and placed as a base in the second row, or built on such a base, if it is possible to do so, but do not yet fill any spaces this may leave in the third row.

When you have got as far as you can, deal the next eight cards face up from stock across the third row from left to right, overlapping any cards that may remain, and beginning to form columns. Then pause, and found base cards or build what you can. When ready, deal eight more across the columns. Continue in this way throughout the game. Always deal eight in a row before pausing and playing. The exposed card of each column is available for founding as a base or building on a suite, its removal releasing the one it overlaps for the same purpose.

There is no redeal, but with careful play the game should come out more often than not.

Miss Milligan (2 packs)

I have heard tell of players who know no Patience game other than Miss Milligan, which suggests that no collection is complete without her. Be warned, however, that the lady is sparing with her favours: one assent to nineteen face slaps seems to be a not unreasonable ambition.

The object is to build eight suit sequences from Ace to King in a row at the top of the table. The Aces are not put in place to start with, but may only be positioned as and when they become available.

Deal eight cards face up in a row. If there is an Ace among them, set it out as a base, and build on it in suit and sequence if the corresponding Two, Three, etc. should also happen to be available. A card may also be packed on another one if it is one rank lower and of different colour than the card it is made to overlap (e.g. red Five on black Six, etc.). Do not fill any spaces yet.

Having done as much as you can and will by way of building and packing, deal eight more cards across the columns, then pause and play again. Follow this procedure throughout the game. After each deal, do any building that may be possible, using only cards exposed at the ends of columns. Such exposed cards may also be packed on one another in descending sequence and alternating colour. A whole sequence of properly packed cards may be shifted to another column, provided that the join follows the rule. If a column is emptied by removal of its last card, it may be filled, but only with a King (together with any sequence of properly packed cards lying with it). When all cards have been entered into the game, continue packing and building until it comes out or blocks.

This game is equipped with a grace (a form of official cheating) known as 'waiving', or perhaps 'weaving'. When the game blocks, it may be exercised as follows. Remove any exposed card of a column and lay it face up in a temporary one-card reserve so as to unblock the card or sequence it was obscuring. Having proceeded further, and re-entered the waived card either by building it or by properly packing it on the tableau, you continue play until it comes out or blocks again. You may waive as often as you like.

Kaiser Bill (2 packs)

A little known Patience, but one that calls for considerable care and well worth making the acquaintance of.

After thorough shuffling, deal the first 27 cards face up in three rows of nine each. Do not overlap any cards – on the contrary, keep them well spaced apart. These form the tableau. The object is to set apart the eight Aces as and when they become available, and to build each one up in suit and sequence to its King.

Fron now onwards only cards lying in the bottom row may be taken for starting suites (if Aces) or building on them. The removal of a card in the bottom row releases the one lying immediately above it in the same column for building, and its removal in turn releases that in the top row.

Although suites may only be built on with cards from the bottom row, any card in the tableau may be packed upon any other to form descending sequences of the same suit. For instance, ♡5 may be placed on ♡6. Similarly, any such sequence may be placed on an exposed card in the tableau provided that the join follows the rule. Thus the ♡5 with the ♡6 on top of it may be placed together on ♡7. It is obviously useful to spread the cards of each pile slightly so that all are visible. At the same time, it is important not to lose track of the three rows and nine columns, and it is for this reason that the cards should be spaced out to start with.

Having done any packing and building that may be possible, deal the next 27 cards face up over the tableau, from left to right and from top to bottom as in the first deal. Some of these cards will fall on spaces and some on single cards or piles of cards. After this deal, pause and build (from top cards of the bottom row only) or pack (anywhere in the tableau). The removal of a card from the top of a pile releases the one immediately beneath it for packing or (if in the bottom row) building. When a space is made in the bottom row, the card or pile of cards immediately above it in the same column is free for building, and if that, too, is cleared out, cards in the top row may be built.

Keep playing in this way, dealing 27 cards each time the game blocks (or earlier, if it seems advisable), and not playing further until all 27 have been dealt. The fourth such deal will exhaust the pack and you will run out of cards before reaching the end of the bottom row. After that, play by building and packing in accordance with the same rules.

With careful play – like all the best patiences – the game will come out more often than not, but it will fail if you misjudge or miscalculate.

Rainbow (2 packs)

The mechanics of this rarely successful game are fairly straightforward and unremarkable, but if laid out properly it makes a very pretty effect on the table.

Remove one Ace and one King of each suit and place them in the middle of the table as base cards for the eight suit sequences which it is your task to build. (In keeping with the theme of the title, I like to arrange them in a circle and radiating from a common centre, so as to represent the sun.)

The Aces are to be built up in suit and sequence to the Kings, and the Kings down in suit and sequence to the Aces. Suite-to-suite reversal is permitted – i.e. the top card of a suite may be transferred to the top of the other suite of the same suit if it fits, but Aces and Kings must be left where they are.

Deal the next sixty cards face up in fans of three, arranging the twenty fans in an arc starting at the bottom of one side of the table, arching over the 'sun', and falling down to the other side, in representation of a rainbow. Only one card of each fan is exposed; the others, though visible, are overlapped. Only the exposed card of each fan is available for building on a suite or packing on another exposed card in the tableau, its removal releasing the one below it for the same purpose. Packing on the tableau takes place in suit but in either direction. For example, an exposed ♡5 may be placed on ♡6 or ♡4. Ace and King, however, do not count as consecutive. Only one card may be moved at a time.

Whenever a space is made by clearing out a fan from the rainbow, immediately replace it with a new fan of three cards dealt from the stock, so long as any are left. When stuck, or at any time that it seems desirable, transfer the bottom card of each fan to the top, so that it becomes exposed, and continue play. This may be done twice more in a single game.

German Patience (2 packs)

Also rarely recorded, but just as intriguing as Kaiser Bill, German Patience looks deceptively easy at first attempt – but don't let that fool you.

Deal eight cards face up. You may treat any of them as a base, and use any of the others that will fit to build upon it in ascending sequence but not necessarily in suit. If you do build one card on another, fill the space it leaves immediately from stock.

The eventual object is to complete eight thirteen-card sequences and remove them from the game. The sequence always ascends, passing from King to Ace if necessary. It is important to keep track of the number of cards in each such sequence.

When ready, deal cards from stock one by one, and build them on suites if they fit, or else discard them face up to a single waste pile. The top card of the waste pile is always available for building on a suite, and care must be taken to do so when possible, as the waste pile may not be turned and used again when the stock runs out.

The top card of any suite may also be taken and built on a different suite if it fits and you think it advisable. If you manage to clear a space by so doing, you may fill it with the top card of the stock or the waste pile.

Since this game is virtually impossible to bring out in the form described above, it is at least reasonable to assume (though the original source does not mention it) that once a completed sequence has been removed from the table, its space may be occupied by another card to start a new sequence.

Two points may be made about strategy. First, don't build a card turned from stock just because you can – sometimes it may be useful to put it on the waste pile, when you can see some possibility of placing it more advantageously in the near future. Also, try to hold some suites back and forge ahead with others, rather than let them grow at the same pace. If a given card can go on either of two suites, for instance, put it on the larger. In this way you clear spaces more quickly, by completing large piles and removing them from the table, and by transferring cards from small piles to larger ones, so that they too can be whittled away to leave spaces.

Salic Law (2 packs)

The title, for what it's worth, refers to a male chauvinist method of fixing the succession to the throne, much favoured in medieval Europe, and partly serves to explain the slightly pictorial layout. As a game of Patience, Salic Law is the chief representative of a group of similar games with rather distinctive features, as will be seen . . .

Place any King near the top of the table and to one side. Shuffle the rest of the cards and start dealing them face upwards in a column of overlapping cards from the King and stretching down the table towards you. Keep an eye open for any Kings, Queens and Aces as you deal, and deal with them as follows:

Whenever a King turns up, start a new column next to the previous King and start dealing downwards from it again. Whenever an Ace appears, place it in a row above the row of Kings. Whenever a Queen appears, place it in a row above the row of Aces. The Aces act as base cards for eight suit sequences that are to be built up as far as the Jacks. During the deal, therefore, extract and build any cards that can be so built.

At the end of the deal you will have a row of Queens, which remain unused – for decoration only – during the rest of the game; below them a row of Aces on which suites are being built up in suit as far as the Jacks; and below them eight columns of varying lengths, all starting with Kings. The object of play is to build up the Aces to the Jacks, so as to finish with three rows of court cards. For better effect, arrange the cards so that each of the eight positions is occupied with the same suit.

When all cards have been dealt, continue building by taking only the exposed cards of the columns. Cards may not be transferred from column to column (there is no 'packing'); but when a King is cleared, it may be treated as an empty space, to which may be moved an exposed card from another column.

The game should succeed as often as not.

3. CARD GAMES FOR TWO

There are more indoor games for two players than for any other number, and cards are no exception to the rule. Perhaps the reason is not so hard to find: two may be company and three a crowd, but there comes a time when you need to stop holding hands and put your brain back into gear. Two-player card games offer considerable variety and there should be enough here to suit all tastes.

They fall naturally into three groups.

The first half dozen games are of English or American origin and played with a full pack of 52 cards. They are all quite distinctive in character, but generally easy to learn and fast to play without requiring a painful amount of intellectual endeavour. Many may be recommended to children and beginners.

The next few are games of continental origin played with a 32-card pack, or less in some cases. These are all trick taking games, and give maximum opportunity for the development and application of the highest card playing skills. It might be added that Piquet and Bézique, if now little heard of in general conversation, were amongst the most popular two-handed games in Britain until after the First World War, and deserve to be revived.

These are followed by a group of unusual games whose common factor is that both players start with exactly equal opportunities, each one knowing exactly what cards are open to his opponent. In some ways these contradict the character of most traditional card games, and may well appeal to players of Chess and other games that are, literally, open and above board. This does not mean that they require more skill than traditional card games, but only that they call for thinking of a different type. Nor are they necessarily cerebral. Gops, for example, is pure fun and quite incalculable.

CRIBBAGE

An old English game, said to have been invented in the early 16th century by Sir John Suckling, Cribbage remains popular in all those parts of the world that used to belong to the British Empire, including the American colonies. Suckling's exact contribution to the game is not clear, but he may have added some refinements to an earlier game called Noddy. In passing, it might be mentioned that a somewhat simpler version was described under the name Costly Colours in Charles Cotton's *Compleat Gamester* of 1674.

Cribbage remains essentially a pub game in England, and a rural one at that. One of its chief delights is the necessity of recording scores on a traditional piece of equipment called the crib (or noddy) board, whereby pegs are moved in holes drilled into a block of wood in a distinctive pattern. When both players have the same score they are said to be at 'level pegging', and the game ends when one of them has 'pegged out'. The equipment is needed because points are accumulated and recorded in dribs and drabs continuously throughout the game: it is not a question of waiting until you have finished play and then calculating the rewards for what you have succeeded in doing, which is the way of most other card games.

The original form of Cribbage is played by two players with five cards each, but a six-card game has grown up for two players as well, and is now preferred to the five-card game by most Crib players, except stubborn old die-hards like me.

Beginners, of course, should start with the simpler five-card game and work upwards, and that is the order in which we shall introduce the game and its variants.

Five-card Cribbage

Equipment. A standard 52-card pack, a cribbage board, and four pegs or matchsticks to move around it. (See captioned illustration for method of use.) The crib board is slightly more of a necessity than a convenience, and any form of mechanical scorer that may be available is better than pencil and paper.

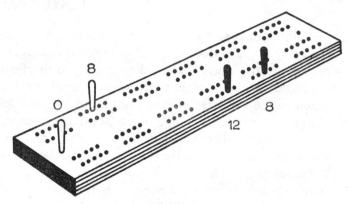

FIGURE 2

A 61-hole Cribbage board. Each player starts with one peg in the centre hole (counting 0 or 61) at either end, and one peg in hand. Scores are pegged up the outside and down the inside of each player's double row of holes by moving pegs alternately. Here, white pegs eight on his first deal and indicates that figure by placing his second peg in the eighth hole from the start. Black also pegged eight on his first deal, and has subsequently pegged four, indicated by moving the previously backward peg four holes in front of the other. By this system each player's total score is indicated by his leading peg, his most recent score by the difference between it and his trailing peg. Mistakes in counting are therefore easy to note and to correct. There are also 121- and 181-hole boards, but it is just as convenient to count twice or three times round the 61 board. Additional central holes are sometimes provided for recording games or circuits of the board.

Game. The winner is the first player to attain 61 points, which will take several deals. It may be agreed that if the loser fails to reach 31, he is lurched (or, in the lurch) and loses double. Alternatively, the game may be played up to 121, in which case the lurch is 91.

Deal. Whoever cuts the higher (Ace low) deals first, and his opponent immediately pegs (scores) 'three for last', which is

meant to compensate him for the disadvantage of not having the
first crib. Subsequently, the turn to deal alternates, but three for
last is not scored again in the same game. Deal five cards to each
player, one at a time, and place the remainder face down on the
table.

Discarding. Each player now looks at his cards, discarding two;
the four discards are laid aside face down to form the 'crib'. The
crib belongs to the dealer. He may not look at it yet, but at the
end of the game any scoring combinations it contains count in
his favour. Meanwhile, any scoring combinations formed by the
three cards left in each hand will count in favour of their holder.
Before discarding, therefore, it is necessary to know what
scoring combinations are to be made at Cribbage.

Scoring combinations. The order of cards in each suit is
A 2 3 4 5 6 7 8 9 T J Q K. Each card has a point value equivalent
to the number of pips on its face, *ie* Ace 1, Two 2, and so on.
For this purpose court cards count 10 each, and it is convenient
to refer to all cards worth 10 (T J Q K) as 'tenths'. The scoring
combinations and the amounts they score are as follows:

Fifteen (any two or more cards totalling exactly 15)	= 2
Pair (two cards of the same rank)	= 2
Prial (= pair royal) (three cards of the same rank)	= 6
Double pair royal (four of the same rank)	= 12
Run (three or more cards in sequence)	= 1 per card
Flush (three cards of one suit in the hand)	= 3
Flush (as above, and start card also of that suit)	= 4
Flush (four crib cards and start card of same suit)	= 5

Some examples of a fifteen are 7–8, 5–Q and A–6–8. A crib
containing A–6–6–8 would count fifteen twice: once for A–8
plus the first Six, and again for A–8 plus the second Six; –

the hand would also score 2 for the pair. But a hand of 7–4–4 counts fifteen only once, because the two Fours must be used once together instead of once each in order to make up the total. They still count 2 for the pair, of course.

A pair only counts if both cards are of exactly the same rank, such as Q–Q. Two different tenths, such as J–K, do not pair. A prial scores 6 because it is made up of three different pairs. For example, ♠7–♡7–♣7 counts as (♠7–♡7)+ (♡7–♣7)+(♠7–♣7). A double pair royal counts 12 by the same system.

A run is three or more cards in sequence, regardless of suit, such as A–2–3 or 9–T–J–Q. The score is 1 per card in the sequence, *ie* at least 3.

If a player's three hand-cards are of the same suit, he may peg 3 for the flush, or 4 if the start card (see below) also matches. If all four cards of the crib are of the same suit, the crib-holder may count the flush *only* if the start is also of that suit, for a total of 5.

A fundamental principle of Cribbage combinations is that a score is credited for each different combination of cards that can be made, and any individual card may be used in different combinations or more than one of the same type. Thus a hand such as 7–7–8–9 is scored cumulatively as follows: 'Fifteen 2, fifteen 4, pair 6 and two runs of three 12'. Note that the Sevens not only count together as a pair, but also can each be used in turn to score two different fifteens and two different three-card runs.

Let us now return to the game. In discarding to the crib, the dealer will naturally seek to throw cards that tend to combine, whereas his opponent will throw cards that bear no relation to each other. At the same time, both will endeavour to retain cards which go together.

The start. After the discarding, non-dealer cuts the pack and dealer takes the top card of the bottom half and lays it face up on the top. This card is known as the start. If it is a Jack, dealer immediately pegs 'two for his heels'.

The play. Before any combinations are scored, the cards are played as follows. Starting with non-dealer, each in turn plays one of his cards face up to the table in front of himself. (The two players' cards must not get mixed up.) Non-dealer announces the face value of his first card, and as each subsequent card appears its player announces the cumulative total of all cards so far played. Thus if the first cards are Four, Nine, Two, the announcements are 'four–thirteen–fifteen' and so on. If either player adds a card which forms a scoring combination when considered in conjunction with the previous card or cards consecutively played, he is entitled to announce and peg for it. For example: Non-dealer 'Four'; dealer (playing a Six) 'Ten'; non-dealer (playing a Five): 'Fifteen 2 and a run of three, 5'. That is, he scores 2 for bringing the count to fifteen, and 3 for forming the three-card sequence 4–5–6, even though they did not actually appear in that order. If now dealer adds a Three, he announces 'Eighteen and a run (of four) 4', as he has thereby extended the sequence into one of 3–4–5–6. Pairs, prials and double pairs royal may be made and pegged in the same way, so long as the cards they combine with were played consecutively, *ie* without interruption by an extraneous card not belonging to the combination. Thus if the first four cards were 6–7–5–5, the first Five would make a run of three and the second would make a pair, but the second would not make a run of three as it has been separated from the Six and Seven by another card. Again, 6–7–4 scores nothing, but if the next card played were a Five it would make a four-card sequence for 4 points. In the play, flushes do not count.

31 and go. The play continues so long as neither player brings the combined count above 31. If a player cannot add a card without exceeding this total, he must pass by announcing 'go', whereupon the other must add as many more cards as he can without exceeding 31. Whoever plays the last card pegs 'one for last', or 'two' if he brings the count to exactly 31.

Counting the hand. Each player now retrieves his cards and scores for any combinations they contain, non-dealer doing so first. For this purpose each player considers the start (turned-up card) as if it formed part of his own hand. For example, if the start were a Six, a player holding 4–5–6 would score 12 altogether. If the three cards of his hand are all of the same suit, he counts 3 for the flush, and if the start is also of that suit, he counts 4 instead. Furthermore, whoever holds the Jack of the same suit as the start pegs 'one for his nob'. After non-dealer has counted his hand, dealer counts his own on exactly the same basis. Finally, dealer turns up the cards of the crib and scores this as if it were yet another hand. Again, the start is counted as part of it, making it a five-card hand altogether, and the Jack of the turned suit scores one for his nob. The only difference is a restriction on flushes: a flush only counts if all five cards are of the same suit – it is not enough for the four discards to be alike in suit if the start is different.

Muggins (*optional*). An optional but recommended rule is that if either player omits to score anything to which he is entitled, his opponent may draw attention to it (with a cry of 'muggins') and score it himself.

Ending. As soon as one player reaches the target score, play ceases at whatever stage it has reached. This may be as the result of turning a Jack for start, or playing to the count, or counting either of the hands or the crib, or scoring by the rule of muggins, or by means of a penalty.

Penalties. A 2-point penalty (added to the aggrieved party's score) is counted for each of the following irregularities: (1) In the deal, exposing one of non-dealer's cards, or dealing him too many; in the former case he may demand a redeal, and in the latter a redeal is compulsory. (2) For touching the undealt pack except to cut and turn the start. (3) During the play, for failing to add a card although able to do so without exceeding 31. Furthermore, if it is discovered that a player has pegged more than his entitlement, he must reduce his score to the correct amount, and the amount by which he overpegged is credited to his opponent.

Six-card Cribbage

(This account assumes knowledge of the five-card game, anything unexplained being the same as described above.)

Game. Game may be set as 121, with (optionally) 91 for the lurch and 61 for the double lurch, or at 181, with 121 for the lurch.

Deal. After cutting for first deal, there is no scoring of three for last. Deal six cards each one at a time.

Discard. Each player discards two cards to a crib, which belongs to the dealer.

Start. Non-dealer cuts and dealer turns up the start, counting 2 for his heels if it is a Jack. (This score seems to be increasingly ignored by modern players.)

Play. Non-dealer leads and cards are played up to 31 as at the five-card game, with scores for fifteen, pairs, runs, 'go' and making 31. If, however, either player has cards left unplayed from hand, those so far played are turned face down and a new series is played with the remaining cards up to (but not over) 31 as before, the first card being led by the opponent of the player who played the last of the previous series. If this still fails to exhaust all the cards, yet a third series is started.

Counting the hand. As before, non-dealer then counts the start as part of his hand and scores for all the combinations he can make from the five cards. Then dealer does the same, and finally counts his crib, consisting of four cards and the start. A flush consists of four cards in hand for 4, plus a fifth if the start is of the same suit. A flush in the crib scores only if the start matches, for 5.

Seven-card Cribbage

As six-card, except that game is 181 and seven cards are dealt to each player. Each discards two to the crib and counts a six-card hand including the start. This form of the game is little played.

Auction Cribbage

This variant, which I suspect to have been invented by the late Hubert Phillips, injects an additional element of judgement and may be commended for that reason, though I have never met anyone who plays it. The principle may be applied to the game whether played with five, six or seven cards, and the idea is that the crib does not necessarily belong to the dealer but may be won by bidding for it. After dealing, the dealer states how many points he is prepared to pay for the privilege of the crib; non-dealer may raise this amount, dealer re-raise it and so on until one of them passes. The other then immediately deducts from his score the amount he is prepared to pay, and play proceeds. The start is turned, both discard as usual, and the opponent of the crib-holder leads the first card and also counts his hand first after the play. Phillips, the only source I know for the game (in *The Pan Book of Card Games*), does not state what happens if neither is prepared to bid. I suggest that if both pass the start should be turned and each have another opportunity to bid. If both still pass, which is unlikely, the hands are thrown in and the next in turn deals.

Square Cribbage

This variation was devised by me and is also intended to increase the skill factor. It may be played auction-wise as described above, but is essentially a six-card game.

1. Deal six cards each and discard two to the crib in the usual way. Do not yet turn a card for start.
2. Starting with non-dealer, or whoever does not have the crib, each in turn scores for any combinations he may hold on his own four cards. Anything he scores for must be shown, but it is not obligatory to declare everything one has.
3. Now the start card is turned in the usual way, dealer scoring 2 for his heels if it is a Jack. The start is placed face up in the middle of the table.
4. Starting with the opponent of the crib-holder, each in turn

plays a card to the table in such a way as to gradually build up a square of $3 \times 3 = 9$ cards, with the start card in the centre. There is no counting up to 31.

5. A player scores for any combination he makes between the card he plays and any other card or cards in the same row, column or long diagonal, as at noughts and crosses (eight directions in all). A three-card flush is valid, but it is impossible to make a four-card run or double pair royal. Combinations may be scored in more than one direction simultaneously, provided that each one involves the card just played. For playing the Jack of the same suit as the centre card (the start), score one for his nob.

6. When all eight cards have been played, the crib-holder turns the crib and counts it in the usual way, including the start (centre card of the square) as part of it. A flush must contain five cards as usual.

The point of this variation is that each player enters it with some knowledge of his opponent's cards, *ie* of those scored at the beginning, and will therefore be guided by this knowledge in his planning of where and when to place cards in the square. Higher scores are made because any given card may be scored in up to three directions at once.

Notes on play (basic 5- and 6-card)

Cribbage has been noted as one of the few games in which memory does not play an important part. At the same time, it is one of the foremost of those in which experience leads rapidly to intuitive and unerringly correct play. The well-practised player does not need to think overmuch about the discard or play of a given hand – similar situations will have come up so often before that he will know by looking at his cards the best course of action to take. The beginner, however, must go slowly at first, and will have to consider several alternatives before making a decision. It is to this end that the following notes may be of help. They are written from the viewpoint of the five-card game, but much the same principles apply to six-card, which is the same thing only bigger.

First, it is important to realise that Cribbage is scored, as I have remarked before, in dribs and drabs – two points here, two points there, one for his nob, and so on. For this reason a fundamental law of the game is that *every point counts*. Look after the pennies, as they say, and the pounds will take care of themselves. Even when deciding which cards to throw to the crib, you must take into account whether or not the cards remaining might enable you, with correct play, to score a go in the play up to 31. There is only one point in it, but it might be vital. The highest possible score in the crib is 29, but an average value is 4, and quite a few are complete duds. In Cribbage you must fight for odd points. Don't sit back and expect them to come out in the wash.

Your first strategic decision in the game is what to throw to the crib. If the crib is yours, throw cards that combine well, such as a Five and a tenth, a pair, or at the very least two cards in sequence, as there is a good chance of improving any of these with the aid of the cards thrown by your opponent plus the start. A Five and a tenth, scoring 'fifteen 2', make a good discard, as the chances are roughly 4 in 13 that the start will be a tenth, while it is often difficult for the non-dealer to avoid throwing a tenth to the crib.

If the crib is not yours, throw cards unlikely to combine well, and certainly not combinable with each other. You cannot guard much against the likelihood that one of your cards will pair with the start or one of the other discards, but you can fight sequences by throwing cards widely separated in rank. From the viewpoint of fifteens it is clearly essential not to throw a Five, as there are too many chances of there being tenths in the crib. There is somewhat less danger involved in throwing a tenth, as the chances are much against your opponent's holding a Five (especially if you have one yourself), or the appearance of one as the start. But keep back a tenth if you can discard anything safer, and always keep back a Jack on the principle of counting the pennies – you may score one for his nob. You must, of course, ensure that the two cards you throw do not total five or fifteen, and ten is to be avoided if possible. There is always also the danger that a start lower than Five will combine to total five with another low card in the crib.

Neither player should bother about a flush in the crib. If the crib is yours you are unlikely to get one, and if it is your opponent's you need not spoil your hand to avoid throwing two of a suit. A flush in the hand is only worth holding as compensation for lack of combining possibilities, and is not worth keeping back at the expense of good cards for the play.

The other side of the discarding coin is consideration of which cards to keep in hand – not only for the combinations they may score between them, but also for the play. In the latter connection it is generally preferable to keep low cards. So, all things being equal, prefer to throw high cards to the crib.

Choice of discards may also be modified by the state of the score. If you have the crib when both are within reach of game, do not waste good cards on a high-scoring crib. Remember that the crib is counted last, and your opponent may peg out before you get a chance to use it. In this case retain cards more likely to score at the earliest opportunity – in the play.

In the play, the best cards to lead from a numerical viewpoint are those lower than Five, as they cannot be fifteened with one card (from which point of view, the worst possible lead is a Five). The best lead is a Four; lower ranks are more usefully retained to score a go as 31 is reached.

From the viewpoint of the structure of your hand, a good lead is one of a pair, in the hope that your opponent will pair it and give you a prial, as the danger of his then making a double pair royal is pretty remote. It is also reasonable to lead cards close in rank, with a view to making a sequence, especially if there is the chance of your making a run of four without his gaining an intervening three.

Playing second and given the choice, prefer to make the lead up to fifteen than to pair the first card, in case it was led from a pair in the hope of a prial. Generally, if your own cards are close in rank you may 'play on' – that is, play ranks close to those of your opponent with a view to making runs. If they are widely separated, it is better to 'play off' by always seeking to play a card remote in rank from the previous one.

Once past the half-way mark, always avoid bringing the count to 21, as there are too many cards in the pack to make it 31 next. It is also important to avoid halving the total needed to make 31 exactly, as your opponent may then score 4 for the pair and the 31. (For example, at 23, which is eight short, don't play a Four. That makes 27, and another Four scores high.)

Finally, keep careful track of both players' positions. When leading, don't mind giving your opponent 2 for a fifteen if you can then pair it for 2 yourself, as he will not gain on you and you will be closer to home. When trailing, however, take every reasonable chance to reduce the difference, and if this is not possible then prefer that neither should score rather than both; e.g., don't pair the lead if you think he can make it 15.

Illustrative deals

Two deals from a game at Five-card Cribbage should show how the game goes and what sort of decisions must be made. Our players are Alf and Bert; the former cuts a King and is 'in the box' first, dealing:

First deal

A: ♡2 ♠5 ◇8 ♣T ♡T
B: ♡3 ◇7 ♣7 ♣8 ◇9

Alf seems to have an embarrassment of riches – three fifteens and a pair, something of which will have to be broken up. If he keeps ♠5 ♣T ♡T, worth 6, he must throw to the crib ♡2 ◇8, which is unlikely to make anything as a Five discarded or turned up is too remote to think of. As there is more chance of a tenth, he discards ♠5 ♣T to his crib and retains ♡2 ◇8 ♡T for the play.

Bert's hand is hardly less prolific, containing a pair, two fifteens and a couple of runs to boot. But ♡3 and ◇9 would make good discards (provided that there is no other Three in the crib), so he breaks the runs and keeps ◇7 ♣7 ♣8.

The ♠A is turned as the start, and Bert leads:

B: ◇7 (= 7)
A: ◇8 (= 15) pegs fifteen–2
B: ♣8 (= 23) pegs pair 2
A: ♡2 (= 25)
B: 'go'
A: pegs 1 for last, as he cannot play further.

Now Bert counts his hand: fifteen 2, fifteen 4, fifteen 6 (counting the start to make ♠A ◇7 ♣7), and a pair 8, plus 2 in play 10.

Alf counts his: nothing in hand, 3 in play. And the crib: fifteen–2, fifteen–4. Total 7. A poor result. Had he discarded his pair of Tens and retained ♡2 ♣5 ◇8 he would have finished with an extra point. In principle, however, the discard of ♠5 ♣T should have met at least another tenth for an extra 2.

Second deal. Bert deals

B: ♠3 ♣6 ♠Q ♠K ◇K
A: ◇2 ◇4 ♠4 ♣J ♡K

Bert's problem is whether to keep the flush for 3, discarding ♣6 ◇K to his own crib, or the pair of Kings intact in hand or crib. If the latter, should he retain ♠Q ♠K ◇K in the hope of turning a Jack for two runs, throwing ♠3 ♣6, or throw the two Kings and keep ♠3 ♣6 ♠Q as being good cards for the play? He chooses the last possibility, discarding both Kings.

Alf has no such problem: he will keep the pair and the Jack, discarding ◇2 ♡K, fairly innocuous-looking cards for his opponent's crib.

The start is ♣5, and play proceeds:

A: ◇4 (= 4)
B: ♠3 (= 7)

A:　♣J (= 17)
B:　♣6 (= 23)
A:　♠4 (= 27)
B:　'go'
A:　1 for last.

Bert hesitated before playing his Six. Bringing the count to 23 gave Alf more scope than bringing it to 27 would have done, but the former has already shown a Four and a Jack. Since Alf must have kept his best cards for the hand, he may well have another Four, which would give him an extra hole for making 31.

Alf now counts his hand (♢4　♠4　♣J and the start ♣5): fifteen–2, pair 4, one for his nob 5, plus 1 for last 6.

Bert's is ♠3　♣6　♠Q and start ♣5, worth fifteen–2 only. His crib, however, brings a rich haul: ♢2　♡K　♢K　♠K and the start ♣5 counts fifteen–2, fifteen–4, fifteen–6, prial 12, total 15 to Alf's 6.

GIN RUMMY

Gin is the simplest, the earliest and probably the best of the large family of Rummy games, which all work on the same principles and differ from one another only in degrees of complication. Though it reached its hey-day during the 30s–40s golden age of Hollywood ('the game of the stars'), it seems first to have been described in more or less its present form during the first decade of the present century. It bears striking similarities to the southern-states negro game of Coon Can, which lies in direct line of descent from the first recorded Rummy game, Con Quian, played in Mexico in the middle of the last century. The whole family has always been particularly associated with Latin America, as witnessed by such later elaborations as Canasta (the word is Spanish and the place of origin Uruguay) and its derivatives Bolivia, Samba and so on.

The object in Rummy games is to collect cards which 'go together', either being of the same rank, like ♠7 ♡7 ♣7, or forming a sequence in the same suit, such as ♠7 ♠8 ♠9. Such a matching collection is called a *meld*. Any cards left in one's hand at the end of a deal which fail to form a meld of three or more are called *deadwood*, and incur penalties equivalent to their combined face values. The method by which cards are collected for this purpose will probably be well known even to non card-players. At each turn you draw a card from a stockpile and throw out an unwanted card to a discard pile, and keep doing so until all the cards you hold can be arranged in matching sets, or melds. It is a method which is to be found in essence in the game of Mah Jong, and which has been borrowed as part of the mechanics of many modern table games. One could even claim to recognise it in Monopoly, by noting that you may not build upon a property until you have formed it into part of a 'meld' of three properties of the same colour.

Gin Rummy is very easy to learn and the rules are clear, simple, and fairly well standardised.

The game

Cards. One standard 52-card pack; no Jokers.

Game. The game is won by the first player to reach 100 points, which normally takes several deals.

Rank and value of cards. Cards rank A 2 3 4 5 6 7 8 9 T J Q K and are worth their face value, with Ace 1 and court cards 10 each.

Deal. Whoever cuts the higher card chooses whether or not to deal first. Thereafter the winner of one hand deals to the next, and the winner of a game deals first to the next. It is important that the cards be thoroughly shuffled before play, dealer having the right to shuffle last. Deal ten cards each, one at a time. Place the remainder face down to form a stock. Take the top card of the stock and lay it face up beside it to form the first 'upcard'. This will form the base of a gradually constituted waste pile of faced cards, the topmost of which is always known as the upcard.

To start. Nondealer may start by exchanging the upcard for any card in his hand. If he refuses, dealer has the same privilege. If either player does so, that constitutes his first turn and the game continues from there. If both refuse it, nondealer must start the game by drawing the top card of the stock, adding it to his hand, and discarding any card face up on the original upcard to continue the waste pile.

Play. Thereafter, each player in turn must draw and add to his hand either the unknown top card of the stock, or the faced upcard surmounting the waste pile. In either case he completes his turn by making one discard face up to the waste pile. It is not permissible to draw the upcard and discard it on the same turn.

Object. The object is to collect cards which together form one or more melds, a meld consisting of either (a) three or four cards of the same rank, or (b) a sequence of three or more cards in the same suit, such as ♠A 2 3 ... or ... ♡T J Q K. (For this purpose, Ace and King are not consecutive.) A hand consisting entirely of melds, with no deadwood, is described as 'gin' and carries a bonus. But a player may end the game as soon as the total value of his unmatched cards is 10 or less, at which point the player with the lower value of deadwood wins. During play, melds are not revealed but retained secretly in the hand.

Knocking. When a player is satisfied with the low value of his deadwood, he ends the game by (theoretically) knocking on the table after he has drawn an eleventh card and before making his final discard. It is now the practice to indicate closure of the game by laying the final discard face down on the waste pile, an action still referred to as knocking. The knocker then spreads his hand of cards face up on the table, arranged in melds and with any deadwood clearly separated from them. His opponent then does the same, but also has the privilege of 'laying off' any cards of his own deadwood which may be matched with any of the knocker's melds, in order to reduce the penalty value of his deadwood. This privilege does not apply, however, if the knocker has a gin hand (no deadwood).

End of stock. The two last cards of the stock may not be taken. If neither player has knocked by the time they are reached, the result is a no-score draw, and the same dealer deals again.

Score. Each player keeps his score cumulatively, the winner of a hand adding his score for the hand to his previous total and writing down the combined amount in order to make clear when 100 has been reached or exceeded.

If the knocker has the lower count for deadwood, he scores the difference between the two deadwood values. If he went gin, he adds a bonus of 25.

If the opponent has an equal or lower value of deadwood, he scores the difference (if any) plus a bonus of 25 for undercut. But he cannot undercut a gin hand, for which the knocker still counts 25, nor may he himself score the bonus for gin, whether he had it already (in which case he should have knocked) or acquired it by laying off.

Game score. As soon as either player has reached or exceeded 100 points, the game ends and a line is drawn beneath both totals, beneath which various bonuses are recorded. First, the winner records a bonus of 100 for game; next, he adds a 25-point 'box' bonus for each hand that he won. Finally, if he won every hand he adds a bonus for 'shut-out'. This is equivalent to twice the basic amount he scored plus another 100 for game. (In some circles, the box bonuses are also doubled. Other bonus systems may be encountered, but the one described here is usual American practice.) The difference between the two final totals is the margin of victory.

Hollywood scoring system. For those who can't get enough of it, this is a method of playing three games simultaneously (or more if preferred, following the same principle). Three sets of double columns are drawn up, each double column headed by the initials of the players. When a player wins his first hand, his score is recorded in the first set only. When he wins his second, it is recorded in the first and second sets. His third, and so on, is recorded in all three, unless and until any of them has been ruled off with a win. As soon as a player reaches 100 in any of the three sets of columns, that set is ruled off and bonuses noted in the usual way. Play continues until all games have been completed and scored.

Oklahoma variant. In this version the maximum count of deadwood with which you may knock is not necessarily 10, but is determined by the value of the initial upcard. For instance, if it is a Six you must have six or less to knock; if a King, ten. It is usually agreed that if the first upcard is an Ace, you must have a gin hand to go out. The variant may be recommended for the variety it adds to the game.

Suggestions for play

Gin is a game of observation, inference and memory, in that order. Each player's management of his own hand is a somewhat mechanical affair in the sense that for any given situation there is a fairly calculable best move. It is because there is a 'best' move that observation is the foremost aspect of skill required. You *observe* what your opponent is discarding and which of your discards he is drawing; from that, *infer* the structure of his hand on the assumption that he is either making the best moves or acting in accordance with a personal style of play to which you have become accustomed; and thereafter *remember* all the cards that have gone and the changing contents of your opponent's hand as the play proceeded.

As to the play of your own hand, the first thing to note is the inadvisability of going all out for gin. The bonus of 25 is not sufficient to compensate for the times when you should have knocked instead of waiting around for glory, and thereby found yourself more knocked against than knocking. And, worse still, being undercut for your pains. A typical game ends about half to two thirds of the way through the pack, so if you get a knocking hand much earlier than that do not hesitate to go down for all you can get.

It is generally better to draw the stock card than the upcard. The more upcards you draw, the more of your hand is known to the other side, and the more of the rest of it can be deduced. You are also taking cards of no use to your opponent, when by drawing the next card of stock you may well be preventing him from going gin. The best exception to the rule is when you need the upcard to convert two matching cards into a meld of three, thus eliminating three pieces of deadwood (including the discard), or, of course, when it enables you to knock immediately. It may also be useful to expand a meld, especially if you thereby eliminate a high unmatched card; but this should be done with caution rather than as a matter of course, as it can do more harm than good. If, for example, you hold

♠K ♡K ♣K, ◊7 8 9, ♠5, ◊5, ♡2, ♣2

it is not worth taking ◊T as the upcard, as you must then throw one of a pair and so halve the number of draws that will enable you to knock. One other conceivable reason for taking the upcard might be to reduce your deadwood when you suspect an imminent knocking from the other side of the table. The lower the rank he discarded, the worse the danger would appear to be.

Because it is desirable to throw high cards instead of low ones, in order to keep your deadwood down, it is also reasonable to retain high-ranking pairs and two-card sequences acquired early in the game, in the hope that your opponent will discard a matching third in exchange for a lower-valued draw. But this should not be kept up too long. When to give up such expectations and start reducing deadwood is a matter for fine judgement.

Keeping track of discards is fundamental to the play. Suppose your opponent throws ♣J. The easy assumption is that he is 'not collecting Jacks', so you discard ♡J at the next opportunity – and are surprised to see him pounce on it. Too late you spot the ruse. He might have held ♡9 ♡T ♣J and thrown the Jack to draw one of the proper suit for the sequence. Even more cunningly, and perhaps at greater risk (depending on how well he knew the contents of your hand) he might have discarded from ♠J ◇J ♣J. Why, then, should he run a risk to bluff the fourth out of you? Because he thereby not only re-forms his meld, but also prevents you from laying off a Jack when he goes out on the next turn, and perhaps undercutting him.

Of course, what's sauce for the gander is sauce for the goose, and you are at liberty to practise such stratagems yourself. And here's another. Suppose he throws a Jack and you have two Jacks. You are tempted to take it immediately and complete a meld. But resist! He might have been playing from a pair. If so, leave it. He will be bound to throw the other Jack, and then you can take it and be certain that he cannot lay off against that meld of yours and be in a position to undercut. For this to work, you must be pretty sure that he was playing from a pair to start with, and that he is not retaining the other Jack as part of a sequence. If all the Tens and Queens have gone, there is no danger of the latter; and if you have held your Jacks for some time, there is a fair chance that his discard was made from two. If it does go wrong, there is still the chance that either you will draw the other Jack or he will draw and discard it before too great damage is done. Unless he knows every card in your hand, he would be unlikely to draw it and keep it.

So much depends upon observation and remembrance of the contents of the waste pile that you must clearly be very careful in your choice of discard. The first card *not* to throw out is the one you have just drawn from stock and are still holding in your hand: if it really is useless, don't let him know. Hang on to it for a turn or two before getting rid of it. On general principles, as we have seen, it is desirable to throw out a high unmatched card in order to reduce deadwood. The time not to do so is when you suspect that it might be of use to your opponent. In particular, he might be deliberately forcing a card out of you by one of the bluffing stratagems described above, in which case you must hold it back for a turn or two. Check this by matching your proposed discard against the current upcard. The less relation it bears to it, by rank and suit, the better. One player of my acquaintance insists that the ideal discard is different in suit from, but adjacent in rank to, the existing upcard.

It is possible to select a discard in such a way as to elicit useful information. Suppose you have to split up ♠K ♡K, ♠Q ♣Q. In this case throw ♠K. If it is picked up you will know he has the other Kings (in which case you keep yours to lay off if necessary), since your own holding of the Queen shows that he cannot need it for the sequence.

In arranging your melds after knocking, prefer to attach a card to a set of four rather than a sequence if it could equally well go with either. In this way you certainly prevent your opponent from laying off against it, whereas with a sequence there is the danger that he may hold (and therefore lay off) an odd card that attaches to one end of it.

In brief, play your own hand with methodical accuracy, and devote all your thinking to the constitution of the waste pile and the probable structure of your opponent's hand. Above all, remain flexible. Don't select a hoped-for meld at the start of play and concentrate upon it fixedly: circumstances will require you to change plans at a moment's notice.

Illustrative deal

The players are Abe and Blondie, which latter deals as follows:

Abe	♠Q 6 A, ♡T 8, ♣K 8 4, ◊J T,
Blondie	♠T 9, ♡5 A, ♣T 3, ◊7 6 4 2,

The upcard is ♡4, which both players refuse. Abe has several pairs and one two-card sequence, but the rest are unrelated and somewhat high in value. He might have done better to take the upcard and start reducing deadwood by discarding ♠Q. Blondie has a pair of Tens and a promising collection of diamonds. In the account below, the first card shown is the card drawn from stock and the one in brackets represents the discard. UP means the upcard (previous player's discard) is drawn.

A: ♡7 (♠6) Makes a two-card sequence.

B: ♡3 (♡5) Her only discard if the Tens are to be kept.

A: ♡9 (♣K) This makes a four-card sequence including ♡T, which can still be detached and used with ◊T if a black Ten is drawn. The discard reduces deadwood and only runs the risk of being taken if Blondie has a pair of Kings or Queen, Jack of clubs. Kings and Aces are good discards because they do not easily enable the opponent to make sequences.

B: ♣J (♠9) Keeping her pair of Tens, and swapping one two-card sequence for another to avoid throwing out the same card as drawn, which might be observed.

A: ♣Q (♣8) Abe splits his Eights, hoping to draw ♡9 to attach to ♡8 and ♡T (not a commendable expectation), and that Blondie might discard a Queen.

B: ♠3 (♣J) This gives her a meld of Threes and enables her to lose a fairly safe piece of high-counting deadwood, as she holds ♣T while ♣K has already gone.

A: ♣5 (◊T) Abe splits his Tens, as the game is progressing without his having drawn anything useful for high-counting combinations.

B: UP (◊2) Blondie grabs this Ten for another meld – though had she read the previous section she might have left it until he discarded the second in order to prevent him from laying off. She doesn't like discarding such a low card (and Abe is duly dismayed by the sight of it), but must keep ♢7–6.

A: ♡K (♢J) He certainly won't throw the other Ten.

B: ♠J (♠J) By discarding the card drawn, Blondie shows that her hand is now ossified, and that she needs one of several specific cards to knock.

A: ♣A (♡K) A valuable draw, reducing deadwood by nine.

B: ♣7 (♢4) This doubles her chances of knocking, for besides ♢8 and ♢5 there are two Sevens that will make a meld on which to go out.

A: ♣6 (♣Q) Makes a club sequence and reduces deadwood by 19.

B: ♠8 (♠8) A useless card.

A: ♡6 (♠Q face down) Knocks.

Abe's melds are: ♡T–9–8–7–6, ♣6–5–4, leaving ♠A and ♣A for deadwood counting 2 against.

Blondie lays off ♣7 against Abe's club sequence, melds T♠–♣–♢, 3♠–♡–♣, and counts 14 for the remaining deadwood, namely ♢7 ♢6 ♡A. Abe wins, counting towards game Blondie's 14 minus his 2, a score of 12.

Note the strong element of luck in those last two draws. Had Blondie drawn ♠7 instead of ♠8 she would have knocked with deadwood of 1 against Abe's 12, giving her 11 to game. Note, too, that the game ended on the fifteenth out of thirty possible draws – exactly half way through the pack.

ALL FOURS

This old English game, of Kentish origin, is the two-player ancestor of the modern American game of Auction Pitch (see the section on *Card Games for Four*). Along with our native Cribbage, to which it has a curiously similar flavour though being quite different in structure, neither it nor any of its relatives have spread to the rest of Europe. As it is now played little in its country of origin, except sporadically as a pub game in a few unconnected localities, it would probably be regarded as extinct were it not for the fact that its emigration to the colonial Americas gave it a new lease of life on the western side of the Atlantic. For much of the last century, All Fours and its derivatives were among the most popular card games in the United States and Mexico. All Fours itself survives in America under the name Seven Up, which is the form described below, along with such derivatives as California Jack (see page 83), All Fives, Pitch, Cinch, and various games which include the name 'Pedro' in the title.

All Fours may be characterised as a fast little gambling game at which success depends less on cerebral calculation than on long experience. The title of the game is presumed to refer to the four major scoring features of play, namely High, Low, Jack, and the Game.

The game

Cards. A standard 52-card pack.

Game. The winner is the first player to reach a previously agreed total, formerly 11 points in the English game but now 7 in the American – whence the alternative title 'Seven Up'. This will take several deals to achieve. Scores may be recorded on paper, though a traditional method is to start with seven counters each and pay them into a pool one at a time for each point won, so that the winner is the first to get rid of his seven counters.

Deal. Whoever cuts the higher-ranking card deals first; thereafter the turn to deal alternates. Deal a batch of three cards face down to each player, then a second batch of three so that each receives a hand of six cards. Lay the remainder face down to one side, and turn the top card face up.

The turn-up. The suit of the turn-up proposes a trump suit for the deal, which may or may not be accepted by either player. If the turn-up is a Jack, the dealer scores 1 point for it.

Object. The object in each hand is to score as many points as possible, single points being available for one or more of the following factors:

> *Turning a Jack*, as explained above.
> *Gift*, as explained below in the bidding.
> *High*, for having been dealt the highest trump in play.
> *Low*, for having been dealt the lowest trump in play (or, if agreed beforehand, for winning it in a trick).
> *Jack*, for winning a trick containing the Jack of trumps, if it is in play.
> *Game*, for capturing, in tricks, the highest aggregate value of scoring-cards, valued thus: each Ace 4, King 3, Queen 2, Jack 1, Ten 10. In the event of a tie this point goes to elder hand (non-dealer) – this is to offset younger's advantage of scoring a point for turning a Jack.

It is to be noted that the first two points (turning a Jack and Gift) will not always occur, and that there can be no point for winning the Jack if it is not in play, *ie* lies in the undealt part of the pack. Two or more of the points for High, Low and Jack may be combined in one card. For instance, if a given card is the *only* trump in play then it counts one for High plus one for Low. Similarly, the Jack of trumps will count an extra point if it is the highest or the lowest in play. In the extreme case, it would count four if it were the only trump in play (High, Low, Jack) and also the only scoring card in play (giving its winner Game).

Bidding. The bidder is the player who eventually chooses trumps. He is not obliged to reach any particular target and is not penalised for losing, but will naturally select a suit which he thinks will yield him more points than his opponent. Elder hand has first choice: he may accept the turned suit as trump by saying 'I stand', or reject it by saying 'I beg'. If he begs, younger may also accept or reject the proposed trump, but it costs him a point to accept. He accepts by saying 'Take it', in which case elder scores 1 point for Gift and play begins. He rejects the suit by putting the turn-up to one side and 'running the cards', as follows.

Running the cards. To find another suit for trumps, younger first deals another batch of three to each player, so that both have nine cards, and turns up the top card of the pack again. If it is a different suit, the same procedure applies: he scores a point if it is a Jack, then elder may stand or beg, and, if he begs, younger may accept the suit by giving elder a point or reject it by running the cards yet again, dealing three more to each. This continues until either the pack runs out, in which case the hands are thrown in and the cards reshuffled and redealt by the same dealer, or a suit is accepted as trump. Whenever the turn-up proves to be of the same suit as one that has already been rejected, the cards are run again automatically. Younger may not score a point for turning the Jack of a suit that has already been rejected.

Play. If the cards have been run, each player makes as many discards as are necessary to reduce his playing hand to six cards again. Non-dealer leads to the first trick, and the winner of each trick leads to the next. Normal rules of trick-taking apply, but with an important exception – namely, that the second to a trick is always entitled to play a trump, even if he can follow suit. It is not permissible, however, to play from a different non-trump suit if able to follow suit to the card led. A trick is won by the higher card of the suit led or by a higher trump if any are played.

Score. At the end of play each reckons his score for high, low, Jack and game. It is to be noted that points are scored strictly in the order stated, and that as soon as one player has the point which brings his total to seven he has won the game. When played for money, each game is settled separately for a fixed amount.

Notes on play

In all games of this family, custom varies as to whether the point for Low is scored by the player who happens to be dealt the lowest trump in play, or by the player who captures it in a trick – which may, of course, be the same player if he uses it to trump with, but need not always be so. In the original game it went always to the player dealt it. In modern games such as Auction Pitch it goes to the player who captures it, though there is a tendency in two-hand play to revert to the original system. There are those who argue that if the point goes to the player who wins it then credit is given for skill rather than luck. On the other hand, it requires hardly less judgement to decide whether or not your lowest trump – the Four, for example – is in fact likely to be the lowest in play. In short, the only matter of any import is that you should agree beforehand which rule to follow.

The strategy of All Fours depends entirely on the score. At love-all you will be looking for a hand that offers at least two and preferably three of the four potential points, and without losing one for gift for the sake of getting it. At the other extreme, with only one point short of game you can safely entrump any suit of which you hold the Ace, as you will win with the inevitable 'one for High' no matter how many of the others your opponent gains.

You are bound to win the point for High if you hold the Ace of trumps. If the cards have not been run, you can reckon the King as high (and, conversely, the Three as low) about nine times out of ten, and the Queen high (Four low) about four times out of five.

Never bank on the point for Jack unless you have it yourself, and well guarded at that, normally with at least two other trumps.

The point for game is the only one that depends upon the skill with which you play your cards. In this connection, it is essential to save any Ten you hold, as its capture is usually enough to swing the point for Game. For the same reason, it is better, if at all possible, to use Aces and Kings to capture adverse leads than to lead them in their own right. As capturing cards they stand to ensure the point for Game by taking others that may also be of value, whereas, as leaders, they risk being trumped.

A hand containing three or more trumps is usually worth playing – the more so if it includes high ranks or the Jacks, the less so if it lacks these or includes an unguarded Ten. A two-trump hand may be playable if it includes the Ace or King. If you are scoring Low for being dealt it, and have the lead, you may also chance your arm on (say) Q–2 by leading the Two and hoping to force out a singleton Ace or King. If it works, you may gain Game and Low against your opponent's High only.

Related games

All Fives. This increases the number of points to be played for. Game is usually set at 61 and progress recorded on a Cribbage board. In addition to the single points for High, Low, Jack and Game, the following trumps score as below to the player capturing them in tricks:

Ace	4
King	3
Queen	2
Jack	1
Ten	10
Five	5

This gives a maximum of 29 points obtainable on one deal if all the value cards are in play. (In counting for 'Game', the Five of trumps is also worth five, but plain suit Fives have no value.) This scoring system may be applied to Pitch (below) and California Jack (page 83).

Pitch. Pitch is a bidding form of All Fours, and for this reason it is generally known as Auction Pitch, more usually played by four than by two. Starting with the non-dealer, each in turn bids to gain a minimum number of game points (High, Low, Jack and Game, as before) in exchange for the right of nominating trumps. Whoever bids the higher number establishes trumps by leading or 'pitching' a card of that suit, which starts the play. Both players score what they actually win, but the pitcher, if he fails to win as many as he bid, is set back by the amount of his bid – *ie*, that amount is deducted from his score. From this feature, the game is also known as Setback.

DRAW GAMES
German Whist – California
Jack – Honeymoon Bridge

Two-hand card game anthologies usually devote separate
sections to the games listed above. Such games, however, are for
the most part makeshift adaptations for two players of trick-
taking games more frequently and more smoothly played by
four, or some other number. All are based on the same method of
changing four hands of 13 cards each into two hands of 26, by
adopting the 'draw' principle as follows:

Deal so many cards each, and place the remainder face down
to form a stock. After playing the first trick in the usual way, the
winner of the trick draws the top card of the stock and adds it to
his hand, waits for his opponent to draw the next, then leads to
the second trick. After each trick there is a draw in the same way.
When all stock cards have been drawn, the cards remaining in
hand are played out to tricks until neither has any left. Thus 26
tricks will have been played in all.

It will be observed that almost any favourite trick-taking game
can be played by two players in this way, the rules and scoring of
the basic game being applied to the procedure described above.
There is one flaw in the whole idea, and that is that the rule
requiring the second player to follow suit to the card led is un-
enforceable during the first half of the game, as there is no way
of telling whether or not the second has revoked. No matter how
much you trust your opponent, or even yourself, it strikes me
that a game so open to temptation on the one hand and suspicion
on the other can hardly be played with complete equanimity.
The most practical way of overcoming this fault in the underlying principle is to introduce the rule followed at Bézique,
which is that the second player need not follow suit but may play
as he wishes. This rule ceases, of course, once the stock is
exhausted.

German Whist

In this game only six cards are dealt to each player. The top card of the stock is turned face up and establishes the trump suit for the whole of that game. The object of play is to win the majority of tricks. Non-dealer leads to the first trick. The second player must follow suit if he can; otherwise he may win by trumping or lose by playing any other card. The trick-winner draws the top card of stock, which is faced, and the loser draws the next. Before leading, the winner faces the next card of the stock so that both may see what it is before the trick is played. The game is a tie if both take 13 tricks.

The most interesting feature of German Whist is the fact that the next stock card is visible. If it is a good card, both players will try to win the trick; if not, they may seek to lose in the hope of drawing a better one from immediately beneath it.

A variation in play, which rather spoils the point of seeing the top card, requires the trick-loser to show his opponent what card he has drawn. It may be preferred by those who like games that exercise memory rather than judgement.

California Jack

This is the draw version of All Fours (page 76). As at German Whist, deal six cards each and turn up the top card of the stock to establish trumps. The winner of each trick draws the top (faced) card of stock and his opponent draws the second (unseen), and the next card is faced again before the next trick is led by the previous winner.

The rules of play and scoring features are as at All Fours, All Fives or Pitch, except that normal Whist rules of trick-play apply – *ie* the second player must follow suit if he can. (A nonsensical rule, for reasons already stated.) One point each is scored for winning High, Low, Jack and Game, as explained on page 77, and the winner is the first to reach a total of 10 points in as many deals as it takes.

Honeymoon Bridge

This game is only recommended for Bridge addicts and a knowledge of Bridge is assumed in this explanation. Deal 13 cards each and form a stock of the remainder. No card of the stock is ever seen except by one player, when he draws and adds it to his hand after a trick is played. During the first part of the game, when it is still possible to draw from stock, tricks are played at no trump and it is obligatory to follow suit. The first 13 tricks are of no account to the score. When they are over, there being no stock and each holding 13 cards in his final hand, the dealer may either bid or pass. Bidding proceeds as at Contract Bridge (or any other form of Bridge as preferred), and a contract is established when a bid, double or redouble is followed by a pass. The defender (non-bidder) leads, and the game is then played and scored as at Bridge. Official rules quote a penalty for revoking during the first half of the game, but do not explain how the fault can be proved other than by self-confession or the employment of an umpire.

CASSINO

There is a distinct family of card games that involves neither playing tricks as in the majority of games, nor collecting sets and sequences as in Rummy, Poker and a large number of others. We might call them 'sweeping games', as the object is to capture cards from the table by matching them with cards played from the hand, and a special score is usually given to 'sweeping the board', which means capturing all the table cards in one fell swoop (or sweep). The whole family is distinctly Mediterranean in flavour and probably of Italian origin, its chief member being Italy's national card game Scopone, for four players.

Of this family, the essentially two-handed Cassino is the 'one that got away' and has most found favour with the English-speaking card world on both sides of the Atlantic, though more on the western than the eastern side, no doubt because of the Italianate population of America. No matter how carefully an account is phrased, Cassino always looks complicated at first reading. Once you start playing, you may at first find it so simple as to be trivial. Closer acquaintance, however, soon reveals hidden depths to the play.

Cassino has long been spelt with a double S. Recent books state that this is a misspelling for Casino, and revert to the 'correct' spelling. I retain the misspelling, which may be regarded as now sanctioned by usage, to avoid any possible ambiguity, as a Cassino game is by no stretch of the imagination a casino game.

There are several variations to the game and the most basic form is described first.

The game

Cards. A standard 52-card pack.

Card values. Each Ace counts as 1, other numerals as face value. Courts do not have values.

Deal. After agreeing who goes first and then shuffling and cutting, deal two cards face down to your opponent, two to the table, two to yourself, and the same again. Each player takes his four cards into hand, and the four table cards are turned face up and arranged in a row. The rest of the pack is put face down to one side to form a stock.

Object. The object at each turn is to capture one or more table cards by matching it (them) in certain prescribed ways with a card played from the hand. If the card played from hand cannot properly match, it is left on the table and so increases the number of cards available for capture. If the card from hand captures all cards on the table, it is called a sweep and scores a bonus. Each player lays his captured and capturing cards face down in a pile, and at the end of the game scores for having:

more cards than the opponent	3
more spades than the opponent	1
◇T, known as Big Cassino	2
♠2, known as Little Cassino	1
each Ace captured	1
each sweep made	1

In brief, the object is to capture as many cards as possible, especially Aces, spades, and the Ten of diamonds.

Play. Each player at each turn plays a card from the hand face up to the table, and may or may not capture as explained below. When neither has any cards left, the same dealer deals four more (in pairs) to each player from the top of the stock, but no more to the table. When the last round is being dealt, the dealer must announce that it is the last.

In playing a card to the table, a player may do one of the following:

1. Capture by pairing, combining or both.
2. Build pairs or totals for subsequent capture.
3. Increase such builds, whether made by himself or his opponent.
4. Trail (none of the above).

Capturing (*'Taking in'*). A court card played from the hand may capture one table card of the same rank by pairing: a King captures a King, and so on.

Numeral cards also capture by pairing, but can capture as many of the same rank as may be available: an Ace can capture one or more Aces, and so on.

Numeral cards, furthermore, can capture by combining. That is, two or more single cards on the table may be captured by playing from hand a card equal to their combined values. For example, a Ten can capture an Ace and a Nine, or two Fives, or two Threes and a Four, and so on.

One numeral card may make as many captures as it can in one turn by pairing and/or combining. But table cards which have been grouped together in builds, as described below, can be captured only as builds, not as individual cards.

Building. Numerical cards (not courts) can be played from the hand in conjunction with cards on the table to form builds for capture on subsequent turns. This may be done by pairing or combining.

A pairing example: If you hold two Fives and there is a Five on the table, you can play one from hand upon the one on the table (announcing 'Building Fives'), then capture both by pairing on your next turn – unless, that is, your opponent held the fourth Five and himself captured them on his intervening turn.

A combining example: If there were a Five on the table and you held a Three and an Eight, you could on one turn play the Three upon the Five (announcing 'Building eight'), and on your next turn use your Eight to capture the build, along with any other captures that may be open to it.

It is obligatory to announce what build is being made, as this could otherwise cause confusion. For instance, if one player plays a Five upon a Five and announces 'Building Fives', that build can be captured only by a Five; but if he announces 'Building ten', it can be captured only by a Ten.

You may only make a build if you are able to capture or increase it on your next turn.

Increasing builds. A pairing build can be increased by the addition of another card of the same rank. For example, if you held three Fives and there were one on the table, you could build one on your first turn, add another on your second, then capture them all on your third.

A combined-total build may be increased by the addition of another card from hand, provided that you hold a card that can be used to capture it on the next turn. For example: Opponent plays a Two to a Three, announces 'Building five', thereby indicating that he can capture it on his next turn with a Five from the hand. You, holding an Ace and a Six, add the Ace to that build and announce 'Building six', hoping that he himself cannot immediately capture with a Six, or increase it further.

It is not permitted to increase a multiple build. For example, if one player builds fours with a Four, a Three and an Ace, the other may not add a Two and announce 'Building ten'. He could do so, however, if the other had declared that combination to represent eight instead of fours when he built it.

A build may be increased only by the addition of a card from the hand, not with one already on the table.

Trailing. If a player cannot or will not take in, build or increase, he 'trails' by playing any card face up to the table, thereby adding to the cards available for capture. But a player may not trail if any build he made is still on the table.

Sweeps. If a player sweeps the board by capturing all the table cards with a single card from his hand, he is credited with making a sweep. To indicate this fact, he should place the card he captured face up (instead of down) on his pile of won cards. At the end of the game, sweeps can then be counted by scoring for each face up card. After a sweep, the opponent can only trail.

End of game. The game ends when there are no cards in stock and both have played out their cards from the hand. Any cards left on the table at the end of play are credited to the player who last made a capture. This does not in itself count as a sweep, though it is possible for the last move of a game to be a valid sweep in the usual way.

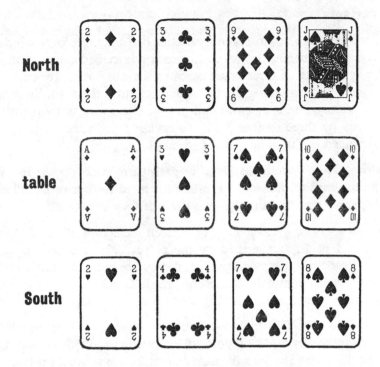

FIGURE 3

North, to move, can immediately capture the table Three by
pairing with the Three from his hand. But he can do better by
adding his Two to the table Ace and announcing 'Building
Threes', adding the table Three to that build. On his next turn he
can use his hand Three to capture all three cards (◇A, ◇2, ♡3).
If it were South's move, he could add his Four to the Three,
announce 'Building Sevens', and on his next turn capture ♣4,
♡3 and ♠7 with his ♡7. But after North's build, he cannot add
the Four to either of the Threes and announce 'Sevens' because
the multiple build of Threes can only be captured by a Three.
Nor could he capture ◇A + ♠7 with his ♠8, as ◇A forms part
of a build and cannot be taken individually.

Score. Each player sorts through his cards and scores according
to the table on page 86. If there is a tie for 'cards' neither scores
for that feature. Each deal is regarded as a complete game when
two play.

Variants

Cassino is subject to several variations in play, some of which have special names. In the basic game as described above, it may be agreed that if three court cards of the same rank are on the table, a player holding the fourth may capture them all. Sweeps are often ignored in two-hand play. (The game is frequently played by three or four.) The following three variants can be combined in the same game, if desired.

Draw Cassino. Immediately after each turn, each player draws the top card of the stock to restore his hand to four cards. This dispenses with making separate deals of four at a time.

Royal Cassino. Jack counts 11, Queen 12, King 13, and Ace either 1 or 14 as specified by the player. The restrictions on court cards do not then apply, and they are used in exactly the same way as numerals. Sometimes Little Cassino scores 2 or 15 to whoever captures it, and Big Cassino 10 or 16. (Optional.)

Spade Cassino. This replaces the blanket score of 1 for capturing more spades by crediting points for capturing individual spades. The Ace, Two and Jack of spades count 2 each to whoever holds them at the end of play, and every other spade counts 1 point. As this increases the maximum possible score from 11 to 26, the game is often played up to 61 and scored on a Cribbage board. If the loser fails to reach 31, the winner's margin of victory is doubled.

SPITE AND MALICE

This fast and furious game seems to be a modern development of such competitive patiences as Russian Bank (Crapette) and Racing Demon (Race Canfield, or Pounce), and the name – very descriptive, as will be seen – may be older than the game, as I have heard it apply to Racing Demon. I nearly avoided referring to it as a form of competitive patience, as there are some card-players who dislike the one-player activity and get put off by the word itself. So let us be quite clear from the outset that this is not a simple case of each player having a game of patience and seeing which one comes out first. This is a real two-player game offering every opportunity for the exercise of – well, spite and malice; and in the long run it will always be won by the more spiteful and malicious of the two.

The game

Cards. Two full packs are used. They should be of the same size and format, but of differing back designs or colours, and are not to be shuffled together at the outset. One of these packs should contain the standard 52 cards, the other a total of 56 cards by the addition of four Jokers. Ideally, the four Jokers should be of the same back design/colour and thus indistinguishable from the rest of their pack. In practice, since most packs contain only two Jokers or at most three, it doesn't matter too much if two Jokers are used from the other pack. This works out better than dispensing with one Joker if a three-Joker pack is used.

Deal. Both packs must be very thoroughly shuffled before play. The importance of this cannot be over-emphasised, as poor shuffling ruins the game. The 52-card pack is divided evenly, each player receiving 26 cards face down. Five cards each are dealt from the second pack, the rest of which is placed face down to one side to form a stock. Each player squares up his 26-card pack, placing it to his right (or left if he is left-handed), and turning the top card of it face up. This pile of cards is his personal pack, and will be referred to here simply as his 'pack', the central pile being known as the 'stock'. The other five cards he takes up as his playing hand.

Object. Each player's object is to be the first to get rid of his pack by playing out all 26 cards to the table, one by one as the opportunity arises. The first to do so automatically ends the game and scores 1 point for each card left in his opponent's pack. This is the sole object: there is no score for doing anything else.

Rank of cards. Cards rank A 2 3 4 5 6 7 8 9 T J Q K. Suits have no significance in the play. Jokers are wild. The holder of a Joker may declare it to represent any rank he pleases and play it as if it were a card of that rank.

Play. The first move is made by the player whose pack has the higher-ranking upcard. (If the upcards are of the same rank, each player shuffles his pack and turns up the top card again.) A move consists of transferring a card from one place to another, and a turn may consist of as many moves as the player is able and willing to make. Few moves are compulsory, and the decision whether to move or not is sometimes a tricky point of strategy. It sometimes happens that one player is unable to move at his turn, or unwilling to do so, in which case the other may take a number of turns in succession.

If the first player holds an Ace he may play it to the centre of the table. Upon this he may play a Two if he has one, upon the Two a Three, and so on, such cards coming either from his hand or from the top of his pack. Each time he plays a card from the top of his pack, he immediately faces the one beneath. Throughout play, any Ace played to the centre of the table forms the base of a pile of cards which is gradually to be built up in sequence as far as the King, regardless of suit. The only way in which either player may reduce his pack is by playing off the upcard to one of these centre piles at the appropriate point. We will call these centre piles 'stacks'.[1]

If the starter has no Ace, or is unwilling to play one, or is otherwise unable to proceed further, he may finish his play by discarding one card face up to the table in front of him. He may not make more than one discard, but is not obliged to make any. He completes his turn by drawing from the top of the stock as many as he needs to restore his hand to five.

It is then the turn of the second player. If his upcard is an Ace he is obliged to start a stack with it; if it is a Two, he is obliged to stack it upon an Ace if one is available; if it is anything else, he is not obliged to stack it (but will be advised to do so if he can). Apart from that, he may start and add to as many stacks as he is able and willing to, and may complete his turn by making one discard before drawing from the stock to restore his hand to five.

Play continues in this way, but with the following added feature. Each player may start up to four discard piles altogether, and may make subsequent discards to any of his own piles, provided that the card it is played upon is of the same rank or one rank higher. (Example: If the first card of a pile is a King, subsequent discards may run: Q J J J T 9 9 8, and so on.) It is never permissible to discard an Ace. The top card of a discard pile is always available for playing to a stack.

Whenever a player succeeds in playing all five cards from his hand, he is entitled to another turn immediately upon drawing five more cards from stock.

Other rules governing play are as follows.

Replenishing stock. No more cards may be added to a stack when it has been built up to the King. Whenever the stock is depleted to fewer than 12 cards, it is replenished by taking all the stacks that have been built up to the King and shuffling them in with the stock. Since some of these cards will be those played off the personal packs, the number of cards available from stock gradually increases during the play. If no stacks have been

---

1. Patience games lack an adequate word for this feature. 'Foundation' is inaccurate, and 'centre pile' long-winded.

completed by the time the stock is exhausted, all the stacks that have been started are gathered up, shuffled, and turned to form the new stock. (The importance of thorough shuffling at these points cannot be overemphasised. The best way of carrying it out is to put the stacks together, deal a row of six or seven cards face down, then another row on top of that, and so on until they are all out. Then pick up the piles in random order, shuffle them once or twice, and place the whole pile beneath the few cards remaining in stock.)

Compulsory/optional play. The following moves, when possible, are compulsory. If a player's upcard is an Ace he must use it to start a stack. If an Ace is available on the table, waiting to be built upon, the player in turn must cover it if his upcard is a Two, or if a Two is visible among his discards (though in this case he *may* cover it from the hand instead). If a player is unable to play, he must pass his turn without compensation. If he is unwilling to play, he may say 'pass' and allow his opponent an extra turn as often as he likes. If both players pass, the first to do so must then play an Ace or a Two from his hand if he can, and his opponent must then do likewise. For this purpose, however, it is not compulsory to play a Joker as such if no Ace or Two is held. If both players are still unable or unwilling to play further, *all* cards in hand and on the table (except the private packs) are gathered up and shuffled together. The new stock is turned down, five more cards are dealt to each, and play begins again as if from scratch.

Jokers. When a Joker is discarded, its holder need not specify which rank it represents until he needs to do so. For example, if the top card of a discard pile is a Nine, and two Jokers are added to it, they may be followed by a Nine, Eight, Seven or Six. A Joker may not be discarded upon a Two[2]. No matter what a Joker represents when it lies on a discard pile, it may be played to a stack at any time, or used as an Ace to start a new one.

---

2. This rule, which causes no hardship, is here recommended to over-come inconsistencies and points of argument that might otherwise arise. The need to invoke it rarely occurs.

Score. Play ceases as soon as one player has played his last up-card, and he scores 1 point for every card left unplayed from his opponent's pack. As there is a natural tendency to play at least three games to a session, here are some suggestions for spicing up the game score:

1. A rubber is won by the first player to win two games, and a bonus of 10 is added for the rubber.
2. Three games are played, and the margin of victory is the difference between the two totals; but if the second and third games are won by the same player his total is doubled (unless this results in a tie).
3. Three games are played, and the winner of a game scores the number of cards in his opponent's pack multiplied by the face value of his upcard (counting numerals at face value, courts 10 each and Ace 11).
4. Three games are played, and the winner of a game scores 100 plus the total face value of all cards remaining in his opponant's pack (counting as above).
5. The Hollywood scoring system devised for Gin Rummy may be used – see page 20.

Other elements of variety might be introduced by (a) permitting a player to resign, in which case his opponent scores the difference between the total of cards left in the two packs, and (b) offering 'double or quits' as in the game of Le Truc (p. 123). The first possibility should be governed by some sort of control against indiscriminate resignation, *eg* by allowing the winner a minimum score of 10.

Suggestions for play

You may find the game gets off to a slow start. This is quite normal, and it will invariably pick up speed later. What often happens is that neither player is dealt an Ace or a Joker, and for several turns the only thing each can do is make a discard and draw one from stock. Even this may get held up. One, for example, may find himself unable to discard after a few turns, in which case he has no choice but to wait until the other has changed the situation by inaugurating a stack. Or again, if one player's upcard is low, say a Three, the other may well hold back the play of an Ace until he can play A–2–3 and so block that opening. Although it is undeniably disadvantageous (not to say annoying) for one player to be stuck this early in the game, allowing the other to play off perhaps half a dozen or more upcards, the possible swings of fortune are such as to give him a fair chance of catching up later.

It is worth noting that, as Aces get played off, the number of potential stacks increases from the original eight (Aces and Jokers) to a maximum of twelve. At a later stage in the game a position is usually reached from which there are so many stacks at different stages of construction that one may be able to play off anything up to ten upcards in succession. It may also be useful to know that at the very start of play there is a slightly better than 1 in 6 chance of drawing any given rank or a Joker, a figure liable to considerable fluctuation as play progresses. It is therefore a marked advantage to be able to play out all five cards from the hand, as you have an immediate second turn with about a 5-in-6 chance of drawing a desired card. Not only should you never miss an opportunity to play out all five, but also you should often refrain from play if there is a chance of reaching this position. For example, holding A–2–3–5–9, you may prefer to discard the Nine and hope to draw a Four (or Joker) rather than play A–2–3 for a new stack. Of course, this principle may be unwise to follow in certain positions. But it quite often happens that a player manages to clear his hand two or three times in succession, and this will always do him more good than harm.

Given the choice, you should prefer to play to a stack (1) from the top of your pack, or, if not possible, (2) from your hand, and only then (3) from your discards. Since the whole object of the game is to empty your pack, while nothing else counts, you should never miss an opportunity to play the upcard, remembering to turn the next one *immediately*, in case it will also go. It is worth playing from your pack even if it gives your opponent an opening too. Perhaps the only time this does not apply is when it gives him a certain play-off and he is considerably in the lead. But whenever you are in the lead, or there is not much in it, always play the upcard when you can.

With the choice of playing from hand or discards, it is usually desirable in principle to play from the hand, as this enables you to draw from stock and so keep up a constant throughput of varying cards. Sometimes, of course, you must play from the discards in order to run through a sequence, and it is usually better to play from the discards in order to get rid of a kink – ie two or more consecutive cards of the same rank preventing access to other cards beneath them. For example, with a pile consisting of 9–8–7–6–5–5 it would be better to play a Five from the table than from the hand, unless perhaps you could otherwise clear the hand and have another turn. (Incidentally, in my circle we spread each discard pile to form a column of overlapping cards so that all are visible, in which case the word 'pile' is not strictly accurate. If they are kept as piles so that underlying cards are not visible, the skill of the game becomes that of memory rather than calculation. Which is preferable is a matter of taste.)

With no choice but to play a discard to a stack, do not bother to do so unless it brings some advantage. It may, for example, enable you to continue with a card from hand or even the upcard, or empty a discard pile to make room for a new one, or build a stack up to the same rank as that of your opponent's upcard, or perhaps raise several stacks to the same level where this looks as if it will hinder him more than yourself. But don't build a stack up to the King just because you can, nor higher than you need in order to block your adversary. Otherwise you may, after next playing your upcard, turn a rank which *could* have been played had you not previously blocked it by purposeless building.

The true test of skill in Spite and Malice lies in the management of discard piles. Never discard without carefully considering the likely consequences: one bad move can hold you up for a long time. The important thing to remember is that you are not obliged to discard, and it is sometimes better to refrain from doing so, especially to avoid creating a kink. A tricky situation often arises in which the only available move involves making a doubtful discard; the question is then whether to make it for the sake of drawing from stock, or to leave it and perhaps allow your opponent several consecutive turns. You just have to play it by ear.

If the game is a long time in starting, with neither player able (or willing) to stack an Ace, do not worry overmuch about using up all four of your depots. Later, however, it is desirable to restrict them to three for as long as possible, in order to leave space for the eventual transfer of a card or cards vital to your game. A positive example would be if you held A–3–4–5–K and your upcard were a Six, in which case you would open a column with the Five and hope to pick up a Two as you built downwards. A negative example would be if you suddenly found yourself drawing third or fourth cards of the same (and useless) rank, in which case you would have to use up that space as a dumping ground for them.

We have already noted that kinks consisting of several consecutive cards of the same rank can be a distinct hindrance to your game, and should therefore be avoided as much as possible. This only applies, of course, where kinks are obscuring access to other cards, and it follows that a run of identical cards can be quite safely played as the base of a discard pile, since they obscure nothing. A good rank to start a pile with is therefore one of which you hold two or three, as you are guaranteed a discard – and a draw from stock – for several turns to come without spoiling your game. If you lack duplicates, it is best to open a pile with the top card of a sequence. For example, holding 2–5–6–7–Q, drop the Seven first, as it assures you of three consecutive discards and draws. Note that it is not important to start all piles with the highest rank possible. Four Kings, for example, are better discarded as the base of one pile than as the bases of four. The ideal arrangement is to run four piles from different bases – say K, J, 8, 5 – so as to maximise your chances of discarding any given rank.

Having started a descending sequence, try to avoid creating a kink by the play of a duplicate. If one duplicate becomes necessary, forming a single kink, do not worry too much as a subsequent play-off as far as the first will unblock the sequence for a later move. But it is usually disastrous to play two or more duplicates in mid-sequence, causing a double or multiple kink, as you will then have to devote as much energy to unkinking it as to playing your upcards, which is self-defeating. The higher-ranking the duplicates are, the more difficult it is to get rid of them: at a pinch, you can allow a run of Twos or perhaps Threes, as it is rarely profitable for either player (hence your opponent) to constipate his hand by holding back Aces and Twos, since the former cannot be discarded and the latter must be played off if no other move is open to either player.

It is useful to stop a sequence at the card next in rank above your own upcard. Suppose that you are trying to play off a Six, that you hold 2–3–6–J–Q, that you have three current discard piles of which one runs T T T 9 8 7, and that you are unable to discard except to the empty depot. In this case you will discard your Six (in hand) not to the Seven but to the spare depot. If you subsequently find yourself able to play off your Six, and then turn up 8, 9, T, J, Q or K, you will be able to play that off with the aid of your sequence, which you would not have been able to do had you blocked it with the Six. This is a good example of the need for a spare discard pile, and hence of the value of clearing out a discard pile whenever you can do so without incurring any tactical disadvantage.

Jokers require careful management too. It is certainly an advantage to be able to discard one without specifying which rank it represents, and then be able to stack it as any other rank you please. Personally, however, I go to every length to avoid wasting a Joker on a discard pile. In my view the primary purpose of a Joker is to enable the upcard to be played. Keep Jokers in your hand for as long as you can, and use them only (and immediately) as part of a sequence leading to the play of your upcard. One other reasonable use of a Joker is to enable you to play out all five cards from hand and draw five more for another turn, though I would not myself use *two* Jokers for this purpose. A Joker on a discard pile is a drawback for two reasons.

First, your opponent can see it, and will adjust his play accordingly, thus lessening its power. Second, you may be forced to cover it with another discard, and once this is done there follows a period during which you might as well not have it at all. Another good way of wasting a Joker is to count it as an Ace and stack it for no other reason than that there was nothing else to do.

Despite all these thoughts about playing off your own upcard, don't forget that at least half your game lies in preventing your opponent from doing the same. Never make a move without examining his upcard, the uppermost stack-cards, the cards which you can see to be available to him in his own discard columns, and the possible cards he holds. Or, as more often applies, the ranks he possibly lacks from his hand. For instance, if his upcard is a Seven, and he keeps discarding and drawing when one of the stacks goes up to Five, then it is evident that he lacks a Six and a Joker from his hand. You, therefore, will avoid stacking a Six until you can cover it with a Seven, and will lose no opportunity to build any stack up to the Seven – perhaps even using a Joker for the purpose if the situation is critical. If several piles are stacked to the Four or Five, and you have low cards to get rid of, it is often worth building up lower stacks to the same rank. If he is going to be able to play anyway once he has drawn a Six, he might as well have half a dozen stacks open to him as two or three.

If his upcard is high – let's say a King – and all the stacks are fairly low, look carefully at his discards and note how many ranks he needs in hand to be able to run up a sequence to the King. For instance, he may have visible access to 6, 7, 8 and T, J. In this case, you would avoid building up to a Five as there is a fair chance that he holds a Nine and Queen (or Joker), but you might build up to a Four, banking on his not holding all three missing ranks.

To summarise, the most important requirements of the game are to keep your eyes open and your wits about you, and never to play a single card without a thorough appraisal of the consequences likely to proceed from it.

PIQUET

The odd thing about Piquet is that although it is widely regarded as the best of all two-hand card games by those in a position to judge, it is nowadays almost equally widely neglected. Not a hundred years ago it was still the everyday card game of the French, occupying in many respects a position equivalent to that of Cribbage in England, but has now ceded pride of place to that Gallic form of Klabberjass called Belote. For many periods between the 17th century and the First World War, though by fits and starts rather than continuously, Piquet found itself a favourite of the English moneyed classes, lying second perhaps only to Whist and later Bridge. American ignorance of the game is and always has been total.

Yet Piquet is a game unlike any other. Unique in format, it is richly varied, unfailingly exciting, and demanding of the highest skills. It has been neglected, I think, partly because like so many other fine card games it has been swept aside by the single-minded tyranny of Bridge; perhaps partly because it looks complicated at first sight and calls for the constant application of even more mental arithmetic than Cribbage (in which connection it may be noted that Cribbage boards are easily obtainable but Piquet markers are now antiques); even, possibly, because it is full of French technical terms which are not pronounced as they are spelt. More probably there is no reason at all, except to say that Piquet is out of fashion. There are fashions in all things, and card games are not excepted.

Pronounced 'picket' in English and 'P.K.' in France, Piquet is traditionally regarded as a French invention and equally traditionally dated back to the 15th century. In fact, legend attributes it to the genius of a certain Stephen de Vignoles, one of Charles VII's chevaliers who, under the title La Hire, is perpetuated to this day as the Jack of hearts in French 'named' packs. (♡K is Charles and ♡Q Judith.) A hundred years later

Rabelais listed the game as one of those played by Gargantua. It was formerly known as Cent, anglicised to Sant or Saunt, from the circumstance of being played 100 up – *ie* the winner was the first player to reach 100 points. The version described below, however, is that known as Rubicon Piquet, as formulated in 1882 by the Portland Club (once the *académie anglaise* of the card world; now given over to Bridge). The 'rubicon' is the scoring of 100 points, but the improvement over the old game lies in the fact that a fixed number of deals are played and the loser is heavily penalised if he fails to cross the Rubicon by reaching 100.

The game

Equipment. At least one pack of 32 cards, consisting of A K Q J T 9 8 7 in each suit. (It is convenient to use two packs, one being shuffled while the other is dealt.) One scoresheet, or one each, and something to write with. Optionally, some form of scorer or marker capable of indicating from 1 to 200 points at least. A proper Piquet marker is illustrated, but a Cribbage board can be turned to use. Serious players announce their cumulative scores verbally as play proceeds, and beginners should aim to dispense with mechanical aids as soon as they know the game.

General idea. A game (or *partie*, to use the needless French word) consists of six deals, and is won by the player with the higher cumulative score. Both players strive to make at least 100 points, as the loser is heavily penalised if he fails to do so. In the event of a draw two more deals are played. It is worth knowing in advance that a player may score anything from zero to 170 on a single deal, but that, on *average*, elder hand (non-dealer) expects to make about 28 to younger's 14 or so. Each deal consists of two parts. In the first, each player throws out some of his cards and draws others from the pack in an attempt to score for acquiring certain combinations of cards. In the second, these cards are played out to tricks at no trump, and the object is normally to win a majority of the twelve tricks. Most of the skill lies in selecting which cards to throw out, but much may also be expended on, if not actually winning the majority of tricks, at least dividing them six-all.

Deal. Whoever cuts the higher card may elect to deal first, and is advised to do so. Thereafter, the turn to deal alternates, so that each deals three times in the course of a game. The dealer is known as younger hand, his opponent as elder. Deal 12 cards each in batches of three at a time (or, if preferred, two at a time; but whichever a player uses on his first deal he must stick to for the rest of the game). Place the remaining eight cards face down in the centre of the table, forming the stock (or *talon*); they should be spread slightly, so that all are easily accessible.

Carte blanche. If either player's hand contains no court cards (Kings, Queens or Jacks), he is entitled to score 10 points for carte blanche provided that he announces this fact before any discarding takes place. He must also prove it by rapidly playing his cards one by one and face up into a pile, but this not until his opponent has discarded for the exchange. If younger has it, therefore, he announces it immediately, waits for elder to discard, and then proves it. If elder has it, he announces it immediately, tells younger how many cards he proposes to leave him in the exchange, waits for younger to make his discard accordingly, and then proves it. (The point of this ritual is that a player is entitled to see his opponent's carte blanche, but not to be influenced by it in deciding upon his discards. In any case, carte blanche is an extremely rare occurrence. The English for carte blanche, by the way, is 'a blank'.

The exchange. The object of the exchange is to improve the hand for the purpose of (a) winning tricks at no trump, and (b) acquiring the best scoring combination of cards in each of these three classes:

Point Most cards in one suit.
Sequence Longest sequence in one suit.
Set Three, or (preferably) four, Aces, K, Q, J or Tens.

Both players are obliged to exchange at least one card. Elder starts by discarding, face down, anything from one to five cards, and drawing the same number from the top of the stock consecutively downwards. If he exchanges fewer than five, he may look at those of the top five which he did not take, without showing them to younger. Younger then discards up to as many as there are left in the stock – usually only three – and similarly replaces them from the top of the stock down. If he leaves any in stock, he may not (yet) see what they are.

Declaring (and sinking). The principle is that 'point' is scored only by the player with the longer or better suit, sequences only by the player with the longest or highest, and sets only by the player with the higher-ranking quatorze (four of a kind) or trio (three) if no quatorze is held. The method is that elder announces his best combination in each class, and younger tells him whether or not he can beat it. Any combination eventually scored for must be fully identified, if not actually shown. But a player is not obliged to declare any combination that he holds, or to declare the whole of it if he does. The practice of keeping any part of it back (and of course losing the right to score for it) is known as 'sinking'. It is an advanced tactic and may be ignored for the moment.

Point. Elder first states the number of cards in his longest suit. To this, younger replies 'not good' if he has a longer suit, 'good' if his best suit is shorter. If equal, he asks elder its total face value ('making ?'), to which elder replies on the basis of adding together 11 for the Ace, 10 for each court, face value for each numeral. If younger's point is of equal value, he says 'equal' and neither may score for point. If elder's point is acknowledged 'good', he scores 1 point per card in that suit, announces what the suit is (and the cards composing it if requested) and passes on to the next declaration.

Sequence. A sequence is three or more cards of the same suit and of consecutive ranks. The six possible sequences and their scoring values are:

tierce (three)	= 3	sixieme (six)	=16
quart (four)	= 4	septieme (seven)	=17
quint (five)	=15	huitieme (eight)	=18

Elder announces the length of his longest sequence, to which younger replies 'good' if he cannot beat it, 'not good' if he has a longer sequence, or 'top card?' if his best sequence is of the same length. In the latter event, elder states the highest card of his sequence, which again younger acknowledges good, not good or equal. If equal, neither player may score for any sequences. If good, elder identifies and scores for all the sequences he may hold.

Set. Finally, elder announces his highest-ranking quatorze (four of the same rank) by saying 'fourteen Aces' or whatever the rank may be, or, if none, his highest-ranking trio ('three Aces', and so on). Any quatorze beats a trio, and a higher-ranking set beats a lower set of the same type. As the names imply, a quatorze scores 14 and a trio 3 points. If younger has a superior set he replies 'not good'. If not, he replies 'good' (equality is impossible), after which elder identifies and scores for as many sets as he holds. Remember that ranks below Ten are not valid as sets.

One for leading. At this juncture, elder announces his total score for combinations so far (if any), leads any card to the first trick, and adds one point for doing so. There is no reason for this: it is just a rule of the game.

Younger's declarations. After elder has led, but before younger replies to it, the latter declares and scores for any combinations he may hold in classes to which he replied 'not good', or which elder passed over because he had nothing to declare. First, however, he must decide whether or not to look at any cards he may have left untaken from the stock, and announce this decision. If yes, he may reveal them to both players at any time until he plays to the first trick, but not after. If he sees them, so may elder; if not, neither may elder. As to his own combinations, younger must count them in the same order as elder. For point, he announces the suit and scores 1 per card in it. For sequence and then for set, he must declare and score for at least one that is better than any claimed by elder, and may also declare and score for any others he may hold. He is then ready to play to the first trick – but there are still two scoring features that may apply, as follows.

Repique. If either player reaches or exceeds a score of 30 for combinations alone before his opponent has scored anything at all, he adds to his score a bonus of 60 for 'repique'. The fact that elder declares before younger is not an advantage, because scores accrue strictly in the following order: carte blanche, point, sequence, set. Thus if younger counted 10 for carte blanche, 6 for point and a quint for 15, he would have reached 31 in time to score repique (making 91) even if elder had managed to score for sets. Equality does not save a repique. If both have the same point and neither scores for sequence, two quatorzes and a trio will win the repique.

Pique. If elder reaches 30+ before younger has scored anything at all, not on combinations alone (which would be repique) but including his one for leading and any other points for subsequently won tricks as may be necessary, he adds to his score a bonus of 30 for pique. Thus if younger has scored nothing for combinations, he must win a trick before elder reaches 30 to avoid being piqued. Younger himself cannot score pique, because if he fails to make 30 on combinations alone elder is bound to score at least one 'for leading'.

Tricks. It is obligatory to follow suit to the card led if possible; if not, any other card may be played but will lose the trick. There are no trumps, and the trick is won by the higher-ranking card of the suit led. The winner of a trick adds 1 or 2 points to his score and announces his cumulative total to date, and leads to the next. Score 1 point for winning a trick led by oneself, 2 points for capturing a trick led by the opponent.[3] Won tricks

---

3. The usual way of expressing the score for tricks is: 'One for leading to a trick, one for capturing an opponent's lead, and one for winning the last trick'. This comes to exactly the same thing.

may be left face up on the table, as either player is entitled to refer to any or all cards already played, as well as to his own discards.

Score for cards. If both players win six tricks, the cards are said to be divided, and neither scores any bonus. For winning a majority of tricks, there is a bonus of 10 'for the cards', and for winning all twelve there is an additional bonus of 30 for 'capot'.[4] Neither of these bonuses counts towards pique.

Scoring. At the end of the deal, each player announces his cumulative total for it, and these figures are entered on the score-sheet. At the end of the sixth deal, each player's scores are totalled, and the higher wins a game score determined as follows. If the loser has 100 or more, the winner scores 100 plus the difference between the two totals (*eg* 196 to 173 wins 123). If the loser failed to reach 100, he is rubiconed, and the winner

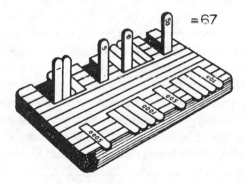

= 67

FIGURE 4

Piquet markers dating from about the turn of the century may still be found in antique shops or even junk stalls. They were made in pairs (one for each player) and consisted of spring-loaded pegs set into an oblong of polished wood of about the size of a playing card. A score is recorded by raising the appropriate peg or combination of pegs. The one illustrated here was also designed for use in the game of Bézique, in which scores range from 5 to over 5000.

---

4. Usually expressed as '40 for capot instead of 10 for cards', which comes to the same thing but disfigures the logic of the game.

scores 100 plus the addition of the two totals (*e.g.* 96 to 73 wins 269). It is not incumbent upon the winner to cross the rubicon. In the event of a tie, two more deals may be played, and if this does not resolve it the game is drawn. An alternative tie-break (proposed by myself) is to credit a game score of 100 to whichever player was younger on the last deal.

Notes on procedure. It must be understood that Piquet is by nature an 'open' game, and not governed by the many rules of secrecy that surround others. We have noted, for example, that no card or cards scored in a combination may remain unidentified: if it is not obvious from one player's own hand exactly which cards constitute a combination for which his opponent scores, he is entitled to ask and must be truthfully answered. (This does not apply, however, to any card undeclared or 'sunk'. For example, if elder holds four Kings but only declares three, and is acknowledged good, younger may ask him which three he is counting – or which one he is not counting – and elder, obliged to give some reply, may announce whichever one he pleases to be 'not counted'. He is not obliged to declare that he has sunk anything.) During the play, each player may refer to his own discards whenever he likes, and may examine previous tricks won by both players. The opponent of a player who has scored for point may, at any time during the trick play, ask his opponent how many he has left of his point suit, and must be answered (if only to save time, since he can find out by examining the tricks).

If a player leads out of turn, his opponent may tell him to take the card back, and there is no penalty; but if his opponent follows to such a lead, the trick stands as good and there may be no correction. If one player revokes (fails to follow suit although able to do so), all cards played from the commission to the discovery are taken back into hand and play proceeds without penalty. To save time, a player holding a suit of unbeatable cards, such as A K T 9 8 7, may play them simultaneously, announcing 'from the top' and requiring the other to play an equal number of cards. The latter, however, should not do so unless he agrees that they automatically win. If not, he need play only to the winning cards, leaving those tricks to his opponent, and may then capture the highest remaining in order to take over the lead. Either player, believing himself to hold all losing cards, may throw his hand in to cede the remaining tricks, but may not then take any back upon discovery of a miscalculation. If one player lays the whole of his remaining cards on the table, being of more than one suit, and claims to win the balance of tricks, his opponent must then either (a) concede, or (b) show that there is at least one losing card amongst them, in which case he himself is deemed to win the whole of the balance. The purpose of this rule, of course, is to prevent one player from discovering whether or not his opponent has made a certain losing discard and profiting from the discovery.

If either player is discovered to hold more cards than he is entitled to, his penalty is to score nothing for that deal. But any combination held good prevents his opponent from scoring in that class, or from scoring pique or repique, and any trick he takes guards him against the capot. It is up to each player to ensure that he has the right number, as there is no compensation (or penalty) for holding too few. In the latter event, tricks to which he cannot play score to his opponent. A misdeal may be corrected without penalty if discovered before either player has taken his cards into hand. If a card is faced in the deal or found faced in the pack, the same player deals again.

If elder announces a combination lower in value than the best he holds, and younger replies 'not good', he may not revise his call but must leave younger to score in that class.

Illustrative deal

The following example, borrowed from the standard work by Cavendish,[5] is provided for no other purpose than to clarify the basic rules of procedure. The only alteration I have made is to change the players from 'A' and 'B' to 'Napoleon' and

---

5. Cavendish, *Piquet* – 6th Edition (LONDON, 1889).

'Josephine'. Josephine deals, making Napoleon elder hand, and the cards are:

> Nap: ♠A K J ♡A Q J 8 ♣J 8 7 ◇9 8
> Jos: ♠T 7 ♡T 9 7 ♣K Q T ◇A Q J T

Napoleon has up to five exchanges, and hopes to draw more hearts and the 'fourteenth' Jack. He therefore discards ♠K and the two low clubs and diamonds.

Josephine must keep her fourteen Tens and discards ♠7 ♡9 ♡7. After the draw, the hands are:

> Nap: ♠A J 9 8 ♡A K Q J 8 ♣J 9 ◇K
> Jos: ♠Q T ♡T ♣A K Q T ◇A Q J T 7

Declarations proceed as follows:

Nap Point of five.
Jos (also having a point of five) Worth?
Nap 49.
Jos (with 48) Good.
Nap In hearts. And a quart major. (*Meaning a sequence of four to the Ace.*)
Jos Good.
Nap That's five for point, four for the sequence nine ... (*Looks for another sequence to count, but fails to find any. His next call is somewhat tentative.*) Three Jacks?
Jos Not good.
Nap (*leading ♡A*) And one's ten.
Jos I count fourteen Tens and three Queens, seventeen.

Tricks are played as follows, each announcing their score upon winning a trick.

Nap	Jos		
♡A	♡T	(1)	*Nap* Eleven.
♡K	◇7	(1)	*Nap (playing all his hearts*
♡Q	◇T	(1)	*simultaneously)* Twelve, thirteen,
♡J	◇J	(1)	fourteen, fifteen.
♡8	◇Q	(1)	*Jos (repeating her score)* Seventeen.

◇K	◇A	(2)	}	*Jos* Nineteen. (*Lays out all her clubs*)
♣9	♣A	(1)		Twenty, twenty one, twenty two,
♣J	♣K	(1)		twenty three
♠8	♣Q	(1)		
♠9	♣T	(1)		
♠A	♠Q	(2)		*Nap* Seventeen.
♠J	♠T	(1)		*Nap* Eighteen, and ten for cards twenty eight.
				Jos Twenty three.

If this hand is played over it will be found that Napoleon would only have divided the cards, failing to score ten for the majority, if he had led spades after his run of hearts. As it is he just comes out ahead of Josephine with an average elder score of 28, whereas Josephine has more than younger usually expects to score and will hope to push ahead as elder on the next deal.

Suggestions for play

The difference in strategy as between dealer and non-dealer is more marked in Piquet than in any other two-hand game save perhaps Cribbage. Elder (non-dealer) starts with all the advantages, being entitled to five of the eight cards of the stock, having the lead and so determining the point of attack, and being alone able to score for pique. Younger's draw of usually only three cards is rarely sufficient to rescue a bad hand from disaster, while only he can find himself in the position of holding all eight cards of a suit and yet lose every trick. As if further proof were needed, statistics show that elder scores nearly twice as much as younger, on average. It follows that elder is in a position to take chances and should play an attacking hand, while younger should see to his defence first and not take chances that might weaken them.

To start, then, elder should always seek to exchange his full entitlement of five cards, for to take fewer is to waste his overwhelming advantage and to give younger considerably more room to manoeuvre. If he takes only four cards instead of five, he has reduced his advantage by 20 per cent but increased younger's by 33 per cent. Cards taken in excess of those he feels necessary to his hand are not wasted, as they are not only denied to younger but also remain unknown to him.

As elder hand, which five cards should you throw out? This is a problem that beginners find hard to solve, as they tend to feel that only non-combinable and non-trick-winning Nines, Eights and Sevens should be discarded, and if they have only three or four such cards will prefer to take less than their entitlement. What you should do, however, is to look at it the other way: decide which cards you must retain for the best chances of combining, and throw out the rest.

Of those to retain, the most important are usually those of your potential point – the suit of which you hold the greatest number of cards, or, if equal, that with the highest pip-values or best chances of turning into a sequence. The point in this hand, for example, is hearts:

♠AKJT   ♡QJT9   ♣AQ   ◇K9

since either of two cards (King or Eight) will convert it to a quint, which is twice as many chances as the solitary Queen that will make a quint in spades. The quint is particularly worth going for as it would be 'good against the cards' – meaning that it is obvious from your own cards that younger could not possibly draw an equal or better sequence. The discards from this hand, therefore, are ♠J ♠T ♣Q ◇K ◇9.

Discards are also made with a view to completing a quatorze, and problems can arise because this combination tends to cut across the discard requirements relevant to point or sequence. The hand above was not complicated by this factor because it contained two each of the valid ranks, thus ensuring that younger cannot score so much as a trio, but not offering strong enough chances of filling a quatorze to allow this hope to influence the discards. Furthermore, the potential quint would have been, if realised, good against the cards. But this superficially similar hand is far from easy:

♠AKJT   ♡JT98   ♣AK7   ◇K

Again, there are virtually twice as many chances of making a quint or better in hearts (5 to 4 against, or 44%) as a quint in spades (3 to 1 against, or 25%). This time, however, it is not good against the cards, as younger might fill, or even have been dealt, an equal or better sequence in diamonds. Furthermore, you have three Kings and would prefer to keep them with a view to drawing the fourth, especially as younger may wind up with fourteen Queens. Since it is vital to restrict younger's entitlement to not more than three cards, you are faced with two possible ways of discarding from this hand.

1. Keep the heart sequence and the Kings, neither of which is at present good against the cards, and discard ♠A ♠J ♠T ♣A ♣7.
2. Keep the Kings and the potential spade quint, discarding the hearts and bottom club and drawing to ♠A K J T ♣A K ♢K.

(A third possibility is to forget the Kings and keep both spades and hearts in the hope of making two quints and repique, but the chances of doing so are too remote since only four cards can be exchanged.)

The chances of drawing the fourteenth King are the same in both cases. In case (1) there is a 1 in 4 chance of making the quint, and in case (2) there are 4 in 9. But although the latter gives better odds, it would lose if younger had a sixieme in diamonds and might tie if he has a quint, whereas the quint major (to the Ace) in the former would be good against a diamond quint. Further, if younger gets only five diamonds instead of six, the retention of spades here stands a better chance of scoring for point because the cards held are higher in value (as it stands, worth 31 against only 27). On the whole, then, case (2) is the safer holding against younger's possibilities, even though case (1) gives better chances on the face of it.

To summarise, elder should nearly always exchange up to his maximum of five cards, unless the hand dealt is so strong as to contain a quint or quatorze and the chance of (re)pique or capot. The longest suit should be kept intact for point, or, if suits are of equal lengths, then that with the highest count or longest sequence should be retained. A trio should be kept intact with a view to the quatorze, except that a trio of Tens or Jacks may be broken if the cards show that younger may hold a higher ranking quatorze and there are other pressures for discarding from them. If it becomes essential to choose between keeping the point or the trio, go for the point. Having classified cards into those that must be kept for combinations and those that need not, prefer to discard unneeded Aces and Kings rather than discard fewer than five, unless this spoils the chance of capot. If discarding requires it, do not hesitate to unguard Kings or Queens. Discard from as few different suits as possible. Unless it contains a card needed for a combination, it is often as well to throw out the whole of a suit as part of it, and sometimes even better.

As younger hand, your approach is quite different. Having normally only three cards to exchange, you have considerably less opportunity to draw to high combinations. The question of tricks is also of greater importance, since – to take an extreme case – you can be capoted though holding a handful of high cards, if they are of suits in which elder is void. Whereas elder can usually expect to win the cards (take more tricks) with an average hand and proper play, younger must usually discard and fight to at least divide them (six each).

Your first concern, then, after looking for carte blanche, is to ensure adequate coverage in all suits to avoid the danger of capot. A hand such as this;

♠A K J 9 8 7   ♡J T 9   ♣Q 9·   ◇8

will lose every trick if elder, as is likely, has no spade in hand. Here it is vital, before thinking about combinations, to cover the three weak suits by discarding spades. Even the lowly ◇8 must be retained, to act as a guard in case the King is drawn. Of course, the probability of drawing one guard in each of the three suits is extremely low, but at least two should be drawn to defend against capot. Even then, it may be hard to find the right discards to elder's winning leads. Quite apart from tricks, the potential combinations are not worth much. From the cards, there is every chance that elder will hold seven diamonds, and even six clubs would be worth more than your six spades. (Assess this quickly by noting that your spade suit lacks cards worth 20 in combined face value, whereas his six clubs would lack only 19, *ie* the Q+9 held by yourself.) And if you drew ♠Q for a quart major, he is likely to hold at least a quint in diamonds.

This hand, however, is an extreme case of weakness for tricks, and is introduced only to point out that a good-looking hand at first sight must be looked at very closely before any discarding decisions are made. As far as combinations are concerned, judge your discards in much the same way as for elder hand. Two points must be noted, though. First, do not aim for a particular combination if it means unguarding a suit or losing a vital trick. And second, although it is best for elder to exchange his full entitlement of five cards, as younger you should not hesitate to take only two or even one if it means throwing good cards after bad. In this case (unlike elder's situations) any cards you leave remain out of play instead of going into your opponent's hand.

To summarise: as younger, discard defensively with a view to retaining coverage in sufficient suits to avoid capot. Do not take all cards available if this means throwing out guards or trick-winners, and do not waste good cards in going after high combinations which are not good against the cards. Other things being equal, always keep your point suit, as it is your best and cheapest defence against pique/repique.

The next important part of the game is not the playing of tricks but the announcement of combinations. Practised players often enter the play with a pretty shrewd idea of their opponent's holding, gleaned from what he has announced in declarations together with an estimate of which of the other cards are more likely to be out of his hand than in it. For this reason it is important not to say more about your holding than you really need in order to establish whether or not your declaration is 'good'. Suppose, as elder, you hold:

♠Q J T 9 ♡A Q J T ♣A K T ◇T

You call a point of four; younger asks its value, and replies 'not

good' to your 40. Your next declaration is fourteen Tens',
with not a word about the sequence. Why? Because if your point
of four is not good at 40, younger must have a point of four worth
41, and from your own holding you can see this to be ◇A K Q J.
Your sequence of four is bound to be not good, so to mention it
at all would only be to give him gratuitous information about
your hand. Again, if as elder you held fourteen Kings after
exchanging five cards, but had not seen hair nor hide of an Ace,
there would be no point in announcing them unless younger
took fewer than three cards, as he would certainly not have
thrown an Ace with Kings against him. Similar considerations
apply to younger. Suppose you hold:

♠A Q J T 7 ♡8 7 ♣Q J T ◇K 9

Your discards were two diamonds and a club. Elder calls a point
of five. Without hesitation, you should immediately announce
'good'. Since his point can only be in hearts, it must be worth at
least 49 to your 48 in spades, and there is no point in giving
away free information.

It is because so many of the opposing cards are known by the
time tricks are played that it has been said, in reference to this
part of the game, that 'in Piquet, there are no surprises' – which
is not quite true, but worth bearing in mind. Elder should
normally lead his point suit from the top down, unless headed by
a tenace (A–Q or, more especially, K–J); younger, when no
longer able to follow, will start discarding from the bottom of his
point, unless he is confident of gaining the lead and winning
tricks with the whole of his point. A time for elder not to lead his
point is when it lacks the top card and there is pique to be made
by leading non-point winner – for example, from

♠K Q J T 8 ♡A K Q ♣A K ◇K Q

elder has point equal, a quart good plus tierce major making 7,
fourteen Kings 21 and a trio of Queens 24, plus 1 for leading 25.
He leads hearts and clubs, reaching 30 in tricks and adding 30
for pique. In defending against elder's point lead, younger must

do everything to avoid unguarding suits, even to the extent of throwing out winners from his own point. For example:

♠Q 8 ♡Q J 9 ♣K 7 ◇A K J T 8

Elder, having counted point six and three Aces, leads his six spades. Younger must throw diamonds from the bottom up after playing his two spades, for if his sixth card is a heart or club he may well be capoted. If possible, of course, younger should keep his point and throw low cards from other suits if this can be done without losing the guard.

The addition of the rubicon has added much interest and excitement to the strategy of the game by sometimes making it vital to play to the score. If your opponent is well in the lead by the sixth deal, while you are still short of the rubicon, you are faced with a nice problem: whether to go all out to reach it, taking chances and playing boldly if need be, or, instead, to go for as few points as possible, by seeking equalities in combinations and playing to divide the cards. (If you are rubiconed, remember, your opponent adds your own score to his, plus 100 for game.)

If elder is trailing at the last deal and feels unable to reach 100, he will do best to sink everything he holds, even if (*especially* if!) this includes a quint or quatorze – in other words, declare nothing and let younger count whatever he holds as 'good'. There is no point in trying to equalise. As elder, you may be convinced that younger has point five and quint major as well as yourself, but if you declare either of them, younger will simply announce 'good' and let you make the score, since it will ultimately be credited to his own account. In trying to divide the cards, elder must not allow younger to manoeuvre him into taking the majority by 'suicide' play to tricks. Younger does not mind who wins the cards, so long as they are not divided.

If the positions are reversed, younger is somewhat better placed for declaring equalities, since elder has to announce first, and younger can sink as much as may be necessary to equalise. For example, suppose you hold a point consisting of K–Q–J–T–7, worth 47. Elder declares a point of four. You ask its value; he replies 'thirty nine'. You announce 'equal', sinking nine from your face value, and neither scores. Elder next announces a tierce to the Queen. Again, you equalise. By sinking the King, you also have a tierce to the Queen.

(Some players only allow whole cards to be sunk, thus making it illegal to sink nine from K-Q-J-T-7 since that value does not correspond to a card held. This nice point, not covered by the Portland Club Laws, should perhaps be agreed beforehand.)

It is easy to see the value of sinking for the purpose of keeping one's score low when certain of being rubiconed, but there are other circumstances in which advantage may be gained from it, or, indeed, when all depends upon it. Here is an extreme example, provided by Cavendish – who pointedly adds 'It is useless to practise this stratagem against an indifferent player who does not count your hand'. In other words, you can't bluff a fool. Elder holds:

♠A K Q J 9 8 7 ♡K ♣A K ◇A K

After equalising on point (younger having seven hearts), elder is in a position to call fourteen Kings. But this would give his hand away. If younger knows he has the singleton ♡K, he will play everything except his red Ace and be assured of taking at least one trick. Elder therefore sinks his red King, knowing his trio of Aces and Kings to be good against the cards, because he himself discarded a Ten and can see that younger cannot hold a quatorze. Younger asks him which King he does not count, and elder (of course) replies 'hearts', which younger may believe or not, as he wishes. This puts younger in the unenviable position of choosing whether to throw all his hearts to elder's lead of spades in order to retain a guard in clubs or diamonds, or to hold back ♡A until the last trick in case elder has not discarded the King. By sinking, elder drops 11 points (counting 3 instead of 14 for Kings); against this, however, he has a good chance of making capot – except, as Cavendish says, 'against a very acute or very stupid player'. There are, of course, circumstances in which, as younger, one would sink an unguarded King in order to avoid being capoted.

Illustrative game

Only the sixth deal of the following illustrative game consists of deliberately concocted hands. The others I dealt normally from a properly shuffled pack specifically for the purpose of these illustrations, which may therefore be regarded as fairly representative. The comments on play may be regarded as those of an impartial observer.

First deal. Josephine cuts the higher card and elects to deal first. Quoting elder hand first, the cards fall thus:

Nap: ♠J ♡AKQJ8 ♣Q7 ◇QJ87
Jos: ♠987 ♡T97 ♣K9 ◇AKT9

Napoleon is faced with the interesting possibility of going for two quatorzes (Jacks and Queens) instead of pressing his point in hearts. But sets are counted last, so even if he were successful he would be unlikely to convert the 28 points into a repique. He therefore keeps his point and the three Queens, making exactly five discards.

Josephine has an unpleasant hand, being unguarded in two suits and holding a point in diamonds that is unlikely to convert into a sequence. In spades and hearts she can keep one and two cards to act as guards against the possible draw of nothing better than a King and a Queen, and accordingly throws ♠8 ♠7 ♡7.

After the draw, the new hands are:

Nap: ♠AQT ♡AKQJ8 ♣QJT ◇Q
Jos: ♠K9 ♡T9 ♣AK98 ◇AKT9

As luck would have it, Napoleon has not improved his point and would have made both quatorzes, giving him a score of 100 on declarations alone. Neither has Josephine improved her diamond point, but she has drawn a King in spades and is glad to have kept a guard for him. She can see five tricks in hand and will hope to be able to divide the cards.

Napoleon counts 5 for point, 4 and 3 for sequences, and 14 Queens for a total of 26. He leads ♡A for 1, then plays the rest of his hearts for 5 trick points. This brings him to 32, plus 30 for pique 62, since Josephine has not yet scored. To these leads she has played two hearts, two clubs and one diamond, from the lowest upwards.

If Napoleon now leads his ♠A he will only divide the cards. Holding a tenace in that suit himself, he must force Josephine to lead into it to give him the extra trick he needs to win 10 for the cards. He knows that she cannot hold more than two clubs and three diamonds, and must therefore stick at five tricks. Accordingly, he leads ♣Q. Josephine wins five tricks for 6, leads a spade, and Napoleon takes the last two for 3. With 10 for cards, Napoleon finishes with a score of 75 to Josephine's 6.

Second deal. Now Napoleon deals and the cards are as follows (elder hand first):

> *Jos:* ♠A K J 7 ♡A K 7 ♣A J 9 8 ◇9
> *Nap:* ♡Q J T 9 8 ♣Q T 7 ◇A T 8 7 (*no spades*)

Elder chooses spades for point, as it is not only worth more but also stands to convert to a better sequence. She must take in an Ace or Queen (or two Kings) to prevent Napoleon from counting a possible 14 Queens. Her discards are, clearly, a heart, a diamond, and the three bottom clubs.

Napoleon's discards are equally obvious. He must keep his point and quint in case he draws a spade with which to beat the elder hand, and must retain his guarded Queen in clubs. Out go the three low diamonds. After the draw:

> *Jos:* ♠A K J T 9 8 7 ♡A K ♣A K ◇K
> *Nap:* ♠Q ♡Q J T 9 8 ♣Q T 7 ◇A Q J

Josephine has not only succeeded in taking the fourth King to beat younger's queenly quatorze, but also wound up with a hand that is almost identical with Cavendish's illustration (p 62) of when to sink a King. This puts Jo in a quandary – shall she follow Cavendish's example, declare only three Kings, and hope thereby to lull Napoleon into believing her void in diamonds so that he will throw his diamonds away and let her win capot? No. For one thing, she has never heard of Cavendish, having flourish-

ed a good half century before him. For another, she knows her
opponent well enough to know that he will hold back his ◇A as
a matter of course. After all, he has seen six of the eight diamonds,
and will not expect the other two to lie in elder's discards.

Battle commences. Josephine declares a point of seven, good,
a quint to the Jack, not good, fourteen Kings and three Aces.
Plus one for leading ♠A, and a score of 25. Napoleon declares a
quint to the Queen for 15. Josephine takes her eleven tricks for
11, plus 10 for more and a total of 46. Napoleon's score is 15 for
the quint plus one trick for 2, making 17. Combined totals to
date: Napoleon 92, Josephine 51.

In retrospect, Josephine might have had second thoughts
about sinking a King. She made the decision not to on the
expectation of a good quint and consequent pique. Finding
Napoleon with a better quint she might well have sought capot
as a consolation.

Third deal. Josephine deals as follows:

 Nap: ♠J 8 7 ♡K Q T 9 7 ♣K Q ◇K Q
 Jos: ♠K T ♡J 8 ♣A T 8 7 ◇J T 9 7

Not an easy one for elder, with only three obvious discards. He
must either spoil his point and go for two quatorzes (not good
against the cards unless he also draws an Ace), or split Kings or
Queens, or discard only three. He decides to throw out two
Queens.

Josephine's hand is no easier, with only two suits guarded and
mediocre chances of a good point or sequence. Preferring to keep
the tierce in diamonds, she eventually throws out the three low
clubs.

 Nap: ♠A Q ♡A K Q T 9 7 ♣K 9 ◇K 8
 Jos: ♠K T 9 ♡J 8 ♣A J ◇A J T 9 7

Having thrown out Queens, Napoleon naturally picks up the
fourth Queen and two Aces, plus a guard to each King – which
he does not really need, having a certain seven tricks. Younger
has raised her point of four to five, but it will not be good, and
she can see little hope of dividing the cards. A mediocre result

all round. Napoleon counts a point of six, good, tierce major in his point suit, good, and three good Kings, total 12, and one for leading, 13. Josephine has nothing to declare.

Napoleon plays his hearts for 6, to which Josephine throws two hearts, a spade and three clubs (the lowest ranks first, of course). If he now plays his Ace for a seventh trick, she will take five tricks for 6. Instead, wishing to keep her score as low as possible with a view to the rubicon (she being only half way there), Napoleon boxes clever with ♣9. She takes it for 2 and returns ◇J. He takes it for 2 and returns ♣K. She takes it for 2 and cashes her ◇A for a fifth trick point – her last, since she must now lead into Napoleon's spade tenace, giving him two tricks for 3 plus 10 for the cards. Total on this deal: Napoleon 34, Josephine 5. Cumulative total half way through the game: Napoleon 126 and well over the rubicon, Josephine 56 and not yet in sight of it.

Fourth deal. Napoleon deals:

    Jos: ♠K Q J 9 ♡Q 8 ♣A K 7 ◇A K J
    Nap: ♠A 8 7 ♡A K 9 ♣J 9 ◇Q T 8 7

As elder, Josephine must keep her point in spades and hope to convert her trio of Kings into a quatorze. As it stands, the trio is not good against the cards, as younger may hold or acquire '14 Tens'. To prevent this, she must find a fifth discard. Rather than spoil her point, she drops an Ace, throwing out ♡Q ♡8 ♣7 ◇A ◇J. (Why not the Ace of clubs ? A fine point – almost a matter of principle rather than practicality. Her diamond suit is marginally stronger than her clubs, therefore his club suit may be marginally stronger than his diamonds, so she had better keep her strength in clubs.)

Napoleon's younger hand is hardly problematical, nor hardly promising either. He keeps his point suit, avoids breaking up clubs in case the Queen appears, and so discards two low spades and the bottom heart. Now:

    Jos: ♠K Q J T 9 ♡T 7 ♣A K T 8 ◇K
    Nap: ♠A ♡A K J ♣Q J 9 ◇Q T 9 8 7

Josephine announces 'five', to which Napoleon replies 'good' immediately, knowing that his diamond point is weaker and not wishing to reveal its length. Josephine adds '. . . in spades, and a quint to the King adds 15', (knowing it to be good against the cards) '20; three Kings 23 and Tens 26; one for leading 27'.

It will be noted that Josephine's trios were also good against the cards, and that her failure to announce three Aces tells Napoleon that she has discarded one – whether it tells him truthfully or not is for him to decide, but there would seem little point in bluffing.

Within three points of pique, Josephine secures the bonus by leading her two top clubs and ◇K, the latter winning because she discarded the Ace. Napoleon played his Jack and Nine of clubs and Jack of hearts, leaving himself with top cards in all suits by the time Jo has announced her score as 60. Whatever she leads next, Napoleon takes nine for 10 plus 10 for the cards, 20 in all. Scores at end of fourth deal: Napoleon 146, Josephine 116 and now over the rubicon.

Fifth deal. Josephine deals:

```
Nap:  ♠Q J T 7  ♡A 7  ♣A K 9  ◇A 9 8
Jos:  ♠A K 9 8  ♡Q T 9  ♣J 7  ◇Q J 7
```

Napoleon has only four obvious discards after keeping his spade point and all Aces and Kings. Should he just exchange four, or spoil his point by throwing the Seven, or throw out ♣K as the fifth card? He decides to dispense with ♠7, which is exactly what I would have done.

Josephine's younger hand is, if possible, even more un-promising. After little thought, out go the numeral spades and bottom club. The Queens must not be unguarded, for younger is often capoted with only one good suit in hand.

```
Nap:  ♠Q J T  ♡A J  ♣A K Q T  ◇A K T
Jos:  ♠A K  ♡K Q T 9 8  ♣J 8  ◇Q J 7
```

A typical quiet hand. Napoleon's point of four is not good, but he counts two tierces for 6, plus 6 for his trios of Ace and Ten, plus one for leading 13. Josephine counts 5 for her point in hearts.

In the play of tricks, elder must prevent younger from establishing hearts by forcing her to throw some of them to his leads. He kicks off in diamonds, hoping to find the Queen bare. Upon receipt of Josephine's Seven, however, he turns to his point in clubs. Younger, after following suit twice, can do neither better nor worse than to discard hearts from the bottom up. At this stage Napoleon cannot find any sure way of taking the last trick – which would give him the advantage of a measly point – so cashes his ♡A and ◇K, allowing Josephine to win the last five tricks for 6. To his opening 13, then, Napoleon has added a point each for seven won tricks, plus 10 for the cards, 30. Totals now, with the last deal coming up: Napoleon 176, Josephine 123.

Sixth deal. Trailing by 53 points, Josephine, as elder on the last hand, looks in need of at least a pique to win the game. The hands are:

   Jos: ♠A T 9   ♡A T 7   ♣A 8 7   ◇T 9 7
   Nap: ♠8 7   ♡J 9 8   ♣K Q J 9   ◇K Q J

Not a promising hand for elder on the last deal – no point suit and no sequences, though the trio of Aces may convert into a quatorze. Of immediate interest, however, is the absence of court cards, which at least gives her carte blanche for 10. 'I have a blank', she announces, 'and am going to exchange five cards. Make your discards before I show it.'

Now Napoleon must assess his hand. He knows the stock contains two Kings and Queens and a Jack. He must be very lucky indeed to take the fourth Jack *and* the Ace which might, if it is there, make those Jacks good against the cards. He discards both spades and the bottom heart.

Josephine now plays her cards rapidly face up to the table, counts 10 for the blank, and makes five discards – two diamonds, two clubs and the lowest heart. After the draw, the hands are:

   Jos: ♠A K Q J T 9   ♡A T   ♣A T   ◇A T
   Nap: ♡K Q J 9   ♣K Q J 9   ◇K Q J 8 (*no spades*)

As elder, Josephine calls a point of six, good, bringing her score to 16; a sixieme, good, 32, repique makes 92 (Napoleon having scored nothing); fourteen Aces and fourteen Tens, 120, plus 1 for leading, 121. With 9 for tricks and 10 for the cards, she reaches 140. Napoleon takes the last three tricks for 4.

The final result: Napoleon 180, Josephine 263. The difference is 83, and Josephine's game score, accordingly, 183.

This hand was deliberately concocted to show the highest score theoretically possible on one deal at Piquet. I say 'theoretically', because in order for it to be reached in practice younger would have to play with the aim of intentionally losing all the tricks. Thus, if Napoleon had suicidally played all his Kings and Queens to Josephine's spades, and then his Jacks to her Aces, she would have added to her original 121 a further 12 for tricks and 40 for capot – a grand total of 173.

The highest score which can be reached in practice is 170. It does not require younger to play stupidly, but does call – rather improbably – for elder's point of three to be 'good'. Holding A–K–Q in all suits, and finding all his combinations good, elder scores 3 for point, 12 for four tierces, 42 for three quatorzes, and repique for 60, total so far 117. One for leading makes 118, followed by 12 for tricks, 130, and capot, 170.

I raise this point because it is often said that the highest possible score on one hand of Piquet is 170. In fact, this is only the highest probable score, the highest *possible* being, as I have shown, 173.

BEZIQUE

A pretty and pleasing game affording much scope for tactical skill without overtaxing the intellect, Bézique may be particularly recommended as an accompaniment to the digestion of a splendid meal.

It is first cousin to the American game of Pinochle, and both appear to be descended from Sixty Six (described later in this section), or something very similar, via such intermediaries as Brusquembille, Briscan and Mariage – whence the terms *brisque* and *marriage* which figure prominently in the game.

The game was first played with a single 32-card pack, like Piquet, and known as Cinq Cents or Five Hundred, the winner being the first to reach that number. Early in the 19th century a two-pack, 64-card version seems to have sprung up in south-western France under the name Besi, which was transformed to Bésigue upon becoming a craze in the Paris gaming houses. This remains the French spelling to date.

A writer in Macmillans Magazine in 1861 sought to interest English players in the popular French game, but it did not really catch on until 1869 – possibly under the patronage of Victoria's son Alfred, Duke of Edinburgh, who picked it up in his travels and became addicted. (Eighty years later, Princess Margaret did much the same for Canasta.) The spelling of the name wavered for some time, only settling down with the discovery of Rubicon Bézique, which became something of a craze during Victoria's latter decades. Rubicon, played with four packs (128 cards), was succeeded by Chinese Bézique, using six, and ultimately by an even more elaborate eight-pack game requiring no fewer than 256 cards all shuffled together.

We will start with two-pack Bézique by way of introduction, and then, if you find this to your liking, proceed to higher things. The name *bézique* refers to the combination of ♠Q and ♢J in one hand, and may be connected with *besicle*, meaning 'spectacles, eye-glasses'. Similarly, Pinochle comes from *binocle*, which denotes the same combination and means the same thing. This may have arisen because in the commonest French pack the ♠Q and ◇J are the only Queen and Jack depicted in profile, thus exhibiting two eyes between them.

Two-pack Bézique

Equipment. Two 32-card packs shuffled together, consisting of A K Q J T 9 8 7 in each suit. It does not matter if they are of different back designs or colours, so long as they are of the same dimensions. Scores are made continually throughout the game, and can be kept on paper, though some sort of mechanical scorer is useful. Patent Bézique markers, of the same design as Whist and Piquet markers, are now antiques, but dial-type scorers are still produced from time to time. Even a Cribbage board will do. All Bézique scores are in tens, so twice round the crib board at 10 per hole gives a maximum of 1210 points, enough to be getting on with.

Rank. In each suit, cards rank: A T K Q J 9 8 7. Note the position of the Ten. It counts higher than King both in play and in cutting for the deal.

Deal. Whoever cuts the higher-ranking card may choose whether or not to deal first. Deal eight cards each in batches of three, then two, then three. Turn up the next card – the seventeenth – and lay it to one side between the two players. The suit of this card is the trump suit for the current deal and, if it is a seven, the dealer immediately scores 10 for it. Place the undealt cards face down across this card to form the stock, so that the turn-up projects from beneath it.

Object. The winner is the first player to reach 1000 points, which may take one or several deals. Points are scored for (a) capturing brisques (Aces and Tens) in tricks, counting 10 points each, and (b) through drawing and discarding, acquiring certain combinations of cards scoring anything from 20 to 500 points each.

Tricks. Non-dealer leads to the first trick. The second player

need not follow suit, but may play any card he chooses. A trick
is won with the higher card of the suit led, or the higher trump
if any are played. If identical cards are played, the first beats the
second. The winner of a trick lays the won cards before him (not
necessarily face down), shows and scores for any scoring combination he may hold in his hand, then draws the top card of stock
to restore his hand to eight. The trick-loser draws the next card
of the stock, and the trick-winner then leads to the next trick.
This continues until the stock is exhausted, when the rules of
play change. The purpose of winning a trick may be to capture
any brisque it contains, though brisques (Aces and Tens) are not
actually counted into the score until the end of the hand, and
do not add up to much. The main advantage of winning a trick
is that only the winner may declare a scoring combination. The
loser may hold one, but he can do nothing about it until he wins
a trick.

Scoring combinations. Upon winning a trick, a player may declare
and score for any one (not more) of the following combinations,
by removing its constituent cards from his hand and laying them
face up on the table before him. Such cards remain on the table,
but continue to count as part of his hand – *ie*, in subsequent
tricks, he may play either from the hand or from a combination-
card on the table before him.

(*a*)	*Sequence* (A T K Q J of trumps)	250
(*b*)	*Royal marriage* (K–Q of trumps)	40
(*c*)	*Common marriage* (K–Q of plain suit)	20
(*d*)	*Hundred Aces* (any four Aces)	100
(*e*)	*Eighty Kings* (any four Kings)	80
(*f*)	*Sixty Queens* (any four Queens)	60
(*g*)	*Forty Jacks* (any four Jacks)	40
(*h*)	*Bézique* (♠Q–◇J)	40
(*i*)	*Double bézique* (♠Q–◇J–♠Q–◇J)	500

Special rules govern the formation and re-formation of such
combinations. The basic principle is that a card which has
already been used as part of a scoring combination (and is there-

fore still lying on the table) may be used again as part of a different type of combination, but not of the same. Cards won in tricks remain out of play and cannot be used to form combinations.

Examples of re-use: If a marriage has been declared in spades, three more Queens might be added on the next turn to score Sixty Queens, and ◇J on the turn after to score bézique, so long as the ♠Q remains on the table throughout and is not played to a trick. If a royal marriage is declared for 40, then so long as both cards remain on the table it is permissible to add A–T–J of trumps and score 250 for the sequence.

Restrictions on re-use: If a marriage has been declared in spades, neither card may be remarried by the addition of another King or Queen (but another spade marriage may be scored by declaring the other King *and* Queen). Once a quartet (of Aces, Kings, Queens or Jacks) has been declared, none of its cards may be added to form another quartet, though it is permissible (if improbable) to declare another four of a kind straight from the hand to the table. It is also not permitted to declare a sequence for 250 and subsequently claim the royal marriage contained within it – as shown above, you must score the lower first and then the higher. Similarly, it is not permissible to score 500 for double bézique and subsequently count each constituent bézique for 40, but it is correct to declare, while winning three tricks, single bézique once, single bézique twice, and then double bézique, so long as all four bézique cards are on the table when double is declared.

It is sometimes stated that a combination is scorable only if at least one of its cards is played directly from the hand. This is not so. For example, it is proper to declare Kings for 80, Queens for 60 at the next opportunity, and then, so long as the appropriate cards remain on the table, a marriage upon winning each of the next four tricks. Or suppose Kings have been declared for 80, and two have been played out, leaving ♡K ♠K on the table. At a later turn, it is permissible to play ♠Q–◇J from the hand and announce 'bézique for 40, and a marriage to score', subsequently counting the ♠K–♠Q upon winning another trick.

Seven of trumps. A player who holds a Seven of trumps may declare it at any time – usually upon playing it to a trick – and score 10 points for it. Alternatively, he may, upon winning a trick, declare it for 10 and exchange it for the turn-up. This, however, counts as a declaration, and prevents him from declaring any other combination at the same time. (There are conflicting rules on the use of the trump Seven. This one is a recommended compromise.)

End-game. When the loser of the 24th trick has taken the turn-up into his hand, and there are no more cards in stock, the rules of play change. Each takes into hand any cards he has left on the table, and the last trick-winner leads to the first of the last eight tricks. The second to a trick must follow suit if he can and must win the trick if he can. If unable to follow, he must trump if he can. No combinations may be declared during this part of the game. The winner of the last trick scores 10 points for it. (*Variants* (a) 10 is scored for winning the 24th trick instead of the 32nd, *ie* the last trick before the stock is exhausted instead of the last trick of all. (b) The last eight tricks may be played as at whist, with Ten ranking between Nine and Jack, and obligation to follow suit if possible but not necessarily to win the trick. Not recommended.)

Score. Each player sorts through his won cards, counting 10 points for each Ace and Ten captured. This total is then added to his total for combinations and the result recorded. As many more deals are played as are necessary, until at least one player has reached 1000 points, the winner being the player with the higher total. If the loser has failed to reach 500, the winner counts double the margin of victory.

Suggestions for play

It is generally not worth winning a trick unless it contains a brisque or you have something to declare. Indeed, other things being equal, it is preferable to lose a trick and play second to the next one, as this gives you more latitude – for example, you know whether or not you can safely win it with a brisque, whereas you will avoid leading one for fear of losing it. On the other hand, situations often arise in which you suspect that your opponent has a valuable declaration to make, in which case you may attempt to keep winning tricks until the stock is exhausted in order to prevent him from declaring it. Bearing in mind that the same will be done against you, try to keep back trumps, especially high ones, to ensure the ability to declare.

It is obvious that good cards to throw to worthless tricks, or lead to those in which you have no interest, are Sevens, Eights and Nines. Often, however, you find yourself with none in your hand, which seems to consist of part-combinations and valuable cards. In this case treat Jacks as dispensable, as Forty Jacks is not a very high scoring combination and not worth spoiling the hand for. Keep hold of a diamond Jack, however, so long as there is the possibility of making bézique. Also be prepared to play a Ten if you can win the trick by doing so, as Tens cannot form part of scoring combinations except in trumps and are therefore not worth keeping from this point of view.

When it comes to breaking up part-combinations, you must weigh the value of each against the probability of making it, to which end you will be guided by what you can see amongst your opponent's declarations and what has already been played to tricks. For example, if he has declared a marriage in spades and you hold both Jacks of diamonds, it is impossible to make double bézique, and so one more Jack becomes available for discarding – unless, of course, you have seen so few of the eight Jacks to date that there seems a fair chance of forming a Jack quartet.

Cards still lying on the table after being declared are suitable candidates for playing to tricks, on the principle that you give your opponent less information about the state of your hand by playing a card he knows you have rather than one he hasn't seen. Marriage partners and quartetted Jacks are particularly good candidates for this purpose. At the same time, however, it is important to retain those which stand a fair chance of being re-used in other combinations, and those which belong to the

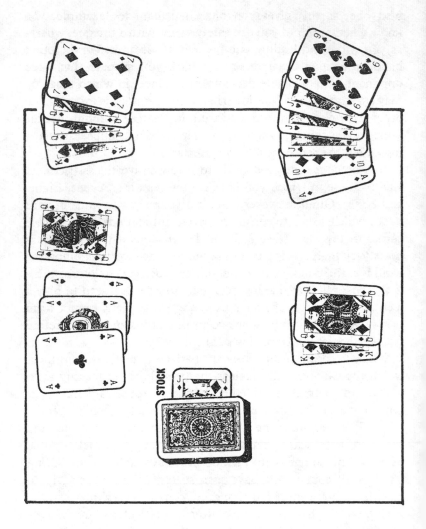

trump suit and may therefore be needed for trick-winning. In particular, never break up (by playing a card from) a single bézique so long as the possibility remains of forming a second and scoring the double, as double bézique is the most valuable combination in the pack and will nearly always win the game.

Given a choice of combinations, it is naturally better to score the more valuable ones first. But there is an exception to this rule, in that (a) given a sequence, you may score 40 for the royal marriage first and then 250 for the sequence for a total of 290, but if you count the higher combination first you are restricted to 250, as the marriage may not then be scored; and (b) the same applies to béziques: you may declare, on three successive turns, a single, a single and a double, for a total of 580, but cannot score for a single after counting the double. In these cases you score more for starting with the lower combination and working upwards. If, however, it seems unlikely that you will have time to make these scores the long way, in view of the number of tricks left to play and the state of your own hand, then it may be better to score the higher combination first and forgo the lower.

In the last eight tricks, the ideal is to play worthless cards of a suit in which your opponent is void, in order to weaken his

FIGURE 5

A situation in Two-pack Bézique. (Players' won tricks are omitted from view, for clarity.) North has evidently scored '100 Aces' earlier on and has since played one of them to a trick. The rules forbid him to add another Ace to those on the table to score the same again, though this is permissible in versions played with more cards. He has also scored either 20 for a marriage in spades, having played out the King, or 40 for single bézique, having played out the Jack. If he draws another Queen, he will be able to declare '60 Queens' by adding it and the Queens in his hand to that on the table. If he has just won a trick, he may exchange the $\diamondsuit 7$ for the turned-up Jack of trumps (for 10) and subsequently add the Jack to either of his spade Queens for bézique. As it happens, South is also much in need of this Jack. He has already scored 40 for the royal marriage in diamonds. Any Jack will give him '40 Jacks' to score, and the $\diamondsuit J$ in particular could be added to his table K–Q and hand A–T to score 250 for the trump sequence.

trumps. Experienced players will know what cards their opponent holds and play accordingly. Experience, in fact, is essential to success at Bézique, as it is a game of judgement rather than analysis. The practised player soon develops an instinctive feel for the state of his opponent's hand, and will know when he can safely lose tricks and when he must keep winning to prevent a high combination from being scored against him.

Polish Bézique

Also known as Fildinski, Polish Bézique differs from the ordinary game in only one major respect – yet the difference is so great as to produce a game of quite different feel, and one that many Bézique players prefer to the main game, finding it more demanding of skill. Certainly one has more control over the cards, and less depends on the luck of the draw.

Polish Bézique is played either with two 32-card packs (64 cards) up to 2000 points, or with three packs (96 cards) up to 3000. The following features are exactly the same as at Bézique: numbers of cards dealt, establishment of trump suit, exchange or declaration of Seven of trumps, method of playing tricks, need to win a trick before declaring, value of brisques and of scoring combinations.

The difference is that declarations can only be made of cards won in tricks. A card may not be played from the hand to the table to form a combination. Upon winning a trick, a player discards Nines, Eights and Sevens as worthless (apart from scoring 10 for the trump Seven, and exchanging it if desired), scores 10 for any brisque it contains, and lays the other cards face up on the table before him. If one or more combinations can be made with either or both of the cards just captured in the trick, they must be announced and scored before the next card is drawn from stock, otherwise they are lost. Cards used in combinations remain face up on the table, but may be played to tricks, and none may be used twice in a combination of the same type.

The play of the last eight tricks follows the same rules as Bézique (follow and head the trick if possible; trump if unable to follow), but combinations may still be declared from cards taken in tricks right up to the end of play. When played with three packs, triple bézique scores 1500.

Rubicon (Four-pack) Bézique

Also known as Japanese Bézique, for those who like artificial ethnic flavouring, Rubicon increases the fun of the game by doubling the number of cards, increasing the number of combinations, and lifting restrictions on re-forming them, with the result that extremely high scores are to be made. Following a similar principle to that of the rubicon in the game of Piquet, that of Rubicon Bézique is set at 1000 points. If the loser of the game fails to reach that total, he is heavily penalised, especially if he is foolish enough to play for money. In the following description, it is assumed that the reader is already acquainted with the basic two-pack game.

Cards. Four 32-card packs shuffled together very thoroughly.

Deal. Nine cards each, either one at a time or in batches of three. Place the remainder face down to form a stock. There is no turn-up.

Carte blanche. If either player has been dealt a hand containing not a single court card, he may claim carte blanche for 50 points by playing his cards rapidly, one at a time, face up to the table in order to prove it. He then takes them back into hand. If the next card he draws from stock during the course of play is also a blank, he may show it and score 50 again, and may do so for as often as he continues to draw a blank on subsequent turns. As soon as he draws a King, Queen or Jack, however, his privilege of scoring for carte blanche ceases for the rest of the deal.

Trumps. There is no trump suit to start with, and a trick can only be won by the higher card of the suit led, or the first played of identical cards. The first marriage declared scores 40, and the suit of that marriage takes immediate effect as the trump suit for the deal. (If a sequence is declared before a marriage, it also establishes trumps, but the royal marriage cannot then be scored separately.)

Tricks. Except that the game is played at no trump until a marriage is declared, the rules of trick-play are the same as at Two-pack Bézique, including the change of rule that obtains when the stock is exhausted and the last nine tricks are being played. It is customary for cards played to tricks to be left face up in the middle of the table until a brisque (Ace or Ten) is played, when the trick-winner gathers up all that have so far been played and stacks them on the table before him.

Briques. The score of 10 per won brisque is not counted until the end of the game, and even then is only used to break a tie. The game therefore depends mainly on scoring combinations.

Declarations. The winner of a trick may declare and score for one of the following combinations. These are basically the same as at Two-pack Bézique, but with the addition of a non-trump sequence and more multiple béziques.

SEQUENCES:

(a)	*Trump sequence* (A T K Q J of trumps)	250
(b)	*Plain sequence* (A T K Q J of a non-trump suit)	150
(c)	*Royal marriage* (K–Q of trumps)	40
(d)	*Common marriage* (K–Q of non-trump suit)	20

QUARTETS:

(e)	*Hundred Aces* (any four Aces)	100
(f)	*Eighty Kings* (any four Kings)	80
(g)	*Sixty Queens* (any four Queens)	60
(h)	*Forty Jacks* (any four Jacks)	40

BÉZIQUES (♠Q–♢J):

(i)	*Quadruple bézique*	4500
(j)	*Triple bézique*	1500
(k)	*Double bézique*	500
(l)	*Single bézique*	40

As a point of difference from the two-pack game, there is no score for a Seven of trumps. A more startling difference is that a single card may be used more than once in the same type of combination, though not in an inferior combination of the same class.

Let us clarify the last point first. It is the same as before: a marriage may be scored first, and other cards subsequently added to score the sequence; but if a sequence is scored first, the marriage within it cannot be scored thereafter. Similarly, béziques may be scored one at a time for the single scores, then later declared as double, triple, and so on, for more; but once (say) triple bézique has been scored, its constituent béziques may not be scored separately thereafter.

Otherwise, the general rule is that as soon as a card has been played out of a combination and into a trick, it may be replaced by an equivalent card and the re-formed combination scored again. For example, if Kings have been declared for 80 and one of them is played to a trick, the quartet may be reconstituted and rescored by the addition of another King, either from the hand or from the table (e.g. forming part of a marriage), as soon as the holder wins another trick. As to béziques, note that a multiple bézique is only scorable if all its cards are visible simultaneously. But if, say, double bézique is on the table, and one of the Queens is played out, another ♠Q may subsequently be declared and the double bézique thereby scored again. Marriages are equally prolific, with partner-swapping allowable on a highly permissive scale. To take an extreme example, suppose four marriages have been declared in the same suit, and all eight cards are still on the table. On each one of his next six opportunities to declare, the holder may play one of these cards to a trick and score for another marriage so long as a King and Queen of the same suit remain. If a card is played from a sequence, it may be replaced on the next turn and the sequence scored again. Furthermore, although a marriage cannot be declared if it lies in a sequence that has been scored, it can be scored by the addition of a second King or Queen if the first is played to a trick, after which the sequence itself is scorable again. Clearly, it is a matter of some importance to keep track of which cards have already been used in the formation of additional marriages.

The only real restriction is that only one score may be made at a time, and that only upon winning a trick. If the addition of cards to the table creates several different combinations, it is desirable to score the highest and announce the others as being 'to score', and to repeat this until the opportunity arises to score them. For example, suppose you have double bézique on the table and then declare eighty Kings, two of them being spades. You announce 'Eighty Kings and two marriages to score'. You draw another King, play a King and win the trick. You are now not obliged to score the marriage, as you can first, more profitably, put the King down and again announce 'Eighty Kings and still two marriages to score' (or, if the King you played was a spade, 'and one marriage to score').

End-game. When the last card has been drawn from stock and the last declaration made, all cards are taken into hand and the last nine tricks played in the same way as the last eight at Two-pack Bézique. There is a bonus of 50 for winning the last trick.

Score. If both players have exactly the same score, brisques are counted in to break the tie, and if they fail to do so the game is drawn. Otherwise brisques are ignored, except to escape the rubicon as explained below. Each player rounds his final score down to the nearest hundred below, and the winner scores 500 plus the difference between the two rounded scores. But the loser is credited with 100 even if he made less, and if the scores round down to the same amount the higher score is rounded up instead.

The rubicon. Regardless of what the winner scored, the loser is rubiconed if he fails to make 1000 points, though if he has won enough brisques to bring his score to this level he may demand that both players count their brisques in and thereby escape the rubicon. If this fails, he does not count his brisques, and the winner scores all points made by both players, plus 1000 for game, plus 300 'for brisques'.

Settlement. This complicated scoring system was made with pecuniary settlement in mind, the game being played at so much per hundred points.

Notes on play. Basic principles of play at Four-pack Bézique are much the same as for the two-pack game, with three major exceptions. First, as we have already noted, the game is essentially one of combinations. As brisques are only counted in the event of ties or being otherwise rubiconed, there is less need to win tricks containing them, and Aces and Tens (especially Tens) are therefore more readily available for winning tricks. Coupled with this is the fact that the almost endless possibilities of combination and re-combination call for a greater degree of judgement – a sharper degree of observation of the possibilities available together with a more accurate assessment of which are worth pursuing and which can be dropped if necessary. The third point arises out of the method of determining trumps. It is often inadvisable to make trumps just because you can. If you are well represented in all suits, holding perhaps a marriage or two, it does not matter too much if your opponent makes trumps first. When you find one of your suits predominating, then is the time for trump-making, with a view to converting into a trump sequence. You may also be guided by what your opponent is discarding. If it is clear that he is keeping back a suit, apparently building it up for greater effect, you might well make trumps earlier in order to upset his plans.

Chinese (Six-pack) Bézique

The difference between what was originally devised as Chinese Bézique and what is now known as Six-pack Bézique is fairly subtle. I believe I'm right in stating that unadulterated Chinese Bézique was no more than Rubicon (Japanese) Bézique played with six packs instead of four, and that the 'Chinese' tag was dropped with the addition of certain 'optional extra' rules which will be carefully noted below so that you may decide beforehand wheth er to follow them or not. Six-pack really is the game for Bézique enthusiasts – amongst whom legend not only numbers the late Sir W S Churchill as a devotee but indeed also credits him with considerable expertise.

Cards. Six 32-card packs shuffled together, 192 cards in all, ranking as at other forms of Bézique.

Optional rule. The dealer (established by cutting, as usual) attempts in one movement to lift exactly 24 cards off the top of the pack, and the non-dealer announces his estimate of how many cards he thinks have in fact been lifted. If the dealer succeeds, he scores 250; if non-dealer's estimate is right, he scores 150. It is, of course, possible for both to score if non-dealer correctly guesses twenty-four. (This optional rule has been criticised as having nothing to do with the game. I do not concur. For one thing it is fun, and for another it strikes me as a more valid exercise of 'skill at cards' than the mere application of memory, for which many existing games give too high rewards.)

Deal. Twelve cards each, one at a time. Place the remainder face down to form a stock.

Carte blanche. As at Rubicon Bézique, but scores 250 each time.

Play. As at Rubicon Bézique, with trumps established by the first marriage (or sequence) declared, and with the following additional scoring features:

Four Aces of trumps	1000
Four Tens of trumps	900
Four Kings of trumps	800
Four Queens of trumps	600
Four Jacks of trumps	400

Other quartets score as at Rubicon, with no score for four Tens if not all trump. Béziques score as at Rubicon, with no extra credit for quintuple or sextuple. The last trick of all scores 250 to its winner. Brisques play no part at all.

Optional trump/bézique rules. Two rules are involved here, it being usual to play either both or neither. First, bézique is redefined as the Queen of trumps plus a Jack of opposite colour. If trumps are spades or diamonds, the Jack is diamonds or spades; if hearts or clubs, it is clubs or hearts. Second, if this rule is followed, the same suit may not be entrumped in two successive games. (This twin optional rule, never much favoured by English players, actually reduces rather than increases the variety of the game. Not recommended.)

Score. Each player's final total is rounded down to the nearest hundred, and the winner scores the difference plus 1000. If both round down to the same hundred, the higher-scoring player rounds up instead. If the loser fails to reach 3000 points he is rubiconed, and the winner scores 1000 plus the total of their two rounded scores (even if he fails to reach 3000 himself). If the final scores are identical the game is a draw – though it is easy, if desired, to devise tie-breakers. For example, (a) credit a final game score of 1000 to the winner of the last trick, or (b) play another game and credit its winner with an additional 1000 for game.

Notes on play. The additional hefty scores for trump quartets – including four trump Tens – may exert considerable bearing on your trump-making plans. Dealt three Aces of the same suit, for example, you will want to go all out to entrump that suit at the earliest opportunity. Without an obvious candidate, however, the decision when and what to make trumps is a matter of judgement born of experience. Much also depends on which rule you follow with regard to béziques. If sticking to the ♠Q–♢J definition regardless of trumps, for example, you may have to decide beforehand whether to go for multiple béziques or for trump sequences and quartets, a dichotomy that does not arise when the bézique Queen is always of the trump suit. In this connection, a reason for preferring the strict ♠–♢ definition of bézique is that games take on a quite different flavour according to whether trumps are spades, diamonds, or neither. Thus if your opponent appears to be collecting béziques, so far as you can tell from the failure of appropriate cards to fall into your own hands, or to be played to tricks by himself, you are in a good position to declare hearts or clubs as trumps. This will make his hand crowded, as he will have difficulty in collecting bézique cards while ensuring adequate coverage in trumps. A bézique suit as trump makes for a more economic hand.

The management of trumps requires some care. Don't bother to keep back small ones for the sake of hoarding, but at the other extreme do keep back trump Aces for maximum effect, both in the winning of tricks – especially towards the end and with a view to the last twelve – and for the possible acquisition (and re-formation) of a trump Ace quartet. But avoid crippling your hand for the sake of trump Tens, as they have no other value. It is better to aim for trump King or Queen quartets, as they can be milked for eighties and sixties while you wait for the appearance of the profitable fourth trump.

For the last twelve tricks it is desirable to retain not only trumps but also a long side suit with which to force the adverse hand. The point at issue is not to make brisques (they don't count) but to win the last trick. It will usually be taken by the better player – partly because he will have kept back better cards, partly because he will have kept closer track of the game and will know his opponent's entire hand, and partly because there is a marked element of skill in making the right moves in the right order, a point at which Bridge, Piquet and Pinochle players will excel. The last trick, at 250, is worth a twelfth of a rubicon and can make a substantial difference to the final game score.

Always keep an eye on both scores throughout the game – partly to check up on accurate score-keeping, but mainly to assess the chances of either player's being rubiconed. If you are in a winning position, be prepared to forgo combinations for the sake of preventing him from declaring enough to get him over the rubicon. If you can see no hope of escaping the rubicon yourself, remember that all scores made by both players will wind up in the winner's account, so win tricks to prevent him from declaring, but avoid declaring yourself. However, follow this course of action only if you are certain that the situation is desperate.

Eight-pack Bézique

This variant differs from Chinese Bézique only in the following particulars:

Cards. Eight 32-card packs, 256 in all.

Deal. Fifteen each.

Scoring combinations. In addition to those of the six-pack game there is quintuple bézique at 9000 points, while five trump Aces, Tens, Kings, Queens and Jacks score respectively 2000, 1800, 1600, 1200 and 800.

Score. As for the six-pack game, except that the rubicon is set at 5000 points.

One-pack Bézique (Binocle)

In case you have only a single pack, and wish to savour the delights of Bézique without rushing out to buy a second, there are several closely related games played with just 32 cards, including Binocle (Swiss), Binokel (German), Cinq Cents (French) and Marjolet (Spanish-French).

Binocle is played like ordinary (two-pack) Bézique, but with these differences:

1. No trump card is turned. Instead, the game is played at no trump until a marriage is declared, which establishes the trump for the rest of the hand.
2. The ♠Q– ◇J combination is called binocle and scores 40.
3. The combination of ♠K–♠Q–◇J is called grand binocle and scores 80.
4. A sequence in trumps counts 150, not 250.
5. Instead of counting brisques at 10 each, certain cards captured in tricks bear point-values as follows: each Ace 11, Ten 10,

King 4, Queen 3, Jack 2. These may be scored as they occur or counted in at the end of play, whichever is more convenient.

6. Game is 500 points.

This game will be found to be remarkably similar to Sixty Six, to which we will turn next. English readers may also like to note that the American game of Pinochle, as played by two, is virtually Bézique but played with only 48 cards, all Sevens and Eights being removed.

SIXTY SIX

This popular German game goes back a long way and is an ancestor of the Bézique/Pinochle family. Though played with only 24 cards – even 20, in one variant – it is remarkably varied and exciting, and gives ample scope for skill. It may be characterised as a fast little game, suitable for play when time is limited or interruptions expected. Why it is not better known in Britain is a mystery, as similar games are quite widespread in Europe.

Sixty Six is said to have been invented in 1652 at an inn in Paderborn (North Rhine/Westphalia) called 'Am Eckkamp 66', and to have achieved such notoriety as a gambling game as to have called forth rapid prohibitions on play from legal and ecclesiastical authorities. (It may be remarked in passing that if such prohibitions did not exist it would be necessary to invent them, as they are essential to the pedigree of any popular game.) The following rules accord with those promulgated by the Sixty Six Research Circle, based in Paderborn.

The game

Cards. Twenty four, consisting of A K Q J T 9 of each suit.

Deal. Whoever cuts the higher card deals first, and the turn to deal alternates thereafter. Deal six cards each in batches of two at a time. Turn up the next (13th) card to establish trumps and lay it face up to one side. Place the undealt cards face down across it to form a stock in such a way that the trump card projects visibly beneath it.

Rank and value. Cards rank in the following order for trick-taking purposes (note the high position of the Ten) and bear a point-value credited to whoever wins them in a trick as follows:

Rank	A	T	K	Q	K	9
Value	11	10	4	3	2	0

Object. Each deal is won by the player who first scores 66 card points, for which he may score one, two or three game points. A game is won by the first to make seven game points, which will take at least three deals. Card points are scored for capturing counters (scoring-cards) in tricks, in accordance with the above table. As there are 30 card points in each suit and 10 points for winning the last trick, the total number of card points available is 130, of which the target number, 66, represents a clear majority. Additional card points are available for the declaration of marriages (each comprising a King and Queen of the same suit), as detailed below.

Tricks. Non-dealer leads to the first trick. The winner of each trick, before leading to the next, draws the top card of stock and adds it to his hand, and waits for his opponent to draw the next card. So long as any cards remain in stock, the rules of trick-play are as follows. The second to a trick need not follow suit but may play any card he pleases. The trick is won by the higher card of the suit led or by the higher trump if any are played. Won tricks are turned face down and may not be referred to. Each player must keep a mental record of the value of cards he has captured so far, it being illegal to record them in any other way.

Marriages. If a player holds the King and Queen of one suit, he may declare and score for the marriage only upon leading one of them to a trick. He must show both cards, and must have won at least one trick, in order to score the marriage. A marriage in trumps scores 40, in any other suit only 20.

Nine of trumps. The player holding the Nine of trumps may exchange it for the trump turn-up at any time, provided that he has won at least one trick, and that the turn-up has not yet been taken or turned down.

End of stock. When the last card of the stock (the trump turn-up or substituted Nine) has been drawn, the method of play changes. Marriages may no longer be declared. The follower to a trick must follow suit if he can and must win it if he can. If unable to follow, he must trump if he can. The winner of the last trick scores 10 for last.

Going out. As soon as a player has reached 66 or more card points, he may claim 'Out!', and play then ceases. If he is correct, he scores one game point, or two if his opponent is 'schneider' (*ie* has less than 33), or three if his opponent is 'schwarz' (has won no trick). If the caller is mistaken, his opponent scores two game points, increased to three if he has not taken any tricks. Note that the player who correctly calls 'Out' wins even if his opponent has taken more card-points, the latter being thereby penalised for failing to call when he could. Note, too, that the caller must already have taken 66 – he cannot count 10 for last if he ends the game prematurely.

If neither player calls, the cards are counted and the appropriate win (of one, two or three game points) goes to the player who has reached or exceeded 66. If both have reached 66, however, and neither has called, then the game point is held over and credited to the winner of the next deal, in addition to whatever score he makes for it in the usual way. If both players take exactly 65, the result is a draw and no game point is scored.

Closing. Either player, when it is his turn to lead to a trick, may close the stock by taking the trump turn-up and placing it face down on top of the remaining undrawn cards. The remaining tricks are then played out in exactly the same way as if the stock had run out naturally. The closer may, but need not, draw a sixth card before closing, so that the end-game may consist of five or six tricks. If he does draw, he must allow his opponent to do likewise. Furthermore, he must allow his opponent the opportunity of exchanging the Nine for the turn-up if so required. If the game is closed, there is no score of 10 for the last trick.

Variants

American Sixty Six. American practice differs in some details from the original game. In particular, marriages may still be declared in the play of the last tricks. One American source also notes that it is not necessary to head the trick in the end-game – that is, you must follow suit if possible, but are not obliged to play higher.

Mariage. This old French game (which explains why there is only one R in it) is virtually identical with Sixty Six. The chief

point of interest is that a meld may be made consisting of the
Ace and Ten of the same suit. This is called an *amour* and scores
30 in plain suits, 60 in trumps.

Illustrative deal

The players are Anton and Bernhard, of whom the latter deals
as follows and turns ♣K for trumps:

Anton:	♣ *none* ◇K Q 9 ♠K ♡T K
Bernhard:	♣T ◇ *none* ♠Q J ♡Q J 9

In the following account, the card in brackets is the one drawn
from stock after the trick has been taken.

Anton	Bernhard	
♡K (♠A)	♡9 (◇T)	As there is no obligation to follow suit, Bernhard would have done better to trump with his Ten. A has 4, B has 0.
◇Q (♠9)	◇T (♣J)	Having won a trick, Anton can now declare his diamond marriage for 20, duly leading one partner to the trick. Now A 24, B 13.
♠9 (♡A)	♣J (◇A)	B leads the only suit which A cannot capture with a high counter, except for the ♣A, which would leave B's Ten in a commanding position anyway. A 24. B 15.
◇9 (◇J)	◇A (♠T)	B takes a chance that A has no trumps, and is rewarded. A 24, B 26.
♠A (♣A)	♠J (♣Q)	A 37, B 26. After the draw, Bernhard, had he held ♣9, could have exchanged it for the turned trump King and made a royal marriage for 40. But now it is too late.
◇J (♣9)	♡J (♣K)	Anton has drawn ♣9 too late to exchange, and Bernhard, though he draws the King, cannot declare the

marriage because the stock is
exhausted. The score so far is A 41,
B 26, and play is now governed by the
strict rules of following to tricks.

♡*A*   ♡Q   A 55, B 26.

♣*A*   ♣Q   A 69, B 26. Anton now declares
himself 'out', and scores not one but
two game points because Bernhard is
'schneidered', having less than 33.
(There is no '10 for last' because the
last trick, which means the twelfth,
was never played.)

Notes on play

Although using little basic material, Sixty Six is a game of
surprising variety and almost pure skill. By half way through the
game, when the stock is exhausted, each knows exactly what
cards the other holds, and can calculate precisely how to play
his own for the best. Even before this it is possible to make well-
informed guesses as to the other's holding. For example, the
absence of a marriage declaration from the other side indicates
that a given King or Queen is yet to be drawn.

In the first part of the game it is essential, so far as possible, to
retain marriages until they can be declared, and to save Aces and
Tens for possible capture of adverse leads instead of leading
them to risk loss by trumping – bearing in mind that there is no
obligation to follow suit. It follows that the safest leads at this
time are Nines and then Jacks.

The best time to foreclose a game is when you are strong in
trumps and high cards, as the effect is to initiate that period of
play in which suit must be followed and tricks won if possible.
It is also necessary to decide whether or not to draw immediately
before closing. Do you need six tricks for your purpose, or will
five suffice ? And which of you is more likely to benefit from the
draw of another unseen card ?

Sixty Six may be a miniature, but it is a jewel of a game.

KLABBERJASS

I can think of no better introduction to this game than that of the late card-game researcher Goodfellow, who told me: 'Klabberjass, which masquerades under a number of different names, must be, next to Bridge, the most widely known game in the world. It is current in almost every capital where European cards are used. Its spread is undoubtedly due to the emigration of Jewish people into the cities of the western world. Every properly brought up Jewish boy of at least the last generation would know something about *Klobiosh*, even if he did not actively indulge in it. It is also widely played by East Londoners of gentile origin. It has a distinct air of Mittel-Europa about it and I am inclined to believe, with Ely Culbertson, that its birthplace was probably Budapest, although it undoubtedly evolved from the earlier, and simpler, game of Jass.'

Jass – pronounced Yass – is a game much played in Switzerland, though considered to be of Dutch origin. The word means Jack, while klabber means 'clubs'. Under the name Kalabriasz it will be familiar to all readers of Damon Runyon, having been probably the most popular game on Broadway before the advent of Gin Rummy. Under the name Belote it will be known to habitués of French bistros and lovers of Byrrh and *boule*. In the Netherlands it is called Smoosjass and in Hungary Alsös. In short, Klabberjass is a centuries-old game of middle European Jewish origin, which has by expansion become one of the most popular pastimes of the western world.

Before starting, it should be noted that the games listed above all differ from one another in many but minor details, and that no two accounts of Klabberjass itself agree in every respect. For this reason I have noted certain rules as options or variants. Beginners should start with the plainest version, and subsequently add optional extras according to taste and previous agreement.

The game

Cards. Standard 32-card pack.

Deal. Whoever cuts the lower card (A K Q J T 9 8 7) deals first, and the deal alternates thereafter until one player reaches a score of 500, which ends the game. Deal six cards each in two batches of three. Place the remainder face down to form a stock. Turn the top card face up and place it beside the stock. The suit of this card is the preferred suit for trumps, but will not necessarily be accepted as such.

Object. After the bidding each player will receive three more cards and play nine tricks. Whoever accepts or nominates the trump suit (the 'maker') thereby undertakes to win the greater number of points for tricks and melds. Trick-points are scored by capturing certain cards with point-values, as shown below. A meld is a sequence of three or more cards in the same suit, or the King and Queen of trumps, known as *bella*.

Rank and value of cards. In non-trump suits cards rank A T K Q J 9 8 7 – note the high position of the Ten. In trumps, the highest card is the Jack, known as Jass, second-highest Nine, known as Menel (accent on the second syllable), then Ace and so on down to the Seven. Cards also have point-values, credited to the player winning them in tricks, as follows:

Jass	20 =	Jack of trumps
Menel	14 =	Nine of trumps
Ace	11 each	⎫
Ten	10 each	⎬ *in every suit*
King	4 each	⎪
Queen	3 each	⎭
(Jack)	2 each	⎫ *except in trumps*
(Nine)	0	⎬
Eight	0	⎫ *in every suit*
Seven	0	⎬

Melds. A sequence of three cards in the same suit counts 20, a sequence of four or more counts 50. The sequential order of cards is A K Q J T 9 8 7 in every suit. (Thus Q–J–T is a sequence of three even though the ranks may not be adjacent in trick-taking power.) The King and Queen of trumps together ('bella') score 20. Melds are not counted until both players have nine cards, and only the player with the best sequence may score for sequences.

Bidding. The rank and value of cards and melds have been described first because bidding can only be carried out on the assessment of one's chances of winning more points than the opponent. It is to be noted that the total value of all the scoring cards in the pack is 152, though not all will be in play, and that the winning of the last trick carries a bonus of 10.

Elder hand starts the bidding by announcing one of three things:

1. *Accept*. In which case he accepts the preferred suit as trumps and becomes the maker.
2. *Schmeiss* (pronounced *shmice*) This is a proposal to abandon the deal. If younger accepts it, the hands are thrown in and there is a new deal. If he refuses, elder is obliged to accept the preferred suit as trump and so become the maker.
3. *Pass*. This is a refusal to become the maker with the preferred suit as trump. Now younger has the same choices: he may accept, schmeiss, or pass. If he passes, elder may either nominate another suit as trump, thereby becoming the maker, or pass. In the latter event, younger may also nominate a suit or pass. If both pass this time, the hands are abandoned and a new deal made.

Play. When one player has become the maker, the dealer deals another batch of three cards to each player from the top of the stock, so that each has nine. Then he takes the bottom card of the stock and places it face up on the top. This card is for information only and has no part in the play. (The purpose of this curious manoeuvre is to ensure that neither player has had the unfair advantage of being the only one to see the bottom card, which may be accidentally or otherwise observed during the deal.)

Dix, pronounced *deece,* is the Seven of trumps if the preferred trump was accepted. If either player has this card he may exchange if for the turned trump-card at any time before the first trick is led. This privilege cannot apply if a different suit was entrumped.

Melds. Before elder leads to the first trick, scores are made for sequences if either player holds any. Only the player who holds the best sequence may score, and he is thereby entitled to score for as many as he shows. (The relevant cards must be revealed.) The best sequence is the one of greatest length; if equal in length, the one with the highest card; if still equal, the one in the trump suit. If neither is in trumps, that of elder hand prevails. Note that the dix may be exchanged either before or after melds are declared, depending on whether the Seven or the card taken is required for a sequence. (Whether or not it is permissible to (a) count the Seven in a sequence of 7–8–9 and then (b) change it for (say) a turned Ace to make and also score another sequence of A–K–Q is a point on which I can find no authority, but I suggest that this should be disallowed.) Bella, if held, is not yet declared.

Tricks. Elder leads to the first trick and the winner of each trick leads to the next. It is obligatory to follow suit, and if a trump is led the second must play a higher trump if he can. A player unable to follow suit is obliged to trump if he can. (In short: you must try to win the trick if the lead is of trumps or a suit in which you are void.)

Bella. If either player holds the King and Queen of trumps he may score 20 by announcing 'bella' upon playing the second of them to a trick.

Last trick. Whoever wins the last trick (sometimes known as *stich,* pronounced *stish*) scores 10 points for it.

Score. Each player announces the total he has made for cards captured in tricks, stich, melds and bella (if any). If the maker has more than his opponent, each counts towards game exactly the amount he has made. If the maker has less, he is said to have 'gone bête' (pronounced and sometimes spelt *bate*); he scores nothing, but his opponent counts towards game the combined total made by both players in that deal. If both have taken the same amount, the maker is 'half bête': he scores nothing, and his opponent scores only the amount he himself has made. The game ends when either player, at the end of a deal, has reached or exceeded a previously agreed total, usually 500.

Variants. Amongst variations and additional rules followed in different countries and localities, the following may be adopted in whole or part.

1. The bid of schmeiss is a comparatively recent addition to the game and may be ignored by purists, though most American and British players like it.

2. In making trumps, first preference is always on clubs and second on the suit of the card turned, if different. This variant is recommended, as it increases demands on good judgement and is in keeping with the name of the game – which, as we have seen, means 'Jack of clubs'.

3. If the suit of first preference has been rejected by both players, either may make a bid of no trump (*sans atout*), which takes precedence over a bid in suit and may be used to overcall it. In this case there is no Jass or Menel, cards rank A T K Q J 9 8 7 in every suit, and each player's final score for the deal is doubled – which makes it attractive to bid no trump on a safe hand, but expensive to go bête on a bad one. If one player bids no trump, the other can overcall him by bidding 'grand' (*tout atout*). In this case there is a Jass and Menel in every suit – in other words, cards rank J 9 A T K Q 8 7 in each suit, and all Jacks are worth 20 and all Nines 14. Otherwise it is played as no trump and also scores double. Grand may only be bid to overcall a previous bid of no trump.

4. In the event of equality for best sequence, the result is a tie and neither may score, instead of declaring elder's to be better by virtue of his position. This is not recommended, as sequences are rare enough already without making them even harder to score.

5. Sometimes a sequence of five or more is valued at 100 points instead of 50 (which is retained for a sequence of four). But such sequences occur so rarely that it hardly seems worth the bother.

6. One source refers to a bonus of 40 for winning all the tricks. It seems reasonable to recognise some sort of bonus for this feat, though the figure quoted would appear to be lifted straight out of Piquet.

7. In the game of Belote (in which there is no bid of schmeiss) additional melds may be scored. Sequences of three count 20, of four 50, and of five or more 100. Also, whoever has the best four of a kind (a *carré* or quartet) may score for any and all quartets he may show, valued thus: four Jacks 200, Nines 150, Aces, Tens, Kings or Queens 100, lower ranks not counting. Game is usually at least 1000 points.

8. If, during the course of play, either player considers that he has reached the target score on melds and/or counting cards so far captured in tricks, he may claim 'out' and end the game immediately – provided that he has already won at least one trick (Belote rule). If he is wrong, he loses the game. Otherwise he wins, even if his opponent has a higher total.

Suggestions for play

Nearly all points are scored for cards won in tricks plus 10 for stich. A whole game may pass without the appearance of a bella or of more than two or three small sequences, and these therefore hardly need to be taken into account in the bidding, unless you are dealt one to start with.

Although the theoretical maximum number of trick-points is 162, it is impossible for all the value-cards to be in play in one deal. In practice, the average number of points in play per deal lies between 100 and 120, of which the maker, if he wins, should expect to score 80–90 against the loser's 20–30. If the game were played with a compulsory trump and no opportunity to pass, each player would expect to take an average of 50–60 points per deal. Since you are called upon to bid on only two thirds of your final hand, you ought to hold 30–40 points in high prospective trumps and supporting Ace-Tens before accepting the preferred suit or nominating another.

It is possible to bid successfully on a hand containing as little as a singleton Jass and two Aces or an Ace–Ten. But this does not mean that all hands are playable. The more expert players become, the more hands they tend to throw in. It does not take more than a few rounds of the game to discover how easily some weak-looking hands win while others, apparently quite promising, fall at the first fence. It is easy enough to recognise a strong hand when you see one, but takes practice to know whether or not to pass or play on something less clear cut. Beginners, I think, should play boldly. You will learn much more from bidding and losing than from passing and never knowing.

In assessing the hand look first for the dix (Seven) of the turned card, unless the latter is an Eight, which is not worth having. In any prospective trump suit it is imperative to hold either the Jack or an accompanied Nine, with preferably an Ace or Ten for company. Do not play a trump suit containing the Ace or Ace–Ten as highest cards, except in the unlikely circumstance of their being accompanied by at least two others of the suit, as there is too great a chance of losing one or more big ones to Jass or Menel in your opponent's hand. Nor be tempted into entrumping a suit just because you have been dealt the King and Queen, worth 20 for bella. If you have a mediocre hand including bella, or a sequence in any suit, the extra value may be just enough to make up either for weaknesses in the hand, or a stout opposition. But never bank on being dealt the marriage partner to a King or Queen already in hand, or a specific card required for a sequence. The odds are more than 7 to 1 against.

A two-card prospective trump including Jass or Menel is sufficient if adequately supported in plain suits, and the mathematical odds favour the appearance of a third in the last part of the deal. (In theory, that is. It never seems to happen to me; but then, I am not one of Dame Fortune's favourites.)

In non-trumps the best holding is an unaccompanied Ace or Ace–Ten, and there is even a goodish chance (4 to 3 in favour) of winning a trick with an ace-less Ten provided that the suit is not held so long as to risk being trumped. A long plain suit, say four or more, is not good for tricks unless it contains low cards which can be used to weaken the opposing trumps – bearing in mind the obligation to trump a suit in which one is void. A void suit in the prospective bidder's hand is a mixed blessing for the same reason. It must, for safety, be accompanied by long trumps, otherwise it will be used to weaken the trump holding.

Younger hand may always bid with greater boldness than elder, since elder's pass is suggestive of weakness. Younger is also in a better position to schmeiss on a hand which is not good for a straightforward acceptance of the turned suit but in which that suit is the only one that stands any chance of succeeding. The fact that elder has passed may justify this move. Elder himself should be very wary of schmeissing, except as a bluff on a good hand, which of course runs the danger of not being called. Otherwise the danger is that younger will accept the schmeiss and prove to hold a fistful of trumps himself.

If you have the lead as maker, your normal strategy on a reasonable hand will be to draw trumps first, partly to test the situation and partly to clear the way for Aces and Tens in plain suits. With a short trump suit or one headed by a tenace (Jack, Ace or Nine, Ten) it is preferable to lead a short plain suit with solid top cards. If you feel that your opponent might hold too many trumps, force them out by leading worthless cards from a long plain suit.

When leading trumps, it is worth starting with the Jack if there is a chance of seizing the Ace or Ten thereby, but (of course) it is dangerous to lead the Nine, Ace or Ten if you lack anything higher. Much of the interest of the game derives from the peculiar positions – third and fourth highest – of the high-scoring Ace and Ten of trumps.

With an average holding of two cards in each suit, it is desirable to win with Aces and Tens as soon as the opportunity arises. If (say) an Eight is led into your Ace/King, it is best to assure yourself of the Ace while you can, rather than hold it back in the hope of catching the Ten with it.

Illustrative deals

First deal. Our two players are Aaron and Bechstein, of whom the latter deals as follows and turns up ♡A:

    Aaron   ♠K ♡9 7 ♣T J ♢A
    Bechstein ♠7 ♡J T 8 ♣Q 8 7

As elder, Aaron has the Menel of the turned suit and can take the Ace by way of the dix. His hand is worth 35 in cards worth counting, and he accepts the turned suit. After three more cards are dealt, and ♠8 turned for information, the hands are:

    Aaron   ♠A K ♡9 A ♣A T J ♢A 9
    Bechstein ♠7 ♡J T 8 ♣K Q 8 7 ♢T

Neither player has improved his trump holding, and it is interesting to note that Bechstein was dealt three trumps including the Jass. With a short trump suit headed only by the second highest, Aaron leads clubs in the hope of retrieving his Ace and Ten before drawing trumps. He takes 21 points on the first two tricks, but then loses his Jack to Bechstein's King (worth a point more than taking it with the Queen). Given the initiative, Bechstein now plans to make the most of his comparatively long trumps. He starts aggressively with the Jass, drawing ♡A for 31 points and the certain knowledge that Aaron has only the Menel in hand, which he next forces out by leading ♡8. Now void of trumps, Aaron plays his Aces, gaining 32 card-points in the process, and continues with ♢9. This Bechstein trumps with his Ten, and concludes with ♣Q, drawing ♠K plus 10 for the last trick. Aaron has just succeeded in his bid, taking 67 to Bechstein's 64. The latter was lucky to hold not only more trumps than his opponent, but also more cards in the same long suit.

Second deal. Aaron turns up ♠T, having dealt:

    Bechstein ♠K 9 7 ♡A K ♢T
    Aaron   ♠J 8 ♡T 9 8 ♣A

Bechstein has three trumps and access to bella by means of the dix. He therefore accepts the turned suit, in which, it will be noted, Aaron holds the top card. The information card, after completion of the hands to the following, is ◇K:

> *Bechstein* ♠9 K Q ♡A K ♣T K ◇T 9
> *Aaron*   ♠J 8 ♡T 9 8 ♣A 8 ◇Q 8

After hearing Aaron declare his sequence in hearts for 20, Bechstein leads. He must allow his clubs and diamonds to be led into, as either Ten could fall needlessly to an Ace if led. He therefore decides to force out any high trumps by means of ♠Q, and is fortunate enough to bring the Jass down, leaving his Menel in charge. He can be sure that the Ace and Ten are not in play, otherwise Aaron would have played one of them and held back the Jass for better things, such as catching the Menel or winning the stich. Aaron continues with ◇8, which is taken by the Ten. The bidder now returns ♠K, announcing 'bella' and scoring 20. This draws ♠8, which Bechstein can be certain is the last trump in his adversary's hand. The remaining tricks are played like bat and ball. Bechstein wins his game, scoring 49 in tricks plus 10 for stich and 20 for bella, 79 in all, to Aaron's 53 in tricks plus 20 for the sequence, 73 in all. The round totals after two deals are A 140, B 143. And it's anybody's game.

ÉCARTÉ

A fast and exciting game of deceptive simplicity, Ecarté is the comparatively modern form of a centuries-old game called Triomphe or French Ruff. The basic idea is simple. Five cards are dealt to each player, and the object is to win at least three of the tricks played, or preferably all five. What makes it interesting, not to say subtle, is the fact that the hands are not necessarily played with the cards first dealt. Instead, both may draw fresh cards in exchange for worthless rejects until one player is satisfied with his hand, at which point play begins. All the fun, and much of the skill, lies in deciding when to stop exchanging and start playing.

Although Ecarté is for two, and makes a pleasant home game for couples who have no need to pay each other[6], it has spent most of its long life as a rather vigorous casino gambling game. One player is put up by the house to take on any and all comers one at a time, while onlookers are able to lay bets on the outcome. Ecarté supplanted Triomphe as the premier game of Parisian casinos early in the 19th century, and even up to 1970 could still be found in a few French establishments, which is not bad going for an industry whose native products are more prone than most to the importation of American substitutes.

It also became popular in English clubs during the last century, and the rules which follow are essentially those of the English form of the game as promulgated by the Portland Club and expounded by 'Cavendish' in the most authoritative monograph to have appeared on the subject.[7]

---

6. Strip Ecarté is a much more workable game than Strip Poker. Ecarté actually means 'discarded', but the reference is to the business of exchanging cards before play.
7. Cavendish, *Ecarté* – 6th Edition (LONDON, 1878).

The game

Cards. Use a 32-card pack, with nothing lower than Seven. It is convenient to use two packs, one being shuffled while the other is dealt, and to have five counters each as a scoring aid (though this is not essential).

Deal. Decide first dealer by any agreed means, after which the deal alternates. Shuffle, offer for cutting, then deal five cards each in batches of two and three. This may be 2+3 or 3+2 on your first deal, but whichever it is you must stick to for the rest of your deals in the same game. Place the undealt cards face down to one side to form a stock. Face the top card and lay it on the table beside the stock. The suit of the turn-up is the trump suit for the deal. If the turn-up is a King, the dealer marks 1 point for it.

Object. In each deal the object is to win three or four tricks (the *point*), for 1 point, or all five (the *vole*), for 2. The game is won by the first to reach 5 points after several deals. If counters are used, each places five on the table at his own left and transfers one to his right for each point marked.

Rank. Cards rank from high to low in each suit as follows: K Q J A T 9 8 7. Note the intermediate position of the Ace.

Discarding. If elder hand is satisfied with his cards, he may begin play by leading to the first trick. If not, he may *propose* a change of cards by calling 'Cards'. In this event, younger may either accept the proposal, in which case both can exchange cards as explained below, or else refuse, in which case elder must lead. (It should be noted that if elder plays without proposing, and loses, he loses double; similarly, younger loses double if he refuses the first proposal and fails to win.)

If the proposal is accepted, elder rejects face down from his hand as many cards as he does not want, announcing this number clearly. Younger does likewise, and then deals from the top of the stock first as many cards as elder needs to complete his hand, then as many as he needs himself. Now the same situation obtains. Elder may play or propose; if he proposes, younger may accept or refuse; if he accepts, more cards are exchanged in the same manner. It should be noted that younger, having accepted a proposal, thereby obliges elder to discard at least one, but need not himself exchange any if he then decides not to.

This continues until either play begins or cards run out, in which case play must begin anyway. Note that the turn-up is not part of the stock and may not be dealt as a replacement. If not enough cards remain to fill both players' hands, such cards as do remain go to elder. If either player is forced to retrieve one or more of his last discards because not enough replacements remain in stock, he must do so before seeing the cards he is dealt.

Marking the King. If either player holds the King of trumps he may mark one point for it provided that he announces 'King' before playing a card to the first trick, or as he does so if he plays it to that trick. If he fails to announce it in time he is too late, as the King may not be marked in retrospect. If marking the King brings a player's score to 5, the hand is not played out.

Play. Elder leads to the first trick, and the winner of each trick leads to the next. The second player must not only follow suit if able, but also win the trick if he can. If unable to follow suit, he must play a trump if he has any. The trick is won with the higher card of the suit led, or the higher trump if any are played. (In leading to the first trick, it is traditional for elder to announce the suit of the card he leads.)

Score. The winner marks 1 point for taking three or four tricks, 2 points for taking all five. But if elder played without proposing and lost, younger scores 2 whether he took three, four or five tricks. Similarly, elder scores 2 if younger lost after refusing elder's first proposal. Note that this increased value applies only if the hand was played with the cards originally dealt, no discards having been made, and only if the player who accepted his hand as good fails to take three tricks.

Revoke. If a player revokes, by failing to follow suit or win the trick or play a trump when able and required to do so, his opponent may upon discovery of the offence call for the hand to be replayed with the same cards. If the offender wins, he scores in the usual way but first subtracts one point from his total as a penalty. If he loses, there is no penalty.

Game. The game may be lengthened by agreeing that a rubber is won by the first player to win two games, for which there is a bonus of two points. Alternatively, play up to a previously agreed total of game points such as 5 or 10. For this purpose it may be preferred to count 1 game point if the opponent has scored 3 or 4, 2 if he scored 1 or 2, and 3 if he scored nothing at all.

Notes on play

The whole point of the game lies in deciding, when you have the choice, whether to play with the cards held or to propose (or accept a proposal) to change cards. Roughly speaking, a hand is playable when it contains at least three cards which are trumps or Kings. Looked at another way, it is advisable to discard all cards which are neither trumps nor Kings, and not to discard fewer than three. But there are exceptions to this principle, governed by such factors as whether you are younger or elder, whether or not you hold the King of trumps, and the state of the score.

From a score of love-all, there are certain types of hand upon which elder's best move is to play rather than propose. Such hands are called *jeux de règle*, 'obligatory plays', for the reason that, in casino play, the house player is obliged to play if dealt one of them – otherwise he is likely to find himself rapidly redundant and without a reference. It should go without saying that anything better than the following minimum *jeux de règles* is equally 'obligatory'. On the other hand, completely mechanical play is boring in its predictability, and more excitement may be squeezed out of playing the occasional shaky hand or sometimes proposing on a good one.

Three or more trumps. No matter how low they are, or what the non-trumps may be, a hand with three trumps is worth playing. Remember that there are only eight cards in each suit, and that one trump – the turn-up – is out of play, thus making it unlikely that younger will have more than one of the other four trumps. Best procedure is to lead the highest trump. If it is not taken you will almost certainly win three trump tricks, and if it is you will expect to win the other two trumps and make an eventual third trick by leading a suit your opponent cannot follow.

Two-trump hands. A hand with two trumps is playable if the other three cards are all of the same suit, or include a King or a guarded Queen. From the first of these, lead the highest card of the plain suit, and keep doing so at every opportunity. Two trumps and a singleton King is playable provided that the other two cards, if of different suits, are not both lower than Ten. Lead the King, unless the other two are of the same suit, in which case lead the higher of them. From two trumps and a guarded Queen (*ie* a Queen accompanied by at least one other of her suit), lead the Queen. Other two-trump hands are playable if the three non-trumps are generally high and not all of different suits, even down to Jack of one suit and Ten, Nine of another. Generally, lead the higher of the two-card plain suit.

One-trump hands. Playable if they contain K–Q–J of another suit, or if the other four cards are of the same suit and include the King, which should be led. Also playable is a hand consisting of a trump, a Queen, and another Queen twice guarded, from which the guarded Queen should be led. Risky is one trump plus two guarded Queens. At least one of the guards should be not lower than Ten.

No-trump hands. A hand devoid of trumps is playable if it contains three Queens or at least four court cards, provided that they are not all Jacks. (But four Jacks and another trump is playable – see two-trump hands.)

By and large, younger may refuse a proposal if he holds a hand that would be a *jeu de règle* with the positions reversed, though some patterns need to be somewhat stronger. Although the fact that elder proposes suggests that his hand is too weak to play, this does not make younger's that much stronger by comparison, since he is likely to be forced into trumping earlier and lacks the initiative to start with his strongest plain suit. In particular, a one-trump hand containing K–Q–J of another suit only merits a refusal if the fifth card is also a court, while a two-trumper with three in a plain suit similarly requires the best plain card to be a court.

Possession of the King of trumps is a key factor in play, as it scores as much as winning the point in its own right, which may prove enough for game, and also increases one's chance of winning the vole whilst ensuring defence against it. The latter considerations also apply to the Queen of trumps when the King has been turned up. It follows that a hand qualifying as a *jeu de règle*, or a refusal, may nevertheless justify one or two discards for the sake of the vole. For example, suppose spades are trumps and you hold

♠K Q ♡K Q ♣7

Although you have a certain four tricks and possible vole as it stands, you may propose in the hope of discarding the Seven and drawing a spade, heart or high card in its place. If refused, you will score 2 for the point in any case.

The *jeux de règle* should be known by heart, as an astute player may learn much from your indecisiveness or air of calculation if you do not play, propose, accept or refuse immediately and evenly. For much the same reason, the astute player, having dealt, will not look at his own cards until elder has made his first decision, in order to avoid giving anything away by inadvertent grimaces (or whoops of delight). And it is the height of folly to give way to force of habit by arranging one's cards in rank and suit.

Normal procedure in play is to lead the top card from one's longest plain suit. This is the suit most likely to force younger into trumping, and it is a general principle that where both players hold the same number of trumps the one first forced is most weakened. If the lead holds, continue the suit until it is trumped; but if you also hold the top trump it may profitably be led second before the forcing suit is continued. Trumps should be led only if four or more are held, or with three in hand if the top two are consecutive. From two trumps, a singleton King and two low cards, lead one of the low cards if both are of the same suit, and the King if both are different. With weak trumps and high plain cards, it is well to lead the high cards and keep changing the suit to avoid being trumped. If you manage to win the first three tricks in this way, lead the trump fourth with a view to the vole.

So far we have considered hands strong enough to have been led from without proposing. What happens when you have to lead from a poor hand on which you have proposed, but have been refused, depends on whether the hand is only poor, or so desperate that the vole may be won against you. In the latter case the important thing is to take a trick as soon as possible. Lead any King, or, if you have none, your highest single card – 'single' in the sense of being the only one in its suit. It is not advisable to lead from a guarded plain suit, such as Q–A, as you have more chance of making a trick from it if your opponent leads into that suit. If the situation is not desperate, prefer to lead one of two consecutive cards in a suit rather than from a non-sequential holding of high cards.

If you win the first two tricks and find your opponent out of trumps, always continue with a non-trump King if you have one, and then lead a trump fourth. He will then prefer to discard from your King-suit if possible in order to preserve a possible defence in some other suit against the fifth lead. If then your fifth card is of the same suit as your King, you will win the vole. If not, you may gain nothing extra in the short run, but will have played consistently and so stand a better chance of succeeding with the ruse when the opportunity next presents itself. Otherwise, an astute opponent will notice that you only play King-then-trump when the King is guarded, and will not fall for discarding the wrong suit to the trump lead.

If left with a trump and a plain card when three tricks have been divided, lead the plain card if you have won two tricks, the trump if only one. This gives you the best opportunity of winning the point.

The best time to mark the King is when about to play to the first trick. This gives younger the advantage of withholding useful information that might otherwise have influenced elder's lead. There is rarely much point in sinking the King (deliberately refraining from marking it). Younger may do so when he stands at three towards game against elder's four and elder plays without proposing, as younger will score two and the game anyway if elder loses, and will lose anyway if elder wins the point. Similarly, elder may sink when he has three to younger's four and younger refuses the first proposal. If when your opponent stands at four points you lack the King and it is not turned up, you should be prepared to play on a riskier hand than normally, as the more exchanging you allow to take place, the greater his chance of winning outright by drawing the King. In these circumstances it doesn't matter if you play immediately or refuse the first proposal, as a score of two is no better than of one to the player with four. Finally, if your opponent proposes when he stands at four points to your three, refuse if you have even an outside chance of winning the point. It is true that he will win the game if you fail, but to have proposed at all at such a score indicates a very weak hand.

Unless, of course, he was bluffing. And this is the point at which all clever stratagems come to nought, for Ecarté, more than any other trick-taking game except Le Truc, is wide open to the sort of intuitive and bluffing play which tends to unnerve 'calculating' players by tying them up in knots.

Illustrative game

First deal. Bertrand deals, the first card going to Armand. He turns up ◊A, and the hands are:

A: ◊J 9 ♠K ♣T 8 *proposes*
B: ◊Q ♠T ♡Q T 7 *accepts*

The new hands are:

    A: ◇J 9 ♠K ♡J ♣7 *proposes*
    B: ◇Q ♠J A 8 ♣J *accepts*

And again:

    A: ◇J 9 ♠K ♣K 9 *plays*
    B: ◇Q 8 7 ♡K ♠9

The play proceeds: ♣K ◇7, ♡K *◇9*, ♣9 *◇8*, ♠9 *♠K*, at which point they have two tricks each. Bertrand's Queen wins the last trick and gives him the point. Had Armand played his original hand he would have won, but by constant exchanging he permitted Bertrand to gain three trumps to his own two. Score: A = 0, B = 1.

Second deal. Armand deals, turning up ♡K for which he marks a point.

    B: ♡T ♣Q T ◇9 ♠9 *proposes*
    A: ♡J ♣J ◇K Q ♠8 *refuses*

Armand considers Bertrand's proposal to be made from weakness and a desire not to lose the initiative, and refuses on the strength of his four court cards. But Bertrand, despite his feeble hand, correctly refrains from leading his guarded suit and succeeds in winning the first, third and fourth tricks as follows: *♠9* ♠8, ◇9 *◇K*, ◇Q *♡T*, ♣Q ♣J, ♣T *♡J*. Bertrand marks two for having won after a refusal, and the scores are now A = 1, B = 3.

Third deal. Bertrand, before turning up ◇9, deals:

    A: ◇J T ♠J ♡Q ♣A *proposes*
    B: ◇Q ♠K 9 ♡8 7 *accepts*

Then after exchanging:

    A: ◇J T 7 ♣7 ♡9 *proposes*
    B: ◇K Q ♠K A T *refuses*

Bertrand, if he had the lead, would hope Armand had not more than two trumps and would play for the vole. As it is, he thinks he has good prospects after a second request for cards. But not so. Armand leads ◇J and Bertrand announces the King as he plays it. There follows ♠K ◇7, ♡9 ◇Q, ♠A ◇7, ♣7 ♠T, and Armand gains the point. Score now: Armand = 2, Bertrand = 4.

Fourth deal. Armand deals, turning up ♠T:

> B: ◇K Q ♡Q T ♣7 *proposes*
> A: ♠K ♣K Q ♡J 8 *refuses*

If Bertrand proposes needing only one point to game, Armand's hand gives him more than a fighting chance. Upon trumping the first trick, Armand marks his King: ◇K ♠*K*, ♣*K* ♣7, ♣*Q* and Armand wins the point. In leading the Queen rather than switching to hearts, Armand hopes that Bertrand either had been dealt no trumps, or, if he were, could still follow suit to clubs, in view of the fact that it was the lowest of all he had thrown to the King. Score: Armand = 4, Bertrand = 4.

Fifth deal. Bertrand deals, turning up ♣8:

> A: ♣7 ♡K Q ♠Q 9 *plays*
> B: ♣T ♡Q T ◇K Q

Armand now plays to the score, preventing Bertrand from drawing the King (if he had it, he would already have announced it and won), and hoping his opponent has not more than one trump if any. It pays off. The play proceeds: ♡K ♡9, ♠Q ♣*T*, ◇K ♣7, ♡Q ♡J – giving Armand the point and the game.

QUINTET

The rags-to-riches story of the man who invented *Monopoly* is an integral part of twentieth century mythology, but nobody, to my knowledge, has ever made a fortune out of inventing a card game. And I speak with all the authority of one who has invented several cards games and failed to make a fortune several times over. It is a curious fact that games which really catch on and become established classics, such as Canasta, can never be traced back to one person, whereas personal strokes of creative brilliance, such as Hoffman's Quinto or R. B. Willis's Calypso (both in the section on *Card Games for Four*), are forgotten in the space of a few years. I feel it not without significance that the millionaire who developed modern Contract Bridge, Harold S. Vanderbilt, is now hardly remembered by name, whereas Ely Culbertson, who waged a brilliantly successful publicity campaign to establish it as a world-wide classic, is now as well known as Hoyle.

No doubt I am cracking a nut with a sledgehammer, for I cannot pretend that Quintet is the greatest two-hander ever devised. But it was invented by Hubert Phillips, who was also responsible for the unjustly neglected Contract Whist described in the section on *Card Games for Four*, and in my book that makes it worthy of closer attention. It is a small scale game of bluff based on Poker hands, and has several points of interest that make it capable of developing into something bigger than the inventor may have envisaged.

The game

Cards. Two separate 32-card packs are used, each consisting of A K Q J T 9 8 7 in each suit.

Deal. Each player takes a complete pack. One shuffles his thoroughly and deals off the top seven cards, face up, leaving himself with 25. The other then removes exactly the same seven cards from his own pack, thereby reducing it in the same way.

Play. Each player now arranges his 25 cards in five Poker hands of five cards each, taking care not to let his opponent see how he is arranging them, and places the five hands in an order of presentation. When both are ready, each player reveals his first hand, and the one showing the better combination scores 3 points. Then the second hands are revealed, and this time the winner scores 4 points. For the third, fourth and fifth hands the winner scores respectively 5, 6 and 7 points. Thus there are 25 points to be played for in all, and it is possible to win by showing the better hand on the last two turns, scoring $6+7 = 13$. In the event of a tie on any hand, the appropriate points for that turn are shared equally.

Poker hands

Poker hands are defined and illustrated in the chapter on Poker (see p. 538), but in Quintet additional information is needed about how hands of the same type rank against each other.

Straight flush. As between two straight flushes, the one with the higher top card wins. Thus A–K–Q–J–T is highest and J–T–9–8–7 lowest. Ties are possible.

Fours. Four of a higher beats four of a lower rank, with Aces best, Sevens lowest.

Full House. The higher-ranking triplet wins. Thus 8–8–8–9–9 beats 7–7–7–A–A.

Flush. Won by the flush with the highest top card, or second highest if equal, and so on. Thus ♠A–J–9–8–7 beats ♡A–T–9–8–7. Ties are possible.

Straight. Won by the straight with the higher top card, as are straight flushes. Ties are possible.

Threes. Won by the higher-ranking triplet. Thus 8–8–8–9–T beats 7–7–7–K–A.

Two pair. Won by the hand containing the higher-ranking pair (e.g. J–J–7–7–8 beats 9–9–8–8–A), or second pair if equal, or odd card if still equal (e.g. K–K–Q–Q–8 beats K–K–Q–Q–7). Ties are possible.

One pair. Won by the higher-ranking pair, or, if equal, decided by the highest odd card. Thus Q–Q–A–9–7 beats Q–Q–A–8–7. Ties are possible.

Nothing. Won by the highest-ranking untied card; e.g. A–J–9–8–7 beats A–J–T–9–8. Ties are possible.

Note about straights. When proper Poker is played with a 32-card pack, it is usual to permit the Ace to count either high or low for the purpose of making a straight or straight flush, so that the lowest possible straight is T–9–8–7–A. Phillips does not state whether this applies to Quintet, and the point should be agreed beforehand. It strikes me as an illogical and unnecessary complication; Ace-low straights are therefore ignored in the rest of this chapter.

Illustrative deal

Here is Phillips's own illustration of play. We will call the players Novice and Oldhand. The cards rejected are ♠K, ♡Q–T–8, ♣Q, ♢J–T, leaving as playing hands:

♠A . Q J T 9 8 7
♡A K . J . 9 . 7
♣A K . J T 9 8 7
♢A K Q . . 9 8 7

First hand. Knowing that the game can be won on the last two hands, Novice starts by putting aside the Queen-high straight flush in spades for his fifth hand and his Jack-high clubs for his fourth, reckoning to do no worse than divide the points. Leaving his rubbish for the first hand, he starts by showing a pair: ♠7 ♡7 ♡K ♡J ♡9. Oldhand beats this with a full house: ♣7 ♡7 ♢7 ♡9 ♢9. Score 3–0 in favour of Oldhand.

Second hand. Novice comes up with a flush: ◇K Q 9 8 7. Old-hand counters with four Aces and the ♡J for ballast. Score now 7–0.

Third hand. Novice's four Aces appear next, along with ♣K, and are overtaken by Oldhand's straight flush in clubs, Jack high. Score 12–0. To avoid loss, Novice must now win the last two hands, or at least tie.

Fourth hand. Novice's club straight flush now falls to Oldhand's straight flush in spades, the Queen beating the Jack. Score 18–0.

Fifth hand. Novice brings his sledgehammer Queen-high spade straight flush down upon Oldhand's three King nut, and succeeds in losing by 18 to 7.

Both players, it will be observed, made three hands the same: the Queen and Jack-high straight flushes and the four Aces. The rest were formed into a pair and a flush by Novice, and a full house and three Kings by Oldhand. Correctly anticipating that Novice would leave his best hands for rounds three, four and five, Oldhand put the same hands to use in rounds two, three and four, thus going one better each time and assuring himself of scoring $4+5+6 = 15$ of the 25 points. In theory, of course, Novice might have foreseen Oldhand's line of reasoning and countered it by planning those same hands for rounds one, two and three, netting 12 points straight off and beating the final three Kings with his flush, for a game score of 19 to 6.

Further thoughts

I described Quintet as a game of bluff, which at this stage is not strictly true: a more accurate description would be that it is a game of judgement. To my mind, the need to decide in advance upon the order in which to present the hands makes the game rather restrictive, as all the strategy must be applied before the hands are played. There are several ways in which an element of bluff might be introduced to give the game a little more variety. For instance:

Any order. In this version, the players do not have to pre-determine the order of showing hands, except the first. Once the first has been decided, each may select which of the four remaining to show second, and so on of those remaining for the third and subsequent rounds. Taking the illustrative deal already described, for instance, it is possible that Novice might have played a straight flush on the second round, in order to compensate for losing his pair to a full house on the first. Oldhand, foreseeing this manoeuvre, might allow Novice to make his 4 points, himself taking the opportunity to throw off his worst hand (three Kings); or he might play his own best hand so as to at least divide the points. Throughout this version, each will be trying to estimate how much the other needs the points for the next round, and what he is likely to play. Opportunities for bluff are thereby introduced similar to those operating in the game of Gops (which is described in the next chapter).

Free hands. This is an extension of the above, in which not even the final playing hands are predetermined. Each player takes his 25 cards, makes a Poker hand, and plays the first round for 3 points as before. For the second round, each selects any five of his remaining cards and puts them face down on the table, both being turned when ready. In other words, the hands are made up as they go along. This considerably increases the skill factor, as both players must note which cards the other has not yet played and estimate their potential in combination.

Slow strip. This takes the element of bluff even further, and increases the scoring potential. It may be combined with any of the versions described above. At the start of every round, each player simultaneously reveals one card of his hand. If neither concedes defeat, a second is turned, and so on until one player concedes. Whoever wins the round, either because he has the better hand when all five are shown, or because the other concedes defeat earlier (in which case the unshown cards are rejected from play without being revealed) scores the value of the round multiplied by the number of cards he had revealed when conceded the win. Thus the first round may be worth anything from 3 to 15, and the last from 7 to 35.

GOPS

The origins of this unusual and unclassifiable game are unknown to me, so I shall plunge into it without further ado. It is a game of psychological warfare rather than mathematical analysis, and it is simple to learn and fast to play.

The game

Preliminaries. Divide the pack into four separate suits. Discard the hearts, which have no part to play, then shuffle the 13 diamonds and place them in a face down pile between both players. Each player then takes an entire black suit as his playing hand.

Object. The object is to capture the greatest value of diamonds, for which purpose each counts its face value from Ace = 1 to Ten = 10, then Jack 11, Queen 12 and King 13. As the total value of the diamond suit is 91, the player capturing 46 or more wins and no draw is possible.

Play Turn the top diamond face up to reveal its value and place it by the side of the stock. Each player then bids for it by choosing any one of his own (black) cards and laying it face down on the table before him. When both are ready, the two black cards are revealed. Whoever played the higher ranking card (Ace lowest, King highest) wins the diamond and places it face up on the table before him. The two black cards are now out of play for the rest of the game, but should be left face up so that each can see what the other has played and therefore, by deduction, know what he has left. The next diamond is then turned from the pack and played for in exactly the same way, and so on until all diamonds have been taken. If at any point both players play a card of the same rank, that result is a tie and the diamond remains untaken, though both black cards still count as spent and may not be taken back into hand. Then the next diamond is faced, and on this turn the winner takes both diamonds. If the result is still a tie, a third diamond is turned and the next winner takes all three, and so on.

Scoring. Each game is a separate event, but as it is boring to play any card game for a simple win/lose result the interest may be increased by crediting the winner with a score equivalent to the difference between the two totals captured (or with the number of points he has taken in excess of 45, which amounts to half the difference between the two).

Additional rules. I usually manage to resist the temptation to tinker about with established games, but all the published rules available to me seem deficient in one respect and rather flat in another.

First, what happens if there is a tie for the last diamond, together with any others that may have been tied in succession before it? The simplest solution is to credit it (them) to the player who made the immediately previous win. One of several alternative rules would be to leave them uncaptured, in which case a draw is possible; further, it might be agreed that if neither player captures a clear majority (46+) then the deal is a tie regardless of the amounts taken.

Second, one deal of Gops is too short to be considered a game in its own right: most players will want to go on playing it for a longer period. Yet if the two are evenly matched, there may only be a few points difference at the end of the whole game, which will seem too small to justify the amount of mental energy expended on the proceedings of the past hour or so. My suggestion for increasing the 'interest' of the relative scoring is one that I frequently apply to card games that score in ones and twos (especially Spite and Malice, of those in this book), and that is to expand the winner's score geometrically as follows:

OVER 45:

PTS TAKEN	1	2	3	4	5	6	7	8	9	10	11	12	13 etc
SCORE:	1	3	6	10	15	21	28	36	45	55	66	78	91 etc

Each successive score is found by adding the next appropriate number in the top row. For example, the score for taking 14 in excess of 45 is $91+14 = 105$, and so on. (If you would like it translated into algebra, the score for any given total n turns out to be $(n^2+n)/2$.) The net result is to give increasingly greater credit for taking increasingly greater totals, so that one player can win the whole game on one good result as opposed to a succession of mediocre ones.

It might also be agreed that the winner is the first player to reach a predetermined target score.

Suggestions for play

Gops is a game of bluff. If you want the next diamond from the stock, you will want to win it as cheaply as possible; if not, you will want your opponent to pay over the odds for it. A player wins cheaply when he captures a card by playing one that is only one or two ranks higher than his opponent's bid card, such as a Seven to a Six, because the latter will then have wasted 6/91 of his strength to no avail. An expensive win is made by the player who captures with, say, a King when his opponent has only played an Ace, for the former will then have paid a value of 11 over the odds for what he has purchased – *ie* he could have bought for 2 what he actually bought for 13. A cheap win is always worth having, no matter what the value of the diamond, but an expensive buy is even worse when the card bought is of comparatively low value – unless, of course, it is just enough to bring you over the 45 mark.

At each turn you both know how many diamonds the other has captured, and how much purchasing strength he has left. Play therefore consists in deciding how much you want the next diamond and how much you are prepared to pay for it, while at the same time estimating how much your opponent is prepared to bid. It is this question of estimating your opponent's strategy, and preventing him from divining your own, that makes Gops a game of players rather than a game of cards – in other words, a game of bluff.

As such, it admits of few guidelines to good play. The essence of most bluffing games is to avoid following the same strategy from game to game, for as soon as you become predictable, you will start being predicted, and to be predicted is to be pre-empted.

Suppose you start by deciding that you will pay for any card you want an amount equivalent to its value – an Ace for an Ace, Two for a Two, and so on. The first diamond turned is a Seven. As soon as your opponent has discovered your strategy, he will automatically play an Eight, thus winning a card of average value for a purchasing difference of one unit. To counter this, you might on the next identical occasion play a Nine, in the hope of overcoming his Eight by one unit and so getting a bargain buy. This time, however, he has predicted you – not by playing a Ten, and winning a Seven for a purchasing difference of one, but by playing his Ace, and making you win the Seven for a purchasing difference of eight – which is not what you had in mind at all!

At all times throughout the play you must bear in mind the relative number of diamond points captured by each of you to date, plus the relative purchasing power still available to each, and particularly the highest purchasing card left. Usually it is the player who is trailing who sets the pace. The one who has paid the greater price but at the same time bought an inferior aggregate cannot afford to waste his good cards on little diamonds. In this position he can only afford to concentrate on relative values, whereas the leading player has no money problems and can therefore direct the whole of his attention to divining his opponent's safest moves, and circumventing them.

Some of the thoughts that might occupy two players' attentions during the course of a deal could be illustrated from the following sample game.

1. *Seven of diamonds.* The card of exactly average value. Each player knows that to bid seven would be a waste, whether overtaken by the other's Eight or undercut by his Ace. Correctly foreseeing that Baker will play his Two for the best result against either manoeuvre, Abel wins it with his Three.

2. *Two.* Abel has more diamonds but Baker has marginally more cash. Neither is prepared to pay much for the Deuce, which in fact Abel wins by four to one. Now Abel is nine up, but has paid four more for that position.

3. *Four.* Baker cannot afford to let Abel win on lots of small diamonds, and ought to think about reducing the difference. To keep an edge on the resources, he can afford to pay perhaps three more than his estimate of what Abel is likely to offer for the Four. He therefore bids six, and very happily overcomes Abel's unexpected five. Now Abel is only five up in diamonds, and Baker three up in cash.

4. *Eight.* If Baker could win this, he would have 12 diamonds to Abel's nine. At this point he decides to have a flutter, playing the unexpectedly high Jack (worth 11, representing the value of the diamond under offer plus the amount of his cash surplus). But Abel anticipates such a move, and plays his Ace. Baker wins expensively, having now bought 12 for 20 as against Abel's nine for 10.

5. *Jack.* Now this is worth having – but how much is each prepared to pay for it? Abel must consider whether Baker will (a) try for it with his King or Queen, or (b) try to force Abel into an expensive win by undercutting with a low bid. Baker is unlikely to waste a card of middling value, which will probably be expensive whether a winner or a loser. He decides to let it go, playing his Two and leaving his hand with nothing lower than Six. Baker, foreseeing Abel's line of reasoning, in fact decided to play a middling card, the Seven, expecting Abel to have bid his Six. He therefore wins the Jack at a cost of five, and the situation now is: Abel 9 diamonds for 15, Baker 23 for 27, giving Baker the edge.

6. *Queen.* Abel, with more cash in hand, offers his Queen, feeling that Baker might play his King. As it happens, Baker followed the same line of thought and also played his Queen. Neither takes the diamond.

7. *King.* Now some hands are being forced: the winner of these two cards will net 25, and if it is Baker, he will have 48 and the game. Abel has no choice but to play his King, for if

this, too, is equalled, he can assuredly win the next turn with his Jack. Naturally, Baker plays his lowest card, the Three, leaving Abel with the 25 in diamonds at a difference in cost of 10 units. Situation so far: Abel has 34 for 38, Baker 23 for 42. A reversal of fortune: Abel is now much better off.

8. *Six.* There are 34 points-worth of diamonds left in play; here are six of them. Can Baker afford to make an expensive bid for this? Can he afford not to, as Abel will then be within six points of a win, and there are still the Nine and Ten to come with a Jack in Abel's hand? Again, Abel has no card lower than Six, but Baker has Four and Five to dispose of. There are several worse diamonds to throw them on, particularly the Ace and Three, which have yet to appear. Baker eventually bids with his Nine, and is gratified to beat Abel's Eight, after which the position is: Abel 34 for 46, Baker 29 for 51. Baker still trailing in both respects.

9. *Ten.* If Abel wins this, any succeeding diamond other than the Ace will give him the game. It is the highest of the diamonds left, and therefore justifies Baker's spending of his King on it. This being so, Abel can be expected to play a low card. In which case, Baker might risk playing his Ten. The danger is that Abel might overtake with the Jack. (A tie would be advantageous to Baker, who could then certainly win more on the next turn.) Baker decides to take that chance, and plays his Ten, Abel coming up with the Six. So far: Abel 34 for 52, with 7, 9, T, J in hand; Baker 39 for 61, with 4, 5, 8, K. This leaves A, 3, 5, 9 in the diamond stockpile. As the Nine will give him game, and Baker holds the highest card in play, he is bound to win.

10. *Five.* As this is the second best diamond left, Abel can afford to play his top card, the Jack. Nevertheless, he plays the Seven, trying to pull a fast one. If Baker anticipates the Jack by throwing his Four, Abel will win nine of the outstanding eighteen diamonds. Baker, however, foresees this manoeuvre, and plays his Eight.

11. *Ace.* Abel takes it. His cards are all as good as one another.

12. *Three.* Abel takes it.

13. *Nine*. Baker, having saved his King, takes the Nine. Result: Abel 38 diamonds, Baker 53 diamonds. That's eight points over the odds, which, by my scoring system, gives Baker 36 towards game. Had Abel's attempt to capture the Five cheaply succeeded, the game would have been 48 to 42, giving Baker only three over the odds for a game score of six.

Bluffing consists in doing the unexpected. This does not mean just doing the unusual or the speculative, because there are occasions on which such moves are expected, and therefore cannot amount to bluff. At move 9, above, Baker made a successful bluff by playing a middling card when common sense would have dictated the play of a high one. The bluff came off, and put him in a winning position. At move 10, Abel sought to reduce the score against him by playing lower than would appear sensible. But the bluff failed to work, because Baker expected it. And the reason why he expected it had nothing to do with mathematics or analysis or common sense. It was entirely due to the fact that Baker had played Abel before, and knew that he could nearly always be relied upon to play recklessly when his game was lost for certain.

MATE

This game was invented by a German, G. Capellen, and first published in 1915. It was rescued from oblivion by the American game-researcher Sid Sackson in his book *A Gamut of Games*, of which the British edition first appeared in 1974. Mate, as Sackson observes, is 'a game that, through unfortunate circumstances, was doomed to an untimely death, but one that eminently deserves to be revived. It is played with only twenty cards. Yet with this limited material an amazing diversity of playing situations develop. And it is, almost unique among card games, completely a game of skill'.

The game

Cards. Twenty, consisting of the Ace, Ten, King, Queen and Seven of each suit. (This constitutes the single Mate pack. A double Mate pack for advanced players is described at the end of this chapter, along with several variations in play.)

Deal. Shuffle the cards thoroughly and deal ten to each player in two batches of five.

Object. To be the last to play a card. Each in turn plays a card to the table in accordance with rules of sequence described below. As soon as one player cannot legally follow the previous card he is 'mated'. His opponent then gets a score based on the value of the card with which he delivered mate, and the number of cards already played.

Rank and value of cards. Within each suit, cards rank from high to low A T K Q 7, and bear point-values which are respectively 11, 10, 4, 3 and 7. As between suits, clubs are highest, followed by spades, hearts, and finally diamonds. In a sense, then, ♣A is the highest card in the pack and ◇7 the lowest. A diagram may clarify this schedule:

♣	A T K Q 7
♠	A T K Q 7
♡	A T K Q 7
◇	A T K Q 7

value: 11 10 4 3 7

Play. Non-dealer leads by playing any card face up to the table before him. Dealer responds by playing any card of the same suit on the table before him, keeping it separate from his opponent's. Whoever plays the higher ranking card leads to the second turn, and so on. If at any turn the second player has no card of the suit led, he must instead play a card of the same rank. In this event the player of the higher suit leads to the next turn. If the second player cannot match the lead by suit or by rank, he is mated and the deal ends. Do not yet mix all the cards up.

Score. The player of the last card now records a score consisting of (a) the value of the last card he played, *multiplied by* (b) the number of the turn on which he delivered mate. Thus if non-dealer led ♠Q and dealer had no Queen or spade with which to follow, the leader would score 3×1 (Queen $\times$ first turn) $= 3$, the lowest possible. At the other extreme, a player delivering mate with an Ace on the tenth and last turn would score $11 \times 10 = 110$.

Game. When the first deal has been played and scored, each player picks up the cards he has played, adds them to those remaining in his hand, and exchanges them for those of his opponent. Now a second round is played and scored, exactly as before except with the hands reversed so that neither player has had the advantage of better cards – or rather, both have had the same advantage. The first lead is made from the same hand as before, but of course by the player who originally dealt. After this round has been played, the cards are gathered up, shuffled, and redealt by the other player. Two more rounds are played in the same way, with hands swapped over as before, and scores are added to determine the final result.

Notes on play

The purpose of swapping hands is to ensure that both players will have made use of the same resources, so that whoever plays better scores more. At least, that's the theory, though it might be held that the second player of the leading hand is in a position to observe the outcome of his opponent's play and either avoid what proved to be weak lines or make improvements to good ones. The playing of a second deal (two more rounds) redresses the balance.

The game as described above is not complete, and an extension of the rules is given at the end of this section. Even so, it is enough to be starting with. At beginners' Stage I it will be sufficient to concentrate on playing the last card. At Stage II you will seek to play in such a way as to make the highest score. The extension referred to later may be regarded as Stage III.

Here are one or two observations that may be made about the different stages.

STAGE ONE: If the cards are fairly evenly divided, with both players holding at least one of each rank and two of each suit, be prepared for a fairly long and intricate game. If, however, there is a marked imbalance, the chances are that the leading hand has a calculable win, and if the first leader muffs it, his opponent may profit from the mistake by avoiding it.

Try to visualise the way in which both hands interlock, perhaps in some such way as illustrated in Figure 6. The process of play may then, if it helps, be translated into terms of a board game.

It is nearly always advantageous to lead to a turn, as you then choose the next point of attack. It is therefore desirable to play the better card at each turn, if this can be done without spoiling the hand.

Try to keep back at least one card of each suit and one of each rank, as you cannot be mated so long as you succeed in doing this. Conversely, concentrate on ridding your opponent of his shortest suit as soon as possible, and play from three of a kind (*ie* three Aces or whatever) when you can.

STAGE TWO: At Stage II, which may be subtitled 'Playing to the Score', get rid of your Kings and Queens first if you are confident of winning, whether because of the cards you hold or because you consider yourself the better player. You can then expect to win with a card of high value for a high-scoring game. Your score will also be higher if you can keep the game open as long as possible, so that more turns will have been played. Conversely, if you have little expectation of winning, try to force an early end to the play. In this event it does not matter what value of cards you hold or play, as they will not affect your opponent's score.

Before describing extensions of the game, I must mention in passing that anyone who knows Germany's national card game, Skat, will recognise some of its influences on the structure of the game. For instance, the order of suits from clubs high to diamonds low comes from Skat, as do the relative ranking of the cards within in each suit and the point-values 11, 10, 4 and 3 for Ace, Ten, King and Queen. (In counting 7 for the Seven, notice how Capellen has picked on a value exactly mid-way between the Ace-Ten and King-Queen averages.) Also characteristic of Skat is the practice of dealing ten cards each in two batches of five – once widely followed though not now officially approved – and even the device of multiplying values to determine a final score. It is fascinating to speculate on how the game would have emerged had the same idea been worked up by an English player of Crib, an American of Poker, or a French of Belote!

Variants

Foreplacing and overmate. When you have played the basic form of the game as described above, you will be ready for the additional feature of 'foreplacing', as follows.

After the deal or exchange, but before the first lead, either or both players may select one card from their hand and put it face down to one side, where it remains out of play for the whole round. The effect of doing so is to increase the winner's score by adding one multiplier to the number of turns, so that, for example, a win on the seventh move multiplies by eight instead of seven. It is clear that you will foreplace if you are confident of winning, so as to boost your own score.

It may be necessary to add that the 'turn factor' is increased by one only, whether one or both players foreplace. But an interesting situation arises if only one player foreplaces, so that he is playing with only nine cards as against his opponent's ten. In this event, the player with only nine cards will, if he gets as far as the tenth move, pick up the card he played on his ninth turn and use it again as his tenth – if, of course, it will follow. If now either player wins on the tenth move, he has given 'over-mate' and scores double. For example, if overmate is given with an Ace on the tenth move, it scores $11 \times 11 \times 2 = 242$, which is the highest possible in the game.

Several other rule variants exist which might be adopted by agreement, being offered for what is described as 'a change of pace'. In my view they do not add much to a game that is already full of riches in its most basic form.

Free move. At any point during the course of play, either player (but only one, and whichever of them happens to use it first) may refrain from following suit even though able, and instead play a card of the same rank.

King's privilege. By this rule, the lead of a King must be followed by another King if possible; if not, suit is followed instead.

Court privilege. Same as King's privilege, but applying to Queens as well. Either version may, by agreement, be combined with the free move rule described above.

Double Mate. This version is played without any Queens, but with the addition of certain doubled cards as follows: $\diamond$A, $\heartsuit$T, $\spadesuit$K, $\clubsuit$7, restoring the pack to twenty. It introduces considerable subtlety to the game, unlike the cheap frills described above.

Self-mate. In this version, proposed by the present author, the first multiplier is the value of the mating card (as before) but the second, instead of being the turn number, is the value of the last card played by the loser. The lowest winning score is therefore $3 \times 3 = 9$ and the highest $11 \times 11 = 121$. If one foreplaces, the winner's score is doubled (maximum 242); if both foreplace, it is trebled (363); and a win by overmate is quadrupled (484).

Illustrative deal

The cards are dealt as follows:

Dr Jekyll ♣...Q7 ♠....7 ♡.TK.. ◇ATKQ7
Mr Hyde ♣ATK.. ♠ATKQ. ♡A..Q7 ◇.....

Mr Hyde can see an easy way to win, taking advantage of Jekyll's weakness in spades and Aces by voiding him of both and then leading ♠A. He does this by leading ♠Q to draw the Seven, then ♣A to draw the ◇A, then ♠A to leave his opponent no saving move. He scores 33, winning with an Ace (11) on the third move.

Now hands are exchanged and Dr Jekyll shows how to make proper use of the hand. He starts by foreplacing ♠K, and the game proceeds thus:

Turn no.	1	2	3	4	5	6	7	8	9	10
Jekyll	♣K	♣A	♣T	♠Q	♠T	♡A	♡Q	♡7	♠A	♠A
Hyde	♣Q	♣7	◇T	♠7	♡T	♡K	◇Q	◇7	◇A	?

Having foreplaced, Jekyll uses his ninth card as his tenth, leaving Hyde unable to play his ◇K, and wins by overmate. His score is 11 for the Ace, times 11 for winning on the tenth move in a foreplaced game, times 2 for overmate, total 242.

FIGURE 6

It may help to visualise one's hand of cards in a pattern of this
sort, bearing in mind that the blanks represent cards held by
one's opponent. The lowest cards are at the bottom and on the
right, the highest at the top and on the left. Tricks may be
thought of as moves on a game-board looking like this. The
hand shown here is one of those used in the illustrative deal.

This game, one of my own invention, is an adaptation for playing cards of a well-known family of games called Nim. In particular, it is most like the Matchsticks Game in which thirteen matches are laid in a row, each player in turn taking one, two or three matches away, and the one who captures the last match is the winner (or the loser, depending on which has been agreed). Like Noughts and Crosses, the Matchsticks Game has an easily discoverable 'best' way of playing, and the game loses its interest once you have discovered it. In Abstrac, however, there is considerably more variety . . . as you will see.

The game

Cards. Twenty four, using only the A K Q J T and 9 of each suit.

Deal. Shuffle thoroughly and then lay the cards face up in a row on the table between the two players. Cards may overlap to save space, but all must be identifiable from their edges.

Object. The object is twofold: (a) to capture sets of three or four cards of the same rank, and sequences of three or more cards in the same suit; but at the same time (b) to avoid capturing any cards you do not need for such combinations, as there is a penalty for taking more than 12 of the 24 cards. Excess cards are safe if they form combinations, but costly if they are unrelated.

Play. Each player in turn takes one, two or three consecutive cards from the top end of the layout and places them face up on the table before him. (The top end is the one with the uncovered card – see diagram.) It is for non-dealer to make the first capture, but he may pass the lead to his opponent if he thinks it advantageous to do so. Thereafter each plays in turn and neither may pass. Captured cards must remain open on the table, and should be arranged by rank and suit so that at any given point each player can see exactly how his opponent is faring. Play continues until all cards have been captured.

Score. There are two parts to the scoring, in accordance with the twofold object of the game. The first is for combinations and the second is for cards.

(*a*) *Combinations* A set is three or four cards of the same rank, a sequence three or more cards of the same suit running in the following order: A K Q J T 9. Any card may be counted as both part of a sequence and part of a set. The scores are:

Set of three	2
Set of four	8
Sequence of three	3
Sequence of four	4
Sequence of five	6
Sequence of six	12

(*b*) *Cards* Each player now takes his total score for combinations and multiplies this by the number of cards captured by his opponent. Thus if both players take twelve each, the multipliers will be the same and the game will be decided, in effect, on combinations alone. If, however, both have scored the same for combinations but have taken different numbers of cards, then the player who took the fewer cards will win.

Game. A game should consist of several deals, each dealing alternately, and the winner is the player first to reach a previously agreed target – say 300 for a short game.

Suggestions for play

If your opponent dealt, make the first move if you can see good purpose in doing so, but pass it if not, so that dealer will have problems to sort out for himself. What constitutes good purpose in doing so is not easy to explain, because it really depends on how far ahead you can calculate. In theory, any given order of cards must permit of a forced win for either the player who moves first or the one who moves second, assuming that both play 'perfectly'.

As non-dealer has the choice of moving first or second, he always has a theoretical forced win (or, at worst, a draw). Therefore, in principle, the decision whether to play first or pass the lead is one on which success or failure depends absolutely. But all this is highly theoretical, as hardly any player in real life can be expected to have the powers of analysis sufficiently well developed to play perfectly. The further ahead you can see, the more you will win. If you can see nothing to be gained by starting, pass the lead.

As a matter of general strategy, you will naturally try to make sets of four and sequences of six (*ie*, entire suits), though you will rarely succeed because your opponent need take only a few specific cards to render that objective unattainable. The defensive side of this coin is to ensure that you do not allow him any quartet or sequence of six; you prevent these by endeavouring to capture at least one card of each rank and one card of each suit. Any card of one rank will do to stop the quartet, but the ideal cards to take in prevention of long sequences are Jacks and Queens, as they restrict runs to only three, namely A–K–Q if the Jack is taken, or J–T–9 if the Queen. At each turn, therefore, always stop to consider which cards you still lack to prevent your opponent from making high-scoring combinations, and play in such a way as to capture them either now or later.

If at any point in the game you are in doubt as to how many cards to take, take only one. If you cannot win on combinations, you may win on cards by taking fewer of them.

Now we come to the fundamental tactic of the game, which you would soon discover for yourself even if it were not drawn to your attention. When it is your turn to play, you can always play in such a way as to capture any one of three desired cards on your *following* turn – or, what comes to the same thing, to prevent your opponent from taking any one of them on his own immediate turn.

Consider the layout illustrated. If the leader takes only one card, the ♢T, then he can also take the fourth card along from it, the ♡K, no matter whether his opponent takes one, two or three cards. If he takes the first two, he also forces the fourth along from ♡T, namely ◇K; similarly, by taking the first three, he secures access to ◇J. Whether he will take one, two or three may therefore depend on which (if any) of the cards ◇A, ♡K, ◇K he may want in addition – or may wish to deny his opponent.

The same principle can be taken even further, for as many steps as you wish. By removing just the first card in this layout (◇T), the leader could also, if they were of use to him, take not only the fourth away (♡K) but also the eighth (♣9), twelfth (◇Q), sixteenth (♠K) and twentieth (♡9). If those particular cards happened to be all of a suit, this is the strategy he would adopt. (To combat this, his opponent would take only one card at each turn, finishing up with a multiplier of 17 as against leader's 7.)

Illustrative deal

Let's look at the illustrated diagram, and see how the game might proceed. Our players are Alpha and Beta.

First, Alpha must decide whether to play or pass. A good move might be to take the first three, winning a pair of Tens and securing, by the rule of four, the ◇J to go with the ◇T and ♠J. If Beta then took the pair of Kings, he (Alpha) would gain a third Jack to boot. But Beta might instead follow the strategy of taking only one card at a time, which would give Alpha too many. He contents himself with taking the pair of Tens only, denying Beta the pair of Kings.

Beta takes just the ♠J, allowing Alpha another pair (in itself useless) but denying him the useful ◇J, and giving himself the advantage of fewer cards.

Alpha next takes three, including the pair of Kings, on the principle that if he is going to take more cards he may as well make as many combinations as possible.

Beta then takes the pair of Jacks, giving himself a highly economical three-card hand worth two points already, and, as they are all Jacks, preventing Alpha from making long runs in three suits. By the rule of four, he can also force the other Jack, increasing his score by 8 points.

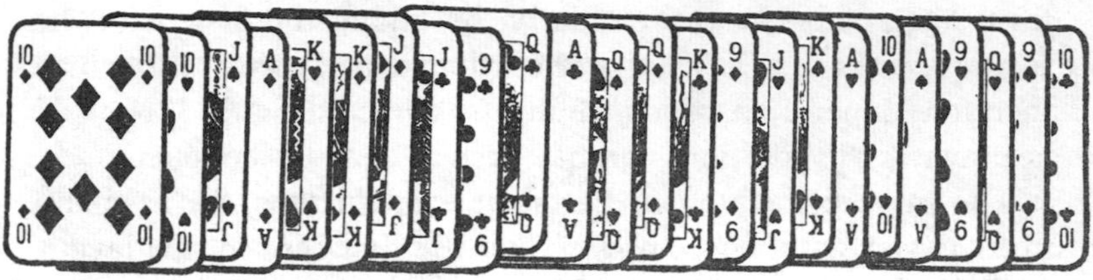

FIGURE 7

The layout of cards at the start of the game discussed in the text. There are over one and a quarter million different ways in which the game might proceed, and millions more different ways in which the cards may be arranged in the first place.

Next available to Alpha are three unconnected clubs, which are useless to himself and not much better for Beta. He takes just ♣9.

To force the ♡J, Beta should now take ♣Q, ♣A and ♠Q. But for better or for worse – and you can work out which for yourself – he prefers not to take so many useless cards and contents himself with ♣Q alone.

Alpha cannot now take ◇Q to add to his King and Ace, otherwise he gives Beta the fourth Jack. He therefore takes two, giving himself ♠Q to guard against Queens and spades in the other hand, and reserving ♡J to himself.

Beta takes ♣K to go with his Ace, Queen and Jack, along with ◇Q. He leaves ◇9, as it is of no real use to either player, and in any case to deny Alpha the ♡A.

Alpha must take ◇9 and the Jack wanted by his opponent, but has no use for ♠K.

Beta takes the next three cards and Alpha the three after that, both for reasons that will be obvious if you are following it through, and Beta has the last two, giving him a total of 11 cards against Alpha's 13.

For combinations, Alpha has a sequence of five hearts to the King, worth 6, plus 2 each for the trio of Aces and Nines, 10 in all. Multiplying by the number of cards taken by his opponent, he finishes with a score of 110.

Beta has sequences of three spades and four clubs for 7, plus 2 for his Jacks, making 9. Multiplying by Alpha's cards, he finishes with a score of 117. The results are about average, though unusually close.

To show that such results are not a foregone conclusion, it will be interesting to see what would have happened had the same layout of cards been played in another way.

If both players had automatically taken three cards at each turn, the leader would have scored 120 and so would dealer – a tie. If they had each taken two per turn, leader would have finished with 144 to 84 – a difference of 60. If they had taken one each alternately, leader would have scored 204 to 120 – a difference of 64. In trying other possible ways of playing the same cards, you may like to note in passing that there are over $1\frac{1}{4}$ *million* different ways in which any single arrangement of cards could be played, while the number of significantly different ways in which the cards can be arranged to start with amounts to 34×10^{27} (that is, 34 followed by 27 noughts).

Variants

There are several interesting ways in which the basic rules can be varied. If you play with a 36-card pack, adding the Eights, Sevens and Sixes, the scores are as follows:

Set of three	3
Set of four	12
Sequence of three	3
Sequence of four	4
Sequence of five	5
Sequence of six	6
Sequence of seven	10
Sequence of eight	15
Sequence of nine	25

Instead of using the combinations described in the basic game, you may prefer to score for making Poker hands, or melds from other favourite games such as Pinochle, Bézique, Cribbage or Cassino.

4. CARD GAMES FOR THREE

Some of the world's best card games are for three players, yet few of them are known in Britain. This may be because British card-play is so dominated by the home-grown games of Cribbage for two and Whist (latterly Bridge) for four that when three get together their natural inclination is to play a three-hand variant of one or the other. Since games designed for specific numbers are put out of balance by such adaptations, the results are unsatisfactory and the players are left thinking that three is an inherently awkward number for any sort of card game. It has even been put to me that there is no real call for three-player games because 'people just don't go around in threes'. This, of course, is a short-sighted view, completely ignoring such famous trios as the Three Graces, the Three Musketeers, Three Men in a Boat, Three Three the Rivals, and Wilson Keppel and Betty, to name but a few.

The following pages present games which are by nature designed for three players – or which at least, though playable by any number, are generally agreed to work best for three. You may be surprised to discover how many there are, for even this collection is not exhaustive. Some are easy and some are hard, but the hard ones are well worth the effort – Skat, for instance, which is Germany's national card game, in the opinion of many experts rivals Bridge in depth, variety and excitement.

What they all convincingly show, I hope, is that three is far from being the awkward number it is usually made out to be. On the contrary, in my own view it is the *ideal* number for a card game, for the following reason. In a two-player game each plays for himself, while most four-player games are a contest between two partnerships. In a typical three-hand game, however, the basic format is that one player, the one with the strongest hand of cards, issues a challenge to the other two, and undertakes to win more tricks or points than the other two combined. It seems to me that this permanent conflict between solo and partnership play gives three-hand games the best of both worlds.

BLACK MARIA

Writers on card games who divide their compendia into sections devoted to different numbers of players – games for two, games for four etc. – usually find themselves short of material when they come to the bit about games for three. But the one candidate they all include with unbridled enthusiasm is Black Maria, under one or another of its many names of varying degrees of propriety. Although it is nominally playable by any number, most agree that it works best for three.

Black Maria is a good family card game, being of simple mechanics and easy to explain. Each plays for himself; no bidding is required (which will please some people) and there are no temporary partnerships – except perhaps when two players individually start getting spiteful towards the third if he is way ahead in the game. Yet for all its surface simplicity, Black Maria both demands and repays close attention, careful play, and that indefinable commodity 'card sense', of which winning is the most prominent symptom. Even such Bridge players as deign to recognise the existence of other games have been known to approve of it. What less can one ask?

The idea of Black Maria is that you play not to win tricks but to lose them – or, to be more precise, to avoid taking tricks that contain certain predetermined penalty cards. Penalty cards score against the players who capture them in tricks, so that the winner at the end of the game is the one who finishes up with the lowest, not the highest, score.

The version described here represents a 'standard' game most favoured by English commentators, in which the penalty cards are all the Hearts and the three highest Spades, Queen of Spades herself being the eponymous lady. American players tend not to penalise ♠A and ♠K, but this makes for an unbalanced score.

Black Maria derives, by the introduction of ♠Q, from an earlier game called Hearts, from which numerous other variations have also been derived. This whole family of trick-taking games has a good pedigree. It is mentioned by Rabelais in the early sixteenth century under the name Coquimbert and was subsequently known to English writers as Losing Lodam, or just Lodam. And for two hundred years the game of Reversis – so called because its object of avoiding tricks is the reverse of that in most games – proved one of the most popular ways of losing money amongst the nobility and gentry for whom an empty purse was a continual feast.

Preliminaries

Cards. Fifty-one – a standard pack from which ♣2 has been removed. Cards rank normally for trick-taking purposes, Ace high, Two low.

Order. Establish first dealer by any agreed means. The turn to deal, the deal and all play proceed clockwise around the table.

Game. For convenience, game may be set at 100 points – it finishes when one player reaches or exceeds that total, bearing in mind that the player with the highest score is the loser.

Deal. Seventeen cards to each player, dealt singly and face down.

Object. After an exchange of three cards, as described below, seventeen tricks are played out at no trump. The object is to avoid taking in penalty cards, which score against players capturing them as follows:

Each Heart	1
♠A	7
♠K	10
♠Q (Black Maria)	13

Play

The exchange. Each player selects from his hand three cards which he does not want and passes them face down to the player on his *right* (anti-clockwise). Having passed them on he takes up into hand the three cards similarly passed to him from the player on his left. The tricks are then played out.

Tricks. The player left of dealer leads any card to the first trick. Usual rules of trick-taking apply. You must follow suit to the card led if possible; if not possible you may discard from any suit. There are no trumps, and the trick is taken by the player of the highest card of the suit led. The winner of a trick leads to the next.

Score. Each player totals the values of all penalty cards he took in tricks and this number is entered against him on the score sheet. The three figures in each round should total 43. Scores are kept cumulatively.

Hints on play

The ideal hand. The exchanging of cards gives players opportunity for the exercise of skill in shaping the final hands from which they play. The judgement called for in determining which cards to oust is compounded by the need to have regard to the cards one is likely to receive from the left. For example, rejecting three Hearts is disastrous if three higher Hearts are received subsequently. Thus, in deciding which cards to pass on it is desirable to have some idea of what constitutes strength and weakness in the final playing hand.

In Hearts, the ideal holding is a number of low cards including Two or Three, and Four or Five as well. Low cards are 'guards' on higher ones: they ensure that if that suit is led you will be able to duck out of taking the trick. If you are safe in this respect it doesn't really matter if you have a long Heart holding and/or a number of high cards, even including the Ace, since you can expect to lose these on tricks led in other suits when you have established voids in the hand. A bad Heart holding is four or more with nothing lower than Five.

Spades lower than Queen are a good suit to hold, in moderation, and must be kept rather than thrown. Penalty Spades (A, K, Q) are bad only if you have no low cards with which to avoid winning tricks with them when that suit is led. Counting as guards anything lower than Queen, you typically need three guards if you hold one or more penalty Spades, four if the holding is Ace only or Ace and King.

In side suits – Clubs and Diamonds – the ideal is high winners and low losers. High winners you lead early in the game, when won tricks are unlikely to contain penalties; low losers you need for safely escaping from the lead when you have taken your fair share of inevitable (clean) tricks. If you have only middling cards the suit is probably safe if you hold four or fewer. A very long side suit can be dangerous if it does not make an early appearance, as you may be left later in the game with the lead of a suit in which the others are now void, but if it contains a safe loser, i.e. Two or Three (but remember Three is lowest in Clubs), then it is probably safer than not.

A void (no cards of a suit) is good defensively, in that it enables you to drop your clangers when led; but if you have too many high cards in other suits and are in danger of too frequently taking the lead then the void becomes a liability. (How often have I wished it physically possible to lead from a void suit!)

Passing on. Having a clear idea of the general framework of a good hand makes it that much easier to select your rejects. Look first at Spades, since that suit accounts for 30 of the 43 penalty points. If you hold one or more penalty Spades, make sure you have enough guards to keep them safe. If so, keep the penalties, as you will be well placed to control their destination; if not, pass on high Spades from Ace downwards. Black Maria herself, if adequately guarded, is always better in the hand than out.

Hearts next, though here there is not so much you can do. There is no need to pass on high Hearts if you are safe in low, or to create a void except as a luxury (and irritant to your victim) if you are safe in other suits.

As to side suits, we have seen that the ideal is voids or long suits containing adequate low cards. A suit with three or fewer may as well be voided, though if it contains losing leaders (Two, Three) it may be more profitable to keep them yourself than donate them to an adversary. If you have a long suit with no low cards get rid of as many of the highest as possible.

The passing on of cards gives their recipient some inkling of the nature of his left-hand opponent's cards, assuming that all tend to discard with the same principles in mind as outlined above. For example, if your neighbour gives you three of a suit including a low one, you can be fairly sure that he has created a void (though it might, of course, be nullified by the other player through discarding from the same suit).

The play. Side suits are usually led first. Theoretically it is safe to lead high cards from side suits in order to take probably inevitable tricks while they are still 'clean'. In practice the procedure comes unstuck as soon as it leads into someone else's void. Since a player can only have voided if he held three or fewer, chances are that the lead of a high card from your side suit will be safe if the suit is short, risky if you have too many.

When following suit and losing the trick it is natural to play the highest card beneath the highest one already showing. Thus if you lead ◇J and the next plays ◇7 you might reasonably assume that he has something lower, making it safe for you to lead Diamonds again. But if third then plays ◇3 or thereabouts, you must be prepared to find him void next time that suit comes round. Drawing such inferences from the appearance of particular cards at particular times is an essential ingredient in the skill of the game.

If you are safe in Spades, and especially lack the penalties in it, they often make a splendid lead. Ideally, play the Jack. If someone else takes the trick it can only be with a penalty, which achieves your object. If not, and the worst you can do is pick up a single Heart, you have the lead and can do the same again – this time with the Ten, if possible.

Heart leads (low, of course, by preference) are not worth making unless you have no other way of losing the lead, and premature Heart leads are the sign of the beginner at the game. But if you have a longish run of Hearts and seem destined to take a trick or two, it is best to do so early and get them over with. If left too late, you may find another player void and pick up a nasty Spade, or you may be left with a lead you cannot escape from. Often, you will lead a dubious Heart (say the Ten from a holding of T 6 4 2) and find it overtaken twice because the others are following the same principle of taking necessary evils early on.

By and large, you should make the tricks you have to make early on, then bow out and stay out for the rest of the round. About the worst thing that can happen to you is to be dealt four or five safe cards in a suit, which you retain, then find your holding increased by the pass-on from your left-hand neighbour, and eventually take the lead at trick ten, with all seven of a suit in which the others are both void.

Sample game

First deal. Charlie deals; the cards fall as follows:

```
Abel     ♠4 2  ♡Q T 8 4 2  ♣Q 6  ◇A K Q T 7 5 4 2
Baker    ♠K Q 7 5 3  ♡9 6 5 3  ♣A K 9 8 5 3  ◇6 3
Charlie  ♠A J T 9 8 6  ♡A K J 7  ♣J T 7 4  ◇J 9 8
```

Abel's hand looks not too bad: he is good in Spades and has

his high Hearts not unreasonably guarded. Going for a void, he ousts ♡Q ♣Q, 6. But what he gets from Baker ruins his Spade holding.

Baker has safe Hearts and good all-round low cards everywhere. He decides to void his Diamonds and pass on ♠K (much to Abel's chagrin), in the hope of losing his Black Maria to the latter. This device is counterbalanced by the cards he now picks up, though the high Hearts need not worry him as he has them well guarded in the original deal.

Charlie has cause for complaint, having a general shortage of cards with which to lose the lead and a particularly bad Hearts holding. He rejects ♠A ♡A, K. The ♡Q picked up from Abel is a nail in the coffin, though the two Clubs are nothing to argue about.

After the exchange, the playing hands are:

Abel 　　♠K42 ♡T842 ♣— ◇AKQT765432
Baker 　　♠AQ753 ♡AK9653 ♣AK9853 ◇—
Charlie 　♠JT986 ♡QJ7 ♣QJT764 ◇J98

Abel can guess that Baker is void in Diamonds, Charlie that Abel is void in Clubs. Abel leads. Winning cards are in **bold** type:

A	B	C	
◇ 7	♠ A	◇ J	Baker could equally well have thrown ♡A. Bad start for Charlie.
♠ 4	♠ 7	♠ J	Charlie hesitated between ♠J and ♣Q lead; decides to throw cat among the pigeons.
♠ 2	♠ 5	♠ T	Looks like the last of Abel's low Spades ...
♠ K	♠ Q	♠ 9	And so it proves. Now Abel forces Charlie to take a penalty ...
◇ 6	♡ A	◇ 8	
♡ T	♣ 9	♣ Q	Not such a lucky lead. Charlie thinks he can escape through Clubs, but it would be as well to void Diamonds first in the hope that Abel will later have to lead them.
◇ 5	♡ K	◇ 9	
♡ 8	♣ 5	♣ 7	Baker is undertaking battle with Charlie in Clubs.
♡ 4	♣ A	♣ 6	
♡ 2	♠ 3	♠ 8	
◇ A	♣ K	♣ J	A clean trick!
◇ K	♣ 8	♣ 4	
		♣ 3	... and Charlie takes the remaining tricks.
23	1	19	Score (against) at end of first round

Second deal. Abel deals as follows:

    Abel   ♠A975 ♡AKJ862 ♣KJ986 ◇Q2
    Baker   ♠KJT63 ♡75 ♣AQ743 ◇AT986
    Charlie ♠Q842 ♡QT943 ♣T5 ◇KJ7543

Abel passes on ♠A, ♡A, ◇Q, preferring to keep ◇2 as an escape card rather than create a void, as he has only one other losing leader (♡2).

Baker may have to take unwanted Diamonds – he discards ◇T 9, 8 (an odd array).

Charlie is better off in low cards than last time. His Black Maria is just about adequately guarded – he will hang on to her, so that if passed a higher Spade he won't run the risk of taking both together. He discards ♡Q, ♣T5.

The revised hands, therefore, are:

Abel   ♠975 ♡KJ862 ♣KJ986 ◇T982
Baker   ♠KJT63 ♡Q75 ♣AQT7543 ◇A6
Charlie ♠AQ842 ♡AT943 ♣— ◇KQJ7543

Baker leads:

A	B	C	
◇T	◇**A**	◇K	So far, so good.
◇9	◇6	◇Q	
◇8	♠K	◇7	Abel expected Baker to have another Diamond.
◇2	♡Q	◇J	
♠9	♠J	♠8	Charlie now feels safe in other suits.
♡K	♡7	♡**A**	Baker leads to get his probable Heart trick over with; the others play with similar aims.
♡J	♡5	♡4	
♠7	♠**T**	♠4	
♣5	♠6	♠**A**	Charlie takes with the lesser of two evils.
♡8	♠**3**	♠2	Tough on Baker!
♣**K**	♣5	♠**Q**	In view of the score to date, Charlie would rather drop Black Maria in one of Baker's tricks; but if he doesn't play her here he might be stuck with leading her later.
♡**6**	♣**A**	♡3	
♡2	♣**Q**	♡**T**	. . . and Charlie takes the rest.
28	1	14	Score
23	1	19	Previous total
51	2	33	Current total

Third deal. Baker deals as follows:

Abel   ♠JT54 ♡AQJ53 ♣875 ♢KJ854
Baker   ♠Q83 ♡KT84 ♣AQJ963 ♢QT63
Charlie   ♠AK9762 ♡9762 ♣KT4 ♢A972

Abel's problem is too many high Hearts, and he debates whether to throw some out or void Clubs in the hope of escaping through that loophole. He decides to void Clubs.

Baker has no safe suit. After some debate he throws out his highest Hearts. He ought to have thrown out ♠Q, as she is inadequately guarded. This mistake will cost him dear.

Charlie, faced with a similar situation to that of Abel, passes ♡976.

The playing hands are therefore:

Abel   ♠JT54 ♡AKQJT853 ♣— ♢KJ854
Baker   ♠Q83 ♡9764 ♣AQJ963 ♢QT63
Charlie   ♠AK9762 ♡2 ♣KT8754 ♢A972

A good result for Charlie, bad for Abel in Hearts; it's a good thing he went for a void, as he may be able to lose Hearts this way. Charlie leads.

A	B	C	
♡ T	♣ Q	♣ K	Charlie decides to work on his worst suit.
♠ J	♠ 8	♠ 9	
♠ T	♠ 3	♠ 7	The usual Spade gambit ...
♠ 5	♠ Q	♠ 6	... which Baker cannot afford to play.
♡ A	♡ 7	♡ 2	
♠ 4	♡ 9	♠ 2	
◇ K	◇ Q	◇ A	
◇ J	◇ T	◇ 9	
◇ 8	◇ 6	◇ 7	As Diamonds seem well distributed, Abel deems it safe to pursue this line ...
◇ 5	◇ 3	◇ 2	... which now clearly peters out.
♡ 5	♡ 4	♠ A	Favouritism: Charlie is hoping to offload ♠Q on Baker.
♡ 3	♡ 6	♠ Q	It works.
♡ K	♣ 3	♣ T	
♡ Q	♣ A	♣ 5	... and Baker takes the rest.
13	28	2	Score
51	2	33	Previous total
64	30	35	Current total

Baker has lost ground, largely through a bad pass-on in the last deal.

Variations

As might be expected with a game popular in many places for a long time there exist numerous variations in the basic format of the play. For example:

Queen only. The game is frequently played without counting ♠A and ♠K as penalties, so that only Hearts and Black Maria count against (for a total of 26). I don't think this is any better or worse than the system described above. (To be honest, I have never been happy with the balance of scores in either of the 'standard' versions. The game of Hearts, in which *only* the Hearts count against, is more balanced in this respect, but somewhat duller on the whole.)

Pass to the left. Some say that cards should be passed to the left, not to the right for the exchange. A moment's thought will show that there is a distinct difference between the two as far as the effect on play is concerned. Passing to the right, as described above, increases the skill factor and should be regarded as standard.

Restriction on the play of ♠Q. Some make it illegal to pass on ♠Q at the exchange, or either of the other Spade penalties if they are counted. Since the decision whether or not to pass her on often calls for niceties of judgment, it seems a pity to thus restrict the skill – and fun – of the game.

Some also state that the player holding ♠Q must play her at the earliest legally available opportunity. Apparently the argument is that it prevents unfairness or 'ganging up' in choosing the player on whom to offload Black Maria. The result is equal unfairness on the player who was dealt her. This rule (invented by a blackmail victim?) is best ignored, as is that which prohibits the lead of a Heart before the third trick.

Hitting the moon. A player who takes all the Hearts scores plus thirteen instead of minus (applies to the game of Hearts, or to Black Maria without ♠A, K penalties). There is something to be said for this variation, which increases opportunities for the player dealt a particularly bad hand, without necessarily making it any easier for him to succeed.

KNAVES

Knaves is not a variation of Black Maria, but another good three-hand game belonging to the same family. It may have been invented by Hubert Phillips (which would be a guarantee of quality).

Cards. Fifty-two.

Deal. Seventeen each; turn up the 52nd card to establish a trump suit.

Object. To take tricks as far as possible, but to avoid capturing any of the Jacks therein.

Play. The turn-up remains out of play. Usual rules of trick-taking apply: follow suit if possible; if not, trump or discard ad lib. Highest card of suit led wins, or highest trump if any are played. Winner leads to the next.

Score. For each trick taken score 1 pt. Each Jack taken counts against, as follows:

$$♡J - 4$$
$$♢J - 3$$
$$♣J - 2$$
$$♠J - 1$$

Thus in each round seven points in all are made (17 for tricks, less 10 for Jacks). Game is 21 up.

FIVE HUNDRED

Five Hundred is the game that three players traditionally turn to if they like Bridge or Whist but find none of the three-hand adaptations satisfying.

Invented about the turn of the century and first copyrighted by the American Playing Card Company in 1904, the purpose of Five Hundred was not primarily to present a good three-hander but rather to provide a game 'intermediate in difficulty between Euchre and Whist'.* Whist at this period had reached its pinnacle of social accomplishment and scientific analysis (as the Victorians liked to call it), and had not yet been usurped by Bridge. Euchre, a derivative of Ecarté said to have originated amongst the Dutch of Pennsylvania, was – and still is – a very popular game of North America, including Canada, and also, for reasons which I cannot trace, is much played in the West country in the UK. It uses the thirty-two card pack, not all of which are dealt out, a point that tends to over-play the element of luck over skill.

Five Hundred has the objectives and bidding of Whist, but uses the whole of the Euchre pack in order to lessen the effects of chance. And because ten is a convenient and natural number of cards to hold, three turns out to be the natural number of players. Adaptations for other numbers followed as a matter of form. Not only does it work best for three, however, but also it is widely regarded by card-players as the best alternative to numerous artificial adaptations of Whist and Bridge for three.

That Five Hundred filled a need and filled it well is indicated by the instant popularity it acquired, a rare thing for an invented card game. For over a decade it remained the leading social card game until supplanted by Auction Bridge;

* Culbertson's Card Games Complete

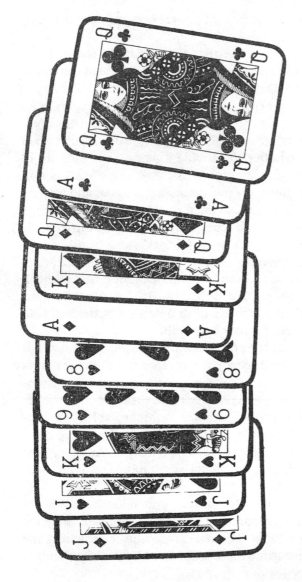

FIGURE 8

With two suits of equal length it is better to nominate the weaker as trump if possible. Here Diamonds and Hearts are of equal length and you hold both Jack bowers. If the stronger suit, Diamonds, were trumps, the side-suit of Hearts would hardly justify a bid of six. But with Hearts trumps you have Diamonds as a strong side-suit and can safely bid up to seven.

even now it is far from dead, and recent correspondence in *Games & Puzzles* reveals that it retains considerable popularity in Australia today.

The term *bower* (rhymes with *flower*) comes from German *Bauer*, which means *farmer* (cf. Dutch *boer*) and is one of several German words for the Jack. Having Right and Left Bowers as highest trumps is a feature of Euchre and clearly Germanic-inspired – compare the use of Jacks in the game of Skat.

Preliminaries

Cards. Thirty-three, consisting of A K Q J T 9 8 7 for four suits, plus one Joker.

Game. Scores are made at the end of each round and game is 500 up. This *can* be achieved in one round, but, more usually, reckon on three to six rounds of play taking about ten minutes each. Scores are best kept on paper divided into three columns.

Order. Choose first dealer by any agreed means; all play and the right to deal passes clockwise around the table.

Deal. A batch of three cards face down to each player, then three face down to the middle of the table to form a 'widow', then a batch of four each and finally a batch of three. Each player receives ten cards in all.

Rank of cards. In games where there is a trump suit, the cards rank as follows (from high to low):

> Joker
> Right Bower (Jack of trumps)
> Left Bower (other Jack of same colour)
> A K Q (J) T 9 8 7 in each suit (except where Jack promoted)

It should be noted that the Left Bower belongs to the trump suit, not to the one marked on it, and is the third highest.

In a no-trump game, the Jacks revert to their normal position between Ten and Queen, and the Joker is the only trump.

Object. Players bid for the right to become Declarer in a contract to take six or more of the ten tricks in whatever suit he specifies as trumps. Declarer has an opportunity to improve his hand by exchanging with the widow. Declarer's opponents play cooperatively to beat that contract, but themselves score for tricks they take individually.

Play

Bidding. Starting with player left of dealer, each in turn must either pass or bid. A player who has passed may not re-enter the bidding; when two have passed the third becomes Declarer and must play the contract he bid; if all three pass the round is abandoned and the turn to deal passes to the left (but see *Variations*).

The lowest possible bid is Six Spades, which is a contract to take at least six tricks with Spades as trumps; the highest is Ten No Trump. Each bid must be higher than the preceding bid. A bid is higher if it is to take a greater number of tricks than the previous bid, or if it is to take the same number of tricks in a higher-scoring suit. For this purpose the lowest suit is Spades, followed by Clubs, Diamonds, Hearts and No Trump. (Thus Six Spades is overcalled by Six anything else, and Six No Trump can only be overcalled by a higher number of tricks.)

The highest bidder becomes Declarer for that round. His contract is the bid he last made; he may not increase it for a higher score.

The exchange and lead. Declarer takes the widow into his hand (without revealing it), then discards any three cards face down, then leads any card to the first trick. The three discards play no further part in the game.

Tricks. The usual rules of trick-taking apply. Follow suit if possible; if not, play a trump or discard ad lib. The trick is won by the highest card of the suit led, or by the highest trump if any are played. The Joker and both Bowers are part of the trump suit if there is one. The winner of a trick leads to the next.

The Joker at No Trump. When there is no trump suit the Joker still counts as the highest (only) trump. If led, its player must specify which suit it calls for; it counts as the highest card of that suit and accordingly wins the trick. He may not, however, ascribe it to a suit which he has already renounced – that is, failed to follow through being void in it. A player holding the Joker must follow suit to other leads if possible, and may only trump with the Joker if unable to follow.

Scoring. The round ends when all ten tricks have been taken. The point value of the various contracts is as follows:

No. of tricks:	6	7	8	9	10
♠ Spades	40	140	240	340	440
♣ Clubs	60	160	260	360	460
◇ Diamonds	80	180	280	380	480
♡ Hearts	100	200	300	400	500
No trumps	120	220	320	420	520

Declarer wins if he takes at least the number of tricks he bid, and scores the value of his contract in accordance with the above table. He gets no credit for taking more than he bid: but if he takes all ten tricks in a contract worth less than 250 then he scores exactly 250 for it, regardless of the nominal contract value.

If Declarer fails to take the number of tricks he bid, the value of his contract is deducted from his score.

Each opponent, whether Declarer succeeds or not, scores ten per trick taken by himself.

FIGURE 9

A certain bid of nine in Clubs for 360, holding the top six trumps. Opponents cannot be expected to take more than a Diamond with the Ace.

Game. The winner is the first player to reach or exceed 500 pts. If two make it on the same deal and one of them is Declarer, Declarer wins regardless of the actual score; if both are opponents, the one who reaches the target first is the winner (and the rest of the hand is not played out, unless there is a possibility that Declarer might also reach 500 on it.)

Hints on play

General. The first thing to be aware of in Five Hundred, if you are already used to other trick-taking games with bidding, is that out of the thirty cards in play no fewer than ten are trumps – that is, one-third of the pack as opposed to only one-quarter in other games. Usually, five or six of the ten tricks are won by a trump (whether to a trump or a plain suit lead).

Assessing the hand. We may first dismiss No Trump hands as somewhat exceptional. A solidly reliable no trumper does not often appear, and can hardly be missed when it does. Certainly you should not attempt it without the Joker, as that is the one and only way of getting back into a suit in which you have a high gap. You will need strength in all four suits besides, since once you allow someone else to establish their suit your good cards will simply be whisked out of your hand before you get back in.

There being ten trumps and only two 'sides' to the game – you versus them – it follows that your minimum requirement is five trumps, together with strength in at least one other suit, in order to establish your 'book' of five tricks (i.e. the basis on which your actual bid must be built). A bid may be considered if you have only four trumps, provided that at least two are in the top three. And don't forget that the top three are the Joker and the bowers: Ace of trumps is only the third highest card.

Strength in side suits means at least an Ace or a high-guarded King. The high guard (Queen, or either Jack or Ten depending on the bower situation) is necessary for you to be able to make the King by leading from below and forcing out the Ace. A side suit headed by a guarded Queen is almost certain not to make a trick; in any case, the three cards involved in a guarded Queen are more strongly employed by being discarded to form a void. Which brings us to the second indicator of strength in a side suit, namely, a void or the possibility of creating one by means of the discard. Finally, a long side suit, one with four or more cards, is a particularly desirable feature.

The widow's worth. The primary purpose of exchanging through the widow is to improve the balance (or imbalance) of your suits by creating a void and/or a long suit – it is not, as the beginner might assume, to furnish the Declarer with one or more winning cards. This is not to say that it will contribute nothing useful to the hand – you can often rely upon it to produce an extra trick if you are already sure of seven, and perhaps two if you are sure of six. But the important thing is not to rely on it to provide a single specific card (such as the Joker) without which a risky bid may be lost as a foregone conclusion. Holding four of a suit, the chances of finding a fifth in the widow are 5 to 3 in favour; holding five, the chances of finding a sixth drop to 5 to 4.

Bidding. The bidding procedure of Five Hundred allows no room for manoeuvre. With most hands you will have only one potential trump suit; only occasionally will you have the luxury of switching to another suit in order to overcall on the same number of tricks. Furthermore, once you have made your bid you must lie on it – you can't increase it for a higher score. If, therefore, you have a probable eight Hearts don't bother to sneak up on it by starting at six. That being the highest suit, neither of the others may wish to raise you to seven, in which event they will pass and leave you to make a certain 100 instead of a probable 300. You must start by bidding the highest you dare, and know in advance whether or not you will allow yourself to be forced up.

Note carefully what the others bid, as this can give you a good idea not only of their strong suits but also of the distribution of the Joker and Bowers.

Discarding rarely presents problems. Retain all trumps, consecutive top cards, and a suit of four or more – in that order. Create a void if possible. (Don't let your discard physically get in the way of your won tricks – beginners have been known to miscount it as a trick and then fall short in the final reckoning! To be on the safe side, spread the discards to form a small fan, and put it out of reach.)

The play. The usual pattern is that Declarer leads into trumps in order to draw his opponents' teeth so that he can later succeed in establishing a long suit of four or more. If you have no long suit, you will gain greater control over potential trick-winners in other suits by letting the player on your left gain the lead rather than his partner. In other words, if not leading, your best position is playing third to a trick. At No Trump, lead from your longest rather than your strongest suit, and return to it whenever possible.

As an opponent of the Declarer, your primary objective is normally to defeat his contract rather than make tricks of your own. (Unusually, you might find yourself playing to the score. Thus, if Declarer is unable to make game – i.e. reach 500 pts. – on succeeding at his contract, but your temporary partner is not only well ahead of you but also only ten or twenty points off target, you will obviously prefer to prevent your partner from taking tricks wherever possible.)

When Declarer leads trumps, prefer to play low if your partner will win the trick, since Declarer's chief preoccupation is to leave himself with all the highest trumps in play. Indeed, you can nearly always afford to undercut his lead as second player if it is obvious that Declarer is trying to force out a higher trump which, since it isn't in your own hand, must be in your partner's. For example, suppose your partner made a bid in Spades before Declarer established his contract of (say)

seven Clubs. Declarer leads ♠K and you have ♠A but nothing higher. You might now, as second player, drop your
next to useless ♠7 and leave the trick to be taken by your
partner. The fact that Declarer led a middling trump means he
is trying to force out something higher; the fact that your
partner bid Spades implies that he must have at least one
Joker and two black Bowers. And the fact that you let your
partner have it means that Declarer will be playing second to
the next trick and you third. All of which is very good – for
the partners.

When leading, generally try to avoid opening up new suits,
and stick by preference to your own longest or strongest.
Once Declarer has shown a void, however, the partners
should lead into it as hard as possible in order to force him to
waste trumps.

A sample game

First deal

> Abel   ♠7 ♡A T 7 ♣K T 8 7 ◇J T
> Baker   ♠K J 9 8 ♡K 9 ♣J 9 ◇9 7
> Charlie Jo ♠Q T ♡J 8 ♣A Q 7 ◇A K 8

Abel's Clubs are long but hopeless – lacking Joker and
either black Bower he has no bid here. Neither do his ♡A
and potential Left Bower (◇J) justify the bid of Hearts he
actually is foolhardy enough to make.

Baker is strong in Spades, with both Bowers, but has weak
supporting cards in side suits. A niggardly widow would ruin
his game.

Charlie's good Diamond suit (counting the Left Bower,
♡J) is better supported on the side by his Clubs.

The bidding goes: Abel 6 ♡ (bluffing!), Baker 7 ♠, Charlie
7 ◇. Abel and Baker pass. Charlie draws from the widow
◇Q, ♡Q, ♠A – a good draw, increasing his trumps and

adding a side-suit Ace. He discards ♡Q, ♡8, ♠T to create a void suit. His hand is good, and probably worth eight tricks, instead of the seven he bid, should the four other trumps lie evenly. Charlie, as Declarer, leads.

A	B	C	
◇ T	◇ 7	**Jo**	
◇ J	◇ 9	♡ J	... They did lie evenly, and the game is assured.
♠ 7	♠ 8	♠ A	
♣ 7	♣ K	♠ Q	
♡ 7	♡ K	◇ 8	
♣ 8	♣ 9	♣ A	
♡ A	♡ 9	◇ A	
♡ T	♠ 9	◇ K	
♣ T	♣ J	◇ Q	
♣ K	♠ J	♣ Q	
1	1	8	Tricks
10	10	180	Score (contract only seven)

Having assured himself of success at trick two, Charlie continued somewhat deviously, perhaps amusing himself by trying to make nine tricks. Such showing off can sometimes have disastrous consequences.

Second deal

  Abel Jo ♠A7 ♡T ♣A97 ◇KQJ
  Baker ♠KQ8 ♡KQJ98 ♣K8 ◇—
  Charlie ♠J9 ♡A7 ♣QT ◇T987

Abel has only four of his best trumps (in Diamonds), but as two of these are of the top three (Joker and Right Bower) he is safe in making a bid, especially as he also has a couple of supporting Aces and a potential void in the fourth suit.

Baker has a nice line in Hearts and a ready-made void, but look again: the other suits stand on nothing stronger than guarded Kings, and even in prospective trumps he lacks the first, third and fourth highest. Odd-numbered gaps like this are weak in any game of trick-taking. A good widow, of course, would be a godsend.

Charlie's hand is unbiddable.

The bidding goes: Baker 6♡, Charlie passes, Abel 7◇, followed by two passes. Abel's widow brings in a lucky Ace, or so it seems: ◇A, ♠T, ♣J. The rest of the draw is highly miscellaneous, and Abel discards, before leading, ♡T, ♠T, ♣7 to give a void in Hearts.

A	B	C
◇ Q	♡ J	◇ 7

The first trick worries Abel. Since he holds Joker and one red Bower, and since Baker bid Hearts, the latter presumably holds the other red Jack. But why drop it so soon, unless it's the only trump he has? If Charlie has the other four Diamonds, things will go ill for Declarer.

A	B	C
◇ K	♡ 9	♡ A
♣ J	♣ K	♣ T
♣ 7	♡ K	♡ 7

Abel puts off parting with a trump as long as he dares, but now he needs the rest of the tricks. If Baker would only lead his Club, Abel would succeed – but Baker knows the value of leading into Abel's void.

A	B	C
◇ A	♡ Q	♣ Q
♠ A	♠ 8	♠ 9
◇ J	♡ 8	◇ 8
Jo	♣ 8	◇ 9
♣ A	♠ Q	◇ T
♣ 7	♠ K	♠ J

5	3	2	Tricks
−180	30	20	Score
−140	40	200	Running total after two rounds

An unfortunate occurrence for Abel, whose bid was perfectly good. It was beaten only by the freak distribution of the remaining trumps (Diamonds) 4–1 in favour of Charlie.

Third deal

Abel	♠8 ♡A K ♣A J T 7 ◇Q J 7
Baker Jo	♠K J T 7 ♡J ♣9 8 ◇A K
Charlie	♠A Q ♡Q T 8 ♣K Q ◇T 9 8

To cut a short story even shorter, Charlie and Abel both passed without hesitation, leaving Baker to wonder where the other Jack was. Seeing three certain losers in his own hand, he reckons the widow will give him an eighth trick and accordingly bids 8♠. Sure enough, widow provides another trump, but nothing else: ♠9, ♡9, ♡7. Baker discards all his Hearts. With two losers now (the Clubs), Baker decides that this best course is to assume a 2–2 distribution of the remaining trumps. Indeed, he has no alternative but to plunge right in:

A	B	C	
♠8	**Jo**	♠Q	So far, so good.
♣J	♠J	♠A	The trumps lay even, and the game now plays itself.
♣7	♠K	◇8	
♣T	♠T	◇9	
◇7	♠9	◇T	
◇J	♠7	♡8	
◇Q	◇A	♡T	
♡K	◇K	♡Q	
♣A	♣9	♣Q	
♡A	♣8	♣K	
2	8	0	Tricks
20	240	0	Score
−150	280	200	Running total after three rounds

Fourth deal

Abel Jo ♠K J T 9 ♡7 ♣— ◇A K 8 7
Baker   ♠8 7 ♡A J ♣A K J 7 ◇J
Charlie   ♠A Q ♡K 9 8 ♣T 9 8 ◇Q 9

Abel has five Spade trumps, including two of the top three, and a promising side suit in Diamonds. He need not hesitate to start at seven. Baker's Clubs are not strong and he ought not to bid at all; Charlie recognises a bad hand when he sees one. Thus: Abel 7♠, Baker 7♣ (sheer bravado), Charlie passes; Abel 8♠.

The widow furnishes ◇T, ♡Q, ♡T (none of which would have been of the slightest assistance to Baker had he been left holding the baby), and Abel throws out the three Hearts to leave himself with a strong two-suit hand. Since it can only be beaten by an unfavourable 4–1 (or 5–0) distribution of trumps in the other hands, he deems it unnecessary to play clever and leads orthodoxly into trumps:

A	B	C	
♠K	♣J	♠Q	Forcing out one of the upper trumps.
♠9	♡A	♡9	Back into trumps via the void Hearts.
Jo	♠8	♠A	That's the Ace gone; now Abel leads his Right Bower and takes the remaining tricks.

9	1	0	Tricks
240	10	0	Score
90	290	200	Running total after four rounds

Fifth deal

Abel   ♠K J 9 8 ♡7 ♣J 7 ◇T 9 7
Baker   ♠7 ♡A 8 ♣Q T 8 ◇A K Q J
Charlie Jo ♠A Q T ♡K Q J 9 ♣A ◇8

Abel holds both Bowers for a Spade bid, but with a non-supporting cast in all three side suits he will do wisely to hold his peace. Baker has a nice-looking Diamond suit and a side Ace to boot. The draw of another Diamond and/or a high Club would make it a biddable hand – the trouble is, it has to be bid before the draw. Charlie's hand has the immediate appearance of a No Trump bid – but again, only *after* a favourable draw. Otherwise, Hearts look promising.

The bidding: Baker 6 ♢, Charlie 6NT, Abel passes, Baker 7 ♢ (pushing it), Charlie 8 ♡, Baker passes. Charlie's bid could have been a mistake for 7 ♡, forgetting that Hearts overbids Diamonds at the same level. Fortunately, he turns up trump in the widow: ♡T, ♣K, ♣9. Discarding ♢8, ♠Q, ♠T, he has now a strong trump suit, a void in Diamonds, singleton Ace in Spades, and ♣A K 9 which could well be worth three tricks should the remaining trumps be badly distributed. Charlie now leads to his contract of eight Hearts.

A	B	C	
♡ 7	♡ A	♡ 9	One tooth drawn, unless you count the Seven, in which case two.
♠ 8	♠ 7	♠ A	Baker could be certain that Charlie's void is Diamonds, and thus creates a void of his own in the hope that C is looking for a couple of Spade tricks.
♢ 7	♡ 8	Jo	Another painless extraction.
♢ 9	♢ J	♡ J	And the last, assuring Charlie of his eight tricks.
♢ T	♢ Q	♡ K	
♣ 7	♢ K	♡ Q	
♣ J	♣ 8	♡ T	
♠ 9	♣ T	♣ A	
♠ J	♣ Q	♣ K	
♠ K	♢ A	♣ 9	And the ninth with the Nine of Clubs, giving Charlie game.
0	1	9	Tricks
0	10	320	Score (for a bid of eight, not nine)
90	300	520	

Footnote to the game: nobody undertook a No Trump contract, though one was mooted; this is quite usual. Nor did any player make all ten tricks; but don't forget that the win of ten tricks scores a minimum of 250, even if the nominal contract is less.

Variations. More in the nature of additions than variations, the first gives an alternative to redealing in the unlikely event of all players passing (few distributions of cards can be entirely unbiddable, in my view), the second is the inevitable introduction of a misère bid. Both variations are widely practised.

All pass. If all players pass, the ten tricks are played out at No Trump, each playing for himself. There is no contract, and the widow is left out of play and unseen. Each player scores ten for every trick he takes.

Nullo. Nullo (misère) is a bid to take no tricks, playing at No Trump. It is a contract worth 250, and therefore ranks in the bidding between eight Spades (which is overcalls) and eight Clubs (which, at 260, is higher). If successful, Declarer scores the 250 and each opponent ten per trick as usual; if not, Declarer is set back 250 and each opponent scores ten for every trick taken by Declarer instead of by himself.

NINETY NINE

Ninety Nine is a three-hand game of my own invention. It was first published in *Games & Puzzles* (Jan 1974), evidently with some success as it continues to attract fan mail from new players. It has since been republished in several languages, the latest to reach me being Japanese!

Ninety Nine, so called because that's the highest score you can make on one hand, follows purely traditional mechanics of trick-play and is therefore easy to learn, even for absolute beginners. But it is skill-demanding and difficult to play well – for reasons that will become apparent as soon as you pick up your cards and find out what the object is.

A feature that most distinguishes it from traditional one-against-two bidding games is that in each round *every* player makes a bid and establishes a contract. You don't have to hang about waiting for a 'good hand' before you can become 'highest bidder' and challenge the others. Every hand is biddable, and it is even possible for all three to succeed in their bids. But only just.

Preliminaries

Cards. Thirty-six plus Joker, ranking normally, i.e. from high to low: A K Q J T 9 8 7 6.

Order. Determine seats and right of first deal by any agreed means. All play is clockwise.

Scoring. Scores are noted at the end of each round. (A typical score sheet is illustrated.)

Game. A game consists of nine rounds and lasts about 45 minutes. Deal passes regularly to the left so that each player deals three times in each game.

Deal. Light shuffling is sufficient. Deal twelve each, one at a time, face down.

Trump. Deal the last (37th) card face up to one side of the table. The suit of the turn-up establishes trumps for that deal. If the turn-up is the Joker or a Nine, the round is played at no trump. Dealer should clearly announce the trump situation.

Joker. The Joker has no independent status, but for the purposes of all play assumes the identity and powers of the turned up card. (Example: if the turn-up is ♣9 then whoever holds the Joker in that round treats it exactly as if it were the ♣9, both for bidding and for playing purposes. He may even, if he wishes, exchange it for the turn-up, though this is disadvantageous as it gives information about one of his cards.)

Object. Each player discards three cards face down and plays out the other nine to tricks. His three discards are called 'bid-cards', and by means of a code explained below they are selected to represent any number from nought to nine. This number constitutes his bid. Each player's object is to take *exactly* the number of tricks he has represented by his bid-cards – no more, no less.

Play

Bidding. This is the strategic crux of the game. A player can bid anything from nought to nine tricks by discarding three bid cards in accordance with the following code:

> Any ♣ discarded means 3 tricks
> Any ♡ discarded means 2 tricks
> Any ♠ discarded means 1 trick
> Any ◇ discarded means 0 tricks

Thus, for example, a player proposing to win three tricks could throw out ♠ ♠ ♠ (1+1+1), or ♡ ♠ ◇ (2+1+0), or ♣ ◇ ◇ (3+0+0). There are three different ways of bidding

3, 4, 5, 6 or 7 tricks, two ways of bidding 2 or 8, and only one of bidding 0 ($\diamondsuit$ $\diamondsuit$ $\diamondsuit$) or 9 ($\clubsuit$ $\clubsuit$ $\clubsuit$).

The ranks of the bid-cards have no bearing at all on the meaning of the bid; it is only the suit that counts. The Joker, of course, counts as the suit of the turn-up.

Each player, then, selects three bid-cards and places them face down on the table before him. They should be spread slightly to avoid being confused with tricks won during the game. Normally, bids remain secret and are not revealed until the end of the game. But each player has the option of making a premium bid for a higher score, which involves giving certain information about his cards, as follows.

Premium bids. There are two premium bids: a declaration and a revelation.

Declaration. When a player declares, he turns his bid cards face up before play so that the others know how many tricks he is proposing to win. It will then be more profitable to them to beat him than to succeed in their own bids.

Revelation. In a revelation, the bidder not only reveals his bid but also plays with his hand of cards face open on the table.

Each of these bids carries a bonus, which goes to the bidder if he succeeds or to each opponent if he fails.

Only one player may make a premium bid in any round, and priority for doing so starts with the player on dealer's left.

After the bid cards have been laid aside, but before any card is led, each in turn, starting at dealer's left, announces whether or not he will declare or reveal. The first to offer to declare is 'on' but he may be overcalled by a subsequent player offering to play open (revealed). In this case the earlier player had one opportunity to raise his declaration to a revelation and so claim priority.

When a declaration is established, declarer immediately

turns his bid-cards face up on the table and leaves them in view throughout the play.

When a revelation is established, revealer immediately turns his bid-cards face up on the table as for a declaration. He then nominates any player to lead (regardless of who dealt) and, after the first card has been led to a trick but before the second is played, lays his hand of cards face up on the table so that all are visible throughout play.

Tricks. Except in a revealed game, the first lead is always made by the player left of dealer. Normal rules of trick-taking apply. Follow suit to the card led if possible; if not possible, either trump or discard from side suit. The trick is won by the highest card of the suit led or by the highest trump if any are played. The winner of a trick leads to the next.

Claims. When the last trick has gone, any player who has succeeded in his bid must turn his bid-cards face up to prove his entitlement to the full score. Any player who has failed is not obliged to reveal his bid (in fact, it is bad policy to do so).

7.4.77				Game 3
Trump	A	B	C	Notes
1 ◇	8	21	50	D+
2 N	3	24	22	
3 ♣	2	35	2	
4 ♣	24	4	21	
5 ◇	14	43	12	D+
6 ♡	5	32	2	
7 ◇	34	1	4	
8 ♠	91	7	1	R+
9 ♡	25	22	2	
Total	206	189	116	

Scoresheet for a game of Ninety Nine (the same grid is also used for recording the results of the nine games of a match, normally producing a grand total of somewhere between 1000 and 2000 per player). In the leftmost column, N denotes No Trump; at far right, D denotes 'declared game' and R 'revealed game', followed by + or — to denote success or failure. As an aid to checking, note that at each round the three figures in the 'units' column of the scores should total nine, and the three 'unit' figures of the final scores should total a number ending in '1'.

FIGURE 10

How Ninety Nine looks in play. Hearts are trumps by virtue of the run-up, whose identity ($\heartsuit$Q) is assumed by the Joker. Note how Abel and Baker have arranged their bid-cards to avoid confusion with tricks won later. Charlie has declared a bid of six ($\spadesuit + \heartsuit + \diamondsuit + \clubsuit = 1 + 2 + 3 = 6$) and accordingly turned his bid-cards face up. Also shown is the hand from which he made the declared bid. For the result, see sample game, round 2.

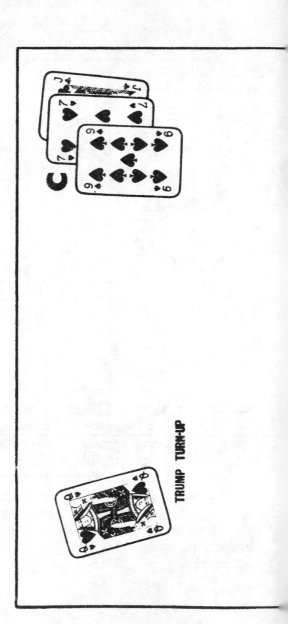

TRUMP TURN-UP

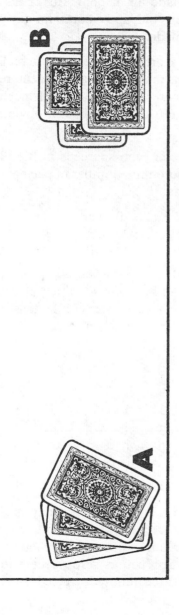

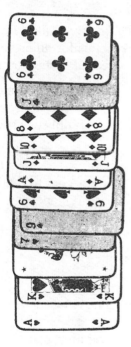

Scoring

Each player's score is made up of points for tricks taken, a bonus for succeeding in his bid, and a bonus for any premium bid that may have been made.

For tricks. Each player scores 1 pt. per trick actually taken, regardless of his bid. This may immediately be entered on the sheet, as bonuses are scored in tens and will not affect it. Trick points between the three players will obviously total nine.

For succeeding. Each player who succeeds in his bid gets a bonus for doing so, based on the number of players who succeeded in that round. Thus:

> If all three succeed ...... 10 each
> If only two succeed ...... 20 each
> If only one succeeds...... 30

For premium bids. In addition to the success bonus, there is a bonus of 30 for a declared bid or 60 for a revealed bid. This bonus goes to the bidder if he succeeds; if he fails, it goes to each opponent, whether or not they also succeeded in their individual bids.

Examples

	A	B	C		A	B	C	
Tricks bid:	4	3	1 dec.		4	3	2 dec.
Tricks taken:	5	3	1		5	3	1
Success bonus:	—	20	20		—	30	—
Premium bonus:	—	—	30		30	30	—
Total score:	5	23	51		35	61	1

*Settlement. If the game is played for money, each pays to any with a higher score than himself an amount proportional to the difference. But scores are adjusted beforehand as follows: anyone failing to make 100 counts zero; a score in the two hundreds is doubled, in three hundreds trebled, and so on.

Hints on play

Approaching the bid. The whole point of the game is that the cards you use to bid with, when removed, alter the hand you are left to play with. This makes for scope and variety. Almost any hand of cards at Ninety Nine is biddable, since there are ten different numbers of tricks to bid and no fewer than 220 different ways of discarding three cards from twelve. Not all the possibilities make sensible bids, of course, but more often than not you will find yourself confronted with a choice of two or three different bids to make and two or three different ways of expressing each bid. Deciding between them is where the basic strategy of the game comes in. You must be guided by various considerations, such as who has the lead, what suit is trumps (a factor which is more significant to the play of Ninety Nine than of any other card game, and to which we must return), what the other players are likely to bid (observing which cards are lacking from your hand helps here), and, above all, which of your cards are to be regarded as trick winners and which as trick losers.

This is the point at which you must begin to assess the hand. In Ninety Nine, you are required to win an exact number of tricks. This means that you are also required to lose a corresponding number of tricks. Thus a bid to win three tricks is the same as a bid to lose six. It follows that your first task is to classify your cards as probable winners (certain Aces, Kings and trumps), probable losers (Sixes and Sevens), and 'incalculables' – those of middle ranks, and especially Jack, Ten, Nine, any one of which is likely to win a trick when you want it to lose, or lose when you want it to win.

What you must aim to do, therefore, is as far as possible to retain extreme cards (winners and losers) and get rid of incalculables by using them to represent the bid. Choosing between several likely bids will often be controlled by the suits – that is, the bid values – of the cards you can most do without. You must enter the play with a clear idea of the intended destination of each card – which are to win tricks, which are to lose tricks, and which can be switched around from winner to loser or vice versa when something goes wrong.

Imbalance of suits. The ascription of values to suits for bidding purposes is unique to Ninety Nine, and it has a correspondingly unique effect on the relative strength in play of the four different suits. The point must be emphasised. In most card games there are a trump suit and three side suits. Apart from the fact that they have different symbols, there is no essential playing difference between one side suit and another. Similarly, one trump suit is as good as another. A game with Spades as trumps may score higher than one with Clubs (as in Bridge), but this has no effect on those suits' relative strength as trumps once the game is under way. The same does not apply in Ninety Nine. In Ninety Nine, Clubs are nearly always a strong suit, and Diamonds nearly always weak. Let us see why.

Not surprisingly, the commonest bid is that of three tricks. ('If in doubt, bid three' is a fundamental principle of Ninety Nine.) This can be represented in three different ways: ♠ ♠ ♠ or ♡ ♠ ◇ or ♣ ◇ ◇. From this bid alone it is apparent that Spades and Diamonds are *more likely* to be laid aside as bid cards than Hearts or Clubs. Studies from actual games confirm that – again, *on average* – the nine cards missing from the play of tricks comprise:

And there is a slightly greater tendency for Diamonds to be out than Spades, as zero is the second commonest bid.

It follows that, in play, Clubs and Hearts tend to be long suits (eight and seven respectively), Spades and Diamonds short (six and five). Players are more frequently void in

Diamonds than any other suit, but only rarely void in Clubs. In side suits, therefore, given a normal distribution of cards, you can usually expect ♣A ♣K to be trick winners, and probably also ♡A, but ♠A is not certain and ◇A is positively risky, standing the most chance of being trumped.

Similarly, at the opposite extreme, if you have the lead and want to lose it, ♣7 is a much safer card than ◇7 – the latter can so easily be undercut by ◇6 and followed by a discard when the third player is void.

Thus in assessing your hand you are concerned not only with the suit of cards, in deciding which to keep and which to use as bidders, but also with their ranks. The ◇T is from all points of view the likeliest candidate for discarding, as it is the most incalculable rank of the most unreliable suit.

This imbalance of suits also has its effect on trumps. Thus if Diamonds are trumps and a player is dealt ◇A K Q he will very often discard them for a certain bid of nought. In which case the player holding ◇J has the top trump and may well be forced to take an unwanted trick with it. Should he therefore count ◇J as a probable winner? Not at all – for an opponent dealt ◇A K Q might equally well keep them in hand and bid at least three.

But at the other extreme of suits, Clubs are reliable as trumps. Thus if Clubs are trumps and your highest trump is the Jack, you can be pretty certain that it's the fourth highest in play. The upper trumps are unlikely to be out in bids, because they imply bids of high numbers of tricks, for which purpose they would need to be retained!

It follows from the above that premium bids (declarations and revelations) tend to be safer in reliable suits (Clubs, Hearts) than in the others.

The Play. You will normally go into play with cards previously earmarked as winners and losers. Inevitably, you will have one or more of middle ranks or weak suits which are winners or losers – in other words, the incalculables. General procedure for all players is to get the lead as early as possible and lead out the incalculables. If they win you can work out in advance which probable winners you must now reclassify as losers. If they lose, you must perform the opposite calculation.

With incalculables out of the way, or if you have none to start with, begin by making your surest winners other than trumps and then lose the lead. Trumps normally play their role as leads at the end of the round, though of course circumstances occur in which they are better led early on.

Note carefully what cards others are playing. Frequently it is possible to work out what they have bid from what they play; even if not, a great deal of scope exists for playing thwarting tactics.

For example, if one leads ◇7 and the other follows ◇6 you can be sure that neither wants the trick. If void in Diamonds it may be better to discard from a side suit than trump, even if you want a trick, solely to discomfit the first player, who probably counted it as a sure loser. On the whole, if you are not sure whether a particular lead means a player wants the trick or not, it generally proves best to let him have it. The fact is – and I offer no explanation for it – that in Ninety Nine players tend to underbid rather than overbid, and therefore more often find themselves trying to lose unwanted strong cards than win with weak ones.

If one player has declared or revealed, it will benefit you to spoil his game (working in collaboration with the other player) rather than make your own bid. If you can do both, of course, so much the better.

Length of suit. Long suits are weak; voids are strong. If you can discard so as to void yourself in a suit you have splendid opportunities for either trumping or losing unwanted cards when that suit is led. Often the desirability of establishing a void is the chief determinant of a suitable bid.

A long suit is bad unless it contains safe low cards. Thus, suppose you hold ♣A Q 9 8 6 when some other suit is trumps.

Normally you expect to be dealt three of each suit, given an even distribution. Here you have five. Chances are that an opponent received two or one and succeeded in voiding himself of Clubs, thus bidding high and intending to trump. With this danger in mind, it is wise not to regard the Ace as a winner. A much safer procedure is to treat all five as sure *losers* and bid accordingly. This particular holding is quite safe: you can never be forced to take with a Club. The situation would be different, however, if the five you held were ♣A Q T 9 8 for now you have neither a sure winner (the Ace may be trumped) nor a sure loser. Leading the Eight would be a sure signal of your intentions, and the others would, on principle, force you to take the trick.

Premium bids. For a declared bid you should have extreme cards in at least three suits and a void if possible. Remember that your bid-cards will be revealed, and that opponents can learn something from them. For example, if you bid three with three Spades they may assume you have a void in that suit, and will probably refrain from leading it. This could be awkward if you were relying on the void as a means of making your trumps or losing some risky cards.

In order to reveal, you must be absolutely certain of the future destination of every card in your hand. Extreme cards or voids are necessary in every suit. It is usually advantageous to select your left-hand opponent to make the lead.

Unbiddable hands. Some hands look unbiddable at first sight. And they may so be, in the sense that you need the same cards for bidding as for making the tricks you bid. For example (with the trump suit quoted first):

◇A 6 ♣J T ♡K J 9 7 6 ♠Q T 7

Here the only sensible bid, of one trick, can only be made by throwing out the very card (◇A) needed to make it with. Two can be bid, by throwing two Spades and ◇6, but the chance of taking a Heart trick is slender indeed.

In this example, it is impossible to make a 'sensible' bid, i.e.

one that you can be sure of fulfilling. What you do instead is adopt the Technique of the Meaningless Bid (TOMB for short), which involves throwing out bid cards solely for the surprise value of their absence from play. In this case the throw-outs are ♢A and both Clubs. The chances of making six tricks are remote, but the likelihood of spoiling your opponent's bids is most promising. See the first player's surprise when you trump his ♣A with ♢6, and the second player's astonishment when he finds you out of trumps and is forced to take with ♢7!

Fortunately, few hands are completely unbiddable in this way, and it is better to avoid the meaningless bid. But laying aside a card for its surprise absence is always good tactics. Strong Aces and high trumps are ideal candidates for this practice.

Sample Game

First deal. Charlie deals. The turn-up is ♠8. As Charlie is dealt the Joker we simply record it as ♠8, as it has no other power.

```
Abel     ♠A J T  ♢J 9  ♣Q T 8 6  ♡K Q 7
Baker    ♠K 7 6  ♢K T 6  ♣A J 7  ♡A 9 8
Charlie  ♠Q 9 8  ♢A Q 8 7  ♣K 9  ♡J T 6
```

A fairly even distribution. Abel has no difficulty in assessing Hearts as one trick and Clubs as none. Spades is an unreliable trump suit and there is a chance that both monarchs are out in bids, leaving his ♠J T high after the Ace. He bids three, discarding ♣Q, ♢J, ♢9 and thus voiding himself in his most awkward suit.

Baker's hand is tricky. There seem to be three winners (Aces and ♠K) and four losers (Sixes and Sevens), giving a sensible bidding range of three to five tricks. One possibility is to discard ♠J, getting rid of a problematical middling card, together with the two high Diamonds for a bid of three. This leaves ♡9, ♡8 as nasty incalculables, for when the Ace is gone a low lead from another player could mean disaster. Another possibility is to discard ♡9, ♡8, ◇T for a bid of four. This relieves him of the problematical Hearts and calls for a fourth trick from either the guarded ◇K or a low trump to a Heart lead after the Ace has gone, In the event, Baker goes for a 'surprise' bid, throwing out his three Spades for a bid of three and putting his trust in his three high cards.

Charlie's hand looks most unpromising at first sight, containing middling ranks, especially in the unreliable trump suit. The only sure loser is ♡6, and the nearest approach to a winner is ♣K. His most sensible bid is two, discarding ♡J, ◇A, ◇Q and intending to win with ♣K and ♠Q.

Abel leads.

A	B	C	
♡ K	♡ A	♡ T	Abel forces out the Ace and gets rid of an unwanted high card.
♣ T	♣ A	♣ 9	
♣ 6	◇ T	◇ 8	
♣ 8	◇ 6	◇ 7	Charlie wins with an unplanned card. He must now revise his tactics and count ♣K as a loser instead of a winner.
♡ Q	♡ 9	♡ 6	Abel makes with one of his planned winners.
♡ 7	♡ 8	♣ K	Baker takes an unwanted trick, but Charlie succeeds in losing his now unwanted King.
♠ J	♣ 7	♠ 9	
♠ T	♣ J	♠ Q	
♠ A	◇ K	♠ 8	
3	4	2	Tricks
20		20	Success bonus
23	4	22	

Obviously, players will not all succeed if their bids do not total nine.

Second deal. Abel deals; Hearts are trumps.

> Abel   ♥JT9 ♠Q87 ♦Q76 ♣AQ8
> Baker   ♥86 ♠AKJT ♦K9 ♣KT97
> Charlie ♥AKQ7 ♠96 ♦AJT8 ♣J6

Abel has awkward trumps and Clubs. He would like to keep losers in weak suits, but cannot bid four. Instead, he voids Spades for a bid of three.

Baker has two long suits – a decided weakness. He discards ♥6 and voids Diamonds for a bid of two.

Charlie, however, has what appears to be an astonishingly good hand. Running down his Hearts and Diamonds will almost certainly give him eight tricks, though he can't bid it. In any case, he must retain ♣6 as a sure loser. Discarding ♥7, ♣J, ♠9 for a bid of six, Charlie declares and reveals his bid-cards. Baker leads.

A	B	C	
♥ 9	♠ K	♠ 6	Baker really wanted the trick – he only played King as a cover-up
♣ A	♣ T	♣ 6	Charlie now plans to lose the third trick and take the remainder.
♣ Q	♣ K	♦ 8	
♣ 8	♠ A	♥ Q	As Charlie planned. Now to run through his red suits.
♥ T	♥ 6	♥ A	
♥ J	♣ 7	♥ K	
♦ 7	♣ 9	♦ A	
♦ 6	♠ J	♦ J	
♦ Q!	♠ T	♦ T	Pipped at the post.
3	1	5	Tricks
30			Success bonus
30	30		Premium bonus (C declared, failed)
63	31	5	Score
23	4	22	Previous total
86	35	27	Current total

It was unfortunate for Charlie that Abel had a guarded Queen and wanted her to win. The declaration was sound in principle.

Third deal. Baker deals; Diamonds are trump.

Abel   ◇86 ♣AKQ87 ♡KQ7 ♠JT
Baker   ◇AT97 ♣JT ♡AJT9 ♠AQ
Charlie   ◇KQJ ♣97 ♡86 ♠K9876

Abel correctly counts all his Clubs as losers, but one trick must be taken as he cannot bid lower. He discards ♠J, ♠T, ◇8. The intention is to make one trick with a high Heart and the other with either the second high Heart or by trumping a Spade.

Baker can guess from his card distribution that the others will be making low bids. He must therefore bid high, though that gap in Diamonds could be awkward. He discards ♣J, ♣T, ♠Q, for a bid of seven, intending to lose two Hearts.

Charlie has an obvious bid: all Diamonds out for a bid of nought. Despite (or perhaps because of) his defeated declaration in the previous round he decides to make a premium bid of it, and has little hesitation in offering to reveal. He appoints Abel to lead.

A	B	C	
♦ 6			Abel decides that if Charlie has a weakness it might be in trumps. Did he but know it, a lead of ♣6 would beat the revelation. But, in view of his own bid and Charlie's, he would expect Baker to overtake the Club. After this lead, Charlie exposes his cards.
	♦ T	♣ 9	Charlie loses his most dangerous card.
♣ A	♦ 7	♣ 7	Baker needed a loser – but didn't get it. Charlie's game now plays itself.
♡ Q	♡ 9	♡ 8	
♣ K	♡ T	♠ K	Baker makes his second loser and must now make the rest, which, as it happens, fits in with his opponents' individual plans.
♡ 7	♡ J	♡ 6	
♡ K	♦ A	♠ 9	At this point Baker has the lead with three top cards in hand. He therefore exposes them and the others concede him the tricks.

2	7	0	Tricks
10	10	10	Success bonus
		60	Premium bonus
12	17	70	Total
86	35	72	Previous total
98	52	97	Current total

Postscript. I have come across a group of enthusiasts who play as follows. Rather than count nine deals to a game, play continues until one player reaches a score of 200 or more. He is the winner, and anyone who fails to reach 100 is penalised (by paying double).

PINOCHLE

Pinochle is almost totally unknown in Britain, but is America's fourth most popular card game.

According to the author of *Scarne on Cards*, it lay third in 1947 when a poll by the American Institute of Public Opinion showed that about 10½ out of 50½ million card players voted it their favourite game. By 1974 the figures had dropped (according to Scarne's own survey) to six million out of ninety million players, its position having been diminished by the rise in the popularity of Rummy. It is not clear whether this means a particular Rummy, such as Gin or Canasta, or Rummy games in general. If the latter, the contest is unfair. (The current running order is Poker, Rummy, Bridge, Pinochle.)

Even so, Pinochle, as much by its intrinsic merits as by its numerical popularity, ranks as one of the world's great card games, and no self-respecting card-player should fail to include it in his repertoire.

Where Pinochle originated is unclear; how it originated, less so. Two-hand Pinochle is practically identical to Bézique, which is a natural two-hander. Since the earliest references to Bézique are earlier than the earliest references to Pinochle, the former is presumably the parent. Bézique is European – according to one story, a Swedish invention – but its terms and place of expansion are wholly French. Pinochle, and especially its earlier name Penuchle, sounds particularly Germanic; yet there is no evidence of its being played in Europe before the start of its popularity in the U.S. Its germanisms, of both vocabulary and procedure, must therefore surely be ascribed to the German immigrant population of that country. For it is there, wherever the game may first have made its appearance, that Pinochle took root and flourished. To this extent, then, it is wholly an American invention in the strictest etymological sense of the word.

Although two- and four-hand versions are widely played, Pinochle is in my view three-handed by nature. Necessity being the mother of invention, I will go so far as to surmise that it came about as the result of adapting Bézique to the needs of three players, since three-hand Bézique as described in the books is a notably unsuccessful variation. In which case, who more likely to have been responsible for it than the Germans, whether American or European? Germanic card-culture is dominated by three-hand games such as Skat, its forerunner Schafkopf (Sheepshead), and Tarock; unlike France, whose aloofness from central European card tradition is emphasised by a preference for two-hand games such as Piquet, Ecarté, Belote and Bézique.

There are, at that, several different versions of three-hand Pinochle, so the question arises which of them to describe in this book. Let's put them in perspective, in order to introduce the game generally and explain the reasons for our choice.

Basics of Pinochle

The essentials of Pinochle are as follows. A double 24-card pack is used, forty-eight cards in all with nothing lower than Nine in each suit. Tricks are played and points scored according to the pip-value of cards taken in them – the scoring system being that of Skat and its relatives. But before any tricks are played, either all the players, or only the one who bid highest (according to the version followed), may declare and score for scoring combinations (melds) held in the hand. For this purpose, the combinations and scores are those of Bézique.

In some versions, the highest bidder seeks to improve his playing hand by drawing three undealt cards constituting a 'widow'; in others all the cards are dealt to start with and there is no widow. In some versions each deal is a complete game; in others, there is a target score of 1000 points.

Most players agree that the best form of the game is 'Auction Pinochle, with Widow', in which only the player who makes the biggest bid may exchange cards and score for his melds. But this is a difficult game for beginners to play with confidence, and if you are learning Pinochle for the first time – as it is the purpose of this book to assume – then you are best advised to start with the 'Home Game, 1000 up'. In this version, although there is a highest bidder who exchanges some cards, *all* players may claim for melds before the tricks begin. This has the advantage of involving everybody from the outset; the bidding starts at a sufficiently low level for every hand to be worth an opening bid; and it will give you instruction and experience in evaluating the hand as dealt and the chances of improving it.

When you have gained a grounding in the Home Game, you will be in a position to graduate to the full game of Auction Pinochle by following the 'conversion kit' instructions given at the end of the chapter.

Preliminaries

Cards. Forty-eight; two packs containing no card below Nine. It is desirable but not vital that they be of the same back design and colour.

Game. In each round scores are made immediately before and immediately after the play of tricks and are conveniently kept in writing. Game is 1000 up, which may take from three to six rounds; allow ten minutes per round.

Order. Choose first dealer by any agreed means. The deal, turn to deal and all play proceed clockwise around the table.

Deal. Face down, a batch of three cards to each player, a batch of three to the middle of the table to form a widow, then the rest around in batches of three until all cards are out and each player has fifteen.

Objectives. There is a round of bidding, the highest bidder becoming Declarer in a contract to take at least as many points as he bid. Points are scored (*a*) for holding certain 'melds' or combinations of cards as described below, and (*b*) for the pip value of all cards won in tricks. The highest bidder has a chance to improve his hand after the bidding and before the play. Each opponent must succeed in taking at least one trick in order to score for his melds at the end of the round.

Rank and value of cards in tricks. For purposes of trick-taking, the cards rank and score as follows:

Rank	A	T	K	Q	J	9
Score	11	10	4	3	2	0

It will be noted that the total value of each suit is 30 and the total number of pips in the pack 240. Ten points are scored for taking the last trick, so the maximum score possible for tricks alone is 250.

Scoring combinations (melds). There are three classes of melds, as follows:

Flushes	Sequence	(A–T–K–Q–J of trumps)	150
	Royal marriage	(K–Q of trumps)	40
	Common marriage	(K–Q in non-trump suit)	20
Quartets	Hundred Aces	(four Aces, one in each suit)	100
	Eighty Kings	(four Kings, one in each suit)	80
	Sixty Queens	(four Queens, one in each suit)	60
	Forty Jacks	(four Jacks, one in each suit)	40
Others	Pinochle	(♠Q–◇J)	40
	Dix*	(Nine of trumps)	10

No card may be used twice in combinations of the same class. (Thus, if K–Q of trumps are scored as part of a sequence they may not also be scored as a royal marriage; to score two sequences you need ten cards; to score two marriages in the

*Pronounced 'deece'.

same suit you need four monarchs not three; to score two pinochles you need both Queens and Jacks, and to score the same quartet twice you need eight cards of the same rank.)

A card may be used twice in different combinations. (For example, the same ♠Q may count towards pinochle, marriage and Sixty Queens at the same time.)

The dix is a single-card meld – if you have both Nines of trumps you score them both, for 20.

There is no such scoring combination as four Tens, though beginners often claim it!

The maximum score Declarer can meld on a single hand (eighteen cards) is 560; therefore, counting tricks, the highest possible bid is 710.

Play

Bidding. Each player in turn may pass or bid. Having passed, he may not re-enter. The lowest permissible bid is 100; each succeeding bid must be higher than the last and a multiple of ten (but bidding may proceed in irregular jumps as players wish). No bid may exceed 710. When two players have passed, the third becomes Declarer and must make at least as many points as he bid in order to score.

Melding. Declarer takes up the three cards of the widow, adds them to his hand, chooses and announces the trump suit, and declares the melds he is scoring from his hand of eighteen cards. (The cards should be seen to be believed.) He then 'buries' three cards by taking them from his hand and laying them (unseen) face down before him in the manner of a won trick. Any pips it contains count towards his score at the end of the round. He may bury any cards other than those he has melded: melded cards may not be buried. Each opponent then declares the melds he can make from his own hand of fifteen cards. The value of the melds should be noted in his score column for reference, but in order to count them as part of his score at the end of the round he must take at least one trick. If either opponent takes no tricks he crosses out his score for melds. (This does not apply to Declarer, since the cards he buried count as a trick anyway.)

Tricks. Declarer leads any card to the first trick, and the following rules apply to the play of tricks:

(*a*) Each player must follow suit to the card led, if able;

(*b*) if a non-trump suit is led, a player who cannot follow suit *must* play a trump, if able; otherwise, he may discard;

(*c*) if a trump is led, each succeeding player must attempt to win the trick by playing a higher trump than any previously played; if unable, he may play a lower trump; if void in trumps, he must discard.

If two identical cards fall to the same trick, the first counts higher than the second. A trick is won by the highest card of the suit led, or by the highest trump if any are played. The winner of a trick leads to the next.

Scoring

Last trick. The winner of the last trick scores ten for it.

Declarer's score. Declarer adds to his count for melds the value of scoring cards he has taken in tricks (including the three cards he buried). If the total equals or exceeds his bid, he scores everything he makes; if not, the value of his bid is deducted from his score, which may run into negative numbers.

Opponent's scores. If an opponent has taken at least one trick, he scores the total value of all scoring cards contained in them plus whatever he may have counted for melds. An opponent who fails to take a trick scores nothing, even for any melds he might have claimed at the outset.

Game. The winner is the first player to reach or exceed 1000 pts., and for this purpose the Declarer's score is counted first – if he reaches 1000 he has won, even if either or both of the others might have finished with a greater aggregate of points on the same deal. If, however, both opponents reach 1000 and Declarer does not (through having lost his bid), then game is continued up to 1250, and by further increments of 250 each time the same situation occurs.

Hints on play

Assessing the hand. The minimum bid of 100 permissible in this version of Pinochle is so low that it is difficult to envisage a hand not worth bidding on.

Consider first the score for tricks. With 240 pips in the pack, plus the bonus of ten for last, you would expect with an average hand to take about sixty in tricks. But as Declarer – and you bid on the assumption that you will be Declarer – with the choice of trump suit *and* an exchange of cards you should reckon on making at least 100, and more like 120, for tricks alone.

Melds are less easy to assess. Your hand as dealt may contain on average cards with a total meldable value of anything from zero to one hundred plus. Statistics I have kept on the game show opponents melding an average of forty each, representing everything they were dealt on fifteen cards; Declarer, of course, melds from eighteen – so the question naturally arises how many the widow can be expected to add to the meldable value of the hand.

On this topic textbooks generally give the following sort of advice: expect the widow to add about thirty to the total strength of the hand as a whole, but nothing specifically to its meldable value (unless any one of at least five different cards would increase your score, in which case you have an even chance of improving it). In other words, assess how many you can make in tricks, and add thirty, plus what you already hold in melds, but not more.

This advice does not accord with my statistics on the game,

which consistently show Declarer melding an average of over 200 – i.e. about five times what each opponent melds. Not much of this can be due to the fact that Declarer has the advantage of choosing trumps, so the significant extra must derive largely from the widow. However, these two facts are not necessarily discrepant, since the advice given in the textbooks is primarily intended to apply to the standard Auction game in which the minimum permissible bid is normally 300. Since this is about the figure Declarer makes in the Thousand Up version, it is clear that when playing to the 300 minimum you have no leeway for counting on hand improvement, and therefore dare not risk more than you can actually see in your initial hand. This in turn emphasises how low the 100 minimum bid is, and so gives an idea of the worthwhile bidding range.

To sum up, it is always worth bidding in the Thousand Up game at a minimum of 100. An average hand, one that is neither exceptionally weak or obviously strong, and bearing melds already worth forty, can be expected to take at least sixty in tricks and so gives you the requisite one hundred needed to start the bid rolling. As Declarer you should normally expect to be able to make something between 250 and 500 when you take all your advantages into account.

Remember, in assessing the hand, to take one suit and assume it to be the trump – in other words, if you only have one marriage as dealt count it as forty rather than twenty. Conversely, if you fail to become Declarer, remember to reassess your hand when scoring for melds, as there is little chance that the same suit will be trump!

The only useful purpose served by starting the bid low, at 100, is to gauge your opponents' prospects by the amounts by which they jump. For example, if you start at 100 and the others continue 110, 120 they are probably also waiting to see how things develop before committing themselves. If you then jump to 200, a further jump to 210 suggests caution, while a jump to 250 indicates that everyone has a strong hand.

The game is not abandoned if Declarer in fact melds more than he bid, since the others must also have their opportunity to score; personally, however, I would consider it bad etiquette to bid lower than 100 plus ready-dealt melds and would even favour a law forbidding Declarer to meld less than 100 below his bid.

Burying. Bearing in mind that melded cards may not be buried, you should normally bury in such a way as to eliminate side-suit weaknesses. Thus any high-scoring card (Ace or Ten) in danger of capture should be buried so as to count in favour at the end of the game. It may even be advantageous, as shown in one of the sample games following, to leave a meld undeclared for the sake of burying a card that is better out of the hand than in.

A point that takes some getting used to if you are unaccustomed to playing with a doubled pack is the possible need to guard an *Ace*. A singleton Ace in Pinochle is nearly as dangerous as a singleton King in Bridge, Whist or Piquet. Though highest of its suit if led, it will fall to the other Ace should that come out first. Thus from a holding of the form A–T–x it is good to bury the Ten for the sake of its score rather than bank on the negligible possibility of its winning a trick. The small card must be kept as a guard.

To summarise, Declarer should seek to hold cards strong in trumps and at least one side suit, to void in at least one side suit, and to bury scoring cards that might run the risk of loss if kept in play. In the Thousand Up game described above it may be advantageous to withhold a meld in order to permit burial of a vulnerable high-scoring card, but in the standard Auction Pinochle with Widow, Declarer usually needs all the points he can get.

Playing. The play of Pinochle tends to revolve around trumps. Typically, Declarer keeps his own strength (especially trumps) in reserve and leads through his strong side suit(s) in order to denude opponents of their trumps. (This is the opposite of

Skat technique, where Declarer leads trumps in order to draw two for one.) That a player must trump when unable to follow effectively hinders opponents from throwing high-counting cards to each other's won tricks.

After cashing any blank Aces he may have, Declarer should start by leading small (losing) cards and running through his strong suit. Wherever possible, play cards that were melded in preference to others, since these are already known to opponents and their appearance gives them no further information about Declarer's hand.

Opponents are partners and should play together – more so in Auction Pinochle with Widow than in the Thousand Up game, where each may need at least a trick in order to score melds and may even be more concerned with playing against his temporary partner's score than Declarer's. In Thousand Up each should keep his tricks separate; in Auction with Widow opponents usually pile them up together.

Typically, opponents will seek primarily to discover Declarer's shortest suit from his play, and then attack by leading into it at every opportunity, since this forces him to weaken his trump holding. If Declarer seems unduly weak in trumps to start with (or, which may not be the same thing, you as one of his opponents have a surprisingly strong holding), it may prove more profitable to start by playing trumps out.

Other things being equal, it is good technique to let the opponent on Declarer's right win the trick, as he will then have the lead and so place Declarer in the most awkward situation. It is desirable, particularly in Auction with Widow, to swarm by playing high counters to partner's won trick. Thus 'an Ace calls for an Ace' – if your partner leads an Ace and you have the other, put it down if you are playing second (or third, unless Declarer trumps it!).

Pinochle, perhaps more than any other three-hand game of this format, demands and repays close observation and the exercise of card sense (of which the chief constituent is the

ability to draw inferences from the play of every card that
appears). Train yourself to keep track of the score and to
identify strengths and weakness in the others' hands; play no
card haphazardly and in time you may become a good beginner at the game.

Sample game

The following is a game of Thousand Up Pinochle in which
each player melds and scores what he can while Declarer seeks
to make his contract. This is an easier version of the game for
beginners than Auction Pinochle with Widow, of which a
description follows the sample game.

First deal. Charlie deals and the hands are as follows:

```
Abel     ♠T K Q J  ♡K Q Q 9  ♣A T T K  ◇A T Q
Baker    ♠A T K 9  ♡T T K J J  ♣K Q Q  ◇T K J
Charlie  ♠A Q J 9  ♡A A 9  ♣A J J  ◇A Q J 9 9
```

Abel has an even spread, with nothing outstanding. It
melds at present 60 with ♠ trump or 70 with ♡, but neither
is well represented. The draw of ♠A from widow would produce a trump sequence for 250, but is too remote even to
think about.

Baker melds 80 Kings and a (clearly plain suit) marriage for
100, but the hand would need the addition of a ♡A to be
worth a decent bid.

Charlie is well-off for existing melds – 100 Aces, 10 or 20
for dix (depending on trump), 40 for Pinochle makes 150 for a
start. With five Aces and the widow he can see a safe 300.

The bidding goes: A 100, B 110, C 250, pass, pass. Charlie
takes the widow and finds ♣9 9 ◇K – uninspiring for tricks
but giving a marriage. (The widow would not have helped
Baker much, but would have given Abel two dixes.) He
announces Diamond trumps, and, after melding as below,

buries ♠J ♡A 9 (bearing in mind that he is forbidden to bury any cards used in melds).

Abel announces two common marriages for 40.

Baker wishes to declare 80 Kings and a marriage for 100.

Charlie has 100 Aces, royal marriage 40, Pinochle 40, dixes 20, total 200. He leads.

A	B	C	
♡ 9	♡ J	♡ **A**	
♣ **T**	♣ Q	♣ 9	
♣ **A**	♣ K	♣ 9	
♠ J	♠ **A**	♠ 9	
♣ Q	♠ **K**	♣ Q	
♠ K	♠ 9	♠ **A**	
◇ **T**	◇ J	◇ Q	Charlie is now forcing out higher trumps.
♡ Q	♡ J	◇ **9**	
◇ **A**	◇ K	◇ K	. . . and chases an Ace out.
♡ Q	♡ K	◇ **9**	Abel continues his policy of leading into Charlie's void to force his trumps out.
♣ **T**	♣ Q	♣ J	Charlie is saving strength for the end.
♡ K	♡ T	◇ **J**	
◇ Q	◇ T	◇ **A**	Charlie now hopes the remaining Diamonds are evenly split, and is rewarded.
♣ K	♡ T	♣ **A**	
♠ T	♠ T	♣ **J**	A brace of Tens and ten for last neatly extracted.

77	23	150	For tricks
40	80	200	For melds
117	103	350	A typical result

Second deal. Abel deals as follows:

> Abel   ♠A T K Q J 9 ♡A T K Q J 9 ♣9 ◇A K
> Baker   ♠K ♡K J 9 ♣A T T K J J 9 ◇A T Q 9
> Charlie ♠A T Q J 9 ♡A Q ♣A K Q ◇T K Q J 9

An extraordinary deal! Abel has a sequence in either trump suit and a marriage in the other, plus either dix, making 80 without further effort. Baker's hand looks very promising, but is deceptive in melds: as it stands there is only the dix for ten, while the chance of drawing ♣Q for the sequence is minimal. Charlie has royal marriage if Diamonds, plus dix, marriage, 60 Queens and Pinochle for 170.

Baker is to start the bidding. Though he has practically nothing in the way of melds, either of the two ◇K will give him 80 Kings and either ♣Q a trump sequence for 150. He cannot bank seriously on either of these, but the point is that he has an eminently improvable hand. He is therefore prepared to start the bidding at 150, and does so. With 170 in hand, Charlie makes a slightly optimistic bid of 300. But Abel's rejoinder of 350 shuts them both out.

Abel draws ♡T, ♣Q, ◇J (cards that would not have helped Charlie, but would have increased Baker's holding by 150 and given him a strong playing hand). Announcing Heart trumps, Abel melds as detailed below and buries ♣Q 9 ◇K, creating a void in Clubs.

Abel melds: Trump sequence 150, dix 10, marriage 20, pinochle 40, total 220.

Baker claims 10 for his dix (♡9).

Charlie claims 60 Queens, two common marriages and pinochle, total 140.

It should be noted that Abel's Spade holding is not as solid as it may look: there being two of each rank, he holds only every other card except for the purpose of leading. Abel, who leads to the first trick, decides to start by squeezing out the five trumps he does not hold.

A	B	C	
♡ Q	♡ K	♡ A	Playing the Queen would leave Charlie with an undesirable lone Ace.
♠ 9	♠ K	♠ A	
♡ 9	♣ 9	♣ A	Charlie has assumed that Abel's inevitable void was Diamonds – which it could not have been since he melded Pinochle and must therefore hold ♢ J. A mistake.
♡ K	♡ 9	♡ K	
♡ J	♡ J	♢ 9	Last of the trumps.
♠ Q	♣ T	♠ T	Unable to follow or trump, B magnanimously swarms a Ten on a trick that Charlie is sure to win, though he needs one himself in order to score his melds.
♡ T	♣ J	♣ Q	
♢ J	♢ A	♢ T	Baker pounces on this loser to make his needed trick.
♡ T	♣ J	♣ K	

After this, Abel leads 'from the top' and takes the rest, including ten for last.

171	23	56	Tricks
220	10	140	Melds
391	33	196	Total
117	103	350	Previous score
508	136	546	Running total

Third deal. The cards fall:

Abel   ♠ T ♡ A T T K J 9 ♣ A A K J ♢ K Q J 9
Baker   ♠ A T Q J J 9 ♡ J ♣ Q Q J 9 ♢ A K J 9
Charlie ♠ A K K Q 9 ♡ K Q Q ♣ T T K 9 ♢ A T T

All have middling but potentially promising hands, respectively melding 30, 50, 70 with appropriate trump suits. Charlie starts the bidding, which climbs slowly: C 100, A 110, B 120, C 150 . . . To cut a long story short, Charlie overreached himself at 240 and Baker even further at 250, being anxious to get a game in and improve his middling score.

Baker draws ♡A ◇Q – disappointing, though they would have done Abel some good. After declaring Spade trumps and melding, he lays aside the three Clubs other than the Jack, which he must retain after melding.

Abel's melds: marriage for 20.

Baker's: 40 Jacks, pinochle, common marriage, dix for 110.

Charlie's: royal marriage, dix, common marriage, total 70.

Baker leads.

A	B	C	
◇ Q	◇ Q	◇ A	
♠ T	♠ A	♠ 9	A nasty lead.
♣ A	♣ J	♣ T	
♡ A	♡ 9	♡ Q	
♣ J	♠ 9	♣ 9	
◇ 9	◇ A	◇ T	Baker should have led low, but was fishing for a Ten – successfully.
◇ K	◇ J	◇ T	
♣ K	♠ J	♣ K	Baker was obliged to trump.
◇ J	◇ 9	♣ Q	Now he draws out one of Charlie's trumps ...
♡ 9	♠ T	♠ K	and Charlie returns the compliment, leaving himself strong in trumps.
♣ A	◇ K	♠ K	B and C are entertaining a private battle in trumps.
♡ J	♠ J	♣ T	
♡ T	♡ J	♡ Q	
♡ K	♡ A	♡ K	The second of two strangely late Heart rounds.
♡ T	♠ Q	♠ A	And C gets ten for last.
52	107	91	For tricks, and Baker loses his contract, falling 23 short of his bid of 250, which is therefore subtracted.
20	—	70	For melds (B's are disallowed)
27	−250	161	Total
508	136	546	Previous total
580	−114	707	Running total

Baker's bid was certainly unsound, though with an even distribution of trumps in his opponents' hand – instead of a preponderance of them in C's – he might have gathered the requisite 140 in tricks.

Fourth deal. The hands are:

    Abel   ♠T T J 9 ♡A A K Q 9 ♣T K ♢A T K J
    Baker   ♠A Q Q J 9 ♡T T J ♣T Q J ♢A Q J 9
    Charlie   ♠A K K ♡K J 9 ♣A A K J 9 9 ♢T K 9

Abel melds 50 with Hearts; add the statutory 120 for tricks and a starting point is 170. A middling hand. Baker melds 90 with Spades and can therefore bid 210 safely. Charlie melds 100 with Clubs, giving him a bid of 220.

Abel starts the bidding at 100 and drops out when Charlie takes it up to 220. Baker, somewhat rashly in view of his ignominious failure, goes up to 240, and successfully tempts Charlie into the 250 region.

Charlie draws three Queens – ♣ ♡ and ♢ – which would have done everybody good, especially Baker. After declaring Clubs trumps, Charlie buries ♠A K ♢T for 25 and needs 110 in tricks to succeed.

Abel melds a common marriage for 20.

Baker claims 40 Jacks and pinochle for 80.

Charlie counts 80 Kings, two marriages and two dixes for 140. At the lead, he promptly voids Spades, which he was unable to do before being obliged to keep the King after declaring it.

A	B	C	
♠ T	♠ A	♠ K	
♢ T	♢ A	♢ 9	
♢ K	♢ J	♢ Q	
♢ A	♢ Q	♢ K	The opponents are doing well because C's hand is very even and much of it is already known ...
♢ J	♢ 9	♣ 9	and, to add insult to injury, Charlie is obliged to trump rubbish.
♡ A	♡ T	♡ Q	
♡ A	♡ T	♡ 9	
♡ K	♡ J	♡ J	
♡ Q	♣ Q	♣ K	Hoping now that the remaining Clubs are evenly divided (they are), C runs down his trumps and finishes with ♡ K and ten for last.

80	46	124	Tricks
20	80	140	Melds
100	126	264	Total
580	−114	707	Previous total
680	12	971	Score to date.

Fifth deal. The hands are:

    Abel   ♠ATKQ ♡T9 ♣ATQJ9 ♢ATKJ
    Baker   ♠AKJJ9 ♡AKJ ♣TKK9 ♢ATQ
    Charlie ♠Q9 ♡ATKQJ9 ♣AQJ ♢QJ99

Charlie's win seems a foregone conclusion: his opening melds are trump sequence 150, 60 Queens, pinochle and dix for 260, to Abel's pinochle and marriage, and no combination for Baker. (Abel needs one of six cards to substantially increase his hand – an Ace of Hearts for 100 Aces, and a King or a Jack for a trump sequence.)

With ♠T ♡Q ◇K in the widow, Charlie declares Hearts, and the result is:

A	B	C	
45	84	121	Tricks
30	0	220	Melds
75	84	341	Total
680	12	971	Previous score
855	96	1312	Final total

AUCTION PINOCHLE WITH WIDOW

When you have played enough of the Thousand Up game described above to get a feel for the principal characteristics and possibilities of Pinochle, you should graduate to the more highly regarded and most frequently played version as described below. Because Pinochle is so frequently played by so many different people in so many different places there are a number of variations, optional procedures and local rules likely to be encountered in everyday American play. You should therefore not be surprised if the following description differs in small matters from that given in the first American card book you consult or professed by the first American Pinochle players you fall in with. But the discrepancies are very small between one authority and another and do not significantly affect the play of the hand.

To keep things simple, optional rules and variations are relegated to the end of the chapter. The following description is complete in itself, but matters explained fully in the Thousand Up game are kept short here for convenience.

The chief differences between proper Auction Pinochle and Thousand Up are (a) the minimum permissible bid is higher, (b) only one player, the Declarer, scores for melds, and (c), as a result of (b), Declarer's two opponents must play a more positive partnership game to defeat the contract.

Cards. Forty-eight card pack with ranking and pip-scoring as before:

Ace	11
Ten	10
King	4
Queen	3
Jack	2
Nine	0

Game. Three systems are used:

(*a*) Most frequently, each game is complete in itself and is settled in chips, counters or units of currency. Different counting systems are used, but for the simplest it should be sufficient to start with twenty chips or units each.

(*b*) Pencil-and-paper accounting may be used, in which one chip or unit is translated into one game point. The winner is the player with most game points when it is agreed to finish. (A time limit should be set beforehand for this and the chips method above.)

(*c*) The game can be point-scored and played one thousand up, as in the Thousand Up game described above.

Deal. Three to each player, three to widow, and the rest round in threes, so that each player has fifteen cards.

Bidding. Player left of dealer starts. A player who has passed may not re-enter. If there are three passes the deal is abandoned and passes to the left. Every bid must be a multiple of ten and higher than the preceding bid. The highest permissible bid is 650. The lowest is 300 in strict circles, but may, by previous agreement, be set at 250 or even – for beginners – 200 250 is recommended. Bidding may start at any level and jump by any number of tens.

The bid represents the minimum number of points the bidder expects to make both for melds (after drawing three additional cards) and for scoring cards won in tricks. The player making the highest bid becomes Declarer, and the opponents play in partnership to prevent him from making his contract.

Widow, melding, burying. Declarer turns up the three widow cards so that all may see them and adds them to his hand.

From his hand of eighteen cards he now declares his melds – i.e., announces what they are, shows them if requested to do so, and notes their value towards his contract. Valid melds are as follows:

Flush (trump sequence)	150
Royal marriage	40
Common marriage	20
100 Aces	100
80 Kings	80
60 Queens	60
40 Jacks	40
Pinochle	40
Dix	10

The same rules and restrictions apply as in the Thousand Up game.

Declarer announces his selected trump suit (if not already implied by scoring for Flush or Dix), lays aside or 'buries' three cards face down to bring his hand back to fifteen, and leads any card to the first trick. The three buried cards count for him as a won trick at the end of the game. They may contain counters (scoring cards) but may not include any card scored in a meld. If he buries any trumps he must announce that fact, but need not say which they are.

Conceding. On seeing the widow, Declarer may decide that he cannot hope to make his game and is allowed to concede without further play – see 'Scoring'. Alternatively, the opponents may agree to concede Declarer his game without further play. Game may not be conceded after a card is led to the first trick.

Tricks. Each player must follow suit to the card led if he can; if he cannot, he must trump, and only if he cannot trump either may he discard from another suit. If a trump is led each succeeding player must, if he can, win the trick by playing a higher trump. (But if a plain suit lead is trumped the third player is not obliged to overtrump.)

Of two identical cards played to a trick, the first ranks higher. The trick is won by the highest card of the suit led or by the highest trump if any are played. Opponents keep their won tricks together in a common pile. The winner of a trick leads to the next.

When the last trick has been taken (counting ten to the side that takes it), the final scores are ascertained and agreed for the two sides – i.e. what opponents have taken in tricks, and Declarer in tricks plus melds. Declarer must make at least the number he bid in order to win.

Settlement (*chips*). The value of each game in chips or monetary units is as follows:

BID	VALUE
200+	1
250+	2
300 +	3
350+	4
400+	5
450+	6
500+	7
550+	8
600+	9

(Many possible systems are regularly used; this is the simplest.)

If Declarer succeeds, either by playing and winning or by the opponents' conceding without play, each opponent pays him the value in chips appropriate to the amount of his bid (as above). If Declarer concedes without playing, he pays *each* of them the appropriate value; and if he plays and loses, he pays each of them *twice* that value.

Scoring (game points). The system is the same as for settlement by chips, but recorded on paper. Against each player's initial is entered the value he wins as a plus score, or the value he loses as a minus score.

Scoring, thousand up. If Declarer succeeds (by play or concession), he scores the amount of his bid. If he concedes without play each opponent scores once the amount of the bid, and if he plays and loses they each score twice that amount.

Variants

A few variants and optional rules are worth noting where they affect the play or the chances one takes; others, such as ways of dealing (in threes only, in various combinations of three and four, and so on), are trivial and here omitted.

Widow. The widow may be dealt exposed, in which case each player is allowed only one bid.

Declarer may be allowed to play without looking at the widow, though still counting it towards tricks at the end of the game. In this case he scores (plus or minus) double value.

Kitty and compulsory bid. When playing for chips it is customary to recognise a separate pool, the kitty, which has various uses. Where there is a kitty, the player left of dealer is obliged to make the minimum bid – he may not pass. If, however, he makes that bid and is left with it because the others pass immediately, he may concede game without looking at the widow (in other words, refuse to play). In this case he pays the value of that bid into the kitty. In addition, the kitty may be paid or pay out as if it were a fourth player in the game. The kitty belongs to all three players: it must be contributed to equally when in deficit, and is equally divided at the end of the game.

Tricks. It will be recalled that if a trump is led each succeeding player must 'play over' – i.e., play a higher trump (if possible) than any already showing. In an eminently sensible variant, the second opponent is not obliged to play over if his partner has already overtrumped a trump led by Declarer.

In some localities the rule is tightened rather than relaxed, players being obliged to attempt to win tricks even on plain suit leads.

Premium suits. 'Spades double' is a common optional rule: any game in which Spades are trumps is won or lost at double its normal value (except that, if Declarer announces Spades as trumps but then changes his mind and concedes without play, he is only charged 'single bête', since the rules permit him to change trumps anyway). Less common is 'Hearts triple'.

Bonuses of various sorts may also be recognised. For example, a player holding 100 Aces may claim a chip from each opponent.

RUMMY FOR THREE

Everybody who plays cards can play Rummy in one form or another. Its popularity is a remarkable twentieth-century phenomenon. Indeed, a hundred years ago you wouldn't have found it in a book of card games, though its probable ancestor Conquian (Coon Can) seems to have been well under way in Mexico and the southern states at about that time.

It was Gin that really put Rummy on the map. First put together in 1909, Gin stood at the forefront of a rise in the popularity of Rummy which continued until the advent of modern Contract Bridge in the early thirties, thereupon suffering a distinct decline. But then 1939 saw (amongst other things) an overwhelming craze for Gin that swept the American world of entertainment at a time when Hollywood was the cultural fashion centre of the States, and the States the cultural fashion centre of the world. Another decade, and two-hand Gin was in turn overwhelmed by the popularity of four-hand Canasta, a complex form of Rummy that had been brewing for some years in Brazil.

All Rummies are much alike – even Gin and Canasta are more like close dialects of the same Rummy language than different card game languages – and the extraordinary popularity of two of them may be taken as indicative of the popularity of them all. Rummy is now thought to be the second most popular card game in the United States, being beaten by Poker. And this is a rise in fortunes, for in the forties it only came third. The probable reason for its popularity is its basic simplicity, despite the complexities of Canasta; that chance can sometimes overcome skill gives it a wider appeal than, say, Bridge, where chance plays practically no part in the actual play. You might also like to take into account an observation of my own to the effect that women seem to prefer 'collecting' card games to 'bidding' card games. If true, it's no doubt relevant to the question of popularity.

FIVE HUNDRED RUM

Preliminaries

Cards. Standard 52–card pack, normal ranking, no Jokers or wild cards.

Game is set at 500 pts., which might be achieved in three to six rounds (allow about ten minutes per round). Scores are made at the end of each round. If more than one player exceeds 500, the winner is the player with most points. In the event of a tie, play a tie-breaking round.

Order. Choose first dealer by any agreed means. All play is clockwise and players take turns to deal.

Deal. Shuffle thoroughly. Deal seven cards to each player face down one at a time. Place the remainder face down at one side of the table to form the stock. Turn over the top card of stock and lay it face up beside the stock as the first card of the discard pile.

Object. To collect and lay aside cards in either groups of three or four of the same rank (as A–A–A, 2–2–2–2 etc) or numerical sequences of three or more of the same suit (as ♠A–2–3, ♡9–T–J–Q–K–A etc) until you have no more cards in hand. Any such group is called a 'meld'. Scores are made for melds, and penalties charged for cards left in hand when one player goes out. There is no bonus for 'going out'. Scores are related to the rank of cards: high ranks score more than low ranks.

Play

Player left of dealer goes first. Each in turn must draw, may then meld, and must then discard unless he has melded his last card. Following rules apply:

Draw. You may take either the top card of the stock, or any (face-up) card from the discard pile, which should be spread slightly so that all cards in it are visible to all players. Two conditions attach to taking a discard:

(*a*) You may only take a face-up card if you can immediately meld it, whether with cards already in hand, or with other cards taken from the discards, or both, or by 'laying it off' against another meld already on the table.

(*b*) Though you may take any card from the discards, right down to the original turn-up, you must also take into hand all the cards lying above it, whether you can meld them or not.

Meld. You may then make as many melds as you can and wish. A meld consists of three or four cards of the same rank, or three or more in suit and sequence. In sequence, Ace may count high (above King) or low (below Two), but not both ('round the corner' sequences, involving K–A–2, are not permitted). An Ace used in a low sequence counts a low score at the end of the game.

You may also meld cards that belong to any melds already lying on the table. For instance, if one player has ♣3–4–5–6 you may meld ♣2 or 7 or both. This is called 'laying off'. You may lay off cards to your own melds. All cards laid off should be placed before you with your own melds, not physically added to opponents' cards.

If you lay off a card that could belong to two different types of meld, you must state which it is. For instance, if two melds on the table are ♠8–♡8–♣8 and ◇9–T–J–Q and you lay off ◇8, you must state whether it completes the Eights or the Diamond sequence. If the latter, yourself or another player could subsequently lay off (say) ◇7; but if ◇8 is stated to belong to the Eights then the sequence cannot be continued downwards.

Discard. If, after drawing and melding, you have any cards left in hand you must discard one of them face up to the top end of the discard pile.

End of Stock. If the stock is emptied before the end of play, play continues by drawing only from the discard pile. The stock is not reconstituted.

End-play

Going out. A player goes out as soon as he gets rid of his last card, either by melding or by discarding. Play immediately ceases.

Score for melds. Each player scores for all the cards he has melded as follows:

Aces (each)	15 (except in sequence A–2–3–)
King, Queen, Jack	10
Other ranks	face value
Ace (low sequence)	1

Penalty for cards in hand. Each player subtracts from his score for melds the value of all cards left in his hand according to the schedule above, Ace counting 15 (even if forming a low sequence in hand: no credit is given for undeclared melds).

Keeping score. Each player's score is kept cumulatively; the game ends when at least one reaches 500 or more; the winner is the player with the highest score (even if the game ended with somebody else going out).

Hints on play

The beginner's mistake is to start melding prematurely in an attempt to go out fast. Not only is it rarely possible to go out early, unless you have exceptionally well-matched cards (in which case shuffle more thoroughly next time!), but also it is rarely profitable, unless you can be sure of setting your opponents back a bundle. Furthermore, it is better to save up your melds as long as possible, not just in the opening but throughout the whole game, for as soon as you lay a meld out you enable the others to get rid of otherwise unmatched cards in their hands by laying them off against your melds. That means you do all the hard work collecting them, and they reap the benefit.

Correct opening strategy is to increase your holding of cards by as much as you can, as soon as you can. Since you can only do this by taking a large batch from the discard pile (for which privilege, remember, you have to be able to meld the lowest you take) you must watch the discard pile very carefully. Take it too early, and you do not get enough cards to continue with; leave it too long, and someone else may sweep it up first.

A good way of laying claim to the discard pile is to salt it, with low matched cards from your own hand. For instance, if you hold three Twos it is ideal to lay one of them down as a salt: it is unlikely to be taken by the others, and it enables you to take a large batch later when enough other discards have been piled on top of it. Do not fear losing it should it be picked up amongst a batch taken by someone else. Very likely it will soon reappear as a discard and will continue to serve you in the same way. And even if it doesn't the loss will have a minimal effect on your score.

You will naturally hold on to high cards as long as possible and prefer to discard low in the early rounds. Not until you have an inkling that someone may be shortly going out will you dispose of valuable cards to the pile in order to avoid a costly loss.

You will also naturally try to avoid playing a card to the discard pile that closely matches another already there, in case somebody else can then meld them both in conjunction with cards from his own hand. But this is not always easy, and some duplication may be necessary. If so, you should in the early part of the game try to match more recent discards, so that a player taking them both will get only a small batch. Later on, when there is a feeling of going out in the air, it is better to make a match with something much lower down, when an opponent may be considerably less inclined to dig deep into the discard pile and take more cards than he wishes to cope with.

It is worth emphasising again that taking discards in batches is an advantage, because it gives you so many more melding possibilities – few cards subsequently drawn will be entirely useless. When you do take a batch, do not feel obliged to meld everything you can from your hand. Holding back is good as long as you can do it safely.

Five Hundred Rum demands – and repays – particularly close attention to the cards drawn, melded and discarded by your opponents. Their actions will often indicate to you which of your potential melds are probably capable of fulfilment, and which not. You may also get a good idea of the cards they are after, in which case you may be able to offer a *quid pro quo* – that is, let a card go that someone else wants in the hope that it will cause him to regurgitate a card you need yourself. In this connection it is desirable to play to the score by releasing cards only to the lower scoring opponent and doing nothing that might prove favourable to the player currently leading you both.

You will often find that the first few melds determine whether most of those made during the course of the current round will be sequences or sets – the two *tend* to exclude each other. Sets (that is, three or four of the same rank) tend to be restrictive and lead to short games if they predominate, since it becomes easier to match up single cards. Where sets and sequences are evenly balanced, the game tends to be more exciting to play. With sequences, the need for close observation is of particular importance. For example, if one player has melded ♣6–7–8 and you draw ♣4 or ♣T you might, if careless, fail to note that ♣5 or ♣9 has already been laid away by the other player or even yourself, enabling the Four or Ten to be itself laid off. And, of course, never miss an opportunity to take a card from the discard pile that can be laid off against a meld already down. Many a good batch of discards can be taken in this way.

A sample round

```
Abel      ♠—  ♡J 4 2  ♣5  ◇8 7 4
Baker     ♠5 3  ♡3  ♣Q  ◇Q J 2
Charlie:  ♠K Q 2  ♡T 8  ♣9 6  ◇—
Upcard:   ♡7
```

In the following account of play, the first card is that drawn from stock, and the second, preceded by (—) denotes the discard made.

Abel	Baker	Charlie	
♣6 — ◇4	♣8 — ◇2	♣A — ♣6	
♡5			Abel does not like to make matching discards and accordingly lets a high-ish card go:
	— ◇8 ♠4 — ♡3	♡Q — ♣9	Following Baker's discard, Abel wonders whether to take and meld the Three or leave it for another round in hopes of taking a bigger batch. He opts for the latter course.
◇3 — ◇7	◇T — ♣8	♠J — ♠2	B and C now have three-card sequences in hand.
melds			Abel takes ◇4 from

discards, melds it with the Two and Three, and retains a promising hand consisting of a four-card sequence in Hearts and one short of a five-card sequence in Clubs. If he were now to discard either of the Spades, Baker would promptly meld it with his ♠3–4–5, plus the Diamond sequence, and throw ♣Q to go out! The scores would then be A −54, B 44, C −73. More by luck than judgment, however, Abel discards otherwise.

− ◇8 ♣T — ♠3   ♠T — ♡Q   Charlie does not like to discard high but finds no satisfactory alternative.

♠8 — ♠2   . . . .   The Spade discard is now safe, as Baker cannot go out. (Abel was unaware of the danger anyway.)

melds   . . . .   Baker now takes ♠3 from the discards and melds ♠2–3–4–5. Now he neatly discards ◇J – the middle card of a sequence. Is he mad? No. If he melds ◇T–J–Q he will have to fill out *two* high ranks

(Q and T) for success, whereas if he subsequently melds three Queens he will rather hold **T–T than** J–T, since the former requires one of two cards and the latter one specific card to complete . . .

— ◇J! ◇5 . . . . and C lays this off against Abel's sequence. He also melds his Spade sequence, and, preferring to keep the Ace (perhaps unwisely)

— ♡T discards the Ten.

♠9 . . . . which he lays off against C's Spade sequence together with ♠8. He also melds ♡2–3–4–5.

— ◇7 melds and goes out . . . . Baker takes ♡T from discards, melds and goes out, having studied all melds and calculated 74 for himself, 40 for Abel less six cards, 45 for Charlie less two cards.

+40	74	45
−44	0	23
−4	74	22

Final scores made up as follows:

Abel

Melds	$\diamond$2–3–4	= 9
	$\heartsuit$2–3–4–5	= 14
Laid off	$\spadesuit$8, 9	= 17
Penalty	$\spadesuit$6 $\heartsuit$J $\clubsuit$9, 8, 6, 5	= 44

Baker

Melds	$\spadesuit$2–3–4–5	= 14
	Q–Q–Q	= 30
	T–T–T	= 30

Charlie

Melds	$\spadesuit$T–J–Q–K	= 40
Laid off	$\diamond$5	= 5
Penalty	$\clubsuit$A $\heartsuit$8	= 23

Note how Baker assessed the scores before going out. Each card has an average value of about $7\frac{1}{2}$; counting his opponents' unmelded cards he put Charlie at about 15 against and Abel at about 44 against – which proved highly accurate.

OKLAHOMA

Widely regarded as the best Rummy for three, Oklahoma belongs to the same group as Five Hundred Rum described above and is even a step on the way towards becoming Canasta. Played with a double pack, it introduces the unusual features of a special card – the Queen of Spades, of Black Maria fame – which adds a deliberate element of imbalance.

Preliminaries

Cards. 105, consisting of two standard 52-card packs plus a single Joker.

Game. Scores are made at the end of each round, and game is 1000 up, which may be achieved in six to ten rounds. Allow about ten minutes per round.

Order. All play and the turn to deal rotates clockwise.

Deal. Thirteen cards each singly, face down. Place the remainder in a face down pile to form the stock. Take the top card and lay it face up beside the stock as the first card of the discard pile. (The discard pile will be kept squared up, not spread as in 500 Rum.)

Object. All eight Twos and the Joker are wild cards; that is, any one of them may be used by its holder to represent any card he wishes to nominate. The object is to draw and discard in order to make melds of three or four cards of the same rank, or three or more cards of the same suit in numerical sequence, until one player goes out by melding all his cards. It should be noted that cards from Eight up score high and cards from Seven down score low; that wild cards have special values and count heavily against if left in hand at the end of the game; and that the two ♠Q also have a high value. There is a bonus for going out.

Play.

First refusal. Immediately after the deal there is a chance for the upcard to be taken by anyone who can forthwith meld it with cards from his own hand. Player left of dealer has first option; if he passes the player on his left has it; if he passes, dealer has it. If all pass, first play is made by player on dealer's left; if anyone takes it, play proceeds from that seat onwards.

General procedure. Each player in turn must take either the top card of the stock or the discard pile, may then make as many melds as he can and wishes, and must finally, if he has any cards left in hand, discard one to the discard pile. The following particulars apply.

Taking the discard. The discard pile must be kept squared up so that only the top card is visible, and this may be taken by any player in turn instead of the top card of stock. But (*a*) the top card may only be taken if it can be immediately melded, or laid off to another of that player's melds already on the table, and

(*b*) if the top card is taken, the whole of the discard pile must be taken with it.

Melds. Cards may be melded complete, i.e. as groups of three or more at a time, or they may be added in ones or twos to other melds already on the table. Each player may, however, add only to his own melds: he may not 'lay off' cards to those of opponents.

A set of three of a rank may be increased to a set of four, but a set of four is 'closed' and may not be further increased. The cards of a set are not required to be of different suits.

In sequences, an Ace may count high or low (Q–K–A or A–2–3) but not both (K–A–2). A sequence may be extended by the addition of cards one, two or more at a time up to a maximum of fourteen – that is, using two Aces, one high, one low.

Wild cards. Twos are wild, but not necessarily so: a Two may be melded as part of a sequence between Ace and Three, and a set of three or four Twos may be melded in its own right. In the latter case, they count low (in other words, you cannot meld a set of Twos and say they are standing in their 'wild' capacity for a set of higher-scoring cards).

When a Two or the Joker is used as a wild card, it is some-times necessary – and therefore always desirable – to state what card it represents. It cannot then be changed. Thus if ♠A–♡2–♣2 is melded, its player must state whether he intends three Aces, in which case he can subsequently add only another Ace, or a high sequence, in which case he can extend it only with ♠J, or a low sequence, which he can then only extend with ♠4.

Trading the Joker. When a player has melded the Joker, he may later replace it with the card it was stated to represent and take it back into hand for further use. The Joker cannot be captured from another player. Only the Joker, not the Twos, may be traded in this way.

Discarding. A player may not discard a ♠Q if he holds any different card in his hand.

Ending. The round ends either as soon as one player has no cards left in hand, or at the end of the turn in which the last card of the stock is taken. In the latter case there is no going-out bonus unless the player who took the last card goes out in the same turn.

Scoring

Card values. Melded cards are counted in their holder's favour, cards left in hand count against. Special cards left in hand count more against:

	MELDED	IN HAND
Ace	20	20
K Q J T 9 or 8	10	10 except ♠Q, see below
7 6 5 4 or 3	5	5

SPECIAL CARDS		
Joker	100	200
Queen of Spades ♠Q	50	100
Two, standing for 8 or higher	10	20
Two, standing for 7 or lower	5	20

Going-out bonus. A bonus of 100 is scored by a player who goes out.

Game bonus. Game is 1000 up; whoever reaches it first or exceeds it most scores an additional 200 for game. This is shared in the event of a tie.

Going out concealed. A player goes out 'concealed' when, having made no previous melds in the round, he melds all his cards and goes out in one turn (with or without a discard). There is a bonus of 250 for going out concealed, but this does not count towards game immediately: it is noted for reference and not added to that player's score until the game has ended. Further, the bonus does not apply at all if the player goes out on his *first* turn. It must happen on the second turn or later in order to count.

Hints on play

Distinctive features of Oklahoma are the Queens of Spades and the wild cards.

Since a ♠Q cannot be discarded and has a high score you must be constantly alert to the danger of being caught with her in hand at the end of the round. Until both are melded by somebody else, you must be careful to keep hold of other Queens and high Spades in case you hold or draw ♠Q yourself.

The fact that Twos are wild and cannot later be exchanged (unlike the Joker) for their aliases has an interesting and potentially dangerous effect on the balance of cards, since it means that those they replace in melds are more difficult to connect elsewhere. This is aggravated by the fact that you cannot lay off cards to other players' melds. Hence much judgment is needed in the matter of designating Twos – you will obviously not wish to discard them (unless there is a danger of being stuck with them towards the end of the game) and may therefore deliberately use them in melds in order to create good discards.

That sets of cards of the same rank are restricted to a maximum of four is another, related point of interest. One result is that you are often better off melding only three of a kind when you actually hold all four. If you subsequently meld the fourth in a sequence, all well and good. If not, you might later find an opportunity to go out with other cards, at which point you will still be able to throw the fourth to your meld of three. In other words, a meld of three is open and therefore gives you more flexibility than a meld of four.

Because there are eight cards of each rank, a pair is much easier to fill and therefore better to keep than two cards in sequence.

Since the discard pile must be taken as a whole, if at all, you should normally not take it unless you are sure that it will give you more in melds than in rubbish.

Finally, except for the purpose of going out concealed, it is not necessary to hold back potential melds, since others will not be able to lay off cards to them.

SKAT

To describe Skat as a national card game is to damn it with faint praise. It is said that at least half the German population *can* play it, and most of them do so regularly. The number of Skat clubs and tourneys is legion, as may be seen from any issue of the monthly magazine of the German Skat Federation. The game also has a substantial following, albeit in a slightly different version, in those parts of America of chiefly German ethnic background, especially in Wisconsin.

Apart from that, Skat is virtually unknown outside its country of origin. (It was deliberately concocted, shortly before 1820, by members of the Altenburg Tarock Club, by combining elements of such games as Tarock, Ombre, Sheepshead and suchlike.) This is a great pity, as it is universally regarded by serious card players as one of the great games of the world in terms of depth, skill and variety. In this respect it is comparable to Bridge, the overlord of card games, although in practical detail it has almost nothing in common with Bridge except tricks and trumps. In particular, Skat is essentially a three-hand game, with each person playing for himself in the long run, though in any single deal two of them will be combining forces to defeat the 'contract' of the third.

I should mention at this point, however, that four is the widely preferred number of players at a table, each of them taking turns to sit out the hand they deal and act either as a *kibitzer* or as a sort of unofficial *confidant* and commiserator of the current bidder.

The German pronunciation of the name is something like *shkaht*, with a short but broad 'a'. The preferred English pronunciation is *scart* – definitely NOT *scat*. (Mind you, this can cause problems. I once went into the Games Centre in London and asked for a pack of Skat cards in my natural London accent, which the assistant interpreted as 'scout' cards as if they had something to do with that youth movement!)

The following description is that of the official German game as promoted by the German Skat Federation. For additional interest, I will append to this chapter some of the 'unofficial' variations played in various parts of Germany, and some variations practised by my own circle of regular players.

The game

Players. Three, but it is more enjoyable if four take part and each in turn sits out the hand he deals to.

Cards. 32, i.e. no cards lower than Seven.

Game. A game may be of any length provided that all players deal the same number of times. Scores are kept on paper ruled into columns. There should be one column for each player, and another to note the value of each game won or lost so as to check the scores. Each player's score is recorded cumulatively. As it is possible to lose points, an individual score may go below zero. This is usually indicated by drawing a circle round the minus figure, and that player is said to be 'in the hole'.

General idea of the game. Each player receives ten cards and the odd two are left face down on the table forming what is known as 'the skat'. There is an auction to determine which player is offering to play the game of highest value. The highest bidder becomes the soloist and endeavours to win the game he bid against the combined forces of the other two, who play as a partnership. The skat belongs to the soloist and he may or may not add those two cards to his hand in exchange for two comparatively useless ones, depending on how strong he thinks his hand is. If he wins the game he bid, he scores its value (possibly with bonuses); if not, he loses its value (possibly with extra penalties).

Card values. Although Skat is a game of tricks and trumps, tricks have no value in themselves. It is individual cards which have point values, and the point of winning tricks lies in the values of the cards they contain. The total value of cards in the pack is 120, made up as follows:

Each Ace 11, Ten 10, King 4, Queen 3, Jack 2 (total 30 per suit). Sevens, Eights and Nines carry no point value. To succeed at most games that may be bid, the soloist must capture more than half the points in the pack, i.e. 61 or more; the partners therefore try to beat him by capturing at least 60 between them.

Shuffle and deal. Cards are dealt face up to each player until someone gets a Jack: he becomes the first dealer, and after that the turn to deal (and to bid, to play and so on) passes to the left. Shuffle the cards thoroughly and have them cut. Deal cards face down in batches as follows: three to each player, then 'two to the skat' (i.e. face down on the table), then four each and finally three each. (If four play, the dealer takes no cards for himself.) Nobody is yet allowed to see 'what's in the skat', since it belongs to the eventual highest bidder, who has not yet been determined.

Bids and game values

Before detailing the procedures for bidding and playing, it is necessary to know what the various bids are and how they are valued. There are basically three types of game that may be bid, which are, from commonest to rarest, as follows:

1. A suit game. The soloist nominates one of the four suits as trumps and endeavours to win at least 61 card points in tricks. The order of cards in each suit is Ace, Ten, King, Queen, 9, 8, 7. The four Jacks count as the four highest trumps, ranking in order clubs, spades, hearts, diamonds. Thus the club Jack is the highest card in the pack, regardless of the trump suit, and the trump Ace is the fifth highest trump, there being eleven cards in the trump suit and seven in each plain suit.

2. A 'grand' game. The soloist does not nominate a trump suit but still endeavours to capture at least 61 card points in tricks. The four Jacks are trumps, ranking as in a suit game (club, spade, heart, diamond). Hence they form a short, fifth suit of four cards, as opposed to seven in each plain suit (A, T, K, Q, 9, 8, 7).

3. A null game ('null' rhymes with 'pull'). There are no trumps and the soloist's object is to lose every trick – the same as misère in Solo and other card games. For this purpose the cards rank in their Whist/Bridge order, namely A, K, Q, J, T, 9, 8, 7.

Each of these games may be played either *with the exchange* or *from the hand*. In an *exchange* game, the soloist adds the two cards of the skat to his hand upon winning the bid, then discards any two in their place before announcing what his game is. The purpose of this may be to improve the shape of the hand or to lay away a high scoring card which may otherwise be captured in play, or even just to wait and see what the skat contains before deciding on what game to announce. In a *hand* game, the soloist plays with his hand as dealt and neither touches nor examines the skat until play has finished. In either case, the skat belongs to the soloist – i.e. any scoring cards it may contain count in his favour exactly as if he took them in tricks.

The numerical value of a game – i.e. the amount the bidder stands to win or lose if he becomes the soloist – depends on the suit selected as trump, if any, and whether the game is played with the exchange or from the hand, a hand game being worth more. It may also be affected by other factors, the chief of which are *schneider* (rhymes with 'spider') and *schwarz* (pronounced *shvarts*). Schneider is the capturing of 90 or more card points in tricks. This carries a bonus, and a player who thinks his hand strong enough to achieve this target may raise his bid accordingly – that is, bid on the assumption that he will make it. Schwarz is the winning of all ten tricks and carries a bonus additional to that of merely making schneider.

Working out the game value. What the players bid on is the minimum value game they expect to win upon becoming the soloist. Apart from the null bids, which have definite fixed values (see below), the value of a game is found by taking the *base value* of the suit selected as trump and multiplying this by the sum of *matadors* held in the hand plus certain other *game factors*. These are as follows:

1. Base value of trump selected

diamonds	9	grand (only Jacks trump)	24
hearts	10	grand ouvert (ditto)	36
spades	11		
clubs	12		

2. Matadors are top consecutive trumps. If you hold the top Jack (club), then you are playing 'with' as many top trumps as you hold in sequence. For example, holding club J but not spade J, you are 'with 1'; holding the top three Jacks but lacking the diamond, you are 'with 3'; holding four Jacks plus Ace, Ten but not King of trumps, you are 'with 6'; and so on.

If you lack the club Jack, then you are playing 'without' (or, as the Americans more logically put it, 'against') as many trumps as lie above your highest. Thus if your highest is spade J you are 'without 1'; if it is the Ace of trumps, there being no Jacks in your hand, you are 'without 4', and so on.

Whether you are playing with or without is irrelevant to the game value: all that counts is the *number* of matadors you are with or without.

3. Game factors. If you are proposing to play with the exchange, then to the number of matadors concerned you add 1 'for game', or 2 if you think you will make schneider (90+ card points), or 3 if you think you will make schwarz (all 10 tricks). Multiply this new total by the base value of your prospective trump (see above) and you arrive at your prospective game value – that is, the amount you are prepared to bid.

If you are prepared to play 'from the hand' then certain other factors may be taken into account to increase your game value. First of all you count 1 'for game', plus 1 'for hand', plus a third 1 if you think you will make schneider, and a fourth if you think you will make schwarz. If you are prepared to announce your intention of making schneider, so that your opponents may be on their guard against it, then you may add another factor for 'schneider declared'. Similarly, the announcement 'schwarz declared' adds one more factor (on top of schneider declared, that is, since a bid to take all ten tricks, worth 120 card points, takes as read the intention of making schneider).

It should be pointed out that if you *declare* schneider or schwarz, then you *must* make it in order to succeed in your game.

Finally, if you declare schwarz when playing a suit game then you may add a seventh factor by offering also to play *ouvert* – that is, with your hand of cards exposed on the table before the first trick is led. If you declare schwarz in a game at grand, however, you do not add the seventh factor but instead switch to the grand ouvert base value of 36, and multiply this by your matadors plus six game factors (game, hand, schneider, schneider declared, schwarz, schwarz declared).

Null games have fixed and invariable game values, namely:

null	23
null hand	35
null ouvert	46
null hand ouvert	59

The 23 and 46 nulls are played with the exchange of cards in the skat; the 46 and 59 are played with the soloist's hand of cards exposed on the table before the first trick is led.

In determining the prospective value of the game you are going to bid, bear in mind that many hands have more than one possibility. For instance, you may have one of two possible trump suits in mind, depending on what turns up in the skat, or you may be prepared to assume the extra value for making schneider only if you are forced into it by vigorous bidding from the other players. It is important to enter the bidding with a clear determination of the maximum value you are prepared to bid in any circumstances.

The auction and the play

Bidding. The player at dealer's immediate left, who has the advantage of eventually leading to the first trick, is known as *forehand*. The player on his left is *middlehand*, and on his left is *rearhand*. Rearhand does not enter the bidding until middle or forehand has passed.

Middlehand is first to speak. He may either pass, or start the auction by bidding '18', which is the lowest possible game value. If he bids, and forehand is also prepared to play a game worth 18 or more, forehand replies 'Yes'. Middlehand then continues the bidding by announcing the next higher possible game values in sequence, i.e. 20, 22, 23, 24, 27, 30, 33, 35, 36, 40, 44, 45, 46, 48, 50, etc. To each of these forehand replies 'yes' if he is prepared to play a game of equal or higher value, 'pass' if not. This continues until one of the two passes – either forehand, because middlehand has made a higher bid than forehand is prepared to match, or middlehand, because forehand has accepted his last bid and he dare not go higher.

As soon as either of them says 'pass', rearhand is in turn. If he cannot bid higher than the last named bid, he passes, leaving one survivor to become the soloist. If he can, he takes over the bidding from middlehand by announcing the next higher bid, to which the previous survivor replies 'yes' or 'pass', and so on, until one of them also passes.

When two players have passed, the third becomes the soloist, and must then play a game whose value, when completed, is not less than the last named bid.

If middle and rearhand both pass without starting the bid at 18, forehand has obviously 'won the bidding' and may become the soloist for a game of any value. If, however, he does not feel strong enough to do so, he may also pass. In this case no game is played (at least, not under the official rules): the cards are gathered up and the turn to deal passes to the left.

Announcing the game. If the soloist is playing an exchange game, he picks up the skat and adds it to his hand. He then discards any two cards face down and announces his game by stating which of the four suits is trump, or declaring 'grand' or 'null'. Nothing else need be said before play begins, but if he is playing null ouvert he now spreads his hand face up on the table.

TABLE 1: GAME VALUES AT SKAT

These are all the possible game values in orthodox German Skat and the bidding should be raised strictly in this order. Against each value is shown the suit or game and the number of multipliers applicable. G = grand, GO = grand ouvert.

18 ◇2	70 ♡7	144 ◇16 ♣12 G6
20 ♡2	72 ◇8 ♣6 G3	150 ♡15
22 ♠2	77 ♠7	153 ◇17
23 Null	80 ♡8	154 ♠14
24 ♣2	81 ◇9	153 ♣13
27 ◇3	84 ♣7	160 ♡16
30 ♡3	88 ♠8	162 ◇18
33 ♠3	90 ◇10 ♡9	165 ♠15
35 N. hand	96 ♣8 G4	168 ♣14 G7
36 ◇4 ♣3	99 ◇11 ♠9	170 ♡17
40 ♡4	100 ♡10	176 ♠16
44 ♠4	108 ◇12 ♣9	180 ♡18 ♣15
45 ◇5	110 ♡11 ♠10	187 ♠17
46 N. open	117 ◇13	192 ♣16 G8
48 ♣4 G2	120 ♡12 ♣10 G5	198 ♠18
50 ♡5	121 ♠11	204 ♣17
54 ◇6	126 ◇14	216 ♣18 G9
55 ♠5	130 ♡13	240 G10
59 N.H. open	132 ♠12 ♣11	252 GO7
60 ♡6 ♣5	135 ◇15	288 GO8
63 ◇7	140 ♡14	324 GO9
66 ♠6	143 ♠13	360 GO10

If the soloist is playing from the hand, he leaves the skat face down and announces his game plus the fact that he is playing it 'hand'. In addition to announcing the trump (except at null) he may add 'schneider declared' as a warning that he plans to capture 90+ card points, or 'schwarz declared' if he also determines to win all ten tricks, or 'ouvert' if he plans to take all ten tricks with his hand of cards exposed on the table before play begins.

Conceding. The soloist may concede defeat if he finds the skat unhelpful, or if a lead is made which makes his game unwinnable. He may concede at any time up to the end of the first trick, but not after a card has been led to the second. (This prevents him from escaping extra penalties should it become apparent during play that his opponents are not only going to beat him but indeed schneider him by taking 90+ card points between them.) He may, however, concede a null at any time. His opponents may not concede. (At least, there is little point in doing so, and the rules governing their concession are too complicated to be worth bothering about.)

The play. Forehand leads to the first trick, and the winner of each trick leads to the next. Suit must be followed if possible, otherwise any card may be played. (Note that where there is a trump suit the four Jacks belong to it and count as the four highest trumps. Thus the lead of *any* trump, whether Jack or lower, requires the following of any other trump, whether Jack or lower. At grand, the lead of a Jack calls for the play of a Jack, since they form a separate Jack suit of their own. Only at null do Jacks necessarily belong to the suits marked on their faces.) A trick is won by the highest card of the suit led, or by the highest trump if any are played.

Scoring a won game. The soloist wins if (a) he achieves his stated objective (the taking of 61+ card points, or 90+ if he declared schneider, or every trick if he declared schwarz or ouvert, or no trick if he bid null), *and* (b) the value of the game he has won is not less than the value at which he took the bidding. In either case he must again go through the procedure of evaluating his game, since he may in the event have won or lost more than originally envisaged.

For this purpose he again takes the base value of his trump

suit and multiplies it by the number of matadors he held plus the number of relevant game factors. As to matadors, he will now be assessing his hand not on the basis of the ten cards he was originally dealt but on the twelve formed by them plus the skat. For example, though he may originally have counted his game as 'with 1', holding the club, heart and diamond Jacks, the appearance of the spade Jack in the skat (whether he took the skat or played from hand) will complete the sequence, raising his matadors from one to four (or more, if he held more in sequence below the lowest Jack). In a suit game it is even theoretically possible for him to have been playing 'with 11', though at grand, of course, the maximum number is four.

By the same token, however, the appearance of a Jack in the skat may actually devalue his game. Had he been bidding 'without three', for instance, with the diamond Jack as his highest trump, and found the spade Jack in the skat, then his game must be revalued 'without 1'. This may seem unfair, especially if he played from the hand and could not know about the position of the spade Jack; but it is one of the features of the game which must be taken into account for successful play.

As to game factors, he may gain an extra multiplier by having schneidered his opponents, or two by having won all ten tricks.

If, taking all these factors into account, the value of his won game is not less than the amount he bid, the actual won value is added to his score. If not, the game is lost by devaluation.

Scoring a lost game. The value of a lost game is found in the same way as described above, except that it is further increased by one multiplier if the soloist himself is schneidered – that is, fails to take more than 30 card points. (Or even two factors in the extremely unlikely event of his taking no tricks at all.) If the value of the lost game is not less than the amount he bid, then he loses *double* his actual game value if he played with the exchange, or just the game if he played from the hand.

If his actual game value is less than the amount he bid, regardless of whether or not he achieved his stated objective, then he must add as many more multipliers as necessary to reach a value which is not less than his bid. This increased value is then lost singly if he played from hand, doubly if he played with the exchange.

Examples of scoring

Ex. 1: A game won. Soloist took the bidding at 23, took the skat, announced 'clubs', was 'with one', laid a Ten aside in his discard, and captured 82 card points in tricks. The 82 in tricks plus 10 in the skat gives him 92 and gains him an extra multiplier for 'schneider'. Game value: with 1, game 2, schneider 3, times clubs (12) = 36. This is more than he bid; he accordingly scores 36.

Ex. 2: Game lost by devaluation. Soloist took the bidding at 27, holding good clubs headed by the heart Jack, so that he was assuming himself to be 'without 2, game 3, times clubs (12) = 36'. He takes the skat and finds it contains the club Jack, so that his game is now only 'with 1, game 2, times clubs (12) = 24'. This is less than he bid, but rather than concede he continues play in the hope of winning schneider, which would give him the necessary extra multiplier to exceed the amount he bid. He plays, but fails to gain schneider. His loss is calculated as follows: 'With 1, game 2, times clubs (12) = 24, but bid 27, so next higher multiple of clubs is 36, lost double because took the exchange, total penalty = 72'. (Had he himself been schneidered, he would have counted 'With 1, game 2, lost schneider 3, times clubs (12) = 36, took the skat so lost double, score = minus 72'.)

Ex. 3: Lost game. Soloist took the bid at 59 holding a strong club hand headed by the club Jack, the Jacks of hearts and diamonds, and the Ten of clubs. He announced 'Clubs, hand, schneider declared', privately assessing his hand as 'With 1, game 2, hand 3, schneider 4, declared 5, times clubs (12) = 60'. Taking 82 card points in tricks, he turns the skat to find it contains the spade Jack and a worthless card. He has therefore failed to make schneider, although he declared it, and must lose his game value. This is recalculated as follows: 'With 4 (because the spade Jack in the skat completes the top sequence), game 5, hand 6, schneider declared 7, times clubs (12) = 84'. This is greater than the amount he bid and so need not be increased, nor is it lost double, because he played from the hand.

(If the skat had not contained the spade Jack, his game would be valued thus: 'With 1, game 2, hand 3, schneider declared 4, times clubs (12) = 48'. This is less than the 59 at which he took the bid, and would therefore have to be increased to 60 before being deducted from his score.)

Null games. A null game is won or lost without scoring complications, since it has one of the fixed values 23, 35, 46 or 59. A lost null, however, if played with the exchange, is lost double – i.e. a lost simple null loses 46, a lost ouvert 92.

The play of suit-trump games

As we have seen, three types of game may be played at Skat: those with a trump suit, those with only the four Jacks as trumps ('Grand'), and the trumpless Null games at which the object is to take no tricks. It will be easiest to discuss and illustrate them separately, starting with games 'in suit' as they are the commonest and most interesting.

To illustrate the rules of play and show that they are not as complicated as they sound, here is a sample deal. Remember that Forehand has the advantageous position of being the leader to the first trick, and that Middlehand is in second position and starts the bidding by raising against Forehand. In the hands below, the Jacks are listed separately because of their special position as more or less permanent trumps.

	Forehand	Middlehand	Rearhand	
J	♣	♠	♡ ◇	
♣	A K Q 7	T 9 8	*none*	
♠	T	9 7	A K	
♡	Q	K 8 7	A T 9	
◇	A K 7	9	T Q 8	*Skat* ♠Q, ♠8

Nobody, of course, knows the contents of the skat at this stage.

Forehand has an obvious suit game in clubs, worth ('with 1, game 2, times clubs (12) = 24'). It is also obviously not a hand that can be played as it stands – 'from the hand' – but needs the benefit of the two skat cards to improve its shape. A particular weakness is the singleton Ten in spades, which would almost certainly be captured by the Ace for a loss of 21 or more card points. By taking two skat cards and throwing two out, Forehand may hope to void the spade suit and either void or strengthen the hearts. He may possibly pick up another trump. Less probably, but conceivably, the skat may contain cards enabling him to change his game to Grand if he wins the auction. Two more Aces would do it, for example, or two Jacks, or a Jack and an Ace. This would raise his game value to 48; but the chances of making such an improvement are too slim to make it worth while bidding up to 48. For the time being, 24 is his maximum bid.

Middlehand's cards are useless for any game with trumps, but might it be worth considering a Null? For this purpose he mentally rearranges his cards with the spade Jack lying above the Nine and bears in mind that his Ten is not the second highest club but lies in sequence above the Nine. Null is now seen to be risky, if not foolhardy. He is safe in only two suits, namely hearts and spades. (No matter what is led in either of them, he can always get just under the highest played card of the trick and still be left with the lowest in play, as you can verify by experimentation.) He can be forced to take a trick in diamonds if one partner has the Seven and one the Eight. Or he will take one in clubs if the opponent with the Seven delays its lead until he knows that his partner has none (or none left) in the suit. One normally plays null from the hand if one is safe in all four suits or with the exchange if safe in three, hoping by means of the skat to either protect or throw out the vulnerable cards of the unsafe suit. Middlehand has only two safe suits and should therefore not bid.

Rearhand certainly has biddable cards – strong enough, in fact, to play from hand. His game factors are 'without 2, game 3, hand 4, times . . .' whatever he chooses as trumps. Not spades, as a four-trump hand is decidedly weaker than one of five trumps (counting the two Jacks, of course). It is often better to entrump a suit lacking the Ace and to save Ace-headed suits for on-the-side support, which in this case suggests a diamond game worth 36. On the other hand, hearts will yield a game of higher value – 40 – and makes for a markedly stronger trump holding because of the Ace, Ten lying in sequence with the Jacks. Looked at another way, the trumps he is playing *against* are 7, 8, Q, K and the top two Jacks. The opponents are bound to make the top Jacks, but they are only worth four card points, and all Rearhand has to be careful of is losing the Ace or Ten to them – anything else will be no great loss.

The strengths of this hand are –

1   Solid trumps – two Jacks and the Ace, Ten for a strong sequence of four.

2   A void suit (clubs). This is a desirable feature in any hand as it creates the possibility of trumping at least one and possibly both of its big cards. (If this can be done with the trump Ace the trick contains half one's target of card points!) Normally, one hopes to void a suit by discarding after taking the skat, as Forehand has in mind for his bid. If one has it already though, as dealt, the first thing to consider is the possibility of a hand game.

3   High cards in plain suits. The spade Ace is a certain trick worth at least 11, while in diamonds the Ace will probably appear early, together with the King, leaving Ten, Queen established for trick taking at the end of play when the trumps have been disposed of.

It does have a couple of weak points, or points that would be weak if the rest of the hand were not so strong. In spades, for example, the King is not a good accompaniment to the Ace. If the Ace is played without drawing the Ten (which is what normally happens), the King will fall to the Ten to give the opponents 14 card points, practically one quarter of their target – or even more, if the other opponent is then void in the suit and can drop an Ace or Ten on it. Since Rearhand cannot reasonably expect to save the King as a trick winner, he will be concerned to lose it as cheaply as possible, perhaps on a plain suit trick containing no other card points. For this reason an

Ace accompanied by a non-scoring card is a much better plain suit holding than an Ace with the King or Queen. The best result for the King would be to finesse it should the opportunity arise. For example, Rearhand could hope for an opening lead in spades and win it with the King if the Ten does not appear, whereupon he would immediately return the Ace in the hope of catching the Ten by now stripped of its support – bearing in mind that there are only seven cards in a plain suit so that they go round at most twice, and often only once, before being exhausted in one hand. However, the shortness of the suits also means that there is not usually so much scope for finessing in Skat as there is in other games such as Bridge.

The Ten-headed diamond suit could present problems. For example, a situation could arise in which Middlehand leads a low diamond, rendering the Ten unplayable in case it falls to the Ace, after which the same could happen, with the possibility of one opponent now trumping the suit. In short, there is a chance of losing the Ten if the opponents sense any embarrassment on Rearhand's part in respect of this suit.

Let us now suppose that Middlehand rather recklessly decides to go for his Null. He opens the bidding at 18, which Forehand accepts, then announces 20, 22, 23, also all accepted. Now he passes, as he should have done to start with. (The simplest Null is worth 23; he certainly cannot think of bidding it from the hand for 35 or of playing open after the exchange for 46.)

This brings Rearhand into the bidding. He continues with 24, which Forehand accepts, then 27, at which Forehand passes. Rearhand announces 'hearts, hand'. Note that he is pleased to win the auction below the true level of his hand, for there is a chance that one of the black Jacks is in the skat, in which case his hand is devalued to 'with (or without) 1, game 2, hand 3, times hearts (10) = 30'.

The play might begin as follows:

Trick 1   ◇A, ◇9, ◇8

How does Forehand choose his lead? Rule One for the opponents is 'never lead trumps against the soloist', to which we may add 'unless you know you are bound to win thereby' for the very rare circumstances in which the exception applies.

Rule Two, in Skat parlance, reads 'Long route, short suit: short route, long suit'. The route is 'long' when you are leading to a trick to which the soloist is playing last, 'short' when you are leading through the soloist and up to your partner. This is quite a handy general rule, and can be applied whenever you have no good reason for doing otherwise, or when in complete doubt. In this case Forehand is playing 'long' and leads from diamonds in preference to clubs. Why not spades, which is shorter still? The answer is that most players prefer not to lead a singleton Ten in such a position, as there is no way of telling who has the Ace. In this case, Forehand may reason as follows: 'My partner was bidding for null, since he stopped at 23, and therefore is more likely to have low cards than high ones. To play from the hand, Rearhand probably has a void suit. This is unlikely to be spades, since I only have one. He probably therefore has several spades headed by the Ace. I'll keep the Ten, in case he leads a low one, or in case my partner can trump spades later on'.

(It should be added that, in less clearcut cases, one might as well lead a singleton Ten on the grounds that if the soloist has the Ace, he will capture it anyway, sooner or later, whereas there is just as good a chance that one's partner has it. Indeed, the lead of a Ten to the first trick is in many circles accepted as a conventional signal, since such knowledge as may be imparted of each other's hand is usually of greater value to the partners than to the soloist.)

Having chosen diamonds because it is the shortest playable suit, Forehand plays the Ace because, if it is going to win a trick, it can only do so before the soloist has had a chance to void himself in the suit. And if he is void already, at least he will have spent a trump and the opponents will be better able to work out the lie of the cards.

Middlehand has no choice, and Rearhand obviously plays a card of no value. So the opponents have 11 to start with, and Forehand leads again.

Trick 2 ◇K, ♡K, ◇Q

In a hand game, the opponents normally switch suits whenever possible in order to clarify the situation – i.e. to probe for the soloist's weaknesses. In this case, however, Forehand can see that he is on to a good thing. His partner has no scoring diamond, or he would have played it to the first trick. This leaves the Ten and Queen, which lie either with the soloist or between him and the skat. Either way, another diamond lead enables his partner to trump with his highest valued heart. Rearhand is unlikely to be void in diamonds, since it is normal for the soloist to have at least two of a side suit if he has any at all.

Forehand is rather disappointed that his partner lacks the Ace or Ten with which to trump, but at least the lie of some key cards is clear, and the trick brings their takings so far to 22.

Now Middlehand is in the lead and has the advantage of the bidder on his left – never a comfortable position for the soloist.

Trick 3 ♣8, ♡A, ♣7

A disappointment for the bidder, as the ideal circumstance in which to trump a lead in your void suit is when playing third to the lead of Ace followed by Ten! Trumping the lead of a worthless card is something of an anticlimax. However, his choices are to throw the ♠K away to it or seize the initiative with a trump. He opts for the latter course, and, naturally, takes it with his highest valued card, giving him 11 so far (plus whatever may lie in the skat, which is as yet unknown).

Trick 4 ◇J, ♡Q, ♠J

Just as the opponents should normally never lead trumps against the soloist, so the soloist should almost invariably do so against the partners, thereby drawing two of their already fewer trumps for every one of his own. His object is to force the upper Jacks out, leaving him in command of the suit so as to eventually play it out and score with a diamond Ten lead. It is obvious that his trump Nine is too low to serve this forcing purpose, while the Ten is too valuable to risk; hence the red Jack.

His left opponent (whom we must now refer to as 'originally Forehand' since he no longer has the lead) does not want to waste his top Jack on it, preferring to save this until his partner is void of trumps and can throw a valuable card on it. He therefore drops the Queen, and is pleased when his partner takes it with the spade Jack – partly because it brings their count up to 29 (nearly out of schneider) but chiefly because he thereby achieves the lead and puts the soloist in the weakest position, i.e. playing second to the trick.

Trick 5   ♠7, ♠A, ♠T

Now the leader (originally Middlehand) is following the principle of switching suits against a hand contract: spades is the only one not yet played. Unfortunately, the soloist captures with the Ace instead of finessing the King as he might have done (at some damage to himself), and thereby wins the singleton Ten, bringing his count up to 32.

A club lead would have been safer here, for although the soloist is known to be void and may trump, the leader can hardly expect his partner to be forced to throw the Ace to it. The soloist would be undecided whether or not to trump, and the remaining partner can play high or low as he sees fit. (With careful play, this variant nets the opponents 56 card points, and should in principle have been enough to win but for the unfortunate distribution whereby the trump Eight and spade Ten prove to be in the wrong hands.)

Trick 6   ♡9, ♣J, ♡7

The soloist continues to draw trumps, giving the opponents a trick worth 2 card points, which is just enough to get them out of schneider. The rest is academic: if clubs are led, soloist trumps in, draws the last outstanding trump, and wins the last two with his King and Ten leads. If diamond, he has no qualms about throwing the Ten to the second player's inspired trump, as it only gives them 10 more and he wins the rest in the same way as before.

At the end of play, the soloist turns the skat to discover two spades worth a total of 3 card points. Had he taken the exchange, he might have discarded the King and Queen of spades.

He calculates his score as he did for the bidding: 'without 2, game 3, hand 4, times hearts (10) = 40'. This being not less than the amount he bid (27) he adds the 40 to his running total. Had the opponents failed to reach 31, the soloist would have added another multiplier ('. . . hand 4, schneider 5, times hearts (10) = 50'). Had the skat contained one black Jack, his game would have been worth less ('with or without 1' instead of 'without 2'); had it contained both, he would have been 'with 6' and scored considerably more.

Before looking at Grand and Null games, it may be useful to make some general points on bidding and play.

Bidding. Decide on your maximum safe bid and do not be forced beyond it. In particular, do not hesitate before making or accepting the next higher bid, or your opponents will be able to form some idea of what you are bidding on. Always bid in correct values and in sequence, i.e. do not bid meaningless values such as 19, 21 etc. and do not miss any out. For one thing, if you win the auction, you want to do so as cheaply as possible so as to give yourself more choice of possible games when taking the skat, and also in case of 'busting' by picking up a Jack and devaluing your hand. For another, the point at which you cease bidding gives some indication of your strength (e.g. stopping at 22 suggests that you are well off in spades and are with or without one Jack; 23 suggests that you have predominantly low cards, etc.). This information is usually of more value to your partner than to the soloist.

Assessing the hand. A good hand for a suit game is one containing five or more trumps including three of the top six (Jacks, Ace, Ten), a void in one of the plain suits, and at least one plain suit Ace. If all this is dealt, consider playing from the hand. Otherwise, bid an exchange game if you think the taking and discarding of two cards should enable such a hand to be formed. If you are Forehand the requirements may be slightly less, since the opening lead is in itself as good as an Ace or a trump; if Middlehand, they should be slightly greater, as this is the worst position for the first trick especially if you have a weak plain suit such as one of three or more or one headed by the Ten. A hand containing a singleton Ten, or lacking both Ace and Ten of trumps, is rarely strong enough to play without taking the skat, though three or more Jacks may compensate. Remember that in an exchange game you do not announce, and therefore need not choose your trump suit until you have taken the skat. Some hands as dealt may contain two, three or even all four prospective trump suits. Be wary when bidding *without* two or more matadors, as you may be tempted into a high bid, turn up a Jack in the skat, and find yourself 'bust' – e.g. 'with 1' instead of 'without 3'.

There are other ways of looking at a hand as well as a simple count of trumps and Aces. Bearing in mind that your object is to capture over 60 card points, consider how many of the big cards (Aces and Tens) you hold and can win, or do not hold and may be able to capture, or may tuck for safety into the skat. Obviously, six of the eight big cards will be enough to win; with five, you can usually reckon on taking enough courts to bring you up to the mark. You can rarely expect to take enough points if you only finish up with four of the big ones, while three only is hopeless.

Consider, too, how many of your cards are probable trick losers, and calculate roughly how many card points the opponents will be able to pile on to the tricks they fall to. It is *possible* for the soloist to make his game with only two tricks, but equally possible for him to take eight and lose it. Many games are won on four or five tricks, but some lost on six.

Taking the skat. Taking the skat increases your hand to twelve cards, from which you can now determine a suitable trump suit and shape the rest of the hand to support it. With two prospective trumps of equal length it is usually wise to keep the stronger as support, especially if it contains an Ace, and to entrump the weaker. The discard presents you with two objectives: one, to void at least one suit if possible, the other, to tuck away any scoring cards that might otherwise be captured, especially Tens. An ideal discard is often a two card suit headed by the Ten, provided that the remaining plain suits are sound, as it is rarely certain that the Ten can be made, especially if you are Middlehand to the first trick. If you cannot void a weak suit – say K, 9, 7 – then keep the whole of it and find your discards elsewhere. Do not feel obliged to discard two from the same suit. Two Tens is often a good discard, particularly from long suits (three or more) where there is a danger of losing them in tricks.

The discovery of a Jack and/or Ace in the skat may convert the hand from a suit trump to a possible Grand, the requirements for which are considered later; obviously, it is important to be alive to this possibility (such chances have been missed!). Exceptionally, the turn of Sevens or other low cards may provide a Null or even a valuable Null ouvert for 46.

As we have seen, the discovery of a Jack may also 'bust' a hand which appeared to be 'without' two or more when you were bidding it. If the hand is unplayable, announce the cheapest game you can legally lose and give it up gracefully. For instance, if you were bidding on 'without 2, game 3, times diamonds (9) = 27, won the auction at 22, and found either of the black Jacks in the skat, your game would be reduced to 18. If you declare diamonds conceded, your loss must be raised to the next multiple of nine and then doubled (down 54 points). Since you bid 22, however, you may declare spades conceded (even if you have none in hand) and lose only 44. Had you taken the bidding at 23, you could equally legally declare and concede the null for a loss of 46.

But do not automatically assume that a bust hand is unplayable. You may be able to justify the amount you bid by entrumping a slightly weaker but higher valued suit, or the extra

Jack gained from the skat may give you sufficient strength to play for schneider and so increase the value of your game.

The soloist's play. It is usually wrong to follow the beginners' practice of leading Aces and Ace-Tens first. This (known in Skat parlance as 'visiting the villages') tends to capture worthless cards and leave the partners in command of the suits when the trumps eventually get played out. The average playable hand is best played by leading trumps as soon and as often as possible, so as to draw two of the partners' for each of one's own and rapidly reach a point at which only you, as soloist, have any left. Since it is not in their interest to lead trumps against you, they are bound to lead plain suits, thus leaving you in the usually happy position of heading or trumping tricks that are worth having (any trick worth 10 or more card points is worth having), or using worthless tricks as a dump for cards of low or no value, or as a means of voiding a plain suit. In particular, you will want to be the last to play to a trick in a suit of which you hold just Ace, King – with a chance of finessing the King – or a guarded Ten, so as to either make the Ten or throw the guard to the Ace.

Only on the rare occasions that you find yourself, after an awkward skat, with a four-card trump suit, may it be worth while to lead your Aces first, though even then the fact of doing so may warn the partners of your trump weakness, which they can then exploit by leading them against you.

With the average five-card trump holding, you can normally play on the assumption that the other six trumps are split three-three. Your first task, usually, is to try to force out any Jacks, for which purpose it is best to lead them rather than worthless low ones. A frequent opening lead by the soloist is a red Jack. It often happens that Middlehand plays a higher Jack to enable his partner to drop the Ace or Ten of trumps if he has it. This makes everybody happy: the partners because they have saved their big trump and can gauge the soloist's strength to some extent, and the soloist because he has drawn two trumps including a Jack and is now lying third to the next trick – which is a much better position than second.

With both black Jacks you can often start at the top and find that one opponent drops a Jack in order to retain his Ace or Ten. With the top three, an obvious ploy is to lead the heart: Middlehand, if he has Ace or Ten and no Jacks, will often drop it in the hope that his partner has one of the top two.

A common pattern of play from the soloist's viewpoint is to lead 'high, low, high' – for example, club Jack, then a worthless trump, and then (when next able to lead) spade Jack. This is to guard against the situation in which adverse trumps may be split four to two, for at the third trump lead, the player originally with two will now be void in trumps and can drop an Ace or Ten if his partner wins the trump trick. Generally, it is not a bad policy for the soloist to always aim to win the third trump lead, even if it means losing the first or second for this purpose.

Similar patterns of play apply to a six-card trump holding, but beware: a six trump hand is more treacherous than one of five trumps, and is often lost, much to the soloist's surprise. The reason for this is that the outstanding trumps, being five in number, cannot be evenly split, and there is a stronger chance that one opponent holds originally only one trump. This may enable his partner to win two or three of the trump tricks, on which he can drop high counting cards from other suits.

With seven or more trumps one's power is great and the appropriate leads should be obvious.

When using trumps to win plain suit leads in which you are void, it is natural and usually right to do so with the Ace or Ten first in order to secure their value, especially if the trick already contains another big card. But don't be too automatic about this, especially if you hold the Ace and the Ten lies with one of the partners. Sometimes it is better to keep the Ace as a threat over the Ten.

Finally, what should go without saying: remember that there are eleven trumps (one third of the cards in play, as opposed to Bridge, etc. in which they constitute only one quarter), and keep careful track of which ones are out against you and who probably holds them. Remember too that there are seven in each plain suit, which means that they may certainly go round once, usually twice, but only rarely three times before one player is in a position to trump or discard to the lead. Above all, keep careful count of the card points accumulated by the opponents (as well as your own): if they reach 50, you can rarely afford to lose another trick; if they are under 31, try to keep them that way for schneider.

Partner's play. Although each person plays for himself in the long run, there are few games in which so great importance attaches to good, even brilliant, partnership play between the soloist's two adversaries. It is frequently and truly observed that more games are won by the soloist through mistakes in the opposing side than through cleverness on his own. 'Well I, certainly didn't expect to make that!' is an all-too-common cry on the part of more loquacious and indiscreet players.

Yet it is more difficult to analyse what constitutes brilliance on the partners' part in any specific detail, beyond the obvious observation that it depends on calculating, judging or simply divining what one's partner holds and intends from the way he leads or discards.

Two important points can be made from the outset. First, Skat is a game of card points, not just tricks. Therefore, you not only try to win tricks with your highest counting cards, but also throw high counting cards to tricks being won (or, at some points, hopefully being won) by your partner. (This is known in German as *swarming* on a trick, or *fattening* it. American players call it *smearing*, from *schmieren* 'to fatten'. A suitable, good old English word for it might be *stuffing* the trick. Take your choice.) Another way for the partners to take advantage of the card point nature of the game is for them to lead middling cards in a suit of which the soloist has none. Especially if playing second to the trick, and even when third, the soloist can be put into considerable difficulty in deciding whether to use up a trump to capture a few card points, or to discard (say) a King or Queen to it himself for the sake of tying up loose ends in his hand.

The other important point for the partners to watch is that of position. 'Put the soloist in the middle' – playing second to the trick – is always a good maxim, particularly if the lead can then be made through him in a suit of which he has none. It is often even worth overtaking your partner's Jack with a higher one for the sake of achieving this arrangement. It is, of course, absolutely essential for the partners to remember how the soloist has acted or responded in each suit, and in which ones he is certainly or probably void.

Grand

Grand is the Skat equivalent of a no trump game, in the sense that all four seven-card suits are equal. This still leaves the four Jacks as trumps in their usual order from club through spade, heart and diamond.

Success at Grand usually requires the winning of at least six and preferably seven tricks, which in turn means that all four suits should normally be strong in the soloist's hand. It is also obvious that the more Jacks held, the better. But the power of Jacks can be over-estimated, since it is perfectly easy to play 'with four' and lose a Grand, while other distributions enable a Grand 'without four' to be played with complete safety. Jacks serve two main purposes. The offensive one is to draw or force out the partners' Jacks so that the strong plain suits can be played without danger of being trumped. The defensive purpose is to enable the soloist to trump in to the lead if and when he has a void suit – preferably, of course, with the simultaneous capture of a high counting Ace or Ten.

The American Skat expert Joe Wergin has devised a neat method of assessing a Grand hand, which, used properly, I have never known to fail. It draws attention to nine power factors, namely the four Jacks, the four Aces, and the opening lead (i.e. being Forehand). If you have at least five of these, and can win a probable seven tricks, you can play Grand from the hand. From which it follows that you can think about playing Grand with the skat if you have less than this but stand a chance of converting to such a hand after the discard – something like four power factors and six tricks, for example, or a hand with a singleton Ten and just the two red Jacks.

A Grand from the hand may be well balanced as between the four suits, such as:

J ♣ ◇
♣ A
♠ T K
♡ A K Q
◇ A 7

... which, with two Jacks, three Aces, a guarded Ten and six certain, seven possible tricks (depending on whether the outstanding Jacks are divided or in one hand) can be played from any position.

Or it may derive its strength from a long suit accompanied by Jacks and voids, for which purpose you need to be Forehand unless you have particularly strong trumps:

J ♡ ◇
♣ A T Q 9 8 7
♠ A K
♡ none
◇ none

As Forehand, you would play this by leading clubs from the Ace down. This forces the partners to trump with the outstanding Jacks. Each time they do so, you trump their next lead (or head it, if in spades) and play clubs again. They cannot trump more than twice, leaving you with at least seven tricks: the two Jacks, the four low clubs and the spade Ace. Don't worry about leading the Ace and Ten of clubs, as the partners cannot take enough card points to win. High cards *must* be led to tempt the Jacks out. If you lead low clubs, they will throw worthless cards to them and save all their big ones to throw in a lump when their inevitable tricks come round.

Replace the spade King with a third Jack, and such a long suit Grand can be played from any position. You can spend a trump to gain the lead, thus putting you in a similar position to that described above, then lead another to force the odd Jack out, and can still trump in to play off the long suit later.

Grand with the skat may be bid on such a hand as this (dealt to Forehand and therefore offering the opening lead as a power factor):

J ♣ ♠
♣ 9 8 7
♠ T
♡ A T K
♢ A

This has five factors but offers only six tricks and has a number of weaknesses, notably the clubs and singleton Ten. Taking the skat enables you to discard that Ten (unless the skat covers it with the Ace) in company with a King or Queen if the skat contains one. The low clubs are unimportant, as they add nothing to the partners' score when captured.

A Grand 'without 4' can be essayed on the following pattern:

J *none*
♣ A K 7
♠ A T
♡ A 9 7
♢ A T

The skat is needed, not to improve the shape of the hand but to enable two Tens to be laid aside for 20 card points. If all four Aces win, the game is certain; if only three, you still have 53 card points and may make up the rest in any of several different ways. It can be played from any position since any suit led puts you in the lead, which is as good as being Forehand in the first place. Of course, it can be lost, depending on the distribution, but that is no reason to pass up the opportunity.

The soloist's usual object at Grand is to draw the teeth of his opponents' trumps and win tricks with Ace-Tens in several suits or by means of one or two exceptionally long suits. The partners should try to fight fire with fire by leading Aces then Tens in order to weaken the soloist's trumps, and looking for his void suit so that repeated leads made from it will put him in a quandary, especially if he is playing second to such tricks. Not to be recommended are opening leads of a singleton with a view to trumping returns in that suit, and of Jacks unless there is particular reason to think this will be effective. If, for example, a partner has both black Jacks and the opening lead he should certainly not hesitate to lead them. The lead of a low Jack may be effective if it is fairly certain that the soloist has three, but not if there is some chance that the partner has one – a point which emphasises how important it is to listen carefully to the process of bidding and try to deduce how many Jacks each player is bidding with or without.

Null

The null bids, completely out of accord with the card point character of Skat, are exactly like misère bids in any ordinary trick taking game such as Solo or Nap. All you need to know, therefore, is that a void suit is good and any other suit should be based on 7, 8 or 7, 9. A suit consisting of singleton Eight is acceptable, especially if you have the lead and can get rid of it immediately. Some sample deals:

	Null hand ouvert (59)	Null hand (35)	Null (23)
♣	K J 9 7	K J 9 7	K J 9 7
♠	T 9 7	A K 8 7	K 9 7
♡	8 7	8 7	8 7
◇	8	*none*	9

The first of these is virtually unbeatable and should therefore be played from the hand with cards exposed. If the soloist is Forehand he must lead the diamond Eight to get it out of the way. He would only win the trick and lose the game if one of the partners were void and the other played the Seven, a so improbable occurrence as to be not worth bothering about. Thereafter, no matter what is led, he can always play just under the highest card so far played to the trick, so as never to leave one opponent with the lowest card of a suit – except diamonds, in which the soloist is even lower by virtue of being void.

If the soloist is not Forehand an element of risk enters into the play. Theoretically, the partners can so play in the other suits as to enable the one who does *not* have ◇7 to get rid of his

FIGURE 11

A good game in Clubs, playable from the hand (leaving the skat face down). Lead low Clubs, which will give the opponents no more than seven card-points for the King and Queen; subsequently play out the Jacks, as the Ace and Ten of trumps would thereby be left vunerable to subsequent capture by the other Jacks.

diamonds, whereupon the other leads the Seven and ends the game. The soloist, however, will discard the offending Eight as soon as one of the other suits is played out and another lead made in it. Whether or not the opponents can defeat the contract depends on the right distribution, over which they have no control, and brilliant team play, which cannot always be relied upon. Ignorance of the contents of the skat (this being played from the hand, remember) is very much to their disadvantage.

The second hand is perfectly safe in three suits but chancy in spades. It can be beaten if (a) one partner holds three of the outstanding cards 9, T, J, Q and (b) has the opportunity and perspicacity to lead them before the soloist has dumped his Ace and King on other tricks (such as a diamond lead). As this is unlikely, these cards can be played from the hand for 35. They cannot be played ouvert, though, for if one opponent *does* have three of the treacherous spades he and his partner will so manage the play as to allow them to be led.

The third hand is safe in clubs and hearts, but holds two risk cards in the shape of the King and the singleton Nine. Three spade leads will fetch the King out, and the Nine loses if the Eight and Seven are split instead of in one hand. The soloist must take the skat with a view to hiding away both bad cards. Even then, two red cards or one black and a high red in the skat may make the attempt impossible. On the other hand, two clubs or low spades would enable it to be played ouvert for 46.

Whenever the soloist can follow suit, he should do so with the highest card possible which is nevertheless lower than the highest one so far played to the trick. When unable to follow, he must discard whichever of his remaining cards is most in danger of being forced to take a trick.

If an opponent holds the lowest in play of its suit, he should not lead it until he is sure that his partner has none left and will not be forced to take it. Most nulls are lost because the soloist is forced to take a trick on the third or fourth round when one of the partners has become void in the suit and the other leads the lowest. The partners' broad strategy, therefore, is to void their short suits. The opening lead may therefore be made with a singleton, to create an immediate void in one's own hand, or from a very long suit, to enable one's partner (who presumably has but few) to void himself.

Null is a far more interesting and challenging game for the partners to play than the soloist, and it is probably in partnership against a null contract that the true test of a Skat player's 'card sense' resides.

Unofficial Skat

Rather like Poker, Skat is not so much a definite game as a basic theme on which many variations may be played. The form described above is the only one sanctioned by the German Skat Federation, whose adherents may be commended for the self-discipline they exercise in sticking to the rules themselves, while laying themselves open to criticism for the way they try and ram 'pure' Skat down everyone else's throats, combined with ridicule for their supposed justification of it by reference to such irrelevances as logic, consistency, elegance and so on. The sub-game called Ramsch, for example (described below), is very widely played, and clearly belongs to the Skat scheme of things to the extent that the four Jacks are trumps and cards rank in their normal Skat order with their normal Skat values. Yet it is denigrated as 'not Skat' by those very purists who unquestioningly accept Null into the Skat canon, even though Null was stolen from Whist and bears no relation to the true genius of Skat.

The following variant games and rules may be encountered in everyday home play (as opposed to highly organised clubs who follow the official rules), presented in approximate order of frequency. It should be noted that not more than one or two of them are to be found at any one time in the same circle of players.

Grand worth 20. Grand was widely valued at 20 instead of 24 until the Federation decided on the latter in 1928. Many older players still prefer it. Having tried both for some time, I must say I prefer 20 myself. The argument against 24 is that it is too great a jump from the 12 for clubs and that it attaches too great

FIGURE 12

This hand (held by Forehand) is 'without three' (lacking the three top Jacks), but it would be dangerous to bid up to 44 in Spades or 48 in Clubs for fear of drawing another Jack. Having, let us assume, won the bidding at a lower figure, you now take the skat and find in it ♡J—which puts an entirely different complexion on the matter. Now the hand is good for a bid of Grand (only Jacks as trumps), and will be worth 'without 2, game 3, times Clubs (12) = 36'. Discard the low Hearts and avoid leading Jacks, which would almost certainly result in a loss of all ten tricks. (The hand is not suitable for Grand if held by Middle- or Rearhand as it requires the opening lead to be effective.)

a value and importance to a game which is actually less interesting to play than one in suit. The argument for 24 is that the minimum Grand bid, at 48, overcalls a player with low cards who is prepared to take a chance on the risky 46 of a Null ouvert. With Grand at 20, the lowest game is worth 40, which is then overcalled by the Null ouvert. I suppose this carries weight in circles whose members are inclined to take such chances (Null ouvert being rarely a sensible bid), though another way of overcoming it – also to be encountered in practice – is to permit Nulls to be played only from the hand (35 and 59), which I must say has much to commend it.

Ramsch. Ramsch, originally a related but distinct game in its own right, is often played automatically when all three players pass without making a bid. There are several varieties of Ramsch, which all have in common that each person plays for himself, with no element of partnership. Only the Jacks are trumps, so the game is played with the same mechanics as Grand.

In *Simple Ramsch,* the skat remains face down until the end of play, when it is added to the cards taken by the winner of the last trick. The object is to avoid taking card points, or rather to take as few as possible. Whoever takes most is the loser, and deducts 10 from his score. If one opponent takes no tricks, the loser deducts 15; if neither opponent takes a trick, the deduction is 20. If two tie for most they lose 5 each; if all three take 40 each there is no penalty.

In *Point Ramsch* the mechanics of play are the same, but the loser deducts from his score the actual number of card points he takes in tricks, unless he succeeds in taking all ten, when he adds 120 to his score instead. If two tie for most, they each lose that number; if three, there is no penalty.

The variant known as *Shove Ramsch (Schieberramsch)* introduces an intriguing complication. Forehand takes the skat into his hand, passes any two cards face down to Middlehand, who in turn passes any two to Rearhand, who completes the sequence by discarding two to form a new skat, which again goes to the winner of the last trick. As in Point Ramsch, the player who takes most card points deducts that number from his score. Many players insist that it is illegal to pass on Jacks in the preliminary round of 'shoving', but I cannot see the point of this and in my circle we ignore it. An additional feature is that if any player takes and passes on the skat, or two cards from the previous player, without looking at it or changing his dealt hand in any way, he thereby automatically doubles the penalty lost by the loser of the game. If two do so, the penalty is thus quadrupled; if all three, it is octupled!

Middle Ramsch is, so far as I know, now never played (except in my circle), but it has the distinction of finishing with a plus score to the winner rather than a minus score to the loser. The skat is taken and shoved around as described above, but the object of the game is to take the middling number of card points. For example, if one player takes 21, another 35 and the third 64, the one with 35 scores 35. In practice this means that the object of the game is to capture as close to 40 as possible – with 40, you cannot lose: the result at worst is a tie. In my circle the following refinements apply: if two players tie, the third wins and scores what he takes. (If he took none, hard luck!); if all three tie, the winner of the last trick wins the 40 points in question. (A game based on this idea is played in Switzerland under the title *Mittlere*, of which a description is to be found in the 1982 edition of my *Penguin Book of Card Games*.)

Whatever form of Ramsch is played, it may be instigated not only when all players pass but also for a complete round after an 'agreed event'. For example, it may be agreed that any bid lost 60/60 is automatically followed by an entire round of Ramsch, i.e. Ramsch is played automatically on the next three or four deals, depending on the number of players. However, this is often combined with the proviso that it can be overcalled by any player offering to play 'Grand, hand' instead.

Kontra (*Doubling*). As soon as the soloist announces his game, either opponent may announce 'Double' (*Kontra*, in German). In this event the soloist's score if he wins, or penalty if he loses, is doubled. The soloist, in turn, may 'Redouble (*Re-kontra*) if he is confident of winning, in which case the appropriate score or penalty is quadrupled.

In some circles, a player may not double unless he made or accepted at least one bid during the auction, which stikes me as a sensible rule. In others, or even the same ones, the opponents are required to win at least 61 card points if they double, and the soloist to win at least 61 if he redoubles. This strikes me as logically defensible but hardly worth the trouble of remembering.

I once heard of a Berliner Skat circle in which a soloist could double *himself* by announcing 'Erklärt' – e.g. he might say 'Clubs, hand, declared'. This strikes me as rather amusing, but eminently dispensable.

Bock. This is a round of play – three or four deals, depending on the number of players – in which each score is automatically doubled before being added to or subtracted from the soloist's total. Like a round of Ramsch as described above, this follows an 'agreed event', such as a Grand bid made and lost, or one player making exactly (or at least) 100 points on the previous deal. If the same event occurs during a bock round, another such round is instigated when the first one is over – or, more drastically, bocks may be run concurrently rather than consecutively, so that it is theoretically possible to be in double, triple or even quadruple bock, and then be doubled and redoubled on top of it! Quite ridiculous, of course.

Hand lost double. In some circles a hand game is lost double, just as an exchange game is. For once I am in agreement with the Skat Federation purists – it is a silly rule and should be stoutly resisted.

Playing ouvert. In some circles any hand bid can be bid and played *ouvert* (with one's hand of cards exposed on the table) without at the same time declaring schwarz or even schneider, an extra multiplier being added to the score for this feat. Thus one may bid 'Clubs, hand, ouvert' and be counting to oneself 'With 1, game 2, hand 3, ouvert 4, times clubs (12) = 48'. I see no objection to this variant, and can confirm from experience that it makes for an interesting game which is by no means a foregone conclusion.

With a spit (Mit Spitze). The 'spit' is the lowest trump. In some circles the soloist increases the value of his game by one multiplier (whether won or lost) if he wins the last trick with the lowest trump – i.e. the Seven in a suit game, or the diamond Jack at Grand. A better variant is that the spit only counts if it is bid, in which case it *must* be made in order to win the game (rather like schneider declared). For example, one may announce 'Clubs, with the spit', counting one's bid as 'With 1, game 2, spit 3, times clubs (12) = 36'. Less commendable are these variants: (a) one multiplier for winning the last trick with the spit, even if not declared, and another for having declared it as well; and (b) bidding two or more spits – e.g. 'with two spits' is a bid to win the last trick with the lowest trump and the second to last with the second lowest, and so on.

It should be noted that when the spit is bid, it must be made in order to win the game, and the game must also be won with the usual 61 or more card points. A spit bid can, of course, be added to a bid of schneider or schwarz declared for all the extra rewards this may bring.

Spitzengrand. This is a really fascinating bid which ought to be more widely known than it is, especially as it is more in keeping with the spirit of Skat than the vaguely similar bid of Null. At spitzengrand, the four Jacks are trumps and the four suits are equal, all cards having their normal point values as at Grand. The difference is that in each suit the trick-taking order of cards is reversed: the Seven, though worth no points, is the highest ranking card in each suit, and the Ace, worth 11, the lowest! The Jacks are also reversed, with diamond highest and club lowest, but this is merely for the sake of consistency and makes no difference to the play or management of trumps. (In some circles there is the additional requirement that the last trick be won with the diamond Jack, but this is a needless adornment.)

To bid spitzengrand safely, your plain suits must look like

Null patterns (Sevens and Eights rather than Aces) and your Jack holdings like strong Grands. For example:

J	◇	♠
♣	7	8	Q
♠	8	9
♡	7
◇	7	A

Given the lead, you would play this from the hand, allowing the Ace to be lost. If the bidding leads you to feel the Jacks are divided, you might lead the diamond Jack to force them out. Otherwise (or after so doing) you lead spades in the hope of forcing out the Seven and so leaving you in command of all suits. Alternatively, you may start by leading your long suit (clubs), drawing (say) Nine, King on the first round, Ten, Ace on the second (if lucky), and either making a third trick with the Queen or using her to force out an adverse Jack.

From any other position you might prefer to take the skat and tuck away the diamond Ace.

The official base value of this unofficial bid is 16, so the hand above is counted thus: 'Without 1, game 2, hand 3, times spitzengrand (16) = 48' (note that Jacks are counted from the club end, as in the orthodox bids, even though the club Jack is the lowest ranking). The value 16 is suitable if combined with the rule that the last trick must be taken with the diamond Jack; otherwise, however, it is too high. In my circle we value spitzengrand at 13 so that it just overcalls clubs, and this seems to be about right for it.

Nullogrand. This comes from an old book and I have not encountered it in practice. It is a Null game to the extent that the soloist's object is to win not a single trick, but it is played with the Jacks as trumps and four plain suits of equal value ranking in their normal (Grand) order. It has the normal null values of 23, or 35 from hand, 46 ouvert, 59 hand ouvert. It is self-evidently a purer form of Null than the one preferred by the German Skat Federation. However, because it requires much the same type of pattern in the hand, it is not sensible to adopt both Nullogrand and Spitzengrand into the same game.

Tournee. This interesting bid, midway in difficulty between an exchange game and a hand game, used to be an integral part of German Skat but has since dropped out. (In American Skat, however, it still remains, the simple exchange game having been dropped instead.) In my circle, we play German Skat with tournee as an additional bid having its own special score. This is how it is played. The highest bidder, having become the soloist, takes either card of the skat and looks at it. If he is prepared to accept its suit as trump, he shows the card and adds it and the other skat card to his hand, rejecting two and then playing as if it were an ordinary exchange game. If he does not like the first card, he adds it to his hand without showing it, and must then turn and accept the suit of the second skat card as his trump, again playing as if it were a simple exchange game. If the turned card is a Jack, he may either accept its suit as trump or else play Grand.

In order to graft this on to the German game we have given it a base score of 13, regardless of the suit actually turned as trump, so that a tournee with or without so many matadors outbids an exchange game of the same number but is worth less than the equivalent hand game. If a Jack is turned and Grand is played, the value is 20 instead of 13. In the event of a tournee being lost by the soloist, the game value is lost doubled if he chose the second turned card as trump, but only singly if he chose the first. Remember, if playing this way, to add extra values to the bidding sequence, i.e. 26, 39, 52, 65, 78, 91, etc.

A hand is biddable at tournee level if it shows at least two Jacks, preferably including a black one, and offers at least two suits as playable trumps. A particularly good tournee candidate is what the Germans call 'rollmops' – a hand with two Jacks and two cards in each suit – provided that it shows enough high cards to enable you to finish up with the necessary five in tricks and skat.

Uno. This comes from the same old book as above. It is a bid to take exactly one trick – neither more nor fewer – and is played as at Grand (Jacks trump). The quoted game value of 100 after the exchange is far too high for the skill involved. In my circle we have a scale of fixed values for it comparable with those of null, namely: uno simple (after the exchange) 31, uno hand 51, uno ouvert 71, uno hand ouvert 91. Of course, it is out of keeping with the card point character of Skat, but so is Null, and at least Uno is played with cards ranking in proper Skat order. (A bid of duo, in which the object is to win exactly two tricks, is, however, undoubtedly going too far!)

Freak hand – without 11

Skat must be the only game ever devised in which it is theoretically possible to announce a trump suit of which one does not hold a single card in the hand and yet win it! Here is a deliberately concocted freak hand in which the soloist, as Forehand, picks up the skat and discovers the possibility. His twelve cards are:

J	*none*		
♣	*none*		
♠	A	9	8	7
♡	A	T	8	7
◇	A	T	8	7

He discards the two red Aces for 22, announces clubs trump, then leads the top card of each suit. If, by good fortune, the three outstanding cards of each suit are divided 2–1 between the opponents instead of being all in one hand, he is bound to make, in addition to his Ace and Tens for 31, at least seven card points in spades and three each in the red suits, giving him the game with a total of 66 card points. His game value is then 'Without 11, game 12, times clubs (12) = 144'.

It may be mentioned, for completeness, that Grands 'without 4' are not uncommonly bid and made, but suit games without more than five are rare and tend to be lost.

TYZICHA

This delightful game was first published in *Games & Puzzles*, and attributed to the Ukraine. The format seems unremarkable at first sight. The highest bidder becomes contractor, and endeavours to make as many points as he bid in the play of eight tricks from the very short 24-card pack. Points are scored not for tricks themselves but for honours (certain designated scoring cards) contained within them, and for the particular suit or suits established as trumps.

Its most original feature for a bidding game lies in the way trumps are made. Play starts off at No Trump, but during the course of the round any player can make or remake trumps by leading either card from a King/Queen holding in the nominated suit. This is the feature that gives the game its point. Its repercussions are most intriguing.

It would be difficult to single out an ancestor to Tyzicha, but it certainly belongs to the central European tradition. The establishment of trumps through the holding of a marriage – i.e. King and Queen of the same suit – will already be known to anyone who has played Pip-Pip. The marriage combination itself is common to many games, such as Bézique and members of the Stops family.

Tyzicha, pronounced *tizzy*-cha, is short for tyzicha-odin, which is Russian for one thousand and one, the target score to which game is usually played. The transliteration, I am told, is not exact; but fortunately that does not affect the enjoyment of the game.

Preliminaries

Cards. Twenty-four, rejecting 2, 3, 4, 5, 6, 7, 8.

Ranking. A   T   K   Q   J   9 (trick-taking power)
Value.   11 10   4   3   2   0 (taken in tricks)

It should be noted that the Ten ranks below Ace but above King, and that the total value of all scoring cards in the pack is 120. Scoring cards may be referred to as counters.

Suit values. ♡ = 100   ◇ = 80   ♣ = 60   ♠ = 40, scored when made trumps.

Object. A round of bidding establishes a contractor, whose object is to score in tricks and for making trumps the number of points he contracted to make. There is no bonus for making more. He has a chance to improve his hand and increase his bid before playing. The opponents combine to beat him, and individually score whatever they make.

Game. Usually 1001 points up, which takes well over an hour; but 501 is enough for a good game. Scores are recorded in writing at the end of each deal. It is advisable to note by each round who is contractor and the final amount of his bid before play starts. A trump indicator is a useful piece of equipment.

Order. Decide seats and first dealer by any agreed means. All play and the right to deal passes regularly to the left.

Shuffle. Light shuffling is sufficient.

Deal. Deal seven cards each face down, and three to the table forming a 'widow'. The usual method of dealing is one card at a time, forming the widow on the first three rounds. An easier method is three each, three to widow, and the rest in ones or twos.

Play

Bidding. Since Elder (player on dealer's left) will be 'forced' to make a contract if others pass, as explained below, bidding is opened by Younger hand (player on dealer's right). Players may bid or pass; having passed, they may not re-enter. Younger must pass or start at 110; Dealer must pass or raise to 120; and bidding continues to rise in tens until two players are forced out.

The highest bidder becomes contractor for that round, and will have an opportunity to raise his bid after the exchange but before the play. He will not be able to lower it, but will have the opportunity of throwing in the hand if the exchange is bad (see 'Conceding').

Forced bid. If Younger and Dealer immediately pass, Elder is said to be forced. He *may* bid 110 if he wishes, and so reserve the right to increase his bid after the exchange. He is alternatively permitted to make a special low bid of 100 – but if he does so, he may not increase it after the exchange.

The exchange. Contractor now takes the three widow cards and – except in a forced bid – turns them face up for the opponents to see before adding them to his hand. (If the bid was forced he takes them up without revealing them.) He then rejects any two cards from his hand and passes them, face up, one to each opponent. Consequently the players each hold eight cards and contractor has improved his hand. He must now either declare his final bid – a multiple of ten which may equal or exceed his original bid but not undercut it – or, if he thinks the contract hopeless, concede defeat.

Conceding defeat. If after the exchange contractor has not improved his hand and thinks the contract unplayable he may throw in his cards and announce 'forty each'. In this event he is set back by the amount of his contract and the opponents automatically score forty each. (But he will not be advised to do so if he stands a fair chance of preventing them from making forty each by the play of the hand.)

Leading. Having announced his final contract, contractor leads to the first trick.

Trick-play. The usual rules of trick-play apply. (Follow suit if possible; if not, trump (if any) or renounce ad lib; highest card of suit led wins unless trumped; winner of trick leads to next.)

Making trumps. Until a player makes trumps the game is played at No Trump. Any player may declare trumps when he has the lead – including contractor at first trick – provided that he holds at the same time both King and Queen of his declared suit. He must lead one of them out to the trick, announce the trump suit, and immediately score the value of that suit. Other suits may be declared trumps in the same way during the course of the round, which finishes when the eighth trick has been taken.

Scoring

Contractor. Contractor counts all points for counters taken in his tricks and adds the value of any trump suits he made during the round. If this total equals or exceeds his contract he scores just the amount of the contract (no bonuses for exceeding it). If not, the contract value is subtracted from his cumulative score.

Opponents. Each opponent scores the value of any counters taken in his tricks and any trump he has made. (It is customary to round off to the nearest five.) But he is not allowed to score to game in this way: a player may only exceed the target score through succeeding at a contract. Until then he must stick at 995.

Hints on play

The most distinguishing feature of Tyzicha is the call for skill at the management of trumps. Contractor cannot open play by announcing a trump suit *and* win the first trick (unless he also holds the Ace and Ten); and if he lets it go, the trump may change before he comes back in. It is also useless to hold more than one marriage without sufficient high cards to ensure re-entry. A hand consisting of four marriages is not worth 280 for trumps plus 120 for honours – it is worth 100 for a heart trump, but won't win a single trick. The beginner's greatest problem is that of foreseeing and avoiding the danger of opponents' declaring undesirable trump suits.

Contractor's play usually consists of making tricks with Aces and Tens in side suits first, then establishing a trump with the hope of getting back in for a trick or two later on. He must, of course, pay particular attention to the appearance or absence of Kings and Queens in other suits. So long as a marriage remains clandestine it represents a potential trump. When one of its partners appears, that danger is gone.

It will be obvious from the foregoing that contractor cannot reasonably expect to succeed if his final playing hand does not include certain trick-winners, especially an Ace or two. A guarded Ten is a poor substitute, since there are too few tricks to guarantee re-entry into its suit. Besides, whereas one can set an Ace to catch a Ten for at least 21 pts. in honours, the reverse does not hold.

As a nice point of balance in the game, it should be noted that the minimum bid of 110 is – apart from exceptional hands – impossible to make without combining points for tricks with points for trumps. So you need both Aces and marriages in order to succeed.

How many for tricks? Players of Whist and Bridge can look at a hand and intuitively count the number of tricks it is likely to make. But unless you have played Skat or suchlike you may have difficulty in 'seeing' the hand as likely to win a certain number of points for honours.

The obvious method of solving this problem is usually safe to follow. Since there are 120 points for honours to be distributed through eight tricks, just estimate how many tricks you can make (but don't forget the ranking of the Ten!) and multiply by the 'average' trick score of 15 – less if you are timid, more if you are confident. A similar alternative is to count 15 for every Ace and well-covered Ten you hold.

To succeed as contractor, you ought to be able to foresee at least 50 pts. for honours. That's an 'average' of forty per player but adjusted in contractor's favour for his ability to take advantage of the widow.

Whether and what to bid. The bid you can make on the basis of the seven cards dealt may be classified as certain, probable, possible, and suicidal.

A certain bid is a number of points above 100 that you can make even before exchanging cards. For instance, a marriage in hearts guarantees you 100 pts., so if the rest of that hand looks good for your fair share of 120 for honours you have a certain bid of 140. With two Aces and two marriages you can probably count both trumps, depending on the exact distribution.

A probable bid is what you can hope to raise your certain bid to as the result of improving your hand after the exchange. Since you can exchange first and decide after, you need not try to work out all the details, unless someone else is trying to force you up in the bidding.

A possible bid is what you have when the hand as dealt would not produce the minimum number of points, but could achieve that status after the exchange. It might, for instance, contain a marriage and high cards but no Ace; or Aces and high cards including unmatched monarchs – i.e., no marriage. These are the hands that call for nice calculation and careful bidding; and the fact that the majority of hands fall into this category is another sign of the balance of the game.

Any dealt hand offering less than a possible bid should be left severely alone – unless, of course, you are 'forced' into it as Elder hand. If you do find yourself forced into bidding an apparently impossible hand you will probably find it worth while to consider taking a chance on it. Look at it this way. If your hand really is impossible then you're going to lose 100 pts. on a forced bid. But the minimum bid of 100 does not permit you to raise if by some lucky chance you should make a considerable improvement in the draw. Changing to a positive bid of 110, however, allows you to raise if you do make a good exchange, while only losing you a further ten if you fail. And if it's really impossible, you can always throw in to restrict your opponents from exceeding forty in tricks.

There is also the point that the very fact of being forced implies weakness in the others' hands. And that brings us to the question of your opponents' bids. Much can be learned from the round of bidding, particularly about marriages and trumps. For instance, the fact that a player bids at all suggests that he has a marriage or expects one of the widow. A glance at your own merry monarchs may tell you his probable trump suit and enable you to plan accordingly. If you hold three Queens and he bids over 140, you can be pretty sure that the suit of the other Queen is due for a trumphood.

Because you can always raise after the exchange, it is sufficient to bid the minimum. But if dealt a rare hand that looks strong enough to take all 120 pts. in a No Trump slam (lacking a marriage, that is) you might as well open at 120 in order to shut the others out. A player with a better hand will outbid you anyway.

The exchange. We have already looked at the chances of making specific improvements in the exchange. There follows the question of what cards to hand over to your opponents.

It is usually better to think in terms of discarding ranks than voiding a suit, except when you can be certain of trumping your way back into it. With eight tricks and variable trumps life is too short to think seriously of voiding or establishing suits.

Except from long suits headed by the Ace, Jacks and Nines

are the safest discards. You *may* thereby be providing an opponent with a much-needed guard on a Ten; but you can't be expected to tell that from your own hand and the alternatives could be worse.

Obviously, Kings and Queens are not discardable, for fear of their contracting marriages in other hands and giving birth to usurper trumps. But there can be circumstances in which the danger is negligible. For instance, if you hold Ace, Ten and King or Queen and propose to lead from that suit, then it is probably safe to release a possible marriage partner, as you'll have them divorced before they have time to get up to anything. (It can only be beaten if third player is void in that suit.)

The disposal of a Ten is justifiable if you can be sure of winning it with a subsequent Ace or trump, as might be the disposal of an Ace to create a void. But few hands warrant such niceties of play.

On the subject of niceties, perhaps one of the nicest is to break up a marriage in the hand and give one half to each opponent. It has been done!

Contractor's play. With only eight tricks in the play-off, contractor does not have much scope for flexibility once under way. As contractor, you must think about the bids that have been made and the probable distribution of cards amongst the others, pick your line of play and plunge into it. The usual plan is to play out your certain tricks, sign off by establishing trumps, then hope to get back in later. For openers, it's worth noting that a holding of Ace, Ten is capable of bringing in 30 pts. in its suit, while Ace, Ten and King is bound to.

Many points of planning and play revolve around 'catching the Ten'. Holding Ace, King, Queen of a suit it is better to play the Ace than lead King or Queen as trumps, for the latter will certainly be taken by the Ten, while the former stands a 1 in 4 chance of winning it. If you hold a lower card in the suit, the chances rise to 1 in 2.

Opponent's play. In opposition to a contractor you will start with more information about the lie of cards, having seen your original seven, the three of the widow, and contractor's two discards – up to twelve in all, or half the pack. Your ad hoc partner will have seen a like number, but contractor only ten (unless he was forced, in which case he sees ten to your eight – another credit to the balance of the game).

If you play as a partnership, therefore, you have between you some extra knowledge with which to fight contractor's advantage of the initiative. Once he loses that and runs out of steam, you must ensure that he never makes a comeback. Any Ace he hasn't led and you haven't got means a trick for your side if you lead into the suit (at risk of contractor's void).

The practice of 'swarming' – a Skat term – is of value in Tyzicha. It means you play a card of value to a trick won by your partner, to ensure the loss of more points to contractor. Suppose, for instance, you hold a void in one suit and a singleton Ten in another; contractor leads into your void suit and partner wins it. Now's the time to throw the Ten.

For all this sensible advice, based on the fact that it is usually more profitable to beat the contractor than play to your own score, opponents will find it a great temptation to play solo instead of partnership. Of course, if contractor habitually tends to underbid then it won't be worth combining to diddle him out of 20 or 30 pts. Partnership play only comes into its own when players are sufficiently expert to make within ten points of their stated contract.

And you can treat that falling margin of error as a true measure of your rising proficiency at what has been called 'a completely scientific game'.

Some sample deals

First deal. Baker deals; Charlie is forced; Abel bids first.

    Abel   ♠T J ♡Q ♣A T Q ♢A
    Baker   ♠K ♡A ♣K J 9 ♢T 9
    Charlie ♠A 9 ♡K 9 ♣— ♢K Q J

Abel, with a probable 45 in tricks and a one in three chance of making a marriage, tentatively bids 110. Baker has nothing worth having and wisely passes. Charlie has a diamond marriage for 80, though at present not much more than a possible 25 for tricks. He bids 120, and becomes contractor as Abel passes. He draws ♠Q ♡J T, none of which is particularly useful save that there is now no danger of a spade marriage, and discards his two Nines, spades to Abel and hearts to Baker.

Charlie now debates his lead. Should he start with ♠A on the off-chance of catching the Ten unguarded? Perhaps not, now that he has given Abel the Nine. Or shall he announce trumps and hope to come back soon in his void suit, taking the risk of a possible club marriage from elsewhere? Since the others' bidding was low, he opts for the latter course. He does not think his hand strong enough to merit increasing his contract.

The play is as follows – winning cards in **bold** type, point-scoring value of tricks in parentheses; T = trump suit declared for score shown:

A	B	C	
◇ **A(14)**	◇ 9	◇ Q(T80)	....
♣ **A**	♣ K	◇ J(16)	Baker swarms, but Charlie trumps as he had anticipated
♡ Q	♡ **A(18)**	♡ K	
♠ T	◇ **T(24)**	◇ K	
♣ **T(14)**	♣ J	♡ J	
♣ **Q(6)**	♣ 9	♠ Q	
♠ 9	♠ K	♠ **A(15)**	
♠ J	♡ 9	♡ **T(12)**	
34	42	124	

So, despite his perhaps unnecessarily devious play, Charlie justifies his bid of 120 very nicely. Scores so far: 32, 42, 120.

Second deal. Charlie deals; Abel forced; Baker to bid first.

Abel	♠T 9 ♡K ♣Q J ◇T Q
Baker	♠A ♡A J 9 ♣K 9 ◇9
Charlie	♠K Q J ♡T ♣A T ◇J

Baker's two Aces are quite unsupported, and he passes. Charlie's hand looks reasonable at first; but the marriage is the lowest (worth 40) and the most he can see in tricks at present is 30. So he passes; and Abel is forced.

Now, should Abel stick safely to 100, or risk raising to have the chance of going higher? Despite the lack of Aces, he has a fair chance of a good marriage. He raises, and is rewarded for this courage by a splendid draw: ♡Q, giving him the Heart marriage for 100, and ◇A K, giving an additional marriage worth 80. That's 180 without trying. What about trick points? He is bound to make 30 in Diamonds, making 210, and since he holds most of that suit he is bound to make more points in discards to it. So he raises to 220, passing ♠9 to Baker and ♣J to Charlie.

A	B	C	
◇ Q(T80)	◇ 9	◇ J	
(+5)			
◇ K(6)	♠ 9	♣ J	Charlie won't play from spades in case he gets a chance to declare it trumps …
◇ T(12)	♡ 9	♠ J	… but now he must, to avoid giving Abel high scoring cards.
◇ A(14)	♣ 9	♠ Q	
♡ Q(T100)	♡ A(24)	♡ T	
♠ T	♠ A(25)	♠ K	
♣ Q	♣ K	♣ A(18)	
♡ K(16)	♡ J	♣ T	
233	49	18	

Abel's bid of 220 had erred on the optimistic side of accuracy and he was lucky to make so many points on the last trick. The most be ought to have expected to make was 219.

The running totals are now Abel 254, Baker, 91, Charlie 138.

Third deal. Abel deals; B is forced; C to bid.

    Abel   ♠—   ♡A   ♣A K J   ◇T K J
    Baker   ♠A T K   ♡T K 9   ♣—   ◇A
    Charlie   ♠K 9   ♡J   ♣T Q 9   ◇Q

Charlie declines to bid. Abel passes because his hand is risky and he does not want to spoil his good record. Baker is forced.

With only a 1 in 3 chance of making a marriage Baker decides to play safe, bidding the statutory 100 and taking the widow without revealing its contents. But the draw is good – ♠J ♡Q ◇9 – and he now regrets having lost the opportunity to raise his bid.

To prove to himself that he would have been justified in raising to 200, Baker now plays exactly as if that were what he had done. He passes ◇A to Abel and ◇9 to Charlie, giving himself a void in Diamonds in addition to the Club void dealt.

Now he leads ♡Q, announces the trump for 100, and permits his opponents to make a single trick worth 16 (Abel wins with the Ace, Charlie throws the Jack). Because both players passed Baker does not fear the possibility of another trump being declared; and he is right. Abel returns ♣A, Baker trumps with ♡9 and can't avoid taking the rest of the tricks. Any other lead from either opponent would also have been beaten.

So Abel's score is increased by 16 to 254 and Charlie's sticks at 138. Baker, having made 204, scores only the 100 he bid, and carries forward a total of 191 instead of 291.

Which just goes to show that a forced bid is often worth raising to 110.

ZETEMA

Unlike most games in this section, the unusual and delightful Zetema is not essentially a three-player game; but I include it here because it works well for this number of players and it compensates for a general shortage of good three-handed games. Two may play instead of three. If four play, it is a partnership game, with the partners of each side sitting opposite each other and playing alternately. If six play, deal only five cards each (instead of six) and play in two partnerships of three, the members of each side playing alternately.

Zetema seems to have been invented a little over a hundred years ago, and to have died an unnatural death a little under a hundred years ago. The word 'invented' is used advisedly, for it can hardly be said to have evolved or developed from anything else. With its distinctive and curious feature of *five* suits, so that you need two packs to play from, it goes on to combine elements of Bézique and Poker, themselves comparatively new at the time, while in layout and 'self tidying-up' property, whereby you are left at the end of the game with a single pile of cards more or less in order, it resembles the great family of Patience games, which were also in vogue at this period.

I first found Zetema described in Cassell's *Indoor Amusements, Card Games and Fireside Fun* of 1881, but the description is so vague as to be, if not entirely unintelligible, certainly not sufficiently intelligible to inspire confidence in any reconstruction that might be made of it. For the version presented in these pages we are indebted to American games writer and inventor Sid Sackson, who rediscovered the game in H. E. Heather's *Cards and Card Tricks* of 1876. According to Heather, 'Zetema is pronounced, and justly so, by most players, to be far superior to Bézique. This game, however, does not appear to initiate itself in public favour as its merits deserve. It was introduced a few years ago by Messrs Joseph

Hunt and Sons, and issued by them with special markers, cards, and rules, like its more popular rival.' And Cassell confirms that 'Proper sets of Zetema cards may be had of any ordinary card dealer' – though if you should be lucky enough to find any now, they will no doubt be at antique-shop prices, which, you may have noticed, are always considerably ahead of their time. (However, a few days after I wrote these words a friend of mine picked up a set in a street market for £2.50.)

Why Zetema lost out in popularity is a matter for surmise. It could be connected with the inconvenience of playing with an unorthodox pack, which is thereafter useless for anything else, and tinged with the fact that any strongly 'ordering' game (like Patience) necessitates strenuous shuffling between deals (bearing in mind that Zetema died out before the advent of Rummy games). It is odd, however, that whereas its more successful rival, Bézique, is essentially a two-player game – its three-player derivative, Pinochle, being virtually unknown in Britain – Zetema has the advantage of being playable by two to six and is, happily for us, at its best for three.

When Sid Sackson published his account of Zetema in *A Gamut of Games* (1969) he made some modifications to the original scoring system. His modifications are so clearly desirable that I have no hesitation in presenting them here as standard. The original scoring is detailed under 'variations', as it is, I feel, of historical interest only.

Preliminaries

Cards. 65, consisting of a standard 52–card pack plus one entire suit from a second pack of identical back design and colour to the first. It does not matter which suit is doubled, and in the following description we will assume it is Spades should the distinction becomes necessary. What is important is that the cards of the extra suit should not be distinguishable from the back when held in a player's hand.

Game. Game is set at 300 pts., which usually takes from three to six rounds to achieve at about ten minutes per round. Scores

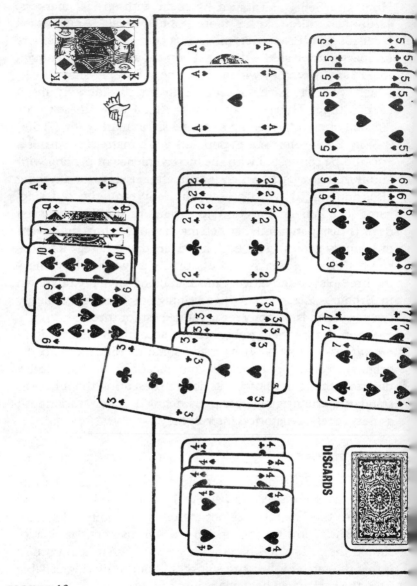

FIGURE 13

How Zetema looks in progress. The player whose hand is illustrated at the bottom of the diagram makes a 'trick' of Threes, scoring 5, and draws a King to produce a sequence worth 20 in the hand. One opponent has nearly a sequence, requiring only an Ace

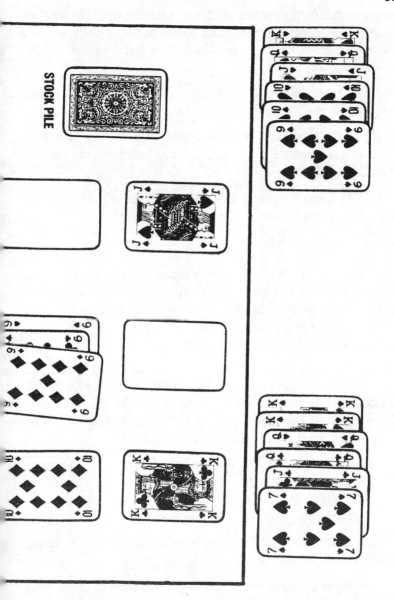

or an Eight in return for a spare Ten, while the other seems well placed in the marriage stakes, although none of the monarchs yet match. (This position comes from the sample game, round 2).

are made during the course of play and may be noted in writing
or on mechanical scorers. The game ends as soon as one
player's cumulative score reaches 300: the rest of that round
is not played out.

Order. Choose first dealer by any agreed means; the deal,
turn to deal and all play proceed clockwise around the table.

Deal. Shuffle the cards very thoroughly and deal six each face
down one at a time. Place the remainder face down at one side
to form a stock.

Object. To make scoring combinations on the table and in the
hand during the course of play.

Play

Procedure. Each player in turn plays a card face up to the
table and draws the top card of the stock to replenish his
hand. The first card played of any rank is placed on its own;
subsequent cards of the same rank are placed on top of it, but
slightly spread so that all are visible.

Tricks. This word does not have its usual meaning. Each pile
of cards of the same rank is called a trick. When a player lays
down the fifth card of the trick he scores for it, and clears
those cards off the layout onto a common discard pile. The
score for a trick depends on its rank, as follows:

King, Queen	50
Jack	20
Ace, Five	15
Other ranks	5

King and Queen tricks score high because they are rarely
made, as will be seen later.

Combinations in hand. If, when it is your turn to play, your
hand consists of six cards in sequence (Ace counting high or
low, e.g. A 2 3 4 5 6 or 9 T J Q K A), or six cards of the same

suit (other than the doubled suit, which is too easy to get), or both, you show your hand and score for it as follows before playing a card to the table:

Sequence	20
Flush (same suit)	30
Flush sequence	50

Note that you do not declare the combination as soon as you draw the card that makes it: you must wait for your turn to come round again. If you score for such a combination, play a card out, and then draw another card which makes the same combination, you may declare and score it again when it is next your turn.

Assembly. If, when it is your turn to play, your hand contains five cards of the same rank, you show your hand and score for Assembly according to the rank of the cards as follows:

Kings, Queens	130
Jacks	120
Aces, Fives	110
Other ranks	100

You do not then play a card to the table, but instead discard the assembly to the rubbish pile, draw five more cards from stock to replenish your hand, and thereby end your turn.

Marriage. A common marriage is the King and Queen of the same suit. An imperial marriage is the *second* marriage made in the *doubled* suit. The score for marriages increases disproportionately according to the number declared at the same time (*see table*), which makes it worthwhile saving Kings and Queens rather than marrying them off as soon as they are obtained. You may make a marriage either by playing it from the hand, or by playing from the hand a King or Queen which matches a Queen or King in the layout, or both.

If you hold one or more marriages in the hand, you may declare and score them. You then throw them to the discard pile, draw the same number of cards from stock, and end your turn without playing to the layout.

If you hold a King (or Queen) which matches a Queen (or King) in the layout, you put the two cards together, declare and score the marriage, discard, and draw from stock without playing to the layout.

You may make as many marriages as you can and wish in one turn, but may not declare and score a marriage *and* a flush or sequence simultaneously in the hand (see round three of sample game).

Table of scores for marriages at Zetema

Number of marriages declared at one time	1	2	3	4	5
Basic score		10	30	60	100	—
Score if one of them is the imperial marriage		20	40	70	110	—
Score if two of them are in the doubled suit		—	50	80	120	150

End-game. When there are no cards left in the stock play continues as before, except of course that no more cards are drawn, and the game ends when all the cards have been played. Players will not necessarily play their last cards at the same time, but simply drop out when they have no more left. Since every card eventually gets taken and discarded as part of a trick, marriage or assembly, the layout will be cleared off leaving all 65 cards in a single waste pile.

Hints on play

As with most card games that involve drawing from a stock-pile Zetema is tactical rather than strategic. Your opening hand contains so few cards that it is impossible to decide in advance on any great plan of play: you must wait and see how things develop. Keep a careful eye on the layout, for you can tell from the cards there whether you have much likelihood of filling out a potential flush or sequence part-formed in your own hand.

In assessing the chances of making various combinations, it is useful to remember that, with 65 cards in the pack and six of them in your hand to start with, you will be drawing about 16 more during the course of play. (The actual number varies according to the number of marriages or assemblies declared from the hand.)

Tricks. Putting out cards to the trick piles in the layout is the means by which you get rid of unwanted cards from your hand in order to build up sequences, flushes and marriages. With a choice of discards, go first to piles containing fewer than four cards, for as soon as you play the fourth, you lay it open for an opponent to capture with the fifth. Obviously, however, it is always safe to play to a trick if you hold two of the same rank, especially if they are the fourth and the fifth of it.

Also aim to play to the lower-scoring tricks, avoiding Ace, Five (15 each) and Jack (20) so long as there is any danger of others capturing these high tricks. It is also desirable not to play a King or Queen to the layout unless you hold its partner, otherwise you give another the chance of scoring the marriage. King and Queen tricks score high as they are rarely taken, and instead are usually split up for marriages. It takes only one marriage to prevent the possible completion of a King or Queen trick, and I have yet to see one taken.

Assemblies are rare enough in the two-player game; with three, they are practically impossible. Certainly an assembly is not worth holding out for, unless you get four of a kind early on and see nothing more promising as a substitute objective.

Sequences and flushes are the staple diet of good scores, the sequence being particularly easy to come by. Flushes are rarer, as you need virtually half the suit to make one. (Don't be misled by experience with odds at Poker: increasing the hand from five cards as in Poker to six as in Zetema makes flushes disproportionately harder to get than sequences.) Flush sequences, in turn, are so rare that they are worth not spoiling the hand for.

But to revert to positive advantages, a sequence or flush in the hand is like a good blackmail subject in that it can constantly be milked for more. Remember to keep sequences open-ended: for example, having scored for A 2 3 4 5 6, discard the Ace rather than the Six, as there are then two ranks (Ace and Seven) which will complete the hand to score again. After scoring a sequence or flush several times over, keep an eye on the layout so that you will know when to give it up. For instance, if you score the sequence A 2 3 4 5 6 and the trick of Sevens has been taken, there is obviously no chance of later concerting it to 2 3 4 5 6 7. If, on examination, there prove to be no Fours (say) on the appropriate trick pile, then discard the Four, since that would appear to be the most likely rank for you to draw from the stock in order to refill the sequence.

Marriages. Do not be in a hurry to declare marriages: the more you can declare at once, as the result of saving them up, the more profitable they are. Beginners often forgot that it is not necessary to keep complete marriages in the hand: if you have the King and Queen of a suit there is no danger at all in playing one of them out in order to match it up later. You might in this connection balk only at laying aside the fourth monarch of a trick, in case someone else has the fifth. If you have not had many Kings and Queens through your hand and can see better combinations to go for do not worry too much about laying aside single monarchs whose partner you lack, except of course in Spades, when someone else may make the imperial marriage. If the draw of a King or Queen gives you a marriage *and* a flush or sequence in the hand, you may not declare them both at once. To score, you need only declare the flush or sequence, then play out any card other than King or Queen, which you retain for scoring later. In other words, reconstitute and score for the flush or sequence as often as possible, and count the marriage only when the former 'dries up'. Note that this does not prevent you from scoring flush or sequence, then playing out King or Queen as part of your turn and thereby marrying it to a partner already in the layout.

End-game. The end-game begins when the last card of the stock has been taken. With three players, the last card will be taken by the one who played second at the outset. Taking the last card is an advantage, for in the last part of the game, which is the most exciting and where the highest scores are often made, it means that you have more opportunity to complete the combinations which others inevitably must lead into. The imperial marriage is often the last combination made, since if two players can each make one in the doubled suit they will each want the other to make it first for the lower score.

A sample game

First deal. Charlie deals, so that Abel leads, and the opening hands are:

```
Abel      ♠Q 4  ♡Q  ♣8 7  ◇9
Baker     ♠9 9 8 8  ♡2  ♣9  ◇—
Charlie   ♠4  ♡J 6 4  ♣A 2  ◇—
```

Abel and Charlie each have three cards to a sequence, which is not very significant as sequences are easy to make anyway. Baker has three cards to°an assembly (the Nines). His apparent four-to-a-flush is useless, as it is in the duplicated suit and therefore not valid; he can only think in terms of keeping the Nines for a few rounds with a view to an assembly, which we know he can't get because Abel has one of them himself.

In the following commentary, brackets enclose the card drawn after playing to the layout.

Abel	Baker	Charlie
♠ 4 (◇ 3)	♡ 2 (♠ J)	♡ 6 (◇ A)
◇ 3 (♣ T)	....	
	♠ 8 (♣ 4)	♠ 4 (♠ 2)
♡ Q (♡ 5)	....	
	♣ 4 (♣ 6)	♠ 2 (◇ T)
♠ O (♡ K)	....	
	♠ 9 (◇ 5)	....
		◇ T (♠ 5)
....	.....	
(◇ 8)	♠ 9 (♣ K)	◇ A (♠ 6)
◇ 8 (♠ K)	◇ 5 (◇ 2)	♡ J (♠ 3)
♠ marriage declared for 10		
(◇ 7)		
	◇ 2 (♠ 7)	....
		♣ A (♣ 5)
◇ 7 (♡ 7)	♣ K (◇ Q)	....
		♠ 5 (♠ 6)
♡ 7 (♠ A)	◇ Q (♡ T)	♠ 6 (♣ Q)
♠ A (◇ J)	....	
....	...	
	♣ 6 (◇ K)	♣ marriage declared for 10 (♠ T)
♡ 5 (♣ J)	....	
	(♠ J)	♠ T (♠ 2)
◇ J (♠ T)	....	
	♠ J (♡ 8)	....

This draw gives Abel three cards to a flush sequence, but this is considerably less promising than his two marriageable Queens.

The drawn Five is useful to a sequence, but it is questionable practice to relinquish a Queen whose King you lack.

Abel has followed the same bad practice on his second Queen, and does not really deserve his luck in drawing the King to his previous discard!
Baker has wisely decided to give up his unlikely assembly of Nines.

Abel declares ♡ marriage for 10.

Abel would have made more by holding on to his first marriage and declaring both at once.
Declares sequence for 20, which by discarding the Ace, he will endeavour to reform as it is now 'open-ended' (needing either Ace or Seven). Baker has little in view save a sequence.

A hard choice, but little alternative.
Baker declares sequence for 20, discards to leave it open-ended.

Baker declares ◇ marriage for 10.

Though Jacks are high-scoring, Abel can safely leave one as he holds another to prevent someone else from taking the trick.
So does Baker, curiously enough! The same applies to other ranks in the next few plays.

Abel	Baker	Charlie
		♠ 2 (♢ 4)
♠ T (♣ 3)	♠ 8 (♠ 7)	♢ 4 (♡ 9)
♢ 9 (♡ 3)	....	....
	♠ 7 (♠ A)	♡ 9 (♢ 6)
♡ 3 (♠ K)	♠ A (♠ 3)	♢ 6 (♡ A)
♣ 3 (♠ 5)	....	....
	♠ 3 (♠ Q)	....
....		
		♡ A tr
♣ 7	♠ 7 tr	
		♣ 2 tr
♣ 8	♡ 8 tr	♠ 3 tr
♣ T	♡ T tr	♡ 4 tr
♠ 5	♣ 9 tr	♠ 6 tr
♣ J	♠ J tr	♣ 5 tr ......
♠ K		
————	————	————
20	85	100

Charlie's hand has nothing of interest, and Baker has the usual promising straight, but the extraordinary feature here is Abel's four Eights: for the time being, it looks worth his while to aim for an assembly. As soon as he sees an Eight in the layout he will know when to stop. Baker leads.

Abel has five Clubs. Counting all those visible on
the layout he decides that there are still five to come,
so he demolishes his sequence in order to seek a flush.
But he has forgotten that two Clubs have been discarded
as a marriage, so there are only three left. (As it
happens, they are in opponents' hands, so the flush is
hopeless; but this he does not know.)

A good draw for Charlie.
Abel avoids playing a 'fourth card' to a trick, and
must retain ♠K.
Baker draws the last card of stock, and is immediately
interested to know where ♠K is!
Declares sequence for 20, plays out the Ace and takes
the Ace trick for 15.
(tr) = takes the trick.

Now the heavies come out: Baker scores 20 for the
Jacks, Charlie 15 for the Fives.
Baker clears the board with the imperial marriage
for 20.
Charlie leads a so far not very exciting game, but the
shuffle produces an interesting hand in the next deal,
made by Abel:

    Abel   ♠8 ♡8 ♣K 8 ◇85
    Baker   ♠— ♡A Q 4 ♣J 7 4 ◇—
    Charlie ♠6 3 3 ♡— ♣A 9 ◇Q

Abel	Baker	Charlie
	♣ 4 (♠ K)	♠ 3 (♠ J)
♢ 5 (♠ 4)	♣ 7 (♣ 5)	♠ 6 (♡ 9)
♠ 4 (♡ 7)	♣ 5 (♢ 3)	♠ 3 (♢ J)
♡ 7 (♠ 4)	♢ 3 (♠ 2)	♡ 9 (♠ 2)
♠ 4 (♢ 7)	♠ 2 (♣ 6)	♠ 2 (♠ T)
♢ 7 (♠ A)	♣ 6 (♣ Q)	♣ 6 (♠ 5)
♠ A (♢ 9)	♡ 4 (♡ 3)	♠ 5 (♢ 2)
♢ 9 (♠ 8)	♡ 3 (♡ 5)	♢ 2 (♠ 9)
♣ K (♠ 8)		
	♡ 5 (♢ T)	....
		♠ J (♠ 6)
....		
	♢ T (♠ K)	....
		♠ 6 (♣ 3)
♣ 2 (♠ 9)	♡ A (♠ 7)	♣ 3 tr (♢ K)
♠ T (♡ 2)	♠ 7 (♢ 6)	....
		♠ T (♠ Q)
♠ 9 (♢ A)	♢ 6 (♠ 7)	♢ Q (♣ T)
♢ A (♠ A)	♠ 7 tr (♠ 5)	....
		♢ J (♢ 4)
♡ 2 tr (♡ 6)	♠ 5 tr (♠ J)	....
		♢ 4 tr
♡ 6 tr	♠ J	♠ 9 tr
♡ T	♣ J	
		♣ T tr
		....
♡ J tr	♡ Q	

Declares ♡ marriage for 10

Success! Abel draws the fifth Eight.
Baker lets the fourth Five go for the sake of retaining
his potential marriages.
Abel declares assembly of Eights for 100; discards
them and draws from stock ♠T ♡K J T ♣2.
With three Nines visibly out, Baker decides to give up hope
of sequence and plan some marriages. The draw was
fortunate.

First trick to Charlie for 5 (*see illustration*).
Charlie declares a sequence for 20.

Charlie declares another sequence for 20.

A worthwhile trick, worth 15 in fact, and Baker takes
the last card of stock. One would normally expect
Charlie to take the last, but the run was thrown out of
kilter when Abel drew five to replace his assembly.

Baker prefers to play the fourth Jack rather than
lose a marriage, but in the event he is not very successful.

Charlie declares ◇ marriage for 10, note Abel scores
20 for Jacks.

Abel	Baker	Charlie
		. . . .
		♠ Q
♠ A		. . . .
		♣ A tr . . . . . .
♠ Q		. . . .
140	60	85
20	85	100
160	145	185

Abel   ♠6 ♡5 3 ♣7 ◇9 5
Baker   ♠8 ♡9 ♣8 5 2 ◇T
Charlie ♠K T 5 ♡8 7 ♣— ◇3

Abel	Baker	Charlie
		◇ 3 (◇ 4)
◇ 5 (◇ A)	♠ 8 (♣ 4)	◇ 4 (♡ Q)
◇ 9 (♠ 2)	◇ T (♠ J)	♠ 5 (♠ 7)
♣ 7 (♠ 6)	♡ 9 (♣ Q)	♠ 7 (♠ 7)
♠ 6 (♡ J)	♠ J (♠ 4)	♠ 7 (♠ 8)
♠ 6 (♡ A)	♠ 4 (♠ K)	♠ 8 (◇ 6)
◇ A (♡ T)	♠ K (♣ K)	. . . .
		♡ Q (♣ 9)
♠ 2 (◇ K)	. . . .
	♣ 8 (♣ 3)	
		♠ K (♠ 5)
◇ K (◇ 2)	. . . .	
	♣ 8 (♠ A)	. . . .

Baker declares ♣ marriage for 10.

Baker declares ♠ marriage for 10.
for 15
Baker declares imperial marriage for 20 and clears the board.

Scores for this round
Scores for previous round
Cumulative scores at end of second round

Although Abel made that rare thing, an assembly for 100, it prevented him from doing much else, and, as in the previous round, all marriages were declared one at a time.

Now Baker deals to the third round as follows:

The deal looks very even and promises the usual chance of sequences.

Baker's draw favours a flush in Clubs: Charlie's is exasperating – fancy drawing the same card as you have just thrown out!
The next worse thing to ♠7.

Abel has drawn his third Heart in a row, and Baker's draw has given him flush and marriage.
Declares flush for 30. There is no need to declare the marriage, for if he does so he must throw it out and so be unable to reconstitute the flush. His object now is to flush as often as possible, and only when he runs out of Clubs will he declare the marriage. As we see, he has another lucky draw.
So does Charlie, though it was questionable play to lay out the King.
Declares flush again for 30.
Declares sequence for 20.

Abel	Baker	Charlie
		♠T (♣6)
◇2 (♡K)	♠A (♡6)	♣6 (♣T)
. . . .	. . . .	. . . .
♡T (◇8)	♡6 (♠9)	. . . .
		♠5 (♠2)
◇8 (♡2)	. . . .	
	♠9 (♣A)	. . . .
		♠2 (♠3)
. . . .		. . . .
♡J (◇Q)	. . . .	
	♣K (♠4)	♠3 (♠J)
. . . .		
	♠4 (♠Q)	. . . .
		◇6 tr (◇7)
♡3 (♠9)	♣2 (♠A)	◇7 (♡4)
♡2 tr (◇J)	♠A (♣3)	♡7 tr (♠T)

♠9	♠3	♣9 tr
◇J	♣3 tr	♡8 tr
♡A	♣A tr	♡4
♡5	♣4 tr	♣T
♣J	♣5 tr	♠J tr
Declares ♠ marriage for 10		

. . . .

105	160	100
160	145	185
265	305	285

Abel's draw was good.
Declares flush for 30.
Declares sequence again for 20.

This draw gives Abel four cards to a flush sequence,
but even if the $\heartsuit$6 had not just been played it would
still mean little.
Strangely enough, this draw puts Baker in the same
position.

Abel declares another flush for 30.
Declares third flush for 30, also plays out King to layout
and marries it to $\clubsuit$Q for 10.
Declares $\heartsuit$ and $\diamondsuit$ marriages for 30; draws $\spadesuit$Q, $\clubsuit$J.
Declares sequence again for 20, and takes the Six trick.

And Charlie draws the last card of stock. The
cumulative scores at this point stand at Abel 255,
Baker 245, Charlie 255 – so it's anybody's game. The
question is whether someone will reach 300 in this
end-game or whether another round will need to start.

Baker's trick was worth 15.

Baker 15, Charlie 20.

Declares imperial marriage for 20, making total score 305.
Game ends without allowing Charlie to play the last
card of all, the $\spadesuit$T which would have given him a final 5 pts.
Scores for this round
Previous cumulative score
Final score: Baker wins

Variations

More of a kind. An American correspondent to *Games &
Puzzles* has suggested that the skill element increases if a
player who holds more than one card of a rank is permitted to
choose how many cards he will play to a trick pile. The point
is valid, since much excitement in the end-game derives from
the number of cards left in the various players' hands. Since
assemblies are so rare, one might pursue the idea further and
introduce a score for laying out four of a kind (say 80 pts.) or
even three (say 30). Alternatively, one might agree that the
normal score for a trick is doubled if you take it by laying out
the fourth and fifth card, tripled if you take it by laying out
the third, fourth and fifth, and quadrupled if you lay out four
of the five cards – all simultaneously, of course. This latter
idea has interesting repercussions: it means that it is *only* safe
to play a single card to a trick if you hold at least one other in
hand, and it may even make King and Queen tricks more
feasible.

Zetema with Joker. I do not like introducing Jokers into card
games just for the sake of it, but by bringing the pack to 66
cards in the three-player game it theoretically equalises the
number of cards available to each player (only theoretically,
because some combinations produce inequalities). I also feel
sure that the inventor of Zetema would have added a Joker
had this card been more common a hundred years ago: nowadays, you fully expect every pack you buy to contain two of
these curious characters.

    Since all the 'real' cards of the pack eventually team up with
one another in scoring combinations, the Joker cannot play
any entirely independent part. Hence its role would be that
of a substitute card. If you hold the Joker you may use it as
any named card to make up a combination (flush, sequence,
marriage or assembly) or as the fifth and capturing card of a
trick. When used as a 'fifth card', an assembly or a marriage
partner, it automatically goes to the discard pile, but should

be laid in it face up instead of face down for ease of location. Whoever then draws the card it stood for may immediately (and not as part of his turn) exchange it for the Joker, which then comes into his hand and may again be used as a substitute card.

When the Joker is shown and declared as part of a sequence, it must be placed in the appropriate trick pile as that player's immediate turn, from which it may subsequently be taken by a card of the same rank. When scored as part of a flush, its holder must, as the continuation of his turn, immediately lay it aside not to the layout (since it belongs to no particular rank) but to the top of the stock, from which it will be drawn by the player next in turn.

The original scoring. As previously noted, the scoring in this description is as recommended by Sid Sackson. In the original game, assemblies of common ranks scored 60, of Aces or Fives 80, of Jacks 90, of Kings or Queens 100. The combination is so rare that the original scoring makes it not worthwhile. Originally both sequences and flushes scored 30, but sequences are far too easy to get, so 20 is a more reasonable score. Finally, the original rules give no credit for the rare but not unattainable flush sequence; a score of 50 for it is eminently sensible, if not a trifle mean.

5. CARD GAMES FOR FOUR

Four is a well served number of players as far as card games are concerned, largely because it is such a common social grouping – two couples, for instance, or an average 'nuclear family'. And it gives a wide choice of games in all categories. The four may play in two partnerships of two each, or, if partnership games are not everybody's favourite, there are many good games in which each plays against all the others. In addition, many of the round games described in the appropriate section work satisfactorily for four.

CONTRACT BRIDGE

Bridge is a peculiar game. Along with Poker and Canasta it is one of the very few card games played throughout the world in a recognisably standard sort of way. Some other card games may be known in different countries, but all are 'national' games to the extent that each country seems to have its own unique list of top favourites. And Bridge, unlike Poker and Canasta but like Chess, is one of the even fewer games to which international tournaments are devoted, and by which people can earn a living as professional players, teachers and writers. No compendium of card games would be complete without a description of the game, yet of all books published each year on the subject of card games some 80 to 90 per cent deal with Contract Bridge alone, making any further descriptions somewhat redundant!

In a book of this nature the only reasonable way of dealing with so vast a subject will be to provide a basic introduction to the background and mechanics of the game, so as to enable four beginners to play it sufficiently well to decide whether or not to take it further – either by reading specialist literature, taking lessons, or, by far the best, joining a Bridge club.

Background and principal features of Contract Bridge

Contract Bridge is a development of partnership Whist (p. 382), which was internationally recognised as the 'king of card games' during the 19th century. (In this connection I must add here my personal belief that nobody should embark upon Contract Bridge without prior experience of Whist.) Both have as their basis the fact that 52 cards are divided between two partnerships, each player receiving thirteen cards and playing to thirteen tricks. Whichever side takes the majority of tricks – seven or more – wins the game, and the first side to win two games wins the match, or 'rubber' as it is properly called. In

Whist, a trump suit is chosen at random by turning up the last card, and all the skill of the game lies in so playing one's cards as to communicate the nature of one's holding to the partner, so that both may then play their remaining cards to best effect. Play therefore begins with no knowledge of anyone else's hand and concludes with complete knowledge.

Amongst serious players, Whist was ousted by the comparatively new game of Bridge in the space of a few years in the 1890s. Bridge introduced two major features and one minor one. First, instead of selecting trumps at random, they were nominated by the dealer after examining his own hand. This may sound like an unfair advantage, but of course the 'fairness' evens itself out over a number of deals (the game now being played up to a target of 30 points, which might take several deals, rather than being determined by the result of one deal). More importantly, it adds an element of skill – partly on the dealer's side, since he must choose the most appropriate suit, and largely because the exercise of this privilege gave some prior information about the lie of the cards, of which *all* players could take as much advantage as their skill would allow. A minor novelty at this stage was the bid of No Trump, which was lacking from Whist but has always been essential to Bridge. Incidentally, the dealer could decline to nominate trumps and pass the privilege to his partner, but this is a small point.

The other major innovation was that the partner of the player who nominated trumps laid his hand of cards face up on the table, leaving the declarer to play from them as well as from his own hand – in proper rotation, of course. The exposed hand – known as the dummy – has been characteristic of Bridge ever since. This, too, had the effect of giving everyone further knowledge as to the lie of cards, and so decreasing yet further the element of guesswork attending the opening tricks.

Further development of Bridge all had to do with decreasing the guesswork and so increasing the skill factor.

Simple Bridge, also known as Bridge-Whist, gave way before 1910 to another major advance under the title Auction Bridge. In this game, trumps were selected not necessarily by the dealer or his partner, but by whichever side bid to take the greater number of odd tricks (tricks in excess of six) using the suit nominated as trumps.

Contract Bridge was foreshadowed in experiments recorded as early as 1915 and acquired a substantial following in France under its title Plafond, but it was not until the late 1920s that it began to displace Auction throughout the world. It was devised in more or less its present form by the American millionaire Harold S. Vanderbilt, and brilliantly promoted and publicised by Ely Culbertson, in partnership with his superior card playing wife Josephine, in the early 1930s, since when it has remained the only card game to win recognition as a social accomplishment.

The essential feature of Contract (as it ought properly to be called, to distinguish it from other forms of Bridge) is that full scoring credit is given only for those odd tricks which the declaring side *contracted* to win. Any extras or 'overtricks' gain bonus points which are placed, as it were, in a separate account, and do not count towards the winning of the game. Another essential feature is that of so-called 'vulnerability', which we will come to in due course – suffice here to say that Auction and Plafond players despised it heartily while the battle for supremacy still raged.

This business of separate scoring accounts is the last feature to need explanation before embarking on the game itself. In Whist and early forms of Bridge, bonus points were scorable for 'honours', which simply meant for the fact of being dealt a majority of the top trumps. This was obviously out of keeping with the rewards for skill embodied in the score for winning tricks. In some games, therefore, the practice grew up (if not of abolishing honours altogether) of keeping a separate record of the score for honours, and using them to determine not whether or not a side won or lost the game, but to what extent bonuses or penalties were applicable after the game had been won on points for tricks only.

In Contract, this works in the following way. Each side's scoresheet is divided into a top and bottom half by a horizontal line drawn about half-way down the page. Scores made for winning contracted tricks are entered below the line and added up as they go along. When they reach the target of 100 points the game is won, another line is drawn, and the next game starts from zero again below it. This continues until one side has won two games. The winning of the game is determined only by scores made below the line, and scores are only made below the line by the contracting side and only for those tricks they contracted to win. All other scores – overtricks, honours, scores for beating the contracting side – are entered above the line and listed upwards towards the top of the page. They are entered into and have some bearing on the *amount* by which the winners beat the losers, but do not alter the *fact* that who wins and who loses depends on scores made below the line.

At this point we can explain the purpose of 'vulnerability'. Since a rubber is won by the first side to win two games, a side which has made one game may be tempted to overbid its hand in an attempt to prevent the other from making a contract, preferring the other to get above-line scores for defeating a poor contract rather than below-line scores for possibly winning their own. Hence a side which has won one game towards the rubber is branded 'vulnerable', and, as such, is subject to increased penalties and bonuses so that they have a greater incentive towards accurate rather than desperate bidding.

Finally, let us summarise the point of the game. In Whist, skill lay entirely in the play of cards. In early forms of Bridge, more information was given about the lie of cards before play began, so that a proportion of the skill required lay in assessing the hands before playing the tricks. In Contract, an even larger proportion of the skill lies in the auction, i.e. that period of play in which the players are bidding with a view to determining which side will make the contract, for how many odd tricks and with what trump suit. With most card games, descriptions and advice on 'how to play' relate 90 to 100 per cent of the play of the tricks. With Bridge, at least 50 per cent of most accounts are devoted to bidding, and there are many books devoted not just entirely to the bidding, or to one system of bidding conventions, but even to particular aspects of conventions – just as there are Chess books devoted to individual defences or even single lines of play deriving from them.

Preliminaries

Equipment. Contract is played with a standard pack of 52 cards. It is customary to have two packs to hand, one being shuffled while the other is being dealt. This is why Bridge packs are widely sold in boxed pairs, with backs of the same design but two different colours. It is sufficient to record the game on one scoresheet, but usual for both sides to keep independent scoresheets for purposes of checking. Pre-printed Bridge scoresheets are obtainable from most stationers. There should be a column for each partnership, and a horizontal line drawn about halfway down to divide each column into an upper and a lower half. Points scored towards winning the game are entered below this line, all other scores and bonuses above it.

Players. Four play in partnerships of two against two. If partners are to be established at random, the usual way is for everyone to draw a card from a shuffled pack: those drawing the two highest are partners against those drawing the two lowest. Partners sit opposite each other and play alternately.

Game. A rubber is the best of three games; i.e. the first side to win two games wins the rubber. A game is won on reaching or exceeding a score of 100 points below the line. Another line is then drawn below that, with below-line scores in the next game starting from zero again beneath it, until one side has won the rubber, when all the scores are added up to determine the size of the win. It is possible to make 100 points and so win a game on a single deal, but several deals may be necessary before the target is reached.

Shuffling and dealing. Whoever draws the highest card from the shuffled pack deals first. The turn to deal, bid and play passes to the left, i.e. clockwise around the table as viewed from above. Everyone may exercise a right to shuffle, but the dealer has the right to shuffle last. He should then offer the cards to be cut by his right-hand opponent, who may decline, but otherwise should leave at least half a dozen cards in the smaller half of the cut. (Shuffling and cutting should take place before each deal – Bridge does not lend itself to 'stacking' the cards.) Deal thirteen cards to each player, face down, one at a time, starting at dealer's left and proceeding in a clockwise direction.

The auction

The auction takes place as soon as players have arranged their cards in hand, for which purpose it may be noted that in each suit they rank from high to low as follows: A, K, Q, J, T, 9, 8, 7, 6, 5, 4, 3, 2. It is advisable to alternate suit colours in the hand for clarity and to keep low ranking cards on the outside, as their accidental sighting by opponents will do less harm than the careless waving about of high ones.

The purpose of the auction is to determine which side will become the declarers of a contract to win a specified minimum number of tricks with a trump suit of their own choosing, or with no trumps if they prefer. The side offering to take the higher number of odd tricks (tricks in excess of six, since seven is the lowest winning margin) becomes the declaring side, its opponents the 'defenders'. If the declarers win at least as many odd tricks as they bid, they score for tricks bid, or 'contracted', below the line, with any extra tricks counting above it. If they fail to reach that target, the defenders will make an appropriate score above the line.

Starting with the dealer, each in turn may pass (by saying 'No Bid'), make a bid, double a bid just made by an opponent, or redouble a double just made by an opponent. A player who passes on one round is not prevented from bidding or doubling when his turn comes round again. If everybody passes the cards are gathered in and passed on for the next deal.

A bid consists of a number and a trump; for example, 'One heart' is a bid for one's partnership to win at least seven tricks with hearts as trumps; 'Two no trump' is a bid to win at least eight tricks, playing without a trump suit. Each new bid must be higher than the preceding one, regardless of which side made it. For this purpose any higher number is a higher bid.

As between bids involving the same number of odd tricks, the order of priority from lowest to highest is:

clubs – diamonds – hearts – spades – no trump

Hence the lowest possible bid is 'One club', which can be overcalled by any other bid of 'one'. A bid of no trump can only be overcalled by raising the number, e.g. 'Two clubs' overcalls 'One no trump', or indeed one of any suit.

'Double' is announced by a player to indicate that a bid just made by one of his opponents strikes him as beatable, and in his view such a contract should be played for doubled scores since he expects his side to win. In response to this, the maker of the bid, or his partner, may 'Redouble' on his next turn to speak, thereby proposing that the contract be played for quadrupled scores since he firmly expects his side to make it. A double may be made of an immediately preceding bid, not of any bid that went before it, and a redouble of an immediately preceding double. The effect of a double or redouble is cancelled as soon as any higher bid is made, though of course such a bid is itself open to doubling and redoubling until somebody makes a higher one.

The auction ends as soon as three players have passed in succession. The last named bid becomes the contract for that deal. Whichever member of the contracting side first bid the suit in which the final contract was made becomes the declarer, playing from his own hand concealed and from his partner's hand spread face up on the table as a 'dummy' after the first lead has been made.

The play

The opening lead is made by the player sitting at declarer's left. As soon as he has made it, declarer's partner spreads his hand of cards face up on the table, properly in four columns, one for each suit, with the cards in each suit overlapping one another in numerical order. The declarer plays to the opening lead from dummy; the leader's partner plays third to the trick; and declarer plays fourth from his own hand.

Normal rules of trick taking apply. Suit must be followed if possible, otherwise any card may be played. A trick is won by the highest card of the suit led or by the highest trump if any are played, and the winner of each trick leads to the next. Each side's won tricks should be neatly stacked and arranged so that it is always clear how many they have so far taken.

Declarer's partner neither takes part in the play nor may advise declarer what to play, though he is permitted to call his partner's attention to any technical fault he may be committing, such as failing to follow suit. If declarer wins a trick from his own hand he leads from his own hand to the next; if he wins with a card from the dummy, his next lead also comes from the dummy.

The score

The full scoring system appears on p. 367, from which it will be seen that three types of score are possible: one for the declaring side if the contract is made, or another for the defending side if the contract is beaten, and a third applicable to one side or the other independently of the contract just played.

If contract succeeds. In this case the declarers score below the line according to the number of odd tricks they contracted to make. For example, if the bid was 'two diamonds', and they made three (taking nine tricks), they score for two diamond tricks below the line ($2 \times 20 = 40$) and one overtrick above it (20).

Above the line, declarers score for overtricks at the basic rate, which is 20 each in minor suits, 30 in major suits and no trumps. If the contract was doubled, each overtrick counts 200 regardless of suit; if redoubled it counts 400; and the doubled scores are doubled yet again if the declarers were vulnerable – that is, had already won a game and now gained the second required for the rubber. There is also a flat bonus of 50 for winning a doubled or redoubled contract, in addition to all the other perks.

A little slam is a contract to win six odd tricks (twelve in all), a grand slam one to win all seven odd tricks (all thirteen tricks). The table shows bonuses applicable to the declarer's score on winning such a contract; note that they apply only to contracted slams, not to the mere winning of six or seven odd tricks if some lower number was bid.

TABLE 1: CONTRACT BRIDGE SCORING

Contract succeeds

Declarer scores below the line for each trick bid and won	With minor suit trump, ♣♦ : 20	× 2 if doubled
	With major suit trump, ♡♠ : 30	
	At NT for the first trick : 40	× 4 if redoubled
	for each subsequent : 30	

Declarer scores above the line if applicable	Per overtrick:	basic trick value
	Per overtrick if doubled:	100 (200 redoubled)
	Ditto if also vulnerable:	200 (400 redoubled)
	Bonus if contract (re)doubled:	50
	For making a little slam	500 not vulnerable
		750 if vulnerable
	For making a grand slam	1000 not vulnerable
		1500 if vulnerable

Contract fails

Defenders score above the line for each undertrick	If undoubled:	50 not vulnerable
		100 if vulnerable
	If doubled, for 1st undertrick	100 not vulnerable
		200 if vulnerable
	Ditto, per subsequent	200 not vulnerable
		300 if vulnerable

Scores independent of individual contract

For five honours in one hand (AKQJT trumps):	150
For four honours in one hand (trumps, any four):	100
For four Aces in one hand in a no trump contract:	150
For winning rubber in two games:	700
For winning rubber in three games:	500
Unfinished rubber: for one game won:	300
Unfinished rubber: for part-score in unfinished game:	50

If contract fails. In this case the defenders score a certain amount above the line for undertricks, that is, the number of tricks by which the declarers fell short of their contract. Note here that the scores vary according to whether or not the declarers were vulnerable, and whether or not the contract was doubled or redoubled.

Extras. Scores may be entered above the line for 'honours', unless it is previously agreed to ignore them since they have nothing to do with good play. If one player was dealt the top five trumps, his side scores 150 for honours, or 100 if he was dealt any four of them. Similarly, if anyone held all four Aces in a no-trump contract, his side scores 150.

There is a final bonus for winning the rubber, which is 700 if the losers did not win a single game and 500 if they did.

In the event of an unfinished game (house catches fire, dog swallows baby, etc.; but most Bridge players would ignore this!) there is a bonus of 300 for a won game, and 50 for having made any score at all in the game under way when the Last Trump sounded.

Bidding system

At least half the interest of Bridge lies in the auction. At first sight the process of bidding might appear baldly straightforward: you name your best suit and how many tricks you think your side should be able to take with it as trump, and hope that your partner will either agree to it or name another suit which will be satisfactory to you – all the while trusting that your opponents will not bid so high as to keep you out of the auction. But this is to assume that the auction serves no other purpose than to arrive at a contract – which is not the case. On the way to that contract it also enables partners to exchange information about their hands, for example, whether they have cards about evenly divided between the suits or heavily weighted in favour of one suit ('distribution'), how many Aces, high cards or 'quick tricks' they are counting, what their strongest suit is, and so on.

This is possible because of the concept known as 'bidding space'. Suppose you have a hand which is undoubtedly good for a bid of two diamonds. (For the moment, ignore the fact that it takes two to make a contract.) If it is you to bid first and you announce 'two diamonds' immediately, you have told your partner nothing about your hand except that it is strong in diamonds. This is not very helpful if he has no diamonds and nothing else to speak of, nor (at the other extreme) if he has a good two no-trump bid provided that you can support him in, say, clubs. You have wasted bidding space by jumping from nowhere to two diamonds, skipping over six other bids that could have been made on the way, i.e. five bids of 'one' and that of 'two clubs'. To take advantage of this space, what you need is a previous agreement between you that initial 'one' bids are not necessarily true reflections of the contract you hope eventually to arrive at, but merely code bids or 'conventions' which say something about your hand, and require him to respond with a higher bid indicating something about *his* hand. Having made this initial exchange of information, you will both be in a better position to agree on a real contract which makes proper use of the combined strength of both your hands. The declarer, after all, will be playing with 26 cards, not just the 13 he is looking at to start with.

Any bid which does not necessarily mean exactly what it says on the surface is a 'convention'. Even the announcement of 'double' can be a convention, thus increasing bidding space by up to twice as much. Conventional bids are nearly all used, not on their own, but as part of a table of conventions which all work together to build up a picture of the hand. Such a table is called a bidding system. Many such systems have been devised: preference for one or the other varies according to the nationality of the players, whether they are playing sociable rubber Bridge or cold-blooded duplicate Bridge, whether they are beginners or experts, and so on. In order to overcome the chaos that such a multiplicity of systems could give rise to, it is universally agreed that no partnership may employ a system which is peculiar to itself and hitherto unpublished, or vary any of the conventions within a given system without previously

explaining what they are. In short, conventions must not be
private, but must be understandable to both partnerships.

Sociable rubber Bridge as played in Britain commonly uses
the system known as Acol (from the Bridge Club in Acol Road,
London, where it was originally developed). There is a slightly
downmarket version of Acol known simply as the Two Club
system, from its most characteristic conventional bid, but the
two have tended to grow together and are more often referred
to as Acol whether it is strictly accurate or not.

The introduction to bidding on the following pages must be
understood as referring only to Acol, apart from the immediately following section on assessing the hand, which
applies regardless of the system by which the assessment is put
to use.

Assessing the hand

Before you can bid your hand you have to assess it by reference
to various factors which the bidding system you employ will
need to take into account. Three things are important here:
distribution, quick tricks, and point count.

Distribution. You would normally expect to receive, on average,
3 cards in each suit. An average balanced distribution of suits
would therefore be 4. 3. 3. 3 or 4 .4. 3. 2; anything else may be
described as unbalanced, i.e. strongly weighted in favour of the
longest suit it contains. A balanced distribution immediately
suggests a no trump contract if you have strength in all suits,
but nothing otherwise. Alternatively, it may act as strong
support if your partner bids a suit corresponding to one of the
four-card suits in your balanced hand. Whether your first
bid is at no trump or in a long suit will depend on circumstances.

An unbalanced hand usually suggests a contract in a particular suit, for example hearts in the case of ♠ A 3 ♡ K Q T
8 5 ◇ K J 4 ♣ 7 6 3. Difficulties may be encountered in a
distribution favouring two suits about equally, such as ♠ A 3
♡ K Q T 8 5 ◇ A K J 7 6 ♣ 2.

Quick tricks. If you have a suit of short or average length headed by the Ace, the Ace is a virtually certain winner and therefore counts as a 'quick trick' in that suit. A short suit headed by K . Q also counts as a quick trick, because one of them is almost certain to win when the Ace has gone. One headed by the King and any card lower than the Queen is less certain: if the Ace is led by an opponent, you can drop the lower card and be left with a winning King; but you will be in a quandary if a low card is led from the suit and you are playing second to the trick. A suit headed K x, therefore, only counts as half a quick trick.

The value of a suit in terms of quick tricks is expressed in the following table:

Suit headed by	Quick tricks
A K	2
K Q J	$1\frac{1}{2}$
A Q	$1\frac{1}{2}$
A	1
K Q	1
K x	$\frac{1}{2}$
Q J	$\frac{1}{2}$

It should be remembered that the longer a suit is, the greater the danger of its being trumped by the time your best cards in it have been promoted to winners. This is why the K · Q · J headed suit is rated at only $1\frac{1}{2}$ quick tricks instead of two. Note also that x is accepted Bridge code for any card lower than Jack, though in the table above the substitution of J for x does nothing to improve the strength of that suit.

The count of quick tricks is a useful way of assisting the rating of a hand when the point count method outlined below is not sufficient to take account of particular circumstances in the process of bidding. It is also useful in deciding to what extent a partner's bid can be supported.

Reference may sometimes be found to 'stoppers'. A stopper is a high card which prevents an opponent from running down a suit from the top and winning all the tricks in it. An Ace is an obvious stopper; so is a guarded King (K and any lower card), and a guarded Queen (Queen and any two lower cards). A guarded Jack (J x x x) hardly counts, as the suit will be trumped by the time the Jack is promoted, though it may come into its own in a no trump contract.

Strength points. All bidding systems take as their starting point the valuation of the strength of a hand known (after its originator) as the Milton Work count. Point count is therefore the nub of assessment, to which distribution and quick tricks are supplementary aids.

The system works by assigning strength points as follows: each Ace counts 4, each King 3, Queen 2 and Jack 1. The total strength of each suit is therefore 10, and of the whole pack 40. An average hand is worth 10; anything lower is weak in this respect, while 13 is strong enough to make an opening bid. A partnership's combined hands normally require at least 25 strength points for a game, 33 for a small slam, 37 for a grand slam.

Some of the conventions used in any bidding system are designed specifically to give information about the strength of a hand, as opposed to distribution or best suit. Considerable refinement is possible in this respect, since the stronger the hand, the higher the bid, and the greater the amount of bidding space available for the employment of conventional statements.

Strength points may also be added for distribution in the case of an unbalanced hand. Consider: the average or commonest distribution of cards in any one suit is four to one player and three to each of the others. Therefore, on average, a suit will go round three times before being trumped. If you have only two of a suit, you will be in a position to trump it on the third round, contrary to 'average' expectations. This may be counted as the equivalent of one strength point. Similarly, if you have only one of a suit you may add 2 for distribution, while a void may be counted as 3 strength points. Obviously, distributional points are irrelevant in a probable no trumper, partly because there are no trumps with which to take advantage of the principle, and partly because the more balanced a hand is anyway the less likelihood of its containing a short suit.

Here are some hands considered from the rating viewpoints discussed above.

♠ K x x
♥ A Q x
♦ K x x x
♣ A J x

This is a balanced hand (4 · 3 · 3 · 3), and a strong one since it is worth 17 points and is stopped in all suits. This makes it good for a no trump contract.

♠ A Q x x
♥ x x
♦ K Q x x
♣ Q x x

Another balanced hand (4 · 4 · 3 · 2), but with less promise for no trumps as it is weak in two suits (hearts and clubs). It is, however, quite strong, counting 14 points including one for the heart doubleton, and offers $2\frac{1}{2}$ quick tricks. It is therefore good for a suit bid (diamonds or spades), and would be valuable for no trump if the partner's hand were strong in the other two suits.

♠ A K J x x
♥ K x x x
♦ x x
♣ x x

Here we have an unbalanced hand favouring spades and hearts. It is worth bidding since its mere 11 points for cards are increased to 13 with distribution taken into account, and it offers $2\frac{1}{2}$ quick tricks.

♠ K
♥ K x x x x
♦ Q x x x x
♣ Q J

Also obviously unbalanced, but what a difference! It may count 11 for cards plus 3 for distribution, but against these 14 strength points its weaknesses are obvious, as confirmed by the fact that it only offers $\frac{1}{2}$ a quick trick. Some players will invariably open if they have a five-card suit, but in this case a pass is perfectly acceptable – at least, until you have heard anything useful from your partner.

Bidding in practice

Opening one in a suit. The opening bid – the first one made by anyone in the auction – is absolutely critical because it is made on the basis of no information whatever beyond that of your own hand, except that a preceding pass may be taken as an encouraging factor. It is therefore wise, especially for beginners, to faithfully follow agreed principles of bidding so as not to mislead one's partner. Agreed principles are not arbitrary, but the ones found to be most useful in practice, and should be well known to everyone. Individual judgment, or idiosyncratic or even 'psychic' bidding, can only be indulged in later during the auction, as the amount of information coming in from the interplay of bids and counter-bids becomes too complex to be condensed into definite rules.

A hand should be opened at the level of 'one' in the best suit if it has these features:
– 13–20 strength points, including distribution
– at least two quick tricks
– a biddable suit (four or more cards)
– a satisfactory re-bid.

A four-card suit should not be counted as biddable unless it contains at least 3 strength points.

It must be appreciated that the fact of opening one in a suit amounts to a promise to your partner that you will bid again if he also bids at a low level. The purpose of this is to enable him to offer a conventional, or purely information giving, bid without the danger of your dropping out and leaving him to play it as a contract. For this reason you must be able to make a sensible re-bid, whether or not in the suit you originally opened with.

If you have two biddable suits, open with the longer of them;

if they are of equal length, open with the higher ranking. For instance, with good four-card holdings in diamonds and hearts, open one heart. This theoretically enables you to show the other suit as a re-bid at the two level, making it possible to finish in either hearts or diamonds as the case may be. ('Theoretically', because circumstances may change with intervening bids, especially from the opponents. For the sake of argument, however, we must simply assume that they make no bids which spoil the flow of the ideal progress of bidding.) The rule about bidding the higher of two equally long suits may be broken if they are not adjacent to each other in bidding power ('touching'), depending on circumstances.

Even at this level of bidding there is scope for judgment. For example, a hand may be worth less than 13 but strong enough to open, having, for example, a good five-card suit or more than two quick tricks, while a hand worth 14 may have an obvious weakness rendering a pass prudent.

Responding to one in a suit. If your partner opens with one in a suit, you are required to bid something in return unless your hand is absolutely hopeless. Since your partner may have anything up to 20 points, so far as you can tell, and since 25 is normally sufficient for a game, you need only pass if you have less than 5 in strength, or 6 to be on the safe side.

If you have 6 or more but have no promising bid yourself, nor more than three in your partner's suit, you can indicate weakness by bidding one no trump, thus enabling him to come back with his first suit or show another one at the two level. Alternatively, if you have a balanced hand with no biddable suit but no obvious weakness, you can bid two no trump to show good general support, enabling him to finish with at least three in his best suit. One no trump would be made on up to 10 strength points, two no trump on 11 or 12, three no trump on anything higher.

If you have particular strength in your partner's suit, e.g. four or more cards, you can obviously raise the bid in the same suit, using your judgment as to how high this may go. Bear in mind that in the case of a minor suit (clubs and diamonds) it may be more profitable to convert into a lower bid at no trump than a higher one in the said suit. A successful two no trump contract is worth 70 points towards game, whereas three in a minor suit counts only 60.

To respond with a bid in your own best suit requires considerably greater strength (in points, distribution and/or quick tricks) than would be necessary were you in the opening bid position. If you must, do so at the lowest possible level. A response in a different suit at a higher level than necessary is an instruction to your partner to keep the bidding open until a contract is reached which will enable the game to be won. (For which the requirement will depend on how your score stands at the moment.)

Opening two in a suit. Acol bidding is characterised by the Two Club convention, which means that if you have a promising hand which is too good to open at the one level, indicate this fact by opening 'two clubs' (whether or not you have strength in clubs). A promising hand is one that is balanced and worth 24 or more points, or a good 23, such as ♠A Q x ♡A K x ◇K Q J x ♣A Q x (worth 25). Alternatively, it may be worth at least nine tricks by itself; for example ♠K Q x ♡ AK Q x x x ◇A K ♣x x.

The fact of opening two clubs instructs your partner to keep bidding until you have reached a contract which will win you the game, taking into account how your score stands at present.

If the partner is unable to offer anything useful, he may indicate weakness by bidding two diamonds, which is equally conventional. (If he actually has strength in diamonds he can indicate this fact later, but in any case it is always better to go for a major suit or no trump contract.) If the opener then bids a major suit, partner can still assert weakness by (conventionally) bidding two no trumps. This still leaves enough bidding space to decide on a contract at the level of at least three further bids being made in 'real' suits rather than conventional ones.

An opening bid of two in a suit other than clubs may be made on a hand that seems too good to open at the one level but does not meet the requirements of the two club convention. For example, two hearts might be opened on ♠x ♡A K Q J x x ♢K Q x ♣A x x. Partner should not pass immediately, but may indicate weakness by bidding two no trumps.

Opening three in a suit. An opening bid of three in a suit is only made on a hand which has exceptional strength in one suit, with at least seven cards, for example. It is described as a pre-emptive bid, since its purpose is to prevent the opponents from establishing bidding communications with each other. It indicates weakness in all respects save that of the exceptional suit, and is made with the general expectation that partner will pass, while being able to offer at least the support of an 'average' hand, which should be enough to make the contract in that suit. Partner will not pass, of course, if he has some exceptional strength himself.

Opening no trumps. A balanced hand is opened with a no trump bid, at a level appropriate to its strength in terms of point count.

There are two types of one no trump opening bid: the 'strong', made on a hand worth 16 to 18, and the 'weak', worth only 14 to 16. It is customary to open 'strong' unless otherwise agreed. (Or it may be agreed to open strong when the side is vulnerable and weak otherwise.) Two no trumps may be opened on a hand worth 20 to 22. A hand worth 19 is best opened with one in a suit, while one worth 23 may be worth opening with a conventional two clubs. Three no trumps may be opened on a hand worth 26, but it also has a conventional meaning which is beyond the scope of this rather elementary introduction.

Slam bidding. The scoring of Contract Bridge is such – deliberately – as to bring particularly high rewards for success-ful slam bids, i.e. to win six or all seven of the odd tricks. Bidding systems take this into account by proposing ingenious conventional bids designed to give maximum information relevant to the possibility of making a slam contract. One example which, with care, can be safely used by beginners is called the Blackwood convention.

If a side's bidding reaches the three or four level fairly naturally there is a good chance of a slam being on the cards. When both partners realise this, one of them initiates the convention by bidding 'four no trumps'. This is a request that his partner show how many Aces he holds by means of the following code: a reply of 'five clubs' means either none or all four, five diamonds shows one, five hearts two, and five spades three. This response will be followed either by the small slam bid of six in the suit previously agreed as trump, or by another stage of the convention. The latter consists in bidding 'five no trump', which calls for the partner to state how many Kings he has: 'six clubs' means 'none', diamonds one, hearts two, spades three, no trumps all four. As a refinement, a void suit can be shown by a jump in level. For example, if one player initiates Blackwood with 'four no trump', the reply 'six diamonds' (instead of five) shows one Ace and a void suit.

It must be understood that a bid of four no trump is not necessarily a Blackwood call for Aces. If no suit has already been indicated by the previous sequence of bids then it takes its place as a natural no trump bid.

Defensive bidding. So far we have only considered the bidding sequence from the viewpoint of the side which made the opening bid. The other side, however (unfortunately!), may also be looking for a contract. Or you may be on the other side yourself. In this case bidding principles are much the same except for the kick-off, where your first bid follows and may therefore be influenced by the opening bid of the other side.

In order to overcall an adverse bid of 'one' in a suit, you really require a long prospective trump suit of five or more cards and should be prepared to play the contract in the suit you name, as the opponents, by getting their blow in first, reduce the amount of bidding space open to you for conventions and explorations. Thus you could reasonably bid 'one spade' on a hand such as ♠K Q J T 9 5 ♡x x ◇K x x ♣x x, which has length in spades although worth only 11 strength points,

whereas you could not safely do so on ♠A x x ♡x x x ◇A x x
♣A J x x, even though it is worth 13. If your long suit ranks
lower than the one opened by an opponent, so that you have to
open at the 'two' level if at all, you need more strength in
addition to length. Partner should respond in the same suit if
he has three or more of them, otherwise, or with less than 10 in
strength, he should pass.

You could overcall with a genuine no trump bid if you have a
strong balanced hand and are not too worried by the suit
mentioned in the opening bid. With the sort of hand on which,
as opener, you would have indicated strong game possibilities
by opening two clubs, you can employ the 'take-out' convention by which you bid the *same* suit as the opener but at the
next higher level. This indicates a strong hand and requires
partner to continue the bidding, since you obviously will not
want to be left with a (no doubt doubled) contract in an
opponent's best suit.

Doubling and redoubling. A penalty double is one made on the
genuine expectation that the other side cannot make the contract it is offering. Generally, it is safer to double a low contract
than a high one and when the bidding has been competitive
rather than one-sided. But remember that doubling is defensive
rather than constructive: if you have a possible contract of your
own it is better to pursue that than to double, as you will then
be scoring towards game rather than merely above the line. If
a bid of yours is doubled, and you are certain of making it, it
may be worth thinking twice about redoubling. If the contract
is so certain, a redouble may well provoke the opposition into
bidding further so as to get you out of the game. A doubled
contract in the hand is worth one redoubled in the bush.

Doubling may also be used as a convention, in which case
it is described (naturally) as an informatory rather than a
penalty double. It may be employed to alert your partner to the
fact that you have opening strength, i.e. at least 12 points, and
requires him to make some response unless he is prevented by
a ridiculously high bid from the intervening opponent.

The play

As soon as the opening lead has been made and the dummy gone down, your first task as declarer is to study the two hands you can see, and, relating this knowledge to information gleaned from the bidding and the opening lead, decide where your proposed tricks are going to come from, and whether they should be so easy to make as to yield possible overtricks, or so difficult as to call for the execution of special plans and manoeuvres. Usually it is obvious which cards should be trick winners, and which trumps will be required for trumping eventual leads in void suits. But it is not always obvious how the winners are going to be brought into play. You must remember that you are playing two hands, and will have to arrange for the lead to come from the right one at the right time.

In a no trump contract the important thing is to prevent the opponents from establishing a suit, that is, forcing out your winners in that suit early on so that they can come back in and win the rest by running down the suit from the top. For this purpose it may be necessary to hold your winners back and allow some early tricks to be taken in it, so that when your winners do eventually come into their own the opposition will be denuded of the suit and so unable to lead it again.

In a trump contract with strong trumps between the two hands and no marked weakness in any of the non-trump suits, basic procedure (which may be varied according to circumstance) is to lead trumps, thereby taking advantage of your strength in them to force the opposition to disgorge theirs, after which the rest of the hand may be played like a no trump game. With a weak plain suit it is often better to concentrate first on attacking it, perhaps with a view to voiding it in one hand so that it may be trumped when led, or by letting early tricks be lost in it before too much damage can be done.

Certain patterns of play occur with sufficient frequency to have been given descriptive labels and attended with extensive analysis. Any elementary book on Bridge will introduce you to the elegance of the finesse, the agony of the squeeze and the regular necessity of unblocking.

From the defenders' point of view, the opening lead is often critical. In a no trump contract, your main idea will be to establish the strongest suit held between you and your partner. By leading from your partner's best suit, as suggested by the process of bidding, you maximise your chances of taking the first trick and maintaining the initiative. If you have heard nothing to suggest what that suit might be, lead from your own longest suit, thus informing your partner of where your chances lie and encouraging him to return it whenever possible. (But choose your next best suit if your longest is one in which the declarers may have shown an interest in the bidding.) Your lead should not normally come from the top. The conventional lead, which gives useful information and maximises your potential, is the fourth highest you hold of the suit, or highest from a sequence of three or more headed by an honour.

In a trump contract your main object will be to realise as many of your trick winners as possible before they can be trumped, rather than attempt to establish a long suit. For preference, lead the highest card you hold in your partner's best suit (harking back to the auction), or the lowest if you have four of the suit or three headed by King or Queen. If playing from your own best suit, lead the highest of a sequence, or the Ace if you have it, but King from Ace King and at least another card of the suit.

WHIST

Whist is not only one of the greatest games ever devised, but also mechanically the simplest and most archetypal of all card games. The absolute beginner at cards can pick it up in a few minutes, and, having played it a few times, will have gained enough experience in basic card-play to undertake any new card game, however complex, with complete confidence.

Whist, like Cribbage, is essentially an English game. At first it was played only by the unlettered and unsophisticated: in 1674, Charles Cotton forbore to detail it in his *Compleat Gamester*, on the ground that 'every child almost of eight years old hath a competent knowledge in that recreation'. Sixty years later the game was taken up by serious players, and in 1742 Edmond Hoyle published his first treatise on Whist, based on lecture notes compiled in his lucrative capacity as a private Whist-tutor to young gentleladies 'attended upon in their own home'. From it and from subsequent treatises on other games he made a fortune late in life and promptly bequeathed his name to posterity. The last and greatest authority was Dr Henry ('Cavendish') Jones, who in the latter decades of the nineteenth century expounded so brilliantly upon the 'scientific' and 'philosophical' principles of play as (some say) to drive it far beyond the reach of ordinary mortal intellect.

Cavendish may be accused of killing Whist through analysis, but the real culprit was the rising popularity of a closely related game called Bridge, of which modern Contract Bridge is a later development (see *Teach Yourself Contract Bridge*), and to which Whist is the ideal – indeed necessary – introduction. Whist is nowadays played in a less glorious manner as a somewhat old-fashioned family game and as an entertainment at social gatherings ('Whist drives'). Efforts being made to revive it, however, are well worthy of success, and no self-respecting card-player may consider his education complete without a solid grounding in this simple but subtle exercise in partnership play.

The following description is designed for complete (but not unintelligent) beginners at card play, and will serve as an introduction to basic mechanics and principles that underlie most of the other games in this book.

Preliminaries

Whist is a partnership game, the two players of each partnership sitting opposite each other. One member of each partnership should keep the score for both sides, as a double check on accuracy.

A rubber is the best of three games: if the same side wins the first two, a third is not played.

Each game is played 'five-up' – that is, the first side to reach or exceed a score of five points wins the game. As many rounds or deals are played as may be necessary for one side to make five.

Cards. The standard 52-card pack is used. It contains four suits of 13 cards each, designated spades (♠), hearts (♡), clubs (♣), diamonds (◇). The four suits are intrinsically equal in power and value, but at each deal one of them (at random) is promoted to the status of 'trump' suit, as explained later, and has power over the others.

The thirteen cards of each suit are called 'ranks', as they rank in power relatively to one another. Ace is the highest rank, followed by King, Queen and Jack, and Two is the lowest, the complete 'pecking order' being:

A K Q J T 9 8 7 6 5 4 3 2

Shuffle and deal. Decide who is to be the first dealer by any agreed means. The usual method is to spread the cards face down in a row, each player drawing one at random. Whoever draws the highest-ranking card (regardless of suit) deals first. (By tradition, Ace counts lowest, not highest, for this purpose.) If two players tie, they alone draw once more against each other.

The cards must be shuffled before each deal. Any one or more players may shuffle if they wish, but dealer has the right to shuffle last. He then deals the cards one by one face down around the table, starting with the player on his left and finishing with himself. Before adding the last card to his hand, however, he lays it face up on the table so that all can see it.

It should be noted that the deal and all play of the cards proceed clockwise around the table, as does the right to deal – i.e., the player on the left of the first dealer automatically becomes dealer in the second round, and so on.

Trumps. Dealer now adds the face-up (52nd) card to his own hand, announcing the suit of that card as the trump suit for this particular deal. This means that any card of the suit is superior to a card of any other suit in the pack, regardless of their rank. Thus the lowest trump, the Two, is higher than and may capture any non-trump Ace, and the Ace of trumps is the highest card in the pack. The non-trump suits are called plain suits or side suits.

Object. The object is for you and your partner to win more tricks between you than your opponents. The partnership winning the majority of tricks – seven or more – scores one point for every trick they take above six.

There may be an additional score for honours – the Ace, King, Queen and Jack of trumps. If by the end of the deal it becomes known that one partnership has held three or four trump honours between them, having been dealt them at the beginning, they score respectively two or four points. Each player should therefore mentally note before play whether he himself holds one or more of the honours cards.

Play. The usual rules of trick-taking apply. The player left of dealer leads to the first trick. You must follow suit to the card led if possible; if not, you may trump or discard. The trick is won by the highest card of the suit led, or by the highest trump if any are played. The winner of a trick leads to the next.

Revoking. The penalty for a revoke is three points. (A player revokes when he fails to follow suit even though able to do so. If the revoke can be corrected in time there is no penalty, but usually it does not become known until later in the play. If a player can be shown to have revoked, the opposing side may either score three points for itself or deduct three points from its opponents.)

Score. Points are scored strictly in the following order:

Revoke: If a revoke has been committed, three points are added or subtracted as explained above. If, as a result, one side reaches or exceeds five points, the other may not score for tricks or honours.

Tricks: The partnership who took the majority of tricks scores one point for each trick taken above six. (Thus the win of eleven tricks is sufficient for game in one deal.)

Honours: The Ace, King, Queen and Jack of trumps are honours. If it transpires that all four were held by one partnership as the result of the deal (either all in one member's hand or distributed between them), that partnership scores four. If one partnership held three honours, it scores two. There is no score for honours if each partnership were dealt two. *Nor may a partnership score anything for honours if it stands at four points towards game.*

Game score. The partnership winning the rubber (two games) scores a bonus of two points. If three games were played, the score of the losing partnership is deducted from that of the winning partnership to determine the latter's final score.

How to play well

You cannot teach yourself to become a good Whist player, because, strictly, there is no such thing. You can only become a good Whist *partner.* We can see why as soon as we start to consider, as we must before all else, what is the whole point of the game.

You may think that whether or not you and your partner can win more tricks than your opponents depends entirely upon your luck (or lack of) in the original deal. This is not so. If in a single deal one side does happen to receive exceptionally bad cards then they probably will not win it. But in the long run the cards even themselves out and both sides get their fair share of average as well as good and bad hands. And it is the partnership that makes the better play of what they are dealt that will invariably win the majority of games.

If Whist were played with all 52 cards open to view so that everyone could see what everyone else had, the play would be purely analytical, and the game won by whichever side were better at working out all the consequences of various lines of play. It would, in technical terms, be a game of 'perfect information', like Chess.

But it is not. At the start of the first trick you know only the thirteen cards of your own hand (and the trump turn-up, which is insignificant). On the other hand, there are over six thousand million different orders in which they can be played out. You might at this point be said to have the *minimum of information* but the *maximum of flexibility*.

By the time the last trick is being played you will have learned how all 52 cards were originally distributed. But now you cannot take advantage of this knowledge, for the play of your last card is forced. At this stage, by contrast to the opening situation, you have the *maximum of information* but the *minimum of flexibility*.

During the course of the game, then, the information enabling you to make the best of your cards gradually increases from zero to 100 per cent. At the same time, your flexibility, or opportunity to take advantage of that information, gradually decreases from 100 per cent to zero. In principle, there must be a cross-over point about half way through – by the play of the seventh trick, you will have lost half your flexibility but should have acquired at least half your knowledge of the lie of cards.

In practice, however, a good partnership will play with sufficient cooperative skill to ensure that they gain as much information as possible much earlier than half way through, thereby lengthening the period of play during which they have the opportunity to take advantage of it, whereas a poor partnership will learn nothing to guide their play until it is too late. The better partnership is the one that reaches its cross-over point the sooner.

From this we draw the two fundamental lessons of good Whist play. First, it is above all a partnership game: that side wins which, all things being equal, makes the superior use of the twenty-six cards they hold between them. Second, a partnership can only hope to make superior use of its twenty-six cards if each partner plays every card not just with a view to winning the trick, but, whether he is in a position to contest the trick or not, with a view to communicating to his partner information about the cards remaining in his hand.

What sort of information has to be conveyed? Surely not a detailed account of every single card left in the hand? No – that would be impossible, and is unnecessary anyway.

How is information to be communicated? Surely not by agreeing in advance that the play of a particular card always 'means' a specific thing? Yes – more or less. That is the only way in which it can be done, and a very good system it is too.

How, then, having communicated information to each other, are you both to make maximum use of it in the play? This brings us to the whole object and strategy of the game – it is the end to which the communicative play of cards is the necessary means. And we must, of course, look first at what we are trying to do before embarking upon details of communicative play.

All this may sound pompous and long-winded and irrelevant to the enjoyment of cards. But I consider it necessary, firmly believing that you would be wasting your time if you embarked upon a game without knowing in advance what you were supposed to be trying to do. Winning the majority of tricks is only the *object* of the game. The *point* of the game is to win them by a skilfully controlled combined operation, not just by putting down your own high cards and hoping for the best.

Strategy. Unless you are exceptionally strong in trumps, which happens rarely, your normal strategy as a partnership is to establish and bring home your longest plain suit or suits. To establish a suit means to force out the high cards which your opponents hold in it (preferably by winning them in tricks, though not necessarily) so that those remaining in your hand are the highest left in play. Bringing it home means subsequently leading and winning tricks with those cards without having them trumped.

Let us illustrate the principle at work before examining how to do it. Since there are 13 cards in each suit, each player will be dealt an average of $3\frac{1}{4}$ of them. Any suit in which you hold four or more is therefore 'long' as far as you are concerned, since you have more than the average number. Those cards of it which are certain to win tricks (disregarding the possibility of trumping for the moment) are described as 'long cards'.

Suppose you have been dealt ♠A K Q 2, spades not being trumps, and the other players have an even three each. How many of these are long cards? At first sight only the top three. But on closer inspection all four, because your lead of

	Ace draws	3, 4, 5
then	King „	6, 7, 8
then	Queen „	9, T, J

and now no-one has any of the suit left, so your Two is bound to win if led (and not trumped). You have thus established the suit, and if you can reach a position from which you can lead the Two without having it trumped by an opponent, you will have brought the suit home.

Few holdings are as clear cut as that, of course, and you will generally need the assistance of your partner in bringing home your long suit, while he in turn will need your assistance in bringing home his. Your first task, therefore, is to let each other know what your best suit is. Normally this will be your longest suit. If you hold two long suits then strength (high cards) must be considered as well as length. Thus a holding of A K Q 2 in one suit is better than one of 6 5 4 3 2 in another, even though it is normally better to play a five-card than a four-card suit.

Opening lead. The best opportunity you have for declaring your suit is at your first lead to a trick, especially (but not solely) when by virtue of sitting immediately to the dealer's left you are responsible to the first trick of the game.

Lead from your best suit, so that your partner will know which one to return to you when he himself has the lead. And from that suit lead a card which will indicate to him what sort of holding you have in it, so that by deducting his own holding in the suit he will be able to start assembling a picture of where all the key cards are lying.

How can you choose a rank that will convey information to

him, and at the same time stand you the best possible chance of either winning the trick immediately or at least forcing out a high card from the opponents with a view to establishing the suit? In response to this need, nineteenth-century experts such as Cavendish worked out a highly complex system of codes and conventions, to which nothing less than a treatise at least the size of this book could be expected to do justice. Because partnership Whist is no longer played with such intensity, and because we are here addressing ourselves to beginners, it will be sufficient to present the simplest account of all, as originally explained in *Foster's Whist Manual* (R. F. Foster, New York, 1890).

Foster prefaced his description with a useful point to remember. It is that the most commonly led card is the King (more than 50 per cent of the time). Therefore, look first for the King, and if you have it be prepared to lead it – but only if you have also a card adjacent to it, that is, either Ace or Queen. The leads in detail are shown in Table I.

Table 1 *Which card to lead from your best plain suit*

If your best suit is headed by this:	Lead this:
A K or K Q*	King
A – Q J, or A x x x x	Ace
Q J T etc	Queen
K Q J x x	Jack
K – J T	Ten
Anything else	fourth best

*Except K Q J x x, which is the Jack lead
x means any low card, so (for example) A x x x x means 'Ace heading a best suit of at least five cards'.

Fourth best means the fourth highest card of your suit, as, for example, the Five from a holding of J 8 7 5 2. The reason for this convention will become apparent later.

Table 1 is all very well, but what happens if your longest suit is trumps? The answer depends much upon the general strength of the hand. If you have a pretty good hand, with (say) five trumps and some high side-suit cards, lead trumps. If not, lead from your best three-card suit.

Conventional (information-giving) trump leads are shown in Table 2. There are two possible leads from a three-card suit. If it is strong (headed by the Ace, King or Queen) lead the lowest of the suit, as your partner will not go far wrong by interpreting this as the lead of fourth best from the above table. If, however, it consists of Q J x, lead the Queen, for reasons which will become obvious upon little reflection. If it is weak, lead the highest – your partner will soon deduce that you are making a 'forced lead' from his own holding in the suit or from the other cards that fall to the trick.

Table 2 *Conventional trump leads*

If your trump suit is headed by this:	Lead this:
A K Q J	J then Q
A K Q	Q then K
A K + at least 5 cards	K then A
A K + 4 or fewer	fourth best

Following your partner's lead. When your partner leads to his first trick, he will (unless returning your own suit to you) be playing from his best suit and telling you, from the card he plays, what sort of holding he has in it. His signalling will be a waste of time if you do not use your knowledge of the conventional leads, plus observation of your own cards and those that opponents play to the trick, to build up a picture of how the key cards in that suit lie. For example, if he leads a Ten and you hold the Queen, then you will realise immediately that you have K Q J T between you, and that, as soon as the Ace has been drawn from an opponent, your partner's suit is as good as established. So, before playing your own card to the trick, study his lead and make the necessary deductions. With experience, you will do this without pausing.

If he leads a high card, it is usually best to play your lowest in the suit. But be on the look-out for situations in which it is logically best, or at least a very good risk, to do otherwise. For example, suppose he leads a King and you hold the Ace and Jack. Knowing that he also has the Queen, you should play the Ace, taking the trick, and then lead the Jack, enabling him to win with the Queen. This serves the desirable purpose of leaving him in control of his best suit. If you held on to the Jack, you would then be 'blocking' him from establishing it.

If he leads a low card, indicating weakness, take the trick if you can, and with your best card – do not play clever by attempting to finesse. Again, there are conceivable exceptions, and we may note one in particular to illustrate the meaning of 'finesse'. Suppose he leads a small card, and the opponent on your right does likewise, and you hold the Ace and Queen. It is strictly correct to play the Ace, but perfectly acceptable to play the Queen instead. For if your left opponent now wins with the King, you will have the benefit of having cleared out a high adverse card while still retaining control of the suit (in the shape of the Ace); if not – there being a fair chance that the King is held by the other opponent, or even your partner – you will have made a trick with the Queen and will still retain control of the suit with the Ace. To finesse is to attempt to win a trick with a card lower than necessary. If the Queen does win, the finesse will have succeeded.

It is possible to make some valuable deductions from a low-card (fourth best) lead, and to take useful advantage of them. Foster's 'rule of eleven' is well worth applying in particular. The rule says: deduct from eleven the number of pips on the card led, and that will tell you how many higher cards lie against the leader; deduct the number of higher cards held by yourself, and that will tell you how many are held between the opponents'. Let us see it in action.

Suppose your partner leads a Seven, and second hand plays low. Seven from eleven is four, so there are four cards higher than Seven which are *not* held by your partner. Suppose you have two of them – say, Queen and Nine. Then your opponents between them hold two of the following ranks: A K J T 8. They surely hold the Ace or King, if not both, otherwise your partner

would have led the King (see Table 1); equally, they cannot hold
the Ace and the Eight, otherwise he would have held a suit
headed by K J T and accordingly led the Ten. And so on. In
this particular case you would refrain from attempting to finesse
with the Queen, as there is too strong a probability that it will
fall to Ace or King from the left.

If your right-hand opponent fails to follow suit to your
partner's lead, don't panic – just play low and await developments.

If you hold a top sequence in the suit your partner leads, take
with the lowest, in accordance with the general principle of always winning a trick as cheaply as possible.

Returning your partner's lead. If your partner led to a trick before
you did, and you subsequently win a trick, then you in turn have
your first lead and are immediately faced with the question
whether to declare your own suit by leading from it – in accordance with the same conventions applicable to the opening lead –
or to return your partner's suit.

Sometimes you can more or less do both. For instance, if your
best suit is headed by A K you can lead the King and then follow
with your partner's suit. The fact that the King won is enough to
let him know that you also have the Ace. Thus you will have
gained a trick, conveyed useful information, and kept command
of your own suit, which is now known to both of you.

On principle, it is better to show your own suit before returning his, even if you lack the Ace and are likely to lose the lead;
otherwise, at a later stage in the game when he has exhausted his
own suit, he will have no idea what to lead for the best. You
certainly must show your suit if you have reason to believe that
he was making a forced lead, for to lead into such weakness would
be to play into your opponents' hands. On the other hand, if
you have no good suit of your own, and he has not made a forced
lead from a weak three-card suit, return his immediately.

What should you lead when returning his suit? The rule is: if
you have two left in the suit play the higher of them; if more,
play the lowest. Why? If you have two, and play high before
low, your partner will know by convention that you have none

left in the suit. Furthermore, if your higher card is significantly high – say Ten or better – then by playing it you remove the risk of blocking his suit and so preventing him from establishing it. If, however, you have three or more, you must have been dealt the suit long to start with (having already released one to the trick he led in it). In this case the suit is good for both of you, and the need to unblock is less urgent – though you can still do so by playing high to a subsequent trick as required.

If your partner led from trumps, return your lowest.

Playing second to a trick. Play low, unless you know for certain that you can win the trick. Do not try to compete for it: this is the job of your partner, who will have the advantage of playing last and knowing what he has to beat, whereas you would be playing speculatively. If, however, there has as yet been no sign of the Ace, and you hold the King and Queen, by all means attempt a finesse by playing the Queen: you will either win the trick, which is good, or be left with the commanding card, which is also good. There are those who would play the King when holding neither Ace nor Queen. This is a risk that may or may not be worth taking.

If you are void in the suit and do not know whether or not your partner is able to win the trick, should you ruff it or not, on the off-chance? This depends on your trump holding. If it is weak, then the best use you can make of your small trumps is to attempt all reasonable ruffs; if strong, pass it up. You can afford to lose the trick if you have strength in trumps for later play, where trumps come into their own, while, by discarding from a side-suit, you not only get rid of a useless card but also convey potentially useful information to your partner about the rest of your hand.

Playing third to a trick. In this position you are either leading your own suit or returning your partner's, as previously described. You should attempt to win the trick if your partner is not already doing so.

Playing fourth to a trick. In this position your only job is to take the trick if your partner has not already won it, and the only logical requirement for you is to play the lowest you can for either purpose. Be it noted that the rule about winning a trick as cheaply as possible applies even when you are playing from a sequence. For instance, if you are playing fourth to a trick containing (improbably) the Two, Three and Four of a suit, and you hold (say) Seven, Eight and Nine, play the Seven. It is true that any card of a sequence is as good as any of its fellows for trick-taking purposes, but for the purposes of conveying information, the fact that you are known to be playing the lowest can be of considerable significance to your partner.

Discarding. When you are void and prefer not to trump, choose carefully which suit to discard from. It is not right to look merely for the lowest-ranking card regardless of suit, and it is positively wrong to discard from your longest suit or the one you are trying to establish. Prefer to throw the lowest card from your weakest suit. But consider this example: you have the choice of discarding from A Q 2 in one suit or T 9 3 in another. Here it is better to throw the Two, for reasons which you should be able to work out for yourself.

Trumps. If you have five or more trumps, lead them, unless they are all very low and you have a well-headed plain suit. Do not lead trumps if you have only four, although if they include two honours and you have no other clear lead, you may be justified in leading trumps (low).

If you have such strength but do not have the lead, you may still find an opportunity to call for them by the way in which you play to other tricks. The call for trumps – a signal known as the Blue Peter – consists in playing an unnecessarily high card in a given suit, and then following it with one lower at the suit's next appearance. We have already seen something similar at work in the situation where, holding two only of your partner's suit, you return the higher of them first: when you play the second, you thereby indicate that you are void in the suit, and are in a position to trump if it comes round again. The fact that you are not necessarily void in the suit being used for the Blue Peter does not militate against its communicative value: the fact that your partner sees you play high then low should alert him to the fact that you are ready to play in trumps.

There is also the question of forcing trumps, which means leading a suit in which you know somebody else is void. You should always force if you know that your opponents are strong in trumps, for, if effective, this reduces the power left against the establishment of your own suits as well as against your own trumps when trump tricks are led. If the opponents refuse to be drawn, keep on forcing until they dare not do otherwise than to ruff.

You may also force your partner, but only if you are strong in trumps yourself.

Sample games

In the following four deals you are presented, as the player designated South, with the hand of cards from which you play. The other cards – including your partner's (North) – are not fully revealed until the end of the hand. Instead, we take each trick one by one, show what cards are played by your partner and your opponents, and consider your own contribution on the basis only of what can be seen at the time, or deduced from what has gone before. In other words, each deal is described from the viewpoint of you, South, as if in the course of actual play. For the sake of variety and to demonstrate all playing positions, you lead to the first trick in the first deal and thereafter the opening leads come respectively from West, from North and from East.

The deals themselves demonstrate both elementary and advanced lines of play, and are adapted from examples originally provided by the great player Cavendish. You will find it well worth your while to deal the opening hand described, lay the remaining 39 cards face up to one side, and follow each trick through by playing out the cards specified. The winning card of each trick is printed in bold type.

First deal. East deals, turning up ♣J as the trump card, and you have the opening lead to make from the following hand:

♠A Q J T 2 ♡Q 6 ♣A 9 8 3 ◇9 3

Your best suit – the one which you will try to establish, and from which you will lead – is spades. You have some strength in trumps, which is enhanced by the fact that you have two (red) suits of below average length and may therefore be expected to make two tricks by ruffing. It is a pity that your red Queen is unguarded: with two lower cards instead of one she might have been expected to win the third round of hearts.

Trick 1

S	♠ A	A clear cut example of an Ace lead. You tell North
W	♠ 5	that this is the suit you would like returned, and that
N	♠ 4	you have in it high cards lacking the King. A run of
E	♠ 3	low spades played to your lead suggests that the suit
		is fairly evenly distributed.

Trick 2

S	♠ J	Continue the suit, hoping to draw the King – which
W	♠ 6	in fact you do, leaving your Queen high. (You will
N	♠ 8	ask why Jack is led from the sequence Q J T – isn't
E	♠ K	Queen the right card to lead? Yes, it is. The answer
		here is that in Cavendish's full-blown signalling
		system the lead of Ace then Jack shows that your
		complete holding was A Q J T and none lower. I
		have avoided 'correcting' the lead, in order to
		indicate the subtleties of which the game is capable.

Trick 3

E	◇ 6	Now your right-hand opponent leads what is
S	◇ 3	presumably the fourth best of his best suit, though
W	◇ K	not a strong one. As second to the trick, it is proper
N	◇ 2	for you to play low. The fact that West takes it with
		the King suggests that he also holds the Ace, other-
		wise he would not risk losing it to your partner.

Trick 4

W	◇ A	West returns his partner's suit, in preference to
N	◇ 5	opening one of his own, so presumably does not
E	◇ 4	have another certain trick in the form of an Ace. You
S	◇ 9	have only the Nine left, and are ready to ruff if
		diamonds are led again.

Trick 5

W	♡ 4	But he switches suits – and to your surprise gives
N	♡ 3	you a trick with your unguarded Queen.
E	♡ J	Presumably hearts are West's best suit. So far your
S	♡ Q !	partner has not been able to communicate with you,

but from his play so far he does not appear to have
anything exciting to offer.

Trick 6

Now it is your lead again, and your hand is ♠Q T 2, ♡6, ♣A 9 7 3. With the command in spades, a void in diamonds and some ruffing strength to match, you are now well placed to see about drawing some trumps with a view to the ultimate bringing home of your spades. The fact that your opponents have switched suits, yet neither led nor called for trumps, suggests that they are not too well off in that suit. So:

S	♣ 3	You lead low, in accordance with principle. Second-
W	♣ 6	hand plays low, as he ought; your partner competes
N	♣Q	for the trick, as is proper; and East, by playing what
E	♣ 4	is presumably his lowest, demonstrates that the

King does not lie with him. Therefore either West or North has it. And North, at last, can lead to you.

Trick 7

N	♣ 7	This trick, exactly half way through the play, tells
E	♣ 5	you everything you need to know! The only trumps
S	♣ A	now left in play against you are King, Jack and Two.
W	♣ T	East has the Jack, because you saw it turned as

trump indicator. Your partner, North, must hold the Two and that *alone*. If it were held by either opponent, it would have appeared as the lowest card at Trick 6 (assuming, as you must, that everyone plays properly). And if North held K 7 2 at the start of this trick, instead of just 7 and 2, he should have led the latter. Unnecessarily playing high before low is nearly always a signal that the two cards concerned are the only ones held in their particular suit. It now follows that West has ♣K, and you therefore have two trumps to everyone else's one. So now you can draw them out preparatorily to bringing home your spades.

Trick 8

S	♣ 8	The trick falls as expected, leaving you with ♠Q T
W	♣ K	2, ♡6, ♣9. With winning spades and the only
N	♣ 2	trump in play, all you can lose is ♡6 to a top heart.
E	♣ J	If West leads spades you capture, lead the other two

to win, then make your last trump before throwing your Six to the Ace of hearts. If West leads anything else you trump it, then lead spades as before. Whichever way it goes, you score three for tricks, taking nine out of the thirteen.

The deal in full at the start of the game was:

North:	♠84 ♡A 7 5 3 ♣Q 7 2 ◇ J 8 5 2
East:	♠K 7 3 ♡J 9 ♣J 5 4 ◇Q T 7 6 4
West:	♠9 6 5 ♡K T 8 4 2 ♣K T 6 ◇A K

Second deal. And now you deal, turning up ♠8 for trumps and finding yourself lying fourth to the first trick on the following hand:

♠98 ♡A Q 6 5 4 ♣Q T ◇J 6 5 3

This time you are definitely weak in trumps, and have only one good suit, the hearts. And once again, you have an unguarded Queen, for which you might compensate by ruffing the third round of clubs. West is to lead.

Trick 1

W	♣ 4	As happened in the previous deal, you are surprised
N	♣ 5	to take a trick as cheaply as this. Presumably clubs
E	♣ 9	are West's best suit but he lacks the Ace; and,
S	♣ T	presumably, from the result, your partner must

have it.

Trick 2

S	♣ Q	You ought really to declare your hearts by leading
W	♣ K	the Ace, but this club lead is not meaningless, as
N	♣ A	your partner ought to infer that you are voiding the
E	♣ 7	suit. As it happens, the result, which squeezes a
		King out of the opponents, is better than you might
		expect.

Trick 3

N	♡ 7	Now it is your partner's first lead and opportunity
E	♡ 8	to communicate – and, to your surprise, hearts is his
S	♡ Q	best suit as well as yours; if he has led the fourth
W	♡ J	best of it, which is probable but not absolutely
		certain, then he must have K T 9 left, giving your
		side command of the suit. The only trouble is that
		your own shortness of trumps suggests that you will
		be lucky to bring the suit home. You have now to
		lead from ♠9 8 ♡A 7 5 4 ◇J 6 5 3.

Trick 4

S	◇ 3	You are not in a position to lead trumps, nor do you
W	◇ 7	wish to have your hearts ruffed. This leaves only
N	◇ A	diamonds to lead from; if pursued further, they may
E	◇ 4	draw some trumps.

Trick 5

N	◇ T	Partner avoids hearts too, presumably for the same
E	◇ K	reason, and seems equally disinclined to lead
S	◇ 5	trumps. His high-ranking lead suggests that he may
W	◇ 8	be voiding the suit in order to ruff it.

Trick 6

E	♠ Q	It is East's first lead, and out come his big guns –
S	♠ 8	trumps are called for. West appears to have the Ace,
W	♠ K	which bodes ill. Your partner's lowest trump is the
N	♠ 3	Three, so he may have several others.

Trick 7

W	♠ A	So far, so bad; and your last trump has been
N	♠ 4	sounded. Five are left in play – J T 7 6 5 – and of
E	♣ 2	these East must have at least the Jack and Ten to
S	♠ 9	have led the Queen to the previous trick. North
		probably has two of the others.

Trick 8

W	♣ J	Now that *is* interesting. West must be out of trumps
N	♠ 6	to have led as he did, and North has been able to
E	♣ 6	turn a trump to his advantage.
S	♡ 4	

Trick 9

N	♡ 2	An unexpected pleasure: East was obliged to follow
E	♡ 3	suit with what little he had, and West was void in
S	♡ 5	trumps as well as hearts, and so you win with a small
W	♣ 2	one.

Trick 10

And here we are at the crux of the deal. You have to lead from ♡A 6, ◇J 6. Should you now make with the Ace? No! East is sure to trump it, and cannot lead anything to your good. Consider the position. North, you know (from Trick 3), has three hearts, no clubs, and either a trump or a diamond as his fourth card. If his fourth card is the diamond, then East must have four trumps (West being void), and East will take all no matter what you lead. But if his fourth card is a trump (spade), you can force it by playing into his void suit. Therefore:

S	◇ 6!	You lead diamonds, and your partner scores his last
W	◇ 9	trump to give you the odd (seventh) trick. East, of
N	♠ 7	course, wins the final three – but they are not the
E	◇ 2	ones that count.

The other hands were:

North ♠7643 ♡KT972 ♣A5 ◇AT
East   ♠QJT52 ♡83 ♣976 ◇K42
West   ♠AK ♡J ♣KJ8432 ◇Q987

Third deal. Your partner deals you the following hand, turns up
♡6 and leads:

♠A Q J   ♡A K 9 3   ♣J 8 6 2   ◇J 5

This is a hand from which you are glad not to have the opening
lead: its longest plain suit (clubs) is weak, and its strongest plain
suit (spades) in short, while the strongest suit is trumps (hearts),
and far from outstanding at that.

Trick 1

N	◇ K	Diamonds are your partner's best friend, and he
E	◇ 8	appears to have a good holding headed by A K or
S	◇ 5	K Q. Your own shortness in the suit is a strength
W	◇ 4	rather than a weakness – but East's 'lowest card' as

second to the trick looks dangerously high. He also
may be playing from a two-card holding, in which
case he will be ruffing diamonds at their third
appearance, and you will have to overtrump.

Trick 2

N	◇ A	A second trick in the suit, and it is clear to North
E	◇ Q	that both you and East are out of it. You can now
S	♠ J	expect him to lead a different plain suit – or might he
W	◇ 7	turn to trumps ?

Trick 3

N	♠ T	Your favourite suit. From your own holding it
E	♠ 3	seems likely that your partner is leading the top of a
S	♠ J	three-card suit. And from your holding of A Q J it is
W	♠ 2	natural to finesse against the King by playing the

Jack. The finesse succeeds: West does not have the
King. Neither does North, for he would not have
led the Ten from King, Ten alone, while from
King, Ten and small he would have led the smallest.
So East must have the King. Naturally, it would
have been foolish for him to play it second to the
trick.

Trick 4

S	♡ 3	You now have your first lead, and hold ♠A Q
W	♡ 6	♡A K 9 3 ♣J 8 6 2. Your best suit is trumps, and
N	♡ **J**	it is not brilliant, so you lead it low. (You might
E	♡ 5	have played ♠A, but would then leave East's King

in command of the suit.) West has probably played
from a pair of high hearts, and either he or your
partner has the Queen.

Trick 5

N	♡ 4	North returns trumps, as he ought, and you are
E	♡ 8	tempted to slip over East's Eight with your Nine.
S	♡ **K**	But as third hand you are morally obliged to play
W	♡ 7	high, and there is an outside chance that you will

catch a Queen from West.

Trick 6

S	♡ **A**	You ought now to turn to another suit, but it seems
W	♡ **T**	worth while to seek to draw the Queen of trumps.
N	♡ 2	Unfortunately, she lies with West, as it is clear from
E	♠ 4	the cards that your partner is now out of trumps.

Remember that he returned the Four to you in the
previous trick, and has now gone down with the
Two: 'high then low' is the correct play from a
holding of two, so he must now be void. No doubt
you interpreted his previous lead of the Four as
lower rather than higher.

Trick 7

You must now lead from ♠A Q , ♡9, ♣J 8 6 2. Your side has six
tricks, and you need only play the top spade to make your
seventh. Yet there may still be a way to make your trump as well
– bearing in mind that every overtrick counts a point towards
game – and to compensate for your previous rashness in hearts. It
is obvious that your opponents have a trick or three to make in
clubs, so you can afford to let them start their little fling:

S	♣ 2	North attempts to make his King, but the chances
W	♣ 3	are 50/50 in theory, and in practice East makes it
N	♣ K	100 to 0 against by overtaking with the Ace. This
E	♣ A	gives you a slight advantage, in that your Jack is now
		second highest in the suit, instead of only third in
		line of succession.

Trick 8

E	♣ Q	The Queen comes out, and now your Jack is high.
S	♣ 6	
W	♣ 7	
N	♣ 5	

Trick 9

E	♣ 4	You have your odd trick, unexpectedly in clubs –
S	♣ J	thanks to your 'guarded Jack' and the fall of Ace and
W	♣ T	King to the same trick.
N	◇ 3	

Trick 10

You to lead again, from ♠A Q, ♡9, ♣8. Key cards against you are ♣9, held by East, ♠K, also held by East, and ♡Q, held by West. (If ♣9 were held by West, he would have just played it instead of the Ten. For the placing of the other two, see Tricks 3 and 6.) Since East is void in diamonds (Trick 2) and West has the only other trump, East must have three spades with his club. If you force East to lead, he will have to play spades right into your hands, for his King can only win if led into. Then either you make two spades, or West trumps one of them and you make a spade and the other trump. And you *can* force East to lead, as follows:

		Trick 11		*Trick* 12		*Trick* 13	
S	♣ 8	E	♠ 5	W	◇ T	S	♠ A
W	♠ 6	S	♠ Q	N	◇ 6	W	◇ 9
N	◇ 2	W	♡ Q	E	♠ 8	N	♠ 9
E	♣ 9	N	♠ 7	S	♡ 6	E	♠ K

So you finish with a score of three for tricks, having taken nine in all. The other hands prove to have been:

North   ♠T 9 7   ♡K 4 2   ♣K 5   ◇A K 6 3 2

East   ♠K 8 5 4 3   ♡8 5   ♣A Q 9 4   ◇Q 8

West   ♠6 2   ♡Q T 7 6   ♣T 7 3   ◇T 9 7 4

Fourth deal. Your partner, North, deals you the following hand, and turns up ◇5. You will be playing second hand to East's opening lead.

♠4   ♡A K Q T 2   ♣8 7   ◇K T 8 7 3

You are immediately struck by the uneven distribution (5–5–2–1), and must be prepared for the whole deal to be unbalanced. Your strong heart suit, for instance could be ruffed at the first round. Fortunately, you are also strong in trumps, and that is really what counts.

Trick 1

E	◇ 6	Well, well. East's best suit appears to be trumps too.
S	◇ 3	And since North could not overtake West's Jack,
W	◇ J	both Ace and Queen must lie with the opponents –
N	◇ 5	very probably with East.

Trick 2

W	◇ 2	West dutifully returns his partner's suit, and, to
N	♣ 2	your disappointment but not to your great surprise,
E	◇ A	your own partner proves trumpless. Note, however,
S	◇ 7	the suit of his discard: his best suit must be clubs. East, properly, played high, leaving your King in command of the trump suit for the time being. You now expect a change of policy from East...

Trick 3

E	♠ 3	The lead is presumably of East's second best suit,
S	♠ 4	and not a very good one. Your partner finds an Ace
W	♠ Q	to compensate for his lack of trumps, and is now
N	♠ A	placed with the lead.

Trick 4

N	♣ A	As you suspected from Trick 2, your partner's suit
E	♣ K	is clubs, and it is a strong one, as his lead indicates.
S	♣ 7	But the unevenness of the distribution strikes again,
W	♣ 3	for East's response clearly shows that his King was single.

Trick 5

N	♣ J	North must be as aware, as you are, that East will
E	♢ 4	trump; the fact that he pursues his clubs neverthe-
S	♣ 8	less indicates considerable length in the suit.
W	♣ 4	

Trick 6

E	♠ 2	East resumes his quest in spades, and at last you can
S	♢ 8	take the initiative. North will be observing your
W	♠ 7	lead with interest.
N	♠ 6	

Trick 7

You have the lead from ♡A K Q T 2, ♢K T, and both sides have taken three tricks. Hearts, your strong suit, have not yet been played. You are well placed in trumps, holding K T against Q 9, which latter you can place with East. (He must have held five trumps to have legitimately opened them to the first trick.) You must lead from the hearts, otherwise you give East a trick in trumps either now or later. By leading from the top down, you are bound to make the four (at least) you need for game, for as soon as East trumps a heart, both your trumps will win.

Effectively, therefore, the play may be said to end at this point. But Cavendish, not liking to take the easy way out of anything, goes on to show how you can be virtually certain of taking all the remaining tricks between yourself and North!

His argument is based on the knowledge, from certain conventions of play, that East led originally from a holding of five spades (though even if he had led from four, as you yourself can surmise from the play, the following approach would still be correct). That being so, East must have three spades left in hand, plus his two trumps, no clubs (see Trick 4), and therefore not more than two of the outstanding hearts. So he will start ruffing when you reach the Queen. Your partner, however, has a long line of clubs. If East can be induced to drop a trump on a club lead, you yourself can overtrump – preventing him from making another trick. Therefore:

	Trick 8		Trick 9		Trick 10
S ♡ 2 !	N ♣ Q	N ♣ T	N ♣ 6
W ♡ 5	E ♠ 5	E ♡ 8	E ♠ J
N ♡ 9	S ♡ T	S ♡ Q	S ♡ K
E ♡ 7	W ♣ 9	W ♡ 6	W ♡ J

Trick 11	Trick 12	Trick 13
N ♣ 5	N ♡ 4	S ◇ K
E ♠ 9	E ◇ 9	W ♠ K
S ♡ A	S ◇ T	N ♡ 3
W ♠ 8	W ♠ T	E ◇ Q

The play of these last few tricks shows the power of position. If at any point during North's club leads East had attempted to take with a trump, you would merely have overtaken with the next higher trump, led out your next trump to win his last, and then pursued the hearts in complete safety. So long as he feared to do this, you remained quite happy to throw your ♡ A K Q T trick-winning cards to your partner's uncontested ♣ Q T 6 5.

The other hands were :

    North   ♠ A 6 ♡ 9 4 3 ♣ A Q J T 6 5 2 ◇ 5
    East   ♠ J 9 5 3 2 ♡ 8 7 ♣ K ◇ A Q 9 6 4
    West   ♠ K Q T 8 7 ♡ J 6 5 ♣ 9 4 3 ◇ J 2

The potential depth of Whist may not be to everybody's taste, and there is no reason why it should be. But I hope the examples given above are enough to show what scope the game gives for brilliant play, and why, before the advent of Bridge, Whist was universally regarded as one of the great games of the world. It is also the most basic of all trick-taking games, being easy to learn without any previous knowledge of card play. Once play Whist, and you can approach any new card game with complete confidence.

EUCHRE

Euchre is the major representative of a group of trick-and-trump games in which only five cards are dealt and five tricks played, the object being to win the majority (three or more) and preferably the lot, the latter feat being termed 'winning a march' – or perhaps stealing it ? Other five-card games include Ecarte, Nap and Five Hundred.

Euchre is an American game of German-immigrant origin dating from about the 1860s. Specifically, it is traced to the so-called Dutch of Pennsylvania (Dutch = Deutsch = German in this case), and is played mainly in the north-eastern states as well as in Canada. For some curious reason it is also the usual pub-game of Britain's West country, in defiance of the otherwise universal preference for Cribbage. There is, however, no evidence to suggest that it originated in Britain and travelled westwards over the Atlantic rather than vice versa.

There are versions of Euchre for different numbers of players, and variant forms even of those versions, it being a highly prolific and cross-bred family of games. Partnership Euchre, as described below, may be regarded as a, if not *the*, classic form of the game, though two-hand Euchre probably preceded it.

A characteristic feature of Euchre games is the peculiarity of the trump suit. The highest trump is always the Jack, which is called the 'right bower'. This is followed by the other Jack of the same colour as the first, called the 'left bower'. The Ace comes next, being third highest, and so on downwards. Bower rhymes with 'flower'; it comes from the German word *Bauer* which primarily means 'farmer' (as do the related Dutch word *boer* and its English derivative *boor*), but is also one of several words for the Jack or Knave at cards.

The effect of the bowers is to lengthen the trump suit and correspondingly shorten the others, especially the suit of the same colour. Since the game is played with a 32-card pack, only eight in each suit, the numerical imbalance is of some significance to the play. Euchre is a fast game and much fun, but it is also one of deadly subtlety, as you will discover to your cost if you play against an expert. And especially if you are foolish enough to play for money.

The game

Cards. 32, consisting of the A K Q J T 9 8 7 of each suit; lower cards are customarily used for marking the score, as shown in Fig. 3.

Preliminaries. Determine partnerships by drawing cards. Ace counts low (below Seven); the two drawing the lowest cards play the two drawing the highest, and partners sit opposite each other. The player who drew the lowest card deals first. All play proceeds clockwise, including the turn to deal. Game is usually set at five points, though seven and ten are common alternatives.

Shuffle and deal. Anyone may shuffle, but dealer has the right to shuffle last. Deal five cards to each player, not singly but in batches – either two then three, or three then two (but, whichever is adopted, the same for everybody). Place the remaining cards face down to one side of the table, and turn up the top card. The suit of this card is the prospective trump suit, though it may be rejected in favour of another later.

Rank of cards. The normal rank of cards for trick-taking purposes is A K Q J T 9 8 7, but trumps are peculiar. The highest trump is the Jack of trumps, called the right bower; second highest is the other Jack of the same colour as trumps, called the left bower. Ace is therefore the third highest trump, and so downwards. It is important to understand that the left bower belongs to the trump suit and *not* to the suit shown on its face.

Dealer's privilege. If the suit of the turn-up is in fact accepted as trump, dealer is entitled to take the turn-up into his own hand and discard any other card face down in its place. Knowledge of this fact may influence the bidding.

Bidding. The player left of dealer is called eldest; the others may be referred to as secondhand, thirdhand and dealer. Starting with eldest, each in turn passes or accepts the suit of the turn-up as trumps. Whoever accepts the prospective trump is called the maker, and his partnership is thereby obliged to win three or more tricks.

As a matter of tradition, an opponent of the dealer (eldest or thirdhand) signifies his acceptance of the trump by saying 'I order it up' – meaning, in effect, that he is ordering the dealer to take up the turned card. Secondhand accepts by saying 'I assist', meaning that he will assist the dealer to win after the latter has taken the turn-up. Dealer accepts by saying 'I take it up'.

If the first three players pass, and dealer also refuses to accept the trump, he announces 'I turn it down', thereupon taking the turn-up and replacing it (still face up) crosswise at the bottom of the undealt cards so that it is still visible.

In this event there is another round of bidding, starting with eldest, in which each player in turn may either pass again or nominate a different suit as trump. (The suit that has already been rejected may not be nominated a second time.)

If all players pass a second time, the round is abandoned and the deal passes to the left.

As soon as any player has made a positive bid, either by accepting the turned up trump or by nominating another on the second round, the bidding ends and the play begins.

Playing alone. The maker is entitled to play alone against his opponents, which he signifies by stating 'alone' as soon as he has accepted or nominated the trump suit. His partner thereupon lays his cards face down on the table and does not participate in the play. The main advantage of going it alone is that the player scores double for his side if he succeeds in winning a march (all five tricks).

If the maker elects to play alone, either opponent may say 'I defend alone', in which case his partner also lays his cards face down and does not participate.

The play. Eldest leads to the first trick regardless of who is the maker, unless the maker is playing alone, in which case the lead is made by the player at maker's left. The usual rules of trick-taking apply: follow suit to the card led if possible; if not, either trump or discard. The trick is won by the highest card of the suit led, or by the highest trump if any are played. The winner of a trick leads to the next. Remember that the left bower is not a card of the suit marked on its face but is the second highest card of the trump suit.

Scoring. If the making side wins three or four tricks it scores one, whether the game was played in partnership or alone.

If the making side wins the march it scores 2 if played in partnership, 4 if played alone.

If the making side fails to win three tricks it is 'euchred'. The opposing side score 2 if it played in partnership, 4 if defended alone.

Hints on play

Here are the basic facts of Euchre life, which you must bear in mind before you start the game.

Fewer than two thirds of the cards are in play, which means that the assessment of your own hand must be made on the probability that certain key cards – such as the right bower, if you hold the left – are actually in play. Although the distribution of cards is a matter of pure chance, one's judgment of play against the probabilities is a matter of skill and experience. Players who come to Euchre from games in which all cards are dealt, such as Whist and Bridge, may be tempted to underestimate the extent to which experts can play successfully *with* the probabilities rather than *against* them.

The peculiar ranking of Jacks must be borne in mind when assessing your hand. Suppose, for example, you hold ♠7 ♡J 7 ♣— ♢J 7. If the turn-up is a black card your hand is useless. If red, however, then both your Jacks are bowers and one of the Sevens a trump, giving you a certain two and a highly probable three, even without your partner's assistance. Naturally, you will lose no opportunity to entrump a red suit.

With only five cards in hand it is unlikely that a plain suit will

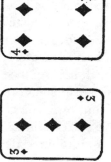

FIGURE 14

Traditional method of score-keeping involves lower cards (Three and Four) not used in actual play. The Three is half-covered to denote a score of '1', the Four half-covered to denote '2', then both respectively uncovered to show '3' and '4'.

go round twice without being trumped. In your original hand, then, a plain suit void is strong because you might be able to trump it, and a one- or two-card suit strong if headed by Ace or even King. Anything longer is likely to be trumped early.

It is, however, often possible to establish a plain suit, and the early drawing of trumps for this purpose is a common strategy. Holding, for example, ♡J, ◇J, ♠A Q 7, with hearts trump, you can reasonably expect to draw all adverse trumps by leading the Jacks and then hope to win all three spades. This would not be 'best' play from the hand quoted, but could be indulged in as an emergency lone hand for a possible four points when your opponents stand at four and your own side at one.

As a general rule, if you have two certain tricks you can expect your partner to contribute a third in order to justify your becoming the maker.

Bidding. Now consider the first round of bidding for acceptance or rejection of the turn-up from each player's point of view.

As eldest, you have no indication of your partner's strength and dealer has an advantage over you by virtue of his privilege of taking the trump turn-up, the rank of which you must take very much into account. In these circumstances you need a secure trump holding to justify a bid, such as one of the bowers and two good trumps. Since you have the lead (except, possibly, against a lone player), a plain suit Ace may be counted as a reliable trick if your holding is not too long.

As secondhand, it is your partner who has the privilege of the turn-up, and you may reasonably bid on the strength of two good trumps or two otherwise reliable tricks.

As thirdhand, your partner must have indicated weakness by his pass; if you bid, the onus will be upon you, and it will be difficult to exercise by virtue of the fact that your partner, as eldest, will have the lead against you. You must therefore have two certain tricks before you may order it up. If you have a good three or more tricks, it may be worth playing alone.

As dealer, three preceding passes will put you in a good position to take it up, though your partner's admitted weakness requires you to be sure of two tricks yourself. Bear in mind that if you turn it down it is your opponents who will have the first opportunity of nominating an alternative trump, for which reason you may be justified in bidding on a risky hand in order to obviate the danger of their winning a march, especially if played alone. Here you may 'play to the score' – a procedure that applies to every player but to dealer most of all. At 0–0 you have little to lose and something to gain from taking the chance, but at 4–2 in your favour you have everything to gain and hardly anything to lose.

If everybody passes, the bidding goes round again, this time for another suit.

As eldest, look first at the possibility of entrumping the other suit of the same colour as the original turn-up (called 'making it next'), since the fact that dealer's side passed first implies that neither of them held a bower.

As secondhand, you will prefer if possible to nominate a suit of the other colour (called 'crossing it') for the same reason that eldest would have preferred to make it next.

As thirdhand, you would also prefer to make it next, but this time warily, since your partner has admitted himself weak.

Dealer, of course, would prefer to cross it, but with the same reservations.

Playing to the score. When the score stands at 0–0, you should only order it up as an opponent of the dealer's side (that is, as eldest or thirdhand) if you are certain of a win and have no alternative suit to nominate, for if all players pass you will have the first opportunity to change suit in addition to the advantage of the lead. Dealer, on the other hand, should take it up at all costs, in order to deprive eldest of the advantage outlined above. The worst outcome of doing so would be to be euchred for a score of 2–0 against, whereas to leave it to the other side might be to invite a lone march resulting in 4–0 against.

If your opponents stand at three points and you are thirdhand or dealer, it is dangerous to become the maker in view of your partner's admitted weakness, coupled with the fact that to be euchred would lose you the game.

A side standing at four points is said to be 'at the bridge'. If you are at the bridge as dealer, and your opponents have less than three, you should take it up even on a poor hand in order to reduce the risk of a lone march from eldest.

Discarding. As a matter of form, dealer should make his discard before the first trick is led but leave the turn-up on top of the pack until he wishes to play it. (It should go without saying that the dealer's exchange privilege applies only when the suit of the turn-up is accepted; when another trump is nominated, there is nothing to exchange.)

There is no problem as to the discard – the best to throw is a plain suit singleton lower than the Ace. With a good alternative, however, a singleton King may be retained, as there is only a 62 per cent probability that the Ace is in play at all and only a 41 per cent probability that it is held by one of the opponents. The chances are therefore better than evens that the King will make a trick. Of two singletons, of course, discard the lower, and if both are of equal rank, discard preferably one of a different colour from trumps.

Playing alone. The chief attraction of playing alone is the possibility of winning a march and scoring four instead of two – indeed, there is little point in going it alone otherwise, unless, as thirdhand or dealer, you feel that your partner is so weak that his participation in the play could be less of a help than a hindrance. One advantage that accrues from playing alone is that the lead is made by the player on your left, thus putting you in the position of playing last to the first trick. It is an advantage that particularly benefits thirdhand, as the worst trick-playing position of all is lying third to the lead from a weak partner. To the dealer, however, it makes no difference, as eldest would lead anyway.

The purpose of defending alone – which may only be undertaken when the maker is playing alone – is to increase your partnership's score in the event of your euchring him. Naturally, you will only undertake a lone defence if you have a particularly strong hand.

(In some circles, only the maker may play alone, and there is no provision for either of his opponents to defend alone. In this case the lone player, if euchred, should lose double in order to penalise a rash attempt made at playing to the score – in other words, his opponents score four instead of two, as he would have done if he had won a march.)

The play. Normal practice is to lead trumps for the purpose of extracting them all round and so establishing a plain suit in which you hold the Ace and more, or (hopefully, bearing in mind the 59 per cent probability) King high. If, however, you have no qualifying plain suit, and are not particularly rich in trumps, it is better to retain what trumps you do hold for the purpose of trumping when void in suits led.

We have already observed that a plain suit is unlikely to go round twice, so there is no point in seeking a finesse. Lead your highest card, especially if it is an Ace or King, at your earliest opportunity, and, when following to the trick, win it if you can unless your partner has already done so. Remember that the trump suit is marginally longer than the others, and that an opponent is as likely to hold three trumps as to be void in them.

Sample game

You are lying thirdhand; the turn-up is ♣Q and your hand is as follows:

    ♣ K
    ◇ T 9 7
    ♠ A
    ♡ —

Not very promising. Your partner passes, and so does second-hand. Your own pass follows as a matter of course. Dealer, you are relieved to hear, turns it down, leaving it to your partner, as eldest, to nominate a suit. But again he passes, indicating considerable weakness, and so does secondhand.

This places you in an interesting spot, as the hints on play advise you not to attempt a game in diamonds; the temptation to do so is great, even though you would be crossing the suit instead of making it same. Your Ace is a sure trick, your King a 41 per cent probable trick (especially since neither opponent accepted clubs as trumps, rendering it conceivable that neither holds the Ace), and your void a very probable trick by virtue of one of your trumps – which, although fearfully low in rank, are reasonably high in length.

It is true that your partner is weak; but on the other hand so are your opponents, and you have twice as many of them, so they must be twice as weak. Convinced by this convoluted logic, and standing at the start of a new game, you nominate diamonds – but do not invite your partner to drop out.

Trick 1

Partner leads ♣J, secondhand plays ♣T, and you play your King. It all hinges on dealer. He plays ♠7. Extraordinary! He is void in both clubs (no wonder he passed first time round) and trumps; and very probably, had you passed the second time, he would have nominated hearts or spades as a sure-fire trump game.

Trick 2

You now hold a plain Ace, ♠A, and your three low trumps, T 9 7. You could surely lead the Ace with success, in view of dealer's void in trumps, and would probably then come back after leading and losing a trump for three or possibly four tricks. But if your right-hand opponent has a good trump at all it would be safer to extract it from him first. So, in the hope that your partner has one good overtaking diamond, you lead ◇T. Dealer throws ♠9, partner ◇A. Where are the bowers? Surely it will be taken? But no; your right-hand opponent plays ◇Q, thus leaving the ball in your partner's court.

Trick 3

He leads ♡7, and secondhand plays ♡Q. You trump with the Seven, and dealer throws ♡8. This leaves you with ◇9 and ♠A.

Trick 4

You lead ♠A. Not the trump – for all you know, your partner may hold the King and lead a wrong suit to the advantage of secondhand, whereas if the latter is void in diamonds you will win the march. Dealer plays ♡K, partner ♠T, followed by ♠8. Very promising.

Trick 4
Your ◇9 is followed by ♡A, ♡9, ♠J. You have four tricks and your partner one, giving you the march for two points. Here are the original hands:

```
Dealer     ♣—  ◇—  ♠9 7  ♡A K 8
Partner    ♣J  ◇A  ♠T   ♡9 7
2ndhand    ♣T  ◇Q  ♠J 8  ♡Q
```

With clubs as the prospective trump, no-one was in a position to take it or order it up, although, with hindsight, your partner could conceivably have made his Ace and right bower together with your Ace for three tricks.

On the second round he had nothing to bid, and no more did secondhand; but, as you surmised from the play, dealer might happily have made game in hearts, probably to the tune of four tricks.

A lone game. The turned up card is ♠Q and the lie of the cards as follows:

```
Eldest     ♠—  ♡K T 8  ♣Q  ◇7        passes
2ndhand    ♠—  ♡Q  ♣9  ◇A Q 9        passes
3rdhand    ♠K  ♡9  ◇Q  ♣K J          passes
Dealer     ♠J 9  ♡A 7  ♣A            takes it up.
```

Thirdhand held the King of prospective trumps (spades) and the left bower (♣J), but with nothing good in hand he correctly refrained from following his partner's pass with a bid.

Dealer can count ♠Q as part of his hand, rejecting ♡7 from the outset, and with the right bower and two good Aces decides to go it alone, as there is a fair chance of winning the march. Secondhand accordingly lays his cards down.

Eldest leads, and the play proceeds:

Eld.	2nd.	3rd.	Del.	
♡ K		♡ 9	♡ A	Having no defence against a possible march, eldest leads his only good card immediately.
◇ 7		♠ K	♠ J	Dealer can only be beaten by a guarded left bower, and plays into the situation at once.
♡ 8		♣ J	♠ Q	Enter the bower, thirdhand having thrown its guard to the previous trick. So much for the march.
♣ Q		♣ K	♣ A	
♡ T		◇ Q	♠ 9	
0		1	4	tricks, scoring 1 to dealer's partnership

Secondhand had, in fact, nothing useful to contribute to the play, and dealer was right to go it alone. He had a good chance of the march, which was beaten only by the holding of a guarded left bower in one opponent's hand. Which goes to show that a guarded left bower is a good defence to an opponent's solo march.

QUINTO

This pleasant little game of tricks was invented around the turn of the century by Professor Hoffman, nom-de-plume of a cards expert with several 'Hoyles' to his credit. Easy to learn and not too demanding, it introduces two quite novel features into the field of Whist-like games from which it is derived. One is the 'hierarchic' order of suits for trumping purposes, which simply means that a card of any higher suit beats one of any lower suit, regardless of rank. (Interestingly, from a historical viewpoint, the order of suits is that of the old form of Bridge. The transference of spades from lowest to highest position produced the modern Bridge order, which is also to be seen in Contract Whist.)

The other novel feature is the invention of 'quints', which gives the game its name. A quint is simply a Five, or two cards of the same suit adding up to five, and it is from the making – and avoiding – of quints that the fun of the game is largely derived.

The game

Cards. 53; a standard 52-card pack plus one Joker.

Game. A rubber is won by the first side to win two games. Game is 250 up, typically reached after two or three deals. Scores may be conveniently recorded on a Cribbage board (each peg counting five) or Bézique markers.

Deal. Twelve cards each, singly; place the last five face downwards to one side of the table to form the 'cachette'. The cachette may not be seen until the end of the round, when it is taken by the side winning the twelfth trick, and counts as a thirteenth.

Object. Points are scored for tricks in themselves, and also for certain combinations of cards – called quints – falling to a trick. Tricks are not counted until the end of the round, but quints are scored as they are taken. If a side makes game (250 points) as the result of winning a trick containing a quint, the rest of the hand is not played out.

Trumps. For trick-taking purposes, suits rank, in ascending order, spades, clubs, diamonds, hearts. A player void of the suit led can therefore trump by playing a card from any higher suit, spades being trumped by any other, clubs by any red suit, diamonds only by hearts, hearts not at all. Thus all 52 cards rank from ♠2 (lowest) up to ♡A, which cannot be beaten.

Quints. The Joker, each Five, and any two cards of the same suit totalling five in face value, are all quints. Thus a trick containing Ace and Four, or Three and Two, of the same suit scores a quint in that suit to its winner. A trick can contain more than one quint – for example, if Ace and Four of a suit fall to the same trick as any Five and the Joker, it contains three quints.

The value of quints is as follows:

Joker (Quint Royal)	25
Any quint in ♡	20
Any quint in ◇	15
Any quint in ♣	10
Any quint in ♠	5

Doubling and redoubling. After the cachette has been laid aside, but before any card is led, each in turn has one opportunity either to double, or to re-double an opponent's double. Doubling affects only the value of tricks, not of quints. Tricks are normally worth 5 each, but if doubled they count 10 each, and if re-doubled, 20 each.

Tricks. Player left of dealer leads to the first trick. Players must follow suit to the card led, except that the holder of the Joker may play it whenever he deems fit (*see below*). If unable to follow suit, a player may discard from a lower suit, or trump by playing any card of any higher suit. The trick is won by the person playing the highest card to it, bearing in mind that all cards have relatives values from ♠2 to ♡A. The winner of a

FIGURE 15

A trick rich in quints. North opens with ♠A. East must follow suit but has only the Four, making a quint in spades for 5. South, assuming his partner's Ace will win, plays Quint Royal for 25. West, void in spades, trumps with a scoring card from a higher suit, giving an additional quint in diamonds for 15. Total quint value 45, in addition to the basic trick score.

trick scores the value of any quint it may contain, and leads to the next.

Joker. The holder of the Joker may play it at any time. It has no trick-taking value, but in its capacity as Quint Royal, worth 25, it counts to the credit of the side winning it in a trick. Its holder will therefore seek to play it to a trick being won by his partner.

(There is no official rule about leading the Joker, but the circumstance can arise in which the holder has no choice but to lead it. For this purpose I recommend that if a player leads the Joker, the player on his left determines the suit to follow.)

Last trick. Whoever takes the last (twelfth) trick takes the cachette of five cards and scores for any quint or quints it may contain. It also counts as an extra trick and scores accordingly.

Score. At the end of the round, each side adds to its score for quints a score for tricks it won, at the rate of 5 undoubled, 10 doubled or 20 re-doubled. If quints are enough to make game (250), tricks are not counted. If both sides make game on tricks, the side with the higher total wins. The first side to make two games wins the rubber, and scores an extra 100 for it.

There is no official ruling about ties, but I recommend that if both sides make equal game on tricks there should be another deal, in which case the first to score a quint is bound to win.

Hints on play

The play of Quinto is entirely shaped by the hierarchic trumping system and the value of the last trick.

The winners of the last trick win the cachette, which is worth playing for, partly for its intrinsic value as the 'odd trick' and partly for the slightly less than one-in-nine chance of its containing at least one quint. Though its average value may be small, the cachette can in certain circumstances be worth 90 to its takers – for if it contains Quint Royal (25) in a re-doubled game (20), that makes 45 to you instead of 45 to your opponents.

The surest way of winning the cachette is for the holder of the unbeatable ♡A to hold on to it until the last moment. Since you

cannot be sure from the outset that your partner does not hold
♡A if you do not have it yourself, there is no point in trying to
force it out early. It is, however, possible to devise some sort of
signalling system whereby a player can, by his choice of lead,
indicate to his partner (and his opponents) whether or not he
holds the top card.

Since it is virtually impossible to establish a black suit – i.e. to
force out the higher red suits in order to lead into a long run of
clubs – normal procedure is to start in spades and gradually progress through the suits in ascending order, leaving hearts till
last. It is sometimes possible to establish diamonds, however, if
you hold the suit long and have also either length or strength in
hearts for the purpose of clearing them out first.

Whoever holds the Joker will be concerned to play it to a
trick won by his partner, which means that if you yourself don't
hold it you must give your partner the earliest opportunity of
dropping it. For this reason leader should start with ♠A if he
has it, or ♣A. Only in default of black Aces or guarded Kings
should ◇A be led for this purpose, and ♡A would in any case be
too valuable.

The making of quints injects some interesting elements into
the play. For example, when playing second to the lead of a top
card you should avoid throwing anything lower than Six for fear
of giving away a quint. The 2+3 quint usually happens by
accident, being forced out (as in the fifth trick of the sample
game given later) when its holder has no choice in the matter.

The A+4 quint can be cooperatively worked up to between
the partners. You may, for example, win a trick with a King
when also holding the Ace, so that with an early return in the
same suit your partner may throw, or even lead, the Four if he
has it. There are two common ways of making the Five quint –
one, which can easily be overlooked if you are not on the ball, is
to trump or overtrump with a Five when unable to follow suit.
Suppose, for example, your left-hand opponent leads ♣A and
your partner drops the matching Four; then your right-hand
opponent, being void in clubs, might profitably trump with ◇5.
If you are also void you may simply be tempted to play a higher
diamond and capture both quints. But of course what you should

look for is ♡5, which gives you the trick and a third quint to boot! The other way of making the Five quint is simply to drop it to a trick you know your partner can win, or is already winning.

It is obvious that a two-card quint cannot be scored if you hold both cards yourself; you can therefore safely lead one of them out, and you should be on the alert for similar play from your partner. Even more significantly, if you hold Ace and Four, circumstances may arise in which you can lead or discard the Four in order to let your partner know you have the Ace as well.

Remember that five cards are out of play, lying in the cachette, so that with an even distribution of cards there may be two or three clean tricks to be made in each suit. With a fairly even distribution, you can expect in the lower suits to make with a guarded King, but possibly not with a guarded Queen. Do not bother to lead from a lower suit when play has reached a higher one. For example, by the seventh trick the play will probably be into diamonds, so it is not worth leading a black card. Reserve the residuals of lower suits to use as discards as necessary at a later stage. This is especially important if, as the result of long black suit holdings, you have kept hold of ♣5 or ♠5. Reserve them in the hope of dropping them, when void, to tricks won by your partner. Leading them out will force everyone to trump or overtrump, and may embarrass your partner considerably.

The lower the suit, the more valuable the void. If you have no spades to start with, you are in a strong position anyway and never more so than when playing second to the trick, as your partner then has a chance to drop his Joker, or the Five quint, or the Four to an Ace lead as the case may be. Since play normally starts in spades there is no point in going out of your way to void them. With two clubs or only one, however, it is often worth clearing them out as soon as possible, even by leading them before spades. A void in diamonds is only worth having if you have plenty of hearts with which to trump them. Needless to say, a void in hearts is useless!

You should certainly double or re-double if you feel you are in a position to do so. Since the cachette counts as the odd trick, one side is bound to take more for tricks than the other, so doubling or re-doubling increases the margin between the two sides. In the sample deal which follows, for example, the side that doubled finished up only 105 points off game and a good 55 in advance of their opponents. Had they not doubled, they would have lain only 30 in advance and a good 150 points off game. The effect is even greater in subsequent deals, where the difference between doubling and not doubling may mean the difference between making game on this round and losing it on the next.

To double or re-double you must be confident that your side will take seven tricks at least, or six and the last. Reckoning your own hand as four may not be enough if your partner can only make two, but if you can make five (or four and last) the opportunity should be seized. Your decision will be influenced, of course, by whether others have called or passed. Note, by the way, that you may only re-double an opponent's double, not your own partner's.

Sample deal

```
                ♡Q J 2
                ◇6 5
                ♣A 5 2
                ♠9 5 4 2
  ♡A K 9 3    ┌─────────┐    ♡7 4
  ◇8 2        │    N    │    ◇K Q J 3
  ♣7 6 3      │ W     E │    ♣T 4
  ♠J 8        │    S    │    ♠A K 7 3
  Jo          └─────────┘
                ♡8 6 5
                ◇A 7 9 4
                ♣K 9 8
                ♠Q T
```

West dealt. North speaks first, and declines to double. East passes, not liking the look of his hearts, though he can probably count on two spade tricks, a trumped club, and a diamond in its own right. South is also unhappy with the trump situation, and passes. West doubles: he can surely trump a spade and a diamond, will make the two top hearts for four, and save one of them for the last trick, five. North leads.

N	E	S	W	
♣ A	♣ T	♣ 8	♣ 6	Possibly North's only opportunity of testing South for the Joker . . . which he has not got.
♠ 9	♠ K	♠ T	Jo	East correctly divines from the previous trick that West has it. 25 to E-W.
♠ 3	♠ A	♠ Q	♠ 8	
♣ 5	♣ 4	♣ K	♣ 7	East has no further use for spades, except as discards, and now proceeds to void clubs. North duly plays the quint to his partner's win, scoring 10.
♣ 2	◊ 3	♣ 9	♣ 3	East happily trumps a two-card quint for 10. He might reasonably have taken high instead, on the off-chance of a later two-card quint in diamonds.
♠ 5	♠ 7	◊ 4	♠ J	East throws a cat to the pigeons, having a weak heart and preferring not to lead diamonds. South, by playing the Four, indicates to his partner that he also has the matching red Ace.
◊ 6	◊ J	◊ 9	◊ 2	
♠ 4	♠ 3	◊ 7	◊ 8	An amusing lead, but South refuses to relinquish his Ace.
♡ J	♡ 7	♡ 5	♡ 9	South gives his partner a quint worth 20.
◊ 5	◊ Q	◊ A	♡ 3!	A good lead of a quint into a partner's known Ace, but un-happily trumped at the last minute.
♡ 2	♡ 4	♡ 6	♡ A	Just by chance, another lovely quint.
♡ Q	◊ K	♡ 8	♡ K	And the last trick.

The cachette contains nothing of value ($\heartsuit$T $\diamondsuit$T $\clubsuit$Q $\clubsuit$J $\clubsuit$6), but gives East-West their ninth trick, well justifying West's double. Thus the scores are:

N-S	E-W	
40	90	for tricks (doubled, 10 each)
50	55	for quints
90	145	total

CANASTA

Canasta is the game you graduate to when you already know one of the basic members of the Rummy family, such as that described on page 161. It is, frankly, about the most complex of all the Rummy games. But not without reason. Few Rummies provide much scope for the exercise of creative skill against the luck of the draw, most of them giving rise to a succession of game positions from which there is always a best move, with no great experience required to determine it. Canasta, however, succeeds in increasing the skill factor by confronting you with a greater variety of options and alternatives, and it is for this reason that alone of the Rummy games it has attracted the attention of serious card players all over the world. It has also given rise to yet more complex derivatives such as Samba, Bolivia and others, but they need not detain us here. Complexity in itself is not a desirable property of card games, and can all too easily be overdone.

Canasta originated in Uruguay during the 1940s. The word itself is Spanish for 'basket', and denotes the high-scoring combination consisting of seven cards of the same rank. Ely Culbertson,* the man who virtually invented Bridge as we know it, explains the image thus:

> The Spanish word for 'weaving' is *tejiendo*. *Tejiendo las cartas*, that is, 'weaving the cards', is a colourful Spanish way of saying that a meld of three of a kind, or more, is being 'woven' together. And when the biggest meld of all, the canasta, is completed, you naturally have woven a 'basket'.

So – let's get weaving.

* Culbertson on Canasta, Faber & Faber, 1950.

The game

Cards. 108, consisting of two standard 52-card packs with four Jokers. They need not all be of the same back design and colour, but must be of the same size.

Game. Partners sit opposite each other, North-South versus East-West. A game may consist of one or more deals and is won by the first side to reach or exceed 5000 points. If both sides reach it on the same deal the one with the higher total wins. Scores are recorded at the end of each deal.

Deal. Decide first dealer by any agreed means; thereafter the turn to deal passes to the left. Deal eleven cards each, in ones. Place the undealt cards face down and squared up in the middle of the table to form the *stock.* Turn up the top card of the stock and lay it face up beside the stock. This starts the discard pile – best referred to as the *pack* – which must also be kept squared up throughout the game. The card on top of the pack is known as the upcard. If the first upcard is a Joker, a Two or a red Three, it must immediately be covered by the next card of the stock, and so on until the upcard is of some other rank or a black Three.

With the stock and the first upcard settled, any player who has been dealt a red Three must place it face up on the table before him and is then dealt the top card of the stock to bring his hand back to eleven cards.

You are now ready to start play, but should first note the following basic facts about the game, which will give you an initial sense of direction.

General information. The object of the game is to collect and display on the table batches of three or more cards of the same rank, such batches being called melds. A meld of seven or more cards is a canasta, and no-one can end the game until his side has made at least one of them.

Jokers and Twos are 'wild' cards: they cannot be melded but can form part of melds based on 'natural' cards by themselves (i.e. ranks from Four up to Ace). Threes have special powers, as outlined below.

All meldable cards have a melding value, which at the end of the game counts to your credit if they are out in melds, but against you if still left in hand. The set values are:

Jokers	50 each
Aces and Twos	20 each
High cards (K Q J T 9 8)	10 each
Low cards (7 6 5 4 and black 3)	5 each

In addition to the melding value of individual cards, each completed canasta carries a bonus of 500 if it consists entirely of natural cards, 300 if it contains one or more wild cards. (These are known respectively as a 'natural' and a 'mixed' canasta.)

Black Threes may only be melded when you are 'going out', as explained later.

Red Threes are bonus cards. Every time you get one you must lay it face up on the table before you. They are worth 100 each (doubled if you get all four) and count in your favour if you have made any melds, but against you if you have not.

The game normally ends when one player 'goes out' by melding in one turn all the cards left in his hand.

Finally, you must be aware that Canasta is essentially a partnership game. Partners keep melds made by both of them together in one place on the table, not separately in front of each. And it is sometimes inadvisable to end the game by going out without first asking your partner's permission.

General procedure. Starting with the person at dealer's left, each player in turn does one or more of three things in the following order:

1. Draw (top card of stock, or discard pile if permitted)
2. Meld (if any possible, and subject to certain restrictions)
3. Discard (unless gone out by melding all cards left in hand).

Draw: You may always take the top card of the stock and add it to your hand. If you draw a red Three, you place it face up before you and draw again.

Instead of drawing from stock, you may take the whole of the pack, provided that you can immediately meld the upcard – either by adding it to one of your existing melds on the table, or by using it to start a new meld in conjunction with two or more matching cards from your own hand (for which purpose a matching natural card plus one wild card is sufficient, though some insist that you must hold a natural pair to start a new meld with the upcard).

But you may not take the discard pile in this way if it is *frozen*, which it is in the following circumstances:

1. It is frozen to you and your partner until your side has made its first meld.
2. It is frozen to everybody whenever it contains a wild card (or a red Three as the result of the initial turn-up).

In these cases you may only take the pack if you can immediately use the upcard to start a new meld in conjunction with at least two matching *natural* cards from your own hand. (If you have none on the table already, this may count as your initial meld provided it meets the initial meld scoring requirement described below under 'melds'.) Furthermore,

3. The pack is 'stopped' to you personally if the upcard is a black Three. In this case you may not take it at all but can only draw from stock.

Melds: All melds made by one partnership are kept together in one place. Subject to rules governing composition and value of melds, you may in your turn (*a*) start one or more new melds, and/or (*b*) add ('lay off') one or more natural or wild cards to any of your partnership's existing melds. Cards once melded cannot be retrieved for further play.

A meld must contain three or more cards, of which at least two must be natural cards, and not more than three may be wild. All natural cards in a meld must be of the same rank.

A canasta is a meld of seven (or more) cards, and may be melded outright or gradually built up by laying off additional cards to smaller melds. Once completed, the cards of a canasta are squared up in a pile, with a red card face up on top if it is a natural canasta (containing no wild cards), and a black card if it is a mixed canasta (containing one or more wild cards).

A canasta is bound to contain at least four natural cards, but there is no limit to the number of wild cards that may belong or be subsequently added to it. As soon as any wild card is laid off to a natural canasta, remember to replace the top red card by a black one.

Red Threes are not melded. Black Threes may only be melded if you go out on the same turn (*see below*).

Initial meld: The first meld or melds made by a partnership must total a certain minimum value (counting each Joker 50, Ace or Two 20, high card 10, low card 5). What that minimum value is depends on your partnership's cumulative score in the current game, as follows:

Score so far	Required initial value
A minus figure	any
Less than 1500	50
1500 but under 3000	90
3000 or more	120

You may count the combined values of more than one meld towards this minimum requirement, but you may *not* count the 500 or 300 point canasta bonus towards it, nor any bonus deriving from red threes.

(Remember that the pack is frozen to your side until it has made an initial meld of the minimum required value. But the initial meld does not *have* to be made from the hand: provided it meets the requirement it may be made by melding the upcard with at least two natural cards from your hand.)

Discard: Having drawn and either melded or not, you complete your turn by taking a card from your hand and placing it face up on the pack, unless in your turn you go out and have nothing left to discard.

You may not discard a red Three. If you discard a black Three, you thereby freeze the pack to your left-hand opponent for one turn only.

If you discard a wild card you thereby freeze the pack to everybody, and it remains frozen until taken. To show that the pack is frozen, you place the wild card not on the top but at the bottom of the pack, face up and sticking out sideways so that it is clearly visible. (It is, however, still the upcard for one turn and theoretically obscures the card visible on top. This means that your left-hand opponent may *not* immediately capture the pack by matching the visible card with a natural pair from his hand; but as soon as he has played, his discard becomes the upcard and thereafter the pack can be taken in accordance with the rule for capturing a frozen pack.)

End of game by going out. A player goes out and thereby ends the game when in one turn he gets rid of all the cards in his hand – either by melding them all, or by melding them all except one and discarding that last one.

You may not go out unless your side has made at least one canasta. But you can meet this requirement by melding or completing a canasta on the turn in which you go out. It is only when you are going out that you may meld black Threes – either three or four of them.

If after drawing from stock you are in a position to go out, you are permitted (not required) to ask your partner whether it suits him. If you do ask, you must do so before melding any card at all. The correct wording is 'May I go out, partner?', to which he must reply either Yes or No. You are then bound by his reply. (Indeed, if he says Yes and you find that you cannot go out after all, you are penalised 100 points.)

You get a bonus of 100 for 'going out blind', that is, if you personally have not previously melded anything during the course of the current deal. But you only qualify for the bonus if all your cards are meldable in their own right – you don't get it if you lay off cards to your partner's melds.

End of game by exhausting stock. Somebody usually goes out before the stock is used up, but in case they don't, this is what happens: if the last card drawn from stock is a red Three, the player faces it, makes any melds he wishes, but does not discard. That ends the deal.

If not, he plays in the usual way and then discards. The next in turn must then take the pack (by melding the upcard) if he can legally do so; if not, the deal ends. If he can do so, he makes his play and then discards. From now on the 'pack' will only ever consist of the previous player's discard. If on your turn the previous discard matches one of your melds, you are forced to take it, lay it off, and then discard. If it does not match, but can still be melded with the aid of cards from your hand, you may either take no action, in which case the deal ends, or you may make your meld(s), in which case you must discard unless you go out.

This continues until any player in his turn either goes out or fails to take the previous player's discard because legally unable or unwilling to do so.

Scores. Each side reckons its score first for bonuses and then for cards; but note that if a side has melded nothing at all then any red Threes it has count against it instead of for it, their value being combined with the penalty for unmelded cards in hand.

Bonuses

For going out	100
or, for going out blind	200
For each red Three	100
or, for having all four	800
For each natural canasta	500
For each mixed canasta	300

To the score for bonuses is added the total meld value of all melded cards, counting thus:

Cards

Joker	50
Ace, Two	20
High card (K Q J T 9 8)	10
Low card (7 6 5 4 and black 3)	5

From the combined total for bonuses and cards, each side now subtracts the total meld value of all cards remaining unmelded in the hand. (The side that went out, of course, will have cards left only in one hand; the other side will have two handfuls to count against them.)

If a player proves to have a red Three in hand, having failed to expose it on the table, it counts 500 against his side.

Hints on play

Canasta is not one of those Rummy games in which the main object is to 'go out' for the sake of the bonus, regarding melds only as a means to that end. It is one of the other sort, in which the main object is to build up a large score by making as many melds as possible. The side that melds first gains an immediate advantage, having, as it were, hatched the goose that lays the golden eggs, and they should go on exploiting this advantage for all it is worth. As soon as the other side has caught up, the first side should be in or approaching the position at which it has the minimum canasta requirement for going out – not for the sake of using it quickly, but for its power as a threat to the opponents.

When going out has become a real possibility, it may eventually be effected for either of two good reasons: first, that despite your lead and initiative your opponents are now beginning to catch up or even threatening to overtake; or second, that your opponents are so far ahead that going out is your only way of defending against a huge loss. There is a third possible reason – that you have been dealt the sort of hand on which the surprise value of a 'quick out' will produce a small, quick profit for the minimum of intellectual investment – but this does not happen very often, and you need not go out of your way to look for it.

The strategy, then, is to be first to break into the scoring vein, get as much out of it as you can while the going is good, and pull out when your advance begins to lessen – or, if you find yourself on the wrong side, to prevent your opponents from succeeding in the same endeavour, even to the extent of pulling out prematurely if you consider the task hopeless. What about the tactics – the means by which this objective is to be achieved?

Inevitably, this aspect of the game revolves around the taking of the pack (i.e. the discard pile). Even if it contains no more than three or four cards the pack is always advantageous to the player who takes it, and most of your play will be directed towards this end. Usually the first side to take the pack is then able to seize the initiative and dictate the course of the game. If your opponents get it first, you must be prepared to play defensively until you can afford to meet them on their own ground.

Initial meld. At the start of the game your immediate objective is to make the initial meld that will entitle you to set out on your scoring spree. So strive for it – but not at the expense of all other considerations. In particular, try to meld as economically as possible. The fewer cards you keep in hand, the less chance you have of taking the pack, so to use up too many on the initial meld is largely self-defeating. For this reason it is unwise to make your initial meld entirely from the hand: wait until you can meld by taking the pack, and deplete your hand no more than necessary.

In subsequent rounds of play, when your initial meld requirement advances to 90 or 120, you may have to accept the sacrifice of more cards in order to compensate for the extra difficulty of meeting the minimum value. Even so, it is wise to expend no more than four cards for the 90, or six for the 120.

Further melding. Having started, make as many melds as you can, in order to keep up the pressure and increase your ability to take the pack. The more melds you can lay off to, the greater difficulty your opponents have in finding safe discards. Don't be frightened of sullying natural canastas by the addition of wild cards, and do not cripple yourself for the sake of working towards the bonus for going out concealed. If your hand happens to lend itself to that fortunate prospect, all well and good; if not, forget it.

There are circumstances in which restraint is worth exercising on the making of melds. The question of economy is one of them, as it was in the case of the initial meld: don't part with too many cards, and in particular don't part with any which may be of use in capturing the pack later. For the same reason it is also sensible to refrain from melding when the discard pile is large: the more cards you keep in hand the more chance you have of capturing it. Defer melding until the pack has been taken, even if not by yourself.

The importance of completing your first canasta is obvious, as it puts you in a position of constant threat (to go out). It is also important throughout the game not to fall behind in the completion of canastas, for which purpose mixed canastas, though less profitable than natural ones, are infinitely better than none at all.

Freezing the pack. It is a beginner's irritating habit to freeze the pack for no better reason than that he happens to be able to, and can think of nothing else to do. There are, of course, times when it is right to freeze the pack and times when it is wrong.

The most important time to freeze the pack is when your opponents have started melding and you have not, as it is your only effective defence against their ability to keep on recapturing it for continual rewards. Freezing is also a good defensive move when your opponents have too many cards in hand and melds on the table, as it enables you with relative safety to discard their players (cards which match their melds and would otherwise enable them to take the pack) and improve the overall meldability of your own hand.

When the pack is frozen it is good to have a hand containing many pairs, as they give you more opportunity to capture it. This does not mean, however, that a hand full of pairs is a good excuse for freezing the pack. It is obviously undesirable to freeze if there is a high probability that the other side will be able to take it. Finally, avoid freezing just because you are unable to find a safe discard. In such circumstances you are likely to do yourself more harm than good.

Black Threes and other cards. If you can find a better discard than a black Three, make it, and save the Three for the time when it is the only solution to an otherwise impossible position. Given a black Three early in the game, a good time to discard it is often when you have just made an initial meld. Since it freezes the pack to your left-hand opponent only, it prevents him from taking the

FIGURE 16

How your side of the table might look at the end of a game in which you have been looking after the melds made by your own partnership. You have just gone out and score as follows:

300 for the mixed canasta (black Seven on top)
100 for the single red Three
100 for going out
300 total value of cards in your melds
−45 for face value of cards left

in your partner's hand (J-J-T-9-5)
Total: 755. Your opponents have:
200 for two red Threes
100 for cards melded
−150 for cards left in both hands
Total: 150. You win.

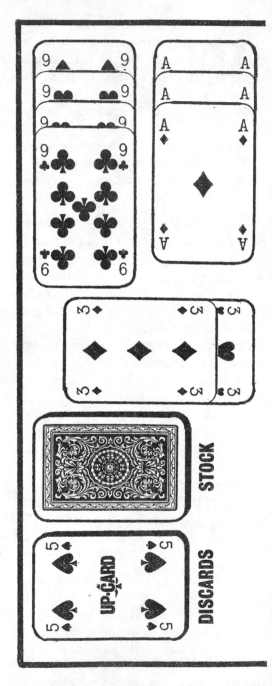

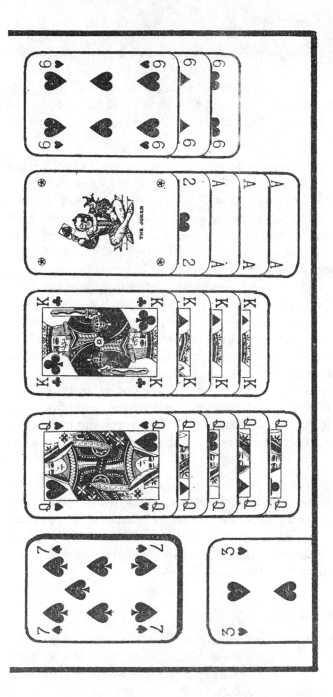

pack before your partner has a chance to take advantage of the position.

Wild cards should be put to work, not hoarded. Every one added to a meld is a bird in the hand when it comes to the score. And do not lightly discard Aces. They, too, are better put to work.

Discarding. Discard low in early rounds, as such cards are not suitable for initial melds. Watch the discards made by your left-hand opponent and try to match them for as long as you feel he is genuinely throwing away unwanted cards. Since your right opponent will be watching you with the same objective in view, don't make things easy for him by sticking rigidly to the discard of singletons. At judicious times have no hesitation in discarding from three or more, so that when he subsequently discards the same rank you can capture the pack and meld. The only time to concern yourself seriously with your partner's discards is when there is a real danger of your opponents' going out. By matching your partner's discards in this situation you may save yourself a lot of penalties.

The time to discard players of your opponents' melds is when the pack is frozen and they appear to have little chance of capturing it. Any cards that are of no use to you but possibly of use to them are best reserved for discarding until the pack is small.

Going out. We have already noted that going out is more of a defensive measure than anything else, either because you are too far behind and want to cut your losses, or because your opponents are beginning to catch up and you do not want to cut your profit margin. Watch the timing. A good time to go out is when your opponents have too many cards in hand.

Sample game

All Rummy games are difficult to notate and inconvenient to play through in sample form, but Canasta, with 108 cards, is virtually impossible. Here instead is an illustration of the end position of a game, showing how the score is calculated.

CALYPSO

This unusual and undeservedly neglected game was invented in the early fifties by R. B. Willis, who named it after the songs of Trinidad where he was living. In Britain, Calypso was avidly espoused, modified, refined and promoted by Bridge master Kenneth Konstam.

It is easy to see why the game attracted initial enthusiasm. It is designed for four, socially the most acceptable number at a card table; it represents a cross between the objectives of Rummy and the mechanics of Whist, two of the most successful card games ever devised; and, at the same time, it is quite original in its ingenious use of these otherwise well-tried features of card play. Above all, it is extremely simple to learn. For my taste, nothing spoils a potentially good card game so much as showy complications that appear to be introduced for effect, often in default of any real depth.

Why it failed to maintain the following it deserved is less easy to determine. A perhaps over-simplified view is that it arrived at the wrong time. Card players of the fifties had gone to great pains to learn the complications of then-fashionable Canasta, and must have been loath to waste this effort by taking on anything else. Perhaps recent memories of years of austerity worked in favour of a game that covered the table with lots of sumptuous card combinations worth millions of points, rather than one of such spartan simplicity as Calypso.

Whatever the reason, it remains high on my list of games worth reviving. Give it a fair trial and see what you think.

The game

Cards. Four standard 52-card packs, making 208 cards in all; it is desirable, but not essential, that they all be of the same back design and colour. They should, however, all be of the same size.

Game. A game consists of four deals, one by each player in turn, and lasts about half an hour. Scores are not noted until the end of the last deal.

Shuffle and deal. It is convenient for each player to shuffle about a quarter of the composite pack and pass it back to dealer, who shuffles them last as best he may and then places them all in a face-down pile to form a stock. Dealer then takes the top quarter of the stock and deals out 13 cards each, in ones. The rest of the stock remains out of play and unused until the hands of the first deal have been fully played out.

Rank of cards, object of play. Cards rank in traditional order, from high to low A K Q J T 9 8 7 6 5 4 3 2. Each player 'owns' a particular suit, as follows:

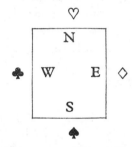

Thus North and South are partners and respectively play hearts and spades against East and West who are respectively associated with diamonds and clubs. Each player's first objective is to collect a complete set of cards, from Ace down to Two, of his own suit. Such a set is called a 'calypso'. Having collected one calypso he can then start collecting another, and so on up to a theoretical maximum of four (because there are four packs in play). His secondary objective is to capture cards that belong to his partner's calypso, as he is permitted to pass cards of his partner's suit across to him when he wins them in a trick. As a third objective, of course, each player will endeavour to prevent players of the opposing partnership from acquiring the cards they need for calypsos in their own suits.

Cards needed for calypsos are captured by winning them in tricks, as described below.

Personal trumps. Before tricks can be played it is essential to understand the way in which 'personal trumps' – a feature unique to Calypso – are used.

The suit that each player is trying to collect is also his personal trump suit. Therefore, when someone leads to a trick he will be leading either from his trump suit (in which case he should announce 'my trump' or something similar), or from one of the others. What happens next depends on which lead is made.

To a non-trump lead each succeeding player must follow suit if possible. The trick is won by the player of the highest card of the suit led. If two identical cards fall to a trick, the first so played ranks higher than the second.

If you cannot follow suit to the card led, you may win the trick by playing any card of your personal trump suit (in which case you should announce 'trump'), or you may lose it by discarding from any other suit. In this case the player of a personal trump wins the trick. If more than one plays from his own personal trump suit, the trick is won by the personal trump of the highest rank (suit does not count for this purpose), and if more than one of the same rank are played then it is the first that takes it.

Note that you can only trump by playing your *own* trump suit, never anyone else's.

To a trump lead each succeeding player must follow suit if possible, and if all do so then the trick is always won by the player who led to it, regardless of rank. In other words, if you lead from your personal trump suit and everyone follows, you automatically win the trick.

If you cannot follow suit to a personal trump lead, then you may win the trick by playing from your own trump suit a card of higher rank than the one led, which can only be overtaken by another player playing a yet higher-ranking card from his own trumps. (You may, of course, lose the trick by playing from a side-suit, but only if you cannot follow.)

In short, when trumps are led the trick is won by the leader unless anyone else legitimately plays a personal trump, in which case the highest-ranking personal trump (or the earliest played of identical ranks) wins the trick.

Tricks and calypsos. The player on the dealer's left leads to the first trick; thereafter the winner of each trick leads to the next. The trick is won by the highest card of the suit led or by the highest personal trump if any are played, except that a trump lead wins the trick regardless of rank unless legitimately over-trumped. Of identical ranks, the first played counts highest.

When you win a trick you first remove from it and place face upwards in front of you any cards of your own suit that you need for building up a calypso – that is, cards of any rank(s) which you have not already got. You may also remove and pass to your partner any card or cards he needs towards his own calypso. However, as only one calypso may be built up at a time, a card that duplicates one already showing in either calypso may not be kept and is lost for the rest of the game. Such duplicates, together with cards of the opponents' suits, are laid aside face downwards to a discard pile. It is convenient for one of the two partners to look after a single common discard pile for his side, rather than to have one each. There is, of course, no need to keep won tricks separate from one another.

There is one exception to the rejection of duplicates. If you win a trick containing several cards of your own (or partner's) suit, as the result of which you can immediately complete your own (or partner's) calypso, you may then complete the calypso and use any surplus cards of the suit to start a new one.

A completed calypso is stacked face up with the Ace on top. The cards of a calypso in the process of being built should be spread face up and in numerical order in a straight line in front of its collector, so that everyone can see which cards it contains and lacks.

End of deal. When 13 tricks have been played, the next 52 cards from stock are taken and distributed singly by the next dealer, that is, the player on the left of the previous dealer. The same procedure is followed in subsequent deals.

Score. The scoring is simple. Each player counts 500 for his first calypso, 750 for his second, and 1000 for any other. He then counts 20 for each card in the calypso he was in course of build-

ing when the game ended. Each partnership's score is found by
adding the two partners' calypso scores together, and finally
adding to that 10 points for every card in their pile of cards won
in tricks.

Hints on play

The play at Calypso is shaped largely by the fact that, although
you must take as many tricks as you can get, you need them not
for their own sake but for the sake of the cards they contain.
Since all cards are good, either because you want them for your
side's calypsos or because you want to keep them from your
opponents, it is correct to play an attacking game, for which
purpose the question of leads when you have the initiative is all-
important. At the same time you must pay particular attention
to how you discard when you do not have the lead and are
unlikely to take the trick yourself. There are good cards to give
to your partner, and bad ones to throw to the opponents.

Your choice is widest when you have the lead, especially at the
start of a new deal. The question is, which suit to play from and
whether to play high or low. As to suits, there are three possibilities: your own, your partner's or either of your opponents'.

Trump lead (own suit). A trump lead, which normally wins the
trick regardless of rank, is standard opening procedure – but it
must be played with understanding. Beginners are tempted to
lead and press their trump suit for as many rounds as it will go
without being overtrumped. This play is faulty. It may well
bring in an average of thirteen cards to your calypso, but so
many are likely to be duplicates, and hence destined for the
waste pile, that it will have been a waste of high trumps to bring
them in.

Given a reasonable holding of trumps, by all means start by
leading them, especially low ones (say Twos to Sixes) that would
be of little value later in the game for purposes of overtrumping.
Leading them is the only chance of putting them to useful work.
High trumps should not be led without due regard to the fact
that they may be more useful for overtrumping at a later stage, or

for winning tricks when your suit is led from other quarters.

Trump leads are inadvisable if you hold the suit too long or too short. With, say, more than six trumps in hand there is a strong possibility that an opponent will be void and take the trick by overtrumping, though of course an Ace lead cannot be overtaken. Three or fewer high-ranking trumps do not invite a trump lead: keep them for overtaking when the suit is led, or for overtrumping when the opportunity arises.

Partner's suit. Not a good lead. Leading partner's suit deprives him of later opportunities to make tricks by trump leads, and unless you can lead an Ace or other master card the chances are nearly two to one against his being able to take it.

An exception to this rule is afforded by the holding of a singleton. If your hand as dealt contains only one card of your partner's suit, and you have a sufficiently early lead, it is good play to lead it in order to create a void that you can trump into (or discard to) later. This play is so obvious as to claim the status of a convention or signal. If it is understood that the lead of a partner's trump implies a void in that suit, the partner stands to gain more by this information than the opponents will.

It should, however, be avoided if you are also weak in your own suit, as you are then less able to take advantage of it yourself by overtrumping.

Adverse suit. The advantage of leading an adverse suit is that only one opponent is in a position to trump it, while the other, whose suit it is, is deprived of later opportunities to make tricks by trump leads.

It is clearly best to lead high; in fact, the lead of a high card in an adverse suit may be regarded as an alternative standard opening to that of a low personal trump. Leading a low adverse trump is justly described by Kenneth Konstam (who refined the mechanics of the game) as 'defeatist', as it is sure to give them the trick and the initiative. One could, however, make a virtue of necessity by proposing a convention that a low adverse lead implies overall weakness.

Which of the two adverse suits makes the better lead? This depends much upon the actual holding, but with comparable strength in both there would be some advantage in leading that of the player on your right, as he will then not be able to trump or overtrump when your partner has played. It is better that the opponent with the greater scope should play before rather than after your partner, so that he can gauge his play accordingly.

If they are not of comparable strength, lead from the stronger, or else from a singleton in order to give yourself a trumpable void.

Other aspects of play. What to play to a trick which you are not winning, or in your estimation are unlikely to win, depends on whether it is going (so far as you can tell) to your partner or to either opponent.

Given a choice of discards, your priorities for throwing to a trick won by partner will be:

1. A card needed for either of your calypsos;
2. A card lacking from an adverse calypso;
3. A low card or singleton from an adverse suit;
4. A duplicate card matching one in either of your side's current calypsos.

Circumstances alter cases, of course. It is obviously better to throw, if you can, the thirteenth card to an adverse calypso than the second to one of your own, especially towards the end of the game. The last card of a calypso is worth at least 260 points, whereas any other is worth only 20 when it comes to the crunch. If an opponent is winning the trick, you will naturally discard in order of preference:

1. An adverse calypso duplicate;
2. A duplicate in one of your own suits.

Principles of trick play appropriate to such games as Whist and Bridge, in which tricks are collected for their own sake, should not be automatically followed in Calypso. Normally, for example, you discard low when unable to contest a trick in the suit led. In Calypso, it is more appropriate to discard duplicates than to preserve higher ranks. If you can do both, by discarding low-ranking duplicates, so much the better.

Bridge players should resist the automatic temptation to finesse, for the whole process is made practically uncontrollable by the facts that (*a*) there are four cards of each rank, and (*b*) which of them are in play during the course of any given deal – except theoretically the last – is beyond reasonable deduction in the time available. To put it briefly, unless you are last to play never try to take with the King if you can take with the Ace instead. There are occasions on which it may be tried in the suit of the player on your right, but it is nearly always dangerous to try it on in other suits.

Memory plays an important part in the game, but, even if it were possible, you have no need to remember the play of all 208 cards. Normally it is sufficient to regard each deal as complete in itself, bearing in mind that the 52 cards dealt will contain gaps and duplicates. But watch those duplicates, especially if two or three of them attract your eye. If any player is prevented from acquiring all four cards of a given rank he will be unable to complete a single calypso. If it happens to you, all your subsequent play must be directed towards helping your partner make his. Similarly, if you can prevent an opponent from making all four, or even from getting further than his first, it is worth playing towards that tactical objective at the expense of normal rules of procedure.

Sample deal

Let's see how things turn out in the first deal of a sample game, to which West dealt. Cards of each player's trump suit are in bold type.

	N ♡	E ◇	S ♠	W ♣
♡	**9887**	A76	KJ4	T76
◇	AJT43	**QQ93**	865	K973
♠	J3	A9	**AQ43**	Q98
♣	76	KJ82	993	**K65**

North, to lead, starts in his strong adverse suit; at this point it is worth noting that suits will not necessarily be evenly distributed – in this deal, for example, there are sixteen diamonds out but only eleven clubs.

N	E	S	W	
◇ A	◇ Q	◇ 5	◇ 3	East throws a duplicate rank . . .
◇ J	◇ **Q**	◇ 6	◇ 7	. . . and makes the trick with his other Queen, giving him four to his calypso.
◇ 3	◇ **3**	◇ 8	◇ 9	Running the risk of being over-trumped, East makes a low trump lead in order to derive some benefit from his Three. North naturally gives him a duplicate, so East loses one of the four to his calypso.
♠ J	♠ A	♠ 3	♠ 8	East, with good adverse cards, switches to South's suit. North avoids throwing ♠3, as one has already been lost.
♠ 3	♠ 9	♠ A	♠ 9	East might reasonably have switched to hearts; apparently he prefers to void spades, considering this to be his best way of subsequently benefiting from his personal trump Nine.
♣ 7	◇ 9!	♠ 4	♠ Q	South expects to make at least one trump lead, and North, void in the suit but banking on his partner's win, throws a card wanted for an adverse calypso. East's previous move pays off, and he saves the club for his partner.
♡ 8	♡ A	♡ 4	♡ 6	Now East decides to have a go at the other opponent, leading into North's trump.
♡ 7	♡ 6	♡ K	♡ 7	South saves the situation and passes three hearts across to his partner's first calypso. It is hard to see why North gave himself a duplicate – perhaps he meant to play an Eight and his hand slipped.

♣ 6	♣ 8	♣ 9	♣ K	South won't lead trumps for fear that his Queen may be over-trumped, especially by West when there have been no clubs visible yet. East avoids playing ♣2 in case he later finds a situation in which it would be better to let West take a trick in clubs.
♡ 9!	♣ K	♣ 3	♣ 5	West is now into his suit (clubs), but to his chagrin North is void and overtrumps. East throws a duplicate, which won't be missed as West already has the King to his first calypso. South, on the other hand, throws a club that would have been useful to it.
♡ 8	♡ 7	♡ J	♡ T	North wins on a personal trump lead, though it stood a strong chance of being overtrumped. But success in this trick is paid for on the next round:
◇ T	♣ 2	♣ 9	◇ K	South could have trumped, but his ♣9 would not have been a promising lead for the last trick and since North appears to be winning this one the Queen should give them two instead of only one trick. West, with luck, seizes a club for himself (Two; the Nine is a duplicate) and two diamonds for his partner.
◇ 6	♣ J	♠ Q	♣ 6	West thinks himself fortunate to finish the deal with a trump lead, but South is even more fortunate in being able to overtrump it, adding a Queen to his own calypso and preventing a Jack to West's.

At the end of the first deal, the following part calypsos have been collected:

North ♡ K J T 9 8 7 6
East ◇ K Q J 9 8 7 6 3 2
South ♠ A Q 9 3
West ♣ K 9 8 7 6 2

And the score so far is North-South 350 (220 in calypsos), East-West 430 (300 in calypsos). In subsequent rounds the initial bias towards diamonds will be counterbalanced in black suits.

CONCERTO

Nearly all partnership card games are of the trick-and-trump variety, which is not much variety at all. Canasta is the one exception, although Calypso at least offers a different objective even while it follows the usual tricky mechanics.

For a change of scenery, then, I include a non-trick partnership game of my own devising, which, far from being trumped up for the occasion, has the merit of having been played for about ten years by a group of players who continue to find it varied and challenging.

Concerto is based on the simple idea of calling upon you and your partner to combine your cards into scoring Poker combinations, but without knowing in advance which cards the other holds. The game has nothing to do with Poker as such, nor is it even a gambling game. Poker hands only come into it because they are widely known and happen to suit the mechanics of the game quite well.

It will, I think, appeal particularly to players of partnership games which encourage the play of cards as a means of conveying useful information about the hand from which they come, so that maximum advantage can be derived from that knowledge while there is still time to pursue it.

Concerto can be played haphazardly, of course, as can Whist or Bridge, but it then loses its point. As with Whist, the actual mechanics of the game are exceedingly simple. All the skill lies in the significant play of cards.

The game

Cards and preliminaries. Use a standard 52-card pack. Partners sit opposite each other. Decide who is to deal first by any agreed means. A game consists of four deals, the turn to deal passing to the left on each occasion, and is won by the side with the greater aggregate of points. (Fig. 8 illustrates a recommended score-sheet.)

Shuffle and deal. The cards must be very thoroughly shuffled before each deal. Deal them one at a time and face down until every player has thirteen.

Object. The members of each partnership have 26 cards between them. Their object is to form these into four scoring Poker hands of five cards each, and to avoid being left with a Poker combination amongst the remaining six cards. Cards are played one at a time to the table, and verbal discussion is prohibited. Each partnership plays in turn – there is no interaction of card play between the two partnerships.

Poker hands. A Poker hand by definition consists of any five cards. If these match one another by rank or suit in certain prescribed ways they constitute a scoring Poker combination. From highest to lowest, the combinations and their scores are as follows:

Combination	*Score*	*Explanation*
Straight flush	15	Five cards in suit and sequence (e.g. ♠A 2 3 4 5).
Four of a kind	12	Four of the same rank (e.g. ♠5 ♡5 ♣5 ◇5), the 5th any.
Full house	8	Three of one rank plus a pair (e.g. ♠5 ♡5 ♣5 ◇Q ♠Q).
Straight	7	Five in sequence but not all of the same suit.
Flush	6	Five of the same suit but not in sequence.
Three of a kind	3	Three of the same rank, plus two odd cards.
Two pair	2	Two of one rank, two of another, the 5th any.
One pair	1	Two of the same rank, the other three unmatched.

A five-card hand containing no combination scores nothing. For the purpose of a straight or straight flush, Ace may count high or low (either A 2 3 4 5 or T K Q K A), but not intermediate (e.g. Q K A 2 3 is not valid). Poker players may wonder why the straight scores more than the flush. The reason is that in Concerto it is harder to make.

Order of play. The player on the first dealer's left is designated North and his partner South; dealer is West and his partner East. North-South play first, with North leading, while East-West merely sit back and observe. Having made and scored their first combination, North places it in front of him in the manner of a won trick, only face up instead of down, and then East leads to the first East-West hand. Play continues in this order, South leading third, then West, and so on until each player has two Poker hands lying face up on the table before him. These hands are kept face up and slightly spread so that all played cards remain visible – Concerto is not intended to be a memory test, but calls for the application of skill to whatever deductions may be made from visible cards.

Method of play. The leader to each round (North, in the first instance) plays any card from his hand face up to the table. He may not pass. His partner may then either pass or add a card of his own to the first. Play continues in this way, each in turn either passing or adding a card, until five cards have been played to the table. The partners then score for whatever combination they may have made; the leader to the hand lays it face up before him; and the player on his left then leads to the next hand to be made by the opposing partnership.

Passing restrictions. The leader to a hand must play the first card – he is not allowed to pass the lead. Thereafter, each in turn may either play a card or pass, but with the following restriction: if one partner passes, and the other passes back, the first may not pass further but must now play. Thus, although there is no restriction on the number of passes a single player can make in the course of a hand (he may pass on all five turns in order to let his partner play out a ready-made combination), no more than two passes may be made consecutively *between* the two partners. In order not to lose count, it is helpful to say 'pass' or 'pass back' as the case may be; then a 'pass-back' cannot be followed by a 'pass'.

Dropping out. Instead of saying 'pass' or 'pass back', a player may drop out of the hand altogether by saying 'play', in which case his partner must then complete the hand entirely by himself.

Game bonus. When each player has two Poker hands lying before him the play ceases and each side totals its four scores. Whichever side has the greater total adds 10 points for game. In the event of a tie, the 10-point game bonus is temporarily held back until the residual bonus has been scored.

Residual bonus. Each side will have six unplayed cards left over, which must now be exposed on the table. Each partnership then examines the other's cards, rejects any one of them from consideration, and scores five times the value of any combination formed by the remaining five cards. (For example, if one side is left with ♠3, ♡Q 3, ♣Q J 2, the other will discount the Jack or the Two and score a residual bonus of 10, being five times the value of a two-pair combination.) If three pairs are left, a sixth card is *not* rejected and the opponents score a residual bonus of 15.

Total score. If the game bonus was held in abeyance because of a tie in the play, it now goes to the side which scored the greater residual bonus. If this also resulted in a tie, it goes to the side that played the first card of the deal. Each side totals its hand score and bonuses (if any), and the result is carried forward towards game.

Hints on play

Whether or not your side has good combinations available depends upon the luck of the deal, but whether or not you succeed in extracting your best possible combinations depends entirely on how well you play your cards. In the long run – and a rubber of four games is long enough for the purpose – the side which made

	N-S	E-W	
1	12	8	1
2	7	15	2
3	12	7	3
4	8	12	4
total	39	42	
game	–	10	
bonus	–	5	
TOTAL	39	57	

FIGURE 17

Concerto score-sheet, showing the actual scores for the illustrative game which follows.

the better play will win, and the luck of the deal will hardly enter into it. What this amounts to is that a partnership needs to play to a system, whereby the cards each one plays and the order in which he plays them conveys information about the rest of his hand. The need for such a system will be evident from a simple example. Suppose you are to lead, and you hold:

♠J T 9 7 ♡A K 9 ♣9 6 3 ◇Q 5 2

You cannot afford to miss a straight flush if one is possible, and your best chance lies in the spade holding, for which you require your partner to hold either ♠8 or, more remotely, ♠K ♠Q. If he cannot help, then your next best possibility is of making four Nines, for which you require him to hold ◇9. Is it possible to play in such a way as to communicate all three possibilities to him, so that he will know whether to play or pass, and if so what to play, while retaining the opportunity to make either a straight flush or four of a kind from the same lead? As we shall see later, the answer is 'yes', provided that you employ a good signalling system by which to do it. First, however, there are some general points to consider.

Distribution of cards. On average, you and your partner can expect to have a straight flush available between you about twice in every five deals, and four of a kind twice in every three. You are bound to hold several middling combinations between you every time (full houses, straights and flushes). It is remotely possible not to have a straight – key cards for which are Fives and Tens; a side with none of either can make no straight – but you will almost invariably have at least three flushes. You would be unusually lucky to hold a ready-made straight flush or four of a kind in your own hand, but the holding of several middling combinations is so usual as to be unremarkable.

The strategy of the game, then, is based on aiming for high combinations first (straight flushes, fours of a kind), and 'converting' these to middling combinations (respectively straights or flushes, and full houses) should the high ones prove unattainable. Low combinations, of pairs or threes, are usually made by accident, and only on the fourth hand. To make no combination at all is a disgrace!

In any given deal, the fall of the cards may tend to favour either long combinations (straights and flushes) or short combinations (things of a kind), and this bias will be shown in the cards of both partnerships. If your opponents start by making a straight flush, the chances are that you may be able to make one too; if they start with four of a kind, there is a fair probability that fours and full houses will figure more prominently than straight and/or flush combinations. Your own hand of cards will give you some indication of which way the bias lies, and you should play accordingly.

Playing and passing. Always lead from the strongest part-combination you have in your hand. Four consecutive cards to a straight flush, for example, is stronger than three of a kind, as there are (except at extremes) two possible cards by which your partner can fill it as opposed to only one for the potential quartet.

The same applies throughout the play of a single hand. At any given stage of the play there is always a best combination that can be made from the card or cards so far played. If you can contribute a card which belongs to that best possibility, play it. If not, pass, in case your partner can further it himself. If he cannot do so either, then he will either start to 'convert' by playing a card to the second best combination that can be made from it, or else pass back to you, in which case, knowing he cannot help, you may convert it yourself.

Do not drop out (by saying 'play') unless you are absolutely certain that your partner has a ready-made combination or can successfully complete the one in progress, for, if he cannot, you may thereby force him to play a card he might otherwise have preferred to retain. This call should only be used when your partner has signalled the fact that he has the best possible cards for the current hand.

There is one occasion on which it is virtually obligatory to pass, and that is when your partner, as leader, has played his first card. A single card tells you nothing. You must pass in order to give him a chance to indicate to you what sort of hand he is aiming for. If, for example, he leads ♡6 and you hold ♡5 ♡4, do not play them until you are sure he is aiming for a straight flush. He would not thank you for a failed straight flush if he were playing from four Sixes! It is not until the leader has played his second card that his partner knows what combination he is playing from. Two cards in suit and range (i.e. potentially belonging to the same straight) signal his intention of a straight flush; two of the same rank signal his intention of trying for four of a kind. Only play immediately if you yourself can turn that first card into a top combination without further assistance, and even then you should wait for his second card before converting a straight flush into four of a kind (which you can afford to do, since the four-combination includes one unmatched card).

Generally, it is the leader to a hand who takes responsibility for directing it and taking the initiative in making conversions throughout the play. The follower to a hand may pass out of caution; the leader may play out of boldness. The roles should only be reversed if the leader passes back on his second turn, having played only one card – this is a signal indicating that he has a weak hand and is leaving it to you to make the decisions.

Finally, note that although there is no direct interaction between the opposing partnerships, you may derive much benefit from observing not only what cards your opponents play but also which ones they fail to play. Suppose, for example, they start with a potential straight flush by playing ♠9 8 7 5, and then convert it into a flush. Holding three Sixes yourself, there is a good chance that your partner has the fourth, otherwise the opponents would have played it for a straight and scored an extra point. If on your next turn you lead a Six, your partner, who is as wide awake as you are, would be justified in dropping his Six instead of making the conventional opening pass.

Because one side can make deductions from observing cards played by the other, the possibility does exist of bluffing your opponents by playing 'wrong' cards, provided you can do so without otherwise spoiling the hand. This, however, is a highly advanced tactic.

Signals. For consistent success at Concerto you and your partner must either be completely telepathic or follow some sort of signalling system whereby the structure of your hand may be communicated by the cards you play and the order in which you play them. Those of us who play the game regularly have devised a series of signals that work sufficiently well in practice to be considered as more or less standard. Here it must suffice to concentrate only on the major signals and to express them, for conciseness, as if they were invariable rules – which they are not. With experience of the game you will soon learn when and how to break them, and quite possibly you will devise other and even better signals of your own.

You make a signal when you have the lead. Since it is virtually obligatory for your partner to pass after your first card, a signal is formed by the first two cards you play.

If the best feature of your hand is three or more cards to a

straight flush, make a straight flush signal, which consists of two
cards of the same suit and in the same range.

If you hold four of a kind, play the 'fours' signal, which is two
cards of the same rank, but of particular suits as explained
below.

If the likeliest possibility you hold is two (or more) sets of
three of a kind, play the 'two threes' signal, which is also two
cards of the same rank, but of particular suits as explained below.

There is also a 'nothing-better-than-a-full-house' signal.

Ready-made straights and flushes are not worth signalling, so
if you have anything less than the combination possibilities outlined above you play the 'no go' signal, which is one card
followed by a pass.

STRAIGHT FLUSH SIGNALS

The left-hand side of the following table shows all the possible
patterns in which you might hold three or more cards belonging
to the same straight flush. X denotes a card held, 0 denotes a
gap in your sequence, and the order is high-low from left to right.
Thus, for example, X X 0 0 X denotes some such holding as
J T – – 7 ,while X 0 X X represents some such holding as J – 9 8.
The Xs in bold type are the cards to play.

No. of cards in range	Pattern of holding (high–low)	Signal
5	**X** X X X **X**	L 3 H
4	**X** X X **X**	L 2 H
	X X **X** 0 X	H 1 L
	X 0 **X** X **X**	L 1 H
	X X 0 X **X**	H 2 L (*two ways*)
3	**X** **X** 0 0 X	H 0 L
	X **X** 0 X	
	X X **X**	H 0 L *or* L 0 H
	X 0 **X** **X**	
	X 0 0 **X** **X**	L 0 H
	X 0 X 0 **X**	H 3 L

On the right-hand side, H-L means play the higher card first and then the low, L-H means play the lower and then the higher. The figure between shows the number of ranks lying between the two signal cards. Thus 'H2L' means 'high card first, two ranks missing, low card second' (e.g. Jack then Eight), while LOH means 'two consecutive cards (no ranks missing), low then high'.

A general principle to be observed in these signals is that you should avoid playing across a gap if at all possible. Only two patterns require you to do so, namely X X 0 X X (e.g. J T – 8 7) and X 0 X 0 X (e.g. J – 9 – 7). The first of these compensates for it by giving you a choice of two (e.g. J, 8 or T, 7); the second offers no compensation but is the worst possible holding anyway.

Reference to the sample hand quoted earlier will not only illustrate the signal in use but also show why it is best to avoid playing across a gap. Given that hand and the lead, your partner would play first ♠J and then ♠9. The signal is H1L, from which you infer that he holds ♠J T 9 – 7 and wants the Eight. Naturally you will play ♠8 if you have it, and be assured of the straight flush. If not, you could still play successfully if you held ♠K and ♠Q, for by *not playing across the gap* represented by the Eight, your partner has allowed for the remoter possibility of making ♠K Q J T 9. If you cannot help either combination, you pass. Now, if you will refer back to that hand, he knows that a straight flush is not possible and can therefore play another Nine. The cards on the table show ♠J ♠9 ♡9, and it is clear from his signal that if you hold a Nine you can play it and expect to make four of a kind, the ♠J remaining as the idle or unmatched card.

FOUR OF A KIND SIGNAL

Given the lead and a ready-made four of a kind in your hand, play two of them, the first from a red suit, the second from a major suit (♠ and ♡ are major, ♣ and ◇ minor, as at Bridge) – e.g. play ♡ ◇ or ♡ ♣ or ◇ ♣. The full set of signals attaches a different 'meaning' to each of these possibilities, but this is enough to be getting on with.

TWO THREES

Lacking three to a straight flush, or four of a kind, the next best possibility in your hand would be two sets of three of a kind, either of which may, with luck, produce four of a kind with your partner's assistance. The signal for two threes is two cards of the same rank, in any suit combination *other than* the 'red-major' signal for four of a kind. Further refinement of this signal enables you to communicate to your partner the exact rank of the other set of three.

FULL HOUSE

If the best you hold is three of a rank and one or more pairs, you still have a chance of leading into four of a kind. Play two cards of different colour suits, the first from your set of three, the second from a pair. Your partner will play from the first rank if he holds the fourth card, from the second rank if he holds the other two of it.

PLAY AND PASS

If the best you hold is three of a kind and no pairs, play a red card from the set of three and then pass on your second turn. If you hold nothing better than pairs, play a black card (from a pair) and pass. Either of these allows four of a kind to be made if available, and is therefore often a better bet than playing from a ready-made straight or flush. There are also 'straight-or-flush' signals, but these may be left to the imagination.

Practice. One advantage of the lack of direct interaction between the two partnerships is that you can devise and practise signals with a prospective partner. Just deal thirteen cards each, leaving the other twenty-six unseen, and play out your four hands. Test the efficacy of your signals and brilliance of your play by (*a*) noting what score you actually made for the four hands, (*b*) calculating what is the best score you could have made had you been able to see all twenty-six cards from the outset, and (*c*) expressing the former as a percentage of the latter. An average of 75 per cent or more is quite good.

You should always make at least 27 points in the four hands you make between you – anything less is an indicator of less-than-perfect play. It is reasonable to be left with two pairs amongst your six residual cards, but anything more denotes faulty play. That is why the game bonus is set at 10 points – it permits you a penalty of up to two pairs without enabling your opponents to get ahead of your higher score for the better group of four hands.

Doubling. As an optional variant, one partnership may double the game bonus from 10 to 20, and the other re-double it to 40, before play begins. In the event of a tie, the bonus then goes to the opponents of the side that doubled or re-doubled.

Sample game

```
North    ♠984 ♡Q75 ♣98 ◇Q8763
South    ♠A652 ♡A983 ♣QJ76 ◇9

East     ♠KJT ♡JT2 ♣AT3 ◇KJ54
West     ♠Q73 ♡K64 ♣K542 ◇AT2
```

N	S	
◇8	—	South makes the statutory pass.
◇7	—	North calls for two lower diamonds, so pass again;
♠8	♡8	North converts to four of a kind and South can now help.
♣8		
12		N-S score for four of a kind.

E	W	
♠T	—	
♠J	—	East calls for two higher spades, so West must pass;
◇J	—	West still cannot help.
♡J	—	
♡T		
8		

E-W make a full house on their first round. Had East played a Ten instead of a Jack they would have made four of a kind. There was no way of knowing this, but, with a more refined system of play, East might have passed on his third turn to indicate that he held three of each rank, in which case West would have played the Ten. In the actual play, a good principle is followed: all other things being equal, it is better for one person to play more cards out than the other throughout the game, since the player with more in hand at the end can exercise control over breaking up residual combinations. The worst end situation is to have three each.

N	S	
	♠ A	
—	♠ 2	
—	—	With no good continuation, South cedes the initiative;
♠ 4	♠ 5	North has nothing brilliant either;
◇ 3		Whoever had a Three was bound to play it 'for the best'.
	7	

E	W	
	♣ 5	
—	♣ 4	West calls for two lower clubs;
♣ 3	♣ 2	East has them and plays accordingly;
♣ A		A neat piece of text-book play.
	15	The first straight flush of the season.

N	S	
♣ 9	—	North has nothing good, plays the statutory 'black and pass';
—	◇ 9	South correctly assumes North has a pair of Nines;
♠ 9	♡ 9	More text-book play.
◇ 6		
12		

An unexpected four of a kind. Why did North automatically play the fifth (unmatched) card? In accordance with the principle that any odd cards should be played by the player holding fewer in hand, so that the residual six should not be evenly divided between them.

E	W	
◇ 4	—	
◇ 5	◇ 2	Not a signal, because ◇ 6 7 8 are out of play
—	◇ A	
—	♠ 3	
	7	

N	S	
	♣ 6	South plays 'black and pass' from his strongest suit.
—	—	
◇ Q	♣ Q	North plays from his best; South can only copy.
♡ Q	—	South must pass in case North has the fourth Queen.
—	♠ 6	North must pass in case South has a Six, which he has.
	8	

E	W	
	♣ K	
♠ K	♡ K	East seizes the initiative for justifiable reasons;
◇ K	—	West passes, having no combination to break up.
♣ T	—	East discards the Ten, knowing that there is another in play.
	12	This last hand was a lucky break.

The result of the game is as follows:

N-S	E-W	
12	8	
7	15	
12	7	
8	12	
39	42	for combinations
	10	for game
	5	to E-W for the pair of Sevens left in their opponents' hands
39	57	– an unusually high-scoring game.

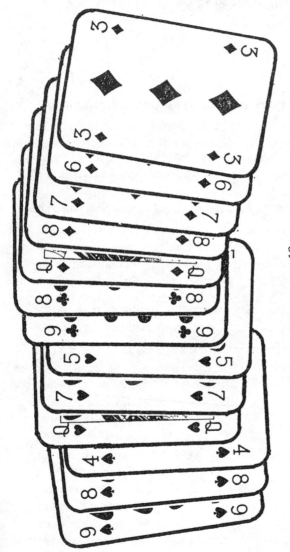

FIGURE 18

Given this hand (North's in the illustrative game above) you are concerned to make either a straight flush in diamonds, built upon your 8-7-6, or, hopefully, four Eights if this fails. You therefore lead ♢8 then ♢7, and, if South passes, continue with another Eight. Now suppose South had the lead, and opened with ♡8. Theoretically, you could immediately play an Eight instead of passing, to show that you can complete the quartet. But this would be over-hasty. For all you know, he may be playing from ♢ J T 9 8, in which case he would next play ♡J and you would add your ♡7 for the straight flush. Wait for his second card before stepping in and making the conversion to four Eights. For more detailed signalling, see the chapter on Concerto in the author's book of *Original Card Games*, Batsford, 1977.

SOLO WHIST

Solo Whist is a popular English gambling game in which one player takes on or 'declares a contract against' the other three, in contrast to the two-against-two structure of classical partnership Whist.

For all its popularity, the game has not attracted as much serious attention as its high qualities undoubtedly merit. Two possible causes of neglect might be suggested. One is that, as an essentially gambling game, it lacks a scoring system of sufficient refinement to appeal to card-players (such as myself) who will not play for money. Another possible demerit may attach to its name. 'Solo Whist' unconsciously suggests a derivative, even a perversion, of some such imaginary concept as 'proper' Whist. This is not so, and the relation between the two games is far from direct. Partnership Whist, though French in origin, is essentially an English development dating back to the seventeenth century. Solo, on the other hand, bears closer relation to the nineteenth-century popular game of Boston, and is widely played in the Low Countries. It may even be described as the national game of Belgium, and in older sources is referred to as Whist de Gand, or Ghent Whist. This circumstance also helps to explain the French terminology particularly associated with the game.

There are two forms of Solo – the classic form described here, and a later development called Auction Solo, which is outlined in an appendix to this chapter. As might be expected, modern Auction Solo is a souped-up version of the original, said to have been designed for greater variety and excitement. There is no universally accepted standard form of either game. The following may therefore be regarded as 'textbook Solo', from which the actual practice of individual schools may differ in various details.

The game

Cards. A standard 52-card pack. Cards rank in their normal order, from high to low A K Q J T 9 8 7 6 5 4 3 2.

Preliminaries. Establish seats and right of first deal by any agreed means. Each deal is usually regarded as a separate event and is settled in chips, of which each player should start with not fewer than twenty. Alternatively, settlements can be recorded in writing (this serving as a crude sort of scoring system). Each new deal is made by the player on the left of the previous dealer, and all play rotates clockwise around the table.

Shuffle and deal. Anyone may shuffle, but the dealer has the right to shuffle last. Deal cards in batches of three at a time to each player, followed by a single card to make thirteen each. The last card of the pack, which belongs to the dealer, must be turned face up on the table. The suit of the turn-up is the 'preferred' trump suit, and as soon as the suit has been positively accepted or rejected as trump the card is taken up into the dealer's hand.

Object. There is a round of bidding to establish which player will undertake a contract against the other three, although there is also a bid – the lowest – by which one player calls on anyone else to support him in a partnership contract against the other two. The values, names and explanations of the possible bids are tabulated here and detailed opposite.

PROP AND COP
The general idea is that this partnership game is only played if no-one has a hand good enough to venture a positive bid on his own: thus the player who can make four tricks in the preferred trump, but not the five needed for a solo bid, has a chance to 'propose', and if anyone else finds himself in the same position he will 'accept' – hence the fixing of the contract at eight tricks (theoretically four each). Some schools of thought do not recognise 'prop and cop', and abandon the deal if no-one bids solo. This practice may be condemned as pointless.

Value	Bid (colloquial in parentheses)	Object
2	Proposal and acceptance (prop and cop)	Partners take 8 tricks with preferred trump
2	Solo	Caller takes 5 tricks with preferred trump
3	Misère	Caller takes 0 tricks at no trump
4	Abondance (abundance)	Caller takes 9 tricks with own trump
4	Abondance royale (royal abundance)	Caller takes 9 tricks with preferred trump
6	Misère ouverte (spread misère)	Caller takes 0 with hand of cards exposed
8	Abondance declarée (declared abundance)	Caller takes 13 tricks at no trump (or with own trump if previously agreed – see note)

SOLO

The caller, playing against the other three, must win at least five tricks, and must accept the preferred suit as trumps.

MISÈRE AND OPEN MISÈRE

Playing without a trump suit, the caller must take no tricks. As soon as he is forced to take a trick he loses his contract without further play. If he considers the hand unbeatable he will play 'open', in which case he spreads his hand of cards face up on the table, though not until the first trick has been played and taken.

ABONDANCE AND ROYAL ABONDANCE

A player bidding 'abondance' must win at least nine of the thirteen tricks. He has the privilege of choosing his trump suit, which may or may not be that of the turned up card, but he does not announce his intended trump suit until the first card is about to be led to the first trick (and, of course, if overcalled by a higher bid he does not announce it at all).

Royal abondance has exactly the same object as abondance, and is merely a bid which enables one player to overcall another who has already bid abondance by offering to take nine tricks using the suit of the turn-up as trumps. If the first bidder was intending to nominate the preferred suit anyway, he can establish priority by announcing that fact, in which case he is not overcalled by the bidder of royal abondance. (Not all authorities agree on this point; many do not even notice that the problem exists.)

DECLARED ABONDANCE

The caller of declared abondance must win all thirteen tricks, and has the privilege (obligatory) of leading to the first trick. Strictly speaking, a declared abondance must automatically be played without a trump suit. In some schools, it is never played at no-trump, but the caller nominates his own trump suit; and in yet other schools this can be overcalled by a bid of declared abondance in the preferred trump. There is no point in such complication, as the bid occurs too rarely to make competition worth while. Players should agree beforehand which system to follow.

Bidding procedure. Starting with the player on the dealer's left, each in turn must either pass or make any bid higher than one that has gone before. Once a player has passed he may not re-enter the bidding, except for the purposes of 'prop and cop' as explained below. As soon as a positive bid has been followed by three passes, that bid is established and the play begins.

If one player proposes, and if the proposal has not been over-called by a solo or higher bid, a subsequent player may bid by saying 'accept'; and if this in turn is not overcalled by a solo or a higher bid, the proposer and acceptant are then obliged to play. (Tricks are still played clockwise around the table – it does not matter if the partners are not opposite each other.)

If eldest hand (the first to bid) passes, and the only other bid made is a proposal, then eldest is permitted to accept if he wishes, in spite of having passed the first time. This privilege of accepting after having passed does *not* apply to any other player.

If a proposal is followed by three passes, there being no acceptant, the proposer may then either raise his bid to a solo or else pass.

If all players pass, 'text-book procedure' is to abandon the hands and let the deal pass to the left. In practice, many schools play one of several varieties of 'all-against-all' games with the hands as dealt, of which the version recommended here is called...

COMPETITIVE MISÈRE

Tricks are played at no trump. The player who takes the most tricks is the loser, and pays the others one unit each.

Play. Before the opening lead is made, the dealer takes up his faced card, and, if the contract being played is abondance, the caller announces the trump suit. The lead to the first trick is always made by eldest hand (the player on the dealer's left) except in a declared abondance, when it is made by the caller. If an open misère is being played, the caller does not expose his cards until the first trick has been played and taken.

The usual rules of trick-taking apply. Follow suit to the card led if possible; if not possible, either trump or discard. The trick is taken by the highest card of the suit led, or by the highest trump if any are played, and the winner of one trick leads to the next.

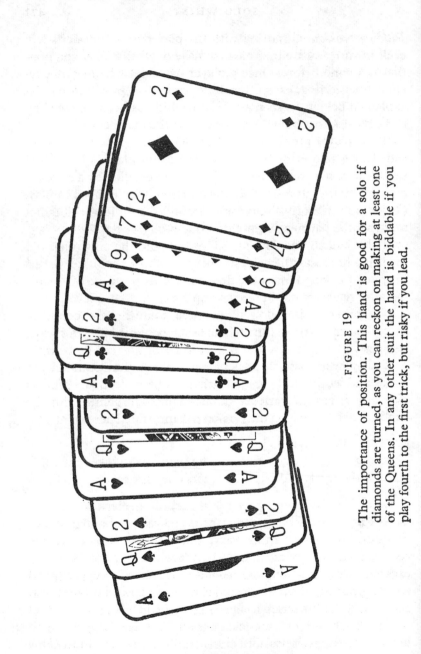

FIGURE 19

The importance of position. This hand is good for a solo if diamonds are turned, as you can reckon on making at least one of the Queens. In any other suit the hand is biddable if you play fourth to the first trick, but risky if you lead.

Settlement. The value of each game is as follows: Solo 2, Misère 3, Abondance or Royal Abondance 4, Open Misère 6, Declared Abondance 8. If the caller wins his game he receives the appropriate value from each player; if he loses, he pays the appropriate value to each player.

There are various methods of settlement for 'prop and cop', of which the simplest is for each member of the winning partnership to receive two units, one from each member of the losing partnership.

A quasi-score may be kept by noting the settlement in writing, preceding each figure by (+) or (−). A figure must be noted against each player's initial on every deal, and the minuses (of course) should always cancel out the plusses.

Example

S	W	N	E	
−4	+12	−4	−4	Successful abondance by West
+2	+2	−6	+2	Failed solo by North
−2	−2	+2	+2	Successful prop and cop by North and East (or failed by South and West).
−3	+1	+1	+1	Competitive misère: South took most tricks.
−7	+13	−7	+1	*Result*

Hints on play

Solo Whist is a subtle game in which it is easy to err in either of two directions – that of excessive caution, and that of extreme recklessness. The over-cautious player will never take a chance on a reasonable but not foolproof bid which the more experienced or imaginative player will undertake promptly; the reckless player will undertake too many long-shot hands and come off worst. If all players are cautious, as usually happens with beginners, the game is dull because there are few bids. This danger is best overcome by playing a Competitive Misère when all pass, as those who lose by taking the most tricks will thereby learn to recognise strength in hand when they see it. If one player is reckless, the game is dull because he hogs the limelight, preventing others from taking a hand with their more reasonable bids, and his frequent losses will be a foregone conclusion. (What makes any game exciting is the fight, not the defeat.) Since dullness can therefore be caused by one reckless player, though not by one cautious player, some argue in favour of playing for money in that the expense incurred discourages reckless overbidding. The point is arguable, in both senses of the word.

Before considering the individual bids that may be made, note first the one important respect in which Solo differs from Bridge, Whist and the majority of other trick-taking games in English card tradition. This lies in the fact that cards are dealt in batches of three, with the result that a balanced distribution of cards amongst the four players is the exception rather than the rule. In Bridge and Whist you normally expect to find the cards of your own hand distributed 4-3-3-3 or 4-4-3-2 amongst the suits, so that any suit longer than five or shorter than two gives you a hand well worth thinking about. In Solo, a hand of the pattern 7-4-2-0 may well give you a good bid, but should not be regarded as anything out of the ordinary. Whether or not the hand is biddable depends not on the distribution but on the quality of the cards you hold.

With this point in mind it is fairly easy to indicate the difference between a slightly risky bid and an out-and-out long shot. A slightly risky bid is one which you will only lose if the remaining cards are unfavourably distributed against you in your opponents' hands. Such a bid is worth making. A long shot is one which you can only win if the remaining cards are distributed amongst the others in your favour. Such a bid is not worth making.

When you are not the caller, remember that you are playing as a member of a partnership of three, and not just for the pleasure of making as many tricks as you can yourself (or losing them, in the case of a misère). It is always to the advantage of the caller's opponents – who, in accordance with card tradition, but in defiance of logic, are known as the defenders – to lead through the caller rather than up to him. In other words, the lead to a trick is always best made by the player on the caller's right, so that he has to play second. Caller's preferred position to a trick is either first (leader) or fourth; the others should therefore play as far as possible to deny him this advantage.

When defending a positive (non-misère) bid, lead low through the caller, and try as much as possible to weaken his hand either by leading trumps or by forcing them out of him by leading suits in which he is void. If playing from a sequence (e.g. from Q J T etc.) always take with the lowest but lead with the highest – though, if you hold Ace, King, lead the King. By following these and other principles derived from partnership Whist your co-defenders will be able to deduce useful features of your hand and play accordingly.

Keeping track of the cards played is important. You need not remember them all, but try at least to count the trumps as they appear, to keep track of the Aces and Kings, and to note when anyone else has a void suit.

Proposal and acceptance

Some schools do not allow the bids of proposal and acceptance, admitting nothing lower than a solo, possibly on the grounds that 'it is too easy to make'. This view is mistaken. If a particular school does find 'prop and cop' too predictably successful, it means they are playing too cautiously and passing up hands on which more experienced players would go solo. The whole point of aiming for eight tricks between two players is that neither of them adjudges his hand good enough for five on its own.

It is to be generally understood – as a matter of convention, but born of common sense – that the player who proposes has some strength in trumps, though not necessarily enough to justify a solo bid. It follows that a player who accepts need not himself have strength in trumps, but should be able to offer further support, especially in side-suits. If neither partner feels strong enough to lead trumps the bid was probably risky, and the defenders will take advantage of this reluctance, when they spot it, to lead trumps themselves.

Position is of some importance in the bidding, and especially so in respect of 'prop and cop'. The best position from which to accept is a fourth hand, as the fact that the proposal has not been overcalled by a solo bid bodes well for the partnership contract. It is risky to accept eldest hand's proposal as second hand, as the third and fourth to bid may well let the contract stand for the sheer pleasure of defeating it.

As eldest hand (first to bid), do not feel obliged to propose if your cards are only just biddable. If your hand is not strong enough for an independent bid, you may safely pass, since you still retain the opportunity to accept should one of the other players propose – a circumstance which automatically suggests that your hand may be stronger than you think. Alternatively, you may well propose on a hand which may or may not be quite good enough for a solo. If a later player accepts, you have a playable game; if not, and all pass, then you may reasonably consider raising your bid to a solo, knowing that it cannot be overcalled.

Here is a hand on which eldest passed, but subsequently accepted a proposal (spades trump):

♠K Q T 4 ♡K 2 ♣T 8 5 4 ◇8 5 2

The proposer's hand was:

♠8 7 6 5 3 ♡A ♣A 9 7 6 ◇T 9 6

This is the sort of combination that makes it criminal to abolish 'prop and cop'!

If you and your partner are sitting side by side, the ideal positioning is for one to be leading to a trick to which the other is playing fourth. As the contracting side, with presumed strength in trumps, you should lead trumps early in order to draw them from your opponents and so establish your side-suits. Against this, however, you should avoid forcing your partner to play trumps if you are weak in them yourself. As in partnership Whist, note what suit your partner leads first, and return it when convenient to do so. Lead from strength – either trumps, or from your strongest suit, whichever you want returned. It is not particularly desirable to lead a singleton.

Solo. Solo is a bid to win five tricks in the preferred trump suit. In order to bid it, you need to have a hand that will enable you to win a certain five tricks in the turned trump. This may sound so obvious as to be trivial, but nevertheless in defiance of all probabilities there are players who will quite happily bid solo, in spades, on a hand such as:

♠K Q 9 4 ♡8 ♣A K Q J 3 ◇T 9 8

The idea is to make two trumps, one of them on a heart lead after the Eight has gone; at least the top two clubs; and one for luck, in either trumps or clubs. Without the lead, a probable outcome is the win of two trumps as anticipated, the possible win of ♣A when led, and, if very lucky, the possible win of ♣K, for a final result of four or even only three tricks. 'Yes,' says one commentator, who shall be nameless; 'Solo is easy enough; just look for five near-certain tricks.'

At the other extreme, there are players so mesmerised by Aces that they will pass up a perfectly feasible solo bid for lack of them – as, for example, on the following hand, again with spades turned:

♠K J 9 8 7 5 2 ♡5 ♣J 9 4 ◇Q 3

Given the lead, this is a good example of the 'slight risk' which we defined previously as being worth taking. With seven trumps in hand, the holder can afford to lose two of them in the not unreasonable hope that those same two tricks will clear the defenders out of their three top trumps (Ace, Queen and Ten). Correct strategy, therefore, is to lead the King.

Even without the lead, you could safely bid solo (spades, again, for convenience) on:

♠K Q T 8 7 6 ♡K T 9 8 ♣K 4 2 ◇—

The side-suit Kings should produce two tricks, the void in diamonds brings in a low trump, and the remaining five trumps are good for the outstanding two.

What, in general, are the minimum requirements for a biddable solo?

The first merit is length or strength in trumps, counting as part of this assessment any void or singleton side-suit which can be ruffed with a low one at the appropriate time. On trumps alone, the borderline between a doubtful and a feasible solo is finely drawn. For instance, a holding of A K Q 9 and one lower is risky, whereas A K Q T and one might be expected to succeed without inducing gasps of astonishment. When holding five trumps, always calculate on the pessimistic assumption that at least one defender may hold five as well. Even a seven-card suit should be headed by nothing less than K J 9.

In side-suits, the chief merit is strength and shortness (not length). The expected failure of the first hand quoted above lies in the undue length of the club suit – A K Q J 3, five in all. The most favourable possible distribution of the outstanding eight is 3-3-2, which means that someone will certainly be trumping by the time you have drawn the odd two with the Ace and King. A more probable distribution is 4-3-1, giving you the Ace but not the King, while there is a strong chance (given the unbalanced distribution of your own hand) of one defender's being void, thus depriving you even of the Ace.

With strength and universal shortness – that is, an unusually even distribution of suits – you may even dispense with strength in trumps. The fact that spades is the turned card does not prevent the following holding from offering a good solo:

♠5 4 3 2 ♡A K 2 ♣A K 2 ♢A 3 2

Of course, it will be beaten if any defender is void in diamonds or holds only one heart or club, but the evenness of the suit distribution in your own hand is good enough to lower the probability of such an event to the acceptable level of 'slight risk'.

Some hands make acceptable solos only if you have the lead; others really require to be led up to. For example, consider the trump holding A K Q T 2 in a hand which does not include a void or easily voidable (singleton) suit. The problem card is the Jack. If you have the lead, you can play out the top trumps in order and without undue optimism hope that the Jack will fall by the time the Queen is out, leaving Ten high and a certain trick with the Two, and giving enough for solo even without side-suit support. Without the lead, the missing Jack is a permanent nuisance. By the time you have voided your short suit you run the danger of ruffing low with the Two and finding it overtaken by a higher trump. On the other hand, a holding that lacks Aces but can place reliance on guarded Kings in short suits will work best if you do not have the lead.

In defending against a solo it is good practice to lead a singleton to the first trick (in which respect the game differs from partnership Whist and also from the play at a 'prop and cop' contract in Solo, where a singleton lead is not to be recommended). With a fairly even distribution, a low trump is also not a bad lead. Otherwise, lead your best card – from not too long a suit – and the highest of a sequence, unless you hold Ace, King, in which case play the King.

Abondance and royal abondance. An abondance is a solo, only more so. As before, you must have length and strength in trumps; in addition, you should have a strong, lengthy side-suit and at least one void. Because the dealing system, 3-3-3-1, produces uneven distributions easily, double voids are not uncommon, and a strong two-suited hand is often a must for abondance.

Since the object of the bid is to make at least nine tricks, one way of assessing the hand is to identify the four cards you can afford to lose – and to make sure there are not five of them (otherwise, you make what is known as an 'eight-trick abondance', which comes expensive).

Given two suits of equal length, do not automatically entrump the stronger. Quite often the 'weaker' suit is not merely the better trump candidate, but indeed affords the *only* way of avoiding loss. On this hand, for example –

♠AKQJT9 ♡T86532 ♣A ◇—

by all means bid abondance, but nominate hearts as trumps, not the apparently stronger spade suit. The reason is perhaps easiest to see if you examine the hand from the viewpoint of the four losers rather than the nine winners. If you make spades trump, how are you going to avoid losing more than four hearts? With hearts trump, however, you can afford to lose four for the sake of extracting your opponents' trumps and so safely establishing the spade suit. You will make one heart by ruffing a diamond lead, and a second either by a ruff in diamonds or clubs, or by virtue of finding your Ten high when the top trumps have gone.

Defending against an abondance, lead from your longest and strongest suit. Remember that the defenders need five tricks to win, and lose no opportunity to make five as soon as possible – that is, before caller can get in with his trumps and dictate the rest of the play. By all means lead suits in which caller is void, thereby forcing him to trump and so weaken his hand. Sometimes caller will be relying on a 'bum card' for a lucky trick: if you can spot this coming you can defend against it. He may, for instance, lead Ace, King of a side-suit, then switch to another line of attack in pretence of being void. By retaining the odd Queen, Jack or even Ten, instead of discarding at the earliest opportunity, you may well find it winning a low one at the thirteenth trick, led to by caller after extracting all the trumps. Again, if caller is hoping to make a risky King or Queen he may be hoping to do so on a bad lead by the defenders, in which case he will be trying to lose the lead – which you can give him back by forcing him to trump.

Declared abondance. This is a bid to win all thirteen tricks, and as the sort of hand which will enable you to do so is unmistakable there is no point in describing it. Or even playing it; for you only declare abondance on a cast-iron hand, and if it really is cast-iron you simply lay it face up on the table and claim your winnings. If any defender can find a way of beating it then the game must be played, and if he is right you will have learnt a valuable lesson.

It will be worth while explaining why a declared abondance is properly played at no-trump, even though many seem to accept it as a trump game. The reason is, quite simply, that *if* you can make thirteen tricks with a trump suit, then you can make thirteen tricks without a trump suit. 'But surely' (you may say) 'You must declare a trump on a hand with a void, such as –

♠A K Q J T ♡A K Q J ♣A K Q J ◇—

– otherwise, at no-trump, the hand is beaten if diamonds are led.'
Objection overruled. It is precisely to obviate this danger that, for
a declared abondance only, caller has the privilege of leading.

Misère and open misère. Beginners may be forgiven for imagining
that a misère, the winning of no tricks at no-trump, is what you
bid when you have no good trick-winners plus a general
miscellany of dribs and drabs. Such a hand is one on which you
do not bid at all. The misère bid is a positive undertaking
to successfully defend yourself against all efforts on the part of
your opponents to force you to take a trick. For this purpose you
need a very good hand – 'good', that is, from the point of view of
beating off such attacks.

Many card-players, especially those who know nothing but
Bridge, tend to look down on misère as a sort of jocular substitute round, played when no-one has a good enough hand on
which to make a 'real' bid. Nothing could be further from the
truth. Both attack and defence at misère call for, and often
receive, some of the finest play that can be observed at the card
table.

To business: in contemplating a misère, there are two good
features to look for. One is low-ranking cards, and the other is a
void suit. Note that the length of any suit you hold is irrelevant
so long as it contains low cards. For example, in this hand

♠32 ♡A Q T 8 6 4 2 ♣7 3 2 ♢—

the hearts are just as safe from attack as the spades: you cannot
be forced to take a trick in either suit. As for low ranks, in a
holding of five or more you must have the Two (you may escape
without it, but the risk is great); with fewer, you may get away
with nothing lower than Three or even Four. If your lowest is
the five, you will be beaten if the Four, Three and Two are evenly
distributed among your opponents. Note, too, that a holding of
alternating low ranks is just as good as a sequence. In the hand
quoted above, for instance, the A Q T 8 6 4 2 of hearts is as
strong as would be 8 7 6 5 4 3 2. To prove it, imagine that the
Three is led; you play the Two, and your Four is then the lowest

of the suit. If the Five is then led, you play the Four and your Six is lowest. And so on.

The advantage of a void is obvious: when it is led, you can throw out your potentially dangerous cards. The recognition of potential dangers can be a subtle affair. Take the hand quoted above. Because the hearts are safe from attack, as we have seen, it contains no dangerous cards, so you need not rush to throw out the Ace or Queen when diamonds are led. Clubs, however, are a different matter, for ♣7 is the most dangerous card in the hand. With three clubs, 6, 5, 4, out against you, you can successfully defend against the lead of only two of them (with 3, 2), and by the time the third is led you may find the other two players void, thus forcing you to take with the Seven. (And do not imagine this to be a case of bad luck – experienced opponents will soon discover your weak suit and exploit it.)

You therefore need the void in diamonds as a means of discarding your dangerous Seven. In general, then, you cannot bid misère with dangerous cards unless you have saving voids to accommodate them, and even then the device may only be expected to work once. Remember, too, to look at things from your opponents' viewpoint. If your hand is good enough for a misère but not good enough for an open misère, then by definition it contains a weakness, and the strategy of your opponents will be to find out where this weakness lies and to exploit it. They need to force you to take only one trick to win; once you have done so, the contract is lost and there is no point in playing further.

In defending against a misère a good lead is any singleton, or, failing that, a middling card from a short suit. Do not play from a long suit, as there is a chance that caller will be void and will immediately throw any dangerous card he may hold. Do not play too low, as you must give your partners an opportunity to get rid of their own high cards in that suit. If you hold a Two, especially in a short suit, you may well hold the means to beat the contract. Save it until the top cards are out, then get the lead and play it – for which purpose retain an Ace or other master card to ensure ability to enter when you judge the time ripe.

Sample game

Proposal and acceptance. East deals, and the exposed card is ◇9:

South	♠K 6 5 ♡Q J 8 6 ♣J 2 ◇J T 8 6
West	♠A J 9 7 2 ♡4 ♣A K 9 6 ◇4 3 2
North	♠Q T 8 ♡K 9 3 ♣8 7 5 4 3 ◇K Q
East	♠4 3 ♡A T 7 5 2 ♣Q T ◇A 9 7 5

South has nothing, and passes. West, taking a calculated risk, proposes, counting a trick for each Ace, one for a ruff on hearts, and hopefully ♣K to boot. North passes. East accepts, on the assumption that his partner has strong trumps (mistakenly) and the other two Aces (correctly). South leads, and having nothing more noteworthy than over a quarter of the trumps available, plunges immediately into that suit.

S	W	N	E	
◇J	◇4	◇Q	◇A	
♡6	♡4	♡3	♡A	Since South seems happy with trumps, East refrains from leading them.
♡8	◇3	♡9	♡2	
♣2	♣K	♣3	♣T	
♣J	♣6	♣4	♣Q	West avoids the Ace – he wants East to take over.
♡J	◇2	♡K	♡2	East, properly, leads into his partner's void. West is now out of trumps, but they need only two tricks.
◇6	♣A	♣5	♠4	Waste of an Ace ? Not at all – it draws a trump out.
♡Q	♣9	♣7	♡5	
♠5	♠A	♠8	♠3	
♠6	♠K	♠Q	◇5	
	4		+4	=the required eight tricks

South's trump lead was a danger signal to East: had he continued trumps at the second trick the contract would probably have failed.

Solo. Now it is South's deal, and the turn-up is ♡7:

    South   ♠K Q 2 ♡A K 7 5 2 ♣K 7 5 4 ◇2
    West   ♠T 7 6 ♡Q J 9 6 ♣T 9 6 ◇K Q J
    North   ♠A J 5 ♡T 8 4 3 ♣A J 8 ◇T 6 4
    East   ♠9 8 4 3 ♡— ♣Q 3 2 ◇A 9 8 7 5 3

West, North and East pass, implying sufficient weakness for South to take a solo upon himself, which he accordingly bids. West leads:

S	W	N	E	
◇2	◇K	◇4	◇3	
♡2	◇Q	◇6	◇5	
♡A	♡6	♡3	♠3	South has no side Aces to make and prefers to have his Kings led up to. So he decides to see how the trumps fall, and is aghast to discover East void: if either of the others had five of the other trumps he would be lucky to escape with his life. East throws a spade to conserve his guarded ♣Q and long diamonds.
♠Q	♠6	♠A	♠4	South has no choice but to slip into another suit, aiming to clear a King.
♡K	♡9	♡T	♠8	A nasty lead. Was South's King a mistake or a necessity? The latter. He must try to make his ♠K.
♠K	♠7	♠5	♠9	Which he now does, for his fourth trick. With four trumps against him in two hands, three of them higher than the Seven, his only chance of another trick lies in the (as yet unseen) club suit. He must force out more trumps to make the clubs safer when they are eventually led. East is void in spades, not so that he can trump (he has none) but because

S	W	N	E	
				the only possible contribution he can make to South's defeat lies either in retaining his guarded Queen or else in leading diamonds.
♡5	♡J	♡4	◇7	
♡7	♡Q	♡8	◇8	West leads a trump and the rest fall out. There was no point in retaining the Queen, as South, if he had two trumps, would win anyway.
♠2	◇J	◇T	◇A	This looks like the chance that East has been waiting for.
♣4	♠T	♠J	◇9	Better late than never. Now there are three tricks to play, and all players have three clubs in hand. East to lead, and it all depends on him . . .
♣5	♣6	♣8	♣2 ?	East has done it wrong!
♣K	♣T	♣J	♣Q	
♣7	♣9	♣A	♣3	
5				And South has made his five.

A fascinating deal, victory bestowed with poetic justice. South's bid of solo was perfectly good in theory: a trick for each black King, a ruff on diamonds, and the top two trumps. In practice, the outstanding eight trumps were divided evenly between two opponents, and South should have been beaten by that unfavourable circumstance. And in reality, he made his bid because of a fatal mistake by East at the eleventh hour (or trick, in this case).

It should be obvious to East that South held ♣K. At the eleventh trick East was ideally placed for regicide, lying to the right of the caller. Had he led ♣Q, South could not have played ♣K, for then the Ace would have appeared, leaving him without a fifth trick. He must, therefore, have played low, in which case, East would have kept the trick and retained the lead in precisely the same position; again, South could not have played the King for precisely the same reason, and his Seven would have been

taken by anything higher except the Ace, to which the King
would fall at the last trick.

This is how the cards lay at the point in question:

South   ♣K 7 5
West   ♣T 9 6
North   ♣A J 8
East   ♣Q 3 2

and it is easy to see that the lead of the Queen is bound to win,
whereas anything else is bound to lose.

Misère. West deals, and a club is turned:

South   ♠A J 4 ♡K J ♣J T 8 5 2 ◇Q T 8
West   ♠Q T 9 5 ♡Q 9 6 3 ♣K 9 ◇K 9 2
North   ♠6 3 ♡A T 7 5 2 ♣6 ◇A 7 6 4 3
East   ♠K 8 6 2 ♡8 4 ♣A Q 7 4 3 ◇J 5

North, as eldest, bids misère, and the others pass. This is a
shaky bid, marginally justified only by the fact that he has the
lead and may get away with his singleton Six at the first trick.

S	W	N	E	
♡ 5	♣ 9	♣ 6	♣ 4	The fates are kind; and besides, if the opponents had all been able to get under there would have been no tale to tell. West keeps his King of clubs with which to come in later should he get a chance to lead ◇2 or ♡3 with advantage.
♡ K	♡ 6	♡ 5	♡ 8	A better lead might have been ◇9.
♡ J	♡ Q	♡ T	♡ 4	
◇ Q	♡ 9	♡ 7	◇ J	East and South discard from their shortest suits.
◇ T	♡ 3	♡ 2	◇ 5	
◇ 8	◇ 2	◇ 7!	♣ Q	West, having made a hash of hearts, now leads his winning diamond prematurely. North is right to play high, for he knows that only K, 9, 8 are left in play; if

they lie with West he has lost his contract anyway, whereas if any of them lies with South the Seven must be taken.

| ♠ 4 | ♠ 5 | ♠ 3 | ♠ K |
| ♠ J | ♠ 9 | ♠ 6 | ♣ 2 |

... at which point, North reveals his cards and victory is conceded. This illustrates the sort of misère hand you may get away with if you are lucky: in fact, as the remaining cards lie, it is not easy to find a way of beating the contract.

Abondance. North deals, and a heart is turned.

South ♠52 ♡AQT52 ♣Q9 ◇QT75
West ♠74 ♡K763 ♣86 ◇A9862
North ♠AKQJ93 ♡— ♣AK432 ◇J4
East ♠T86 ♡J984 ♣JT75 ◇K3

Following a prelude of three passes, North bids abondance in spades. His four losers are to be the two diamonds and two of the three low clubs, and the main point of his strategy must be to ensure the win of the third low club. East leads.

S	W	N	E	
◇ 5	◇ 2	◇ 4	◇ K	East, having no certain trick, starts to clear his shortest suit and successfully takes his two-to-one chance of winning.
◇ 7	◇ A	◇ J	◇ 3	Good for East; since caller didn't have the Ace, he can lead his Three, void the suit, and ensure the second of the five tricks his side needs to beat the contract.
◇ T	◇ 6	♠ J	♡ 4	A good lead – not that South expects to win the trick, but with so many diamonds gone a possible trump by caller may yet be over-trumped. North is considerably put out by it, and feels obliged to

S	W	N	E	
				trump high. Just as well he did – East is happy to throw a useless card, and could indeed have overtrumped if it had come to the push.
♠ 2	♠ 4	♠ A	♠ 6	North must now clear trumps with a view to establishing his clubs.
♠ 5	♠ 7	♠ K	♠ 8	
♡ 2	◇ 8	♠ Q	♠ T	That takes care of the last opposing trump. Now North plays from ♠9 3, ♣A K 4 3 2, needing five tricks more.
♣ Q	♣ 6	♣ 4	♣ 5	He attacks the club suit from below...
♡ A	♡ 3	♠ 3	♡ 8	... ruffs a long-awaited heart lead, and continues clubs...
♣ 9	♣ 8	♣ A	♣ 7	
◇ Q	◇ 9	♣ K	♣ T	That leaves the Jack out against his Three and Two.
♡ 5	♡ 6	♣ 3	♣ J	
♡ T	♡ 7	♠ 9	♡ 9	And in he trumps to lead to the last trick...
♡ Q	♡ K	♣ 2	♡ J	... which it is always a joy to win by the lead of a side-suit Two!
		9		Abondance succeeds.

The abondance would not have succeeded if any opponent had held five clubs, which was a risk worth taking. On the assumption that at least one player held four, North made his little club by leading two low ones to force out two high ones, and two high ones to draw out the other two. The whole manoeuvre depended upon his successfully clearing trumps first.

Footnote: In some schools, the caller of an abondance does not announce his trump suit until immediately after the first card has been led to the first trick.

AUCTION SOLO

Auction Solo is substantially the same as basic Solo, but permits a greater degree of competitive bidding, as follows:

> Proposal/acceptance
> 5-trick solo
> 6-trick solo
> 7-trick solo
> 8-trick solo
> Misère
> 9-trick abondance
> 10-trick abondance
> 11-trick abondance
> 12-trick abondance
> Open misère
> No-trump abondance declared
> Trump abondance declared

The 'preferred suit' is established by cutting a second pack rather than by turning up the dealer's last card. Proposal/acceptance and declared abondance in trumps may only be undertaken with the preferred trump. Other solo or abondance bids may be made in any suit, which remains unspecified until the bid has been accepted, but it is possible to overcall any bid by making the same bid in the preferred trump. In other words, the bid 'solo of five' can be overcalled either by 'solo of six' or by 'five in trumps' – meaning in the pre-selected trump.

Different schools vary in which bids they recognise. Proposal/acceptance and a solo of five in one's own suit are often omitted.

In a no-trump abondance declared the bidder leads to the first trick; if there is a trump suit, however, it is made, as usual, by eldest hand.

The value of each game is as follows:

> | | |
> |---|---|
> | Proposal/acceptance | 6, plus 1 per under/over-trick |
> | Solo | 6, plus 3 per under/over-trick |
> | Misère | 12 |
> | Abondance | 18, plus 3 per under/over-trick |
> | Open misère | 24 |
> | Abondance declared | 36 |

If the caller succeeds, he receives the appropriate value from each opponent. (An over-trick is any trick in excess of the number he bid. In some circles, not more than three over-tricks are paid for in a bid of solo, it being argued that the caller should have gone abondance. Settle this point before play.)

If the caller fails, he pays the appropriate value to each opponent. (An under-trick is any trick short of the number he bid – for example, the win of only five tricks in a bid of seven makes two under-tricks.)

AUCTION PITCH

Auction Pitch derives from an English game of some antiquity called All Fours, which is described in *The Compleat Gamester* of 1674 as being 'very much play'd in Kent'. Nowadays All Fours and its descendants are little heard of in Britain (except, curiously, in the Blackburn area), but the family as a whole retains a faithful following in America, Mexico, the West Indies, and no doubt other corners of the globe – if a globe may be said to possess corners.

Of the many American varieties that have been devised – California Jack, Seven Up and Cinch are a few of the better known – Auction Pitch strikes me as offering the best balance between chance and skill while still remaining true to the original conception of the game. Though playable by any number from two to seven, it is generally considered best for four. (The original two-player game is described on p. 67.)

The All Fours family is probably so called because it attaches importance to four particular features of play – namely, 'high' or highest trump, 'low' or lowest trump, 'Jack', meaning Jack of trumps, and 'game', credited to the player who takes most points in tricks. That the game was well known in the early nineteenth century is indicated by the fact that J. R. Planché, a popular playwright of his time, was able without additional explanation to entitle one of his works 'High, Low, Jack and the Game'.

Auction Pitch may seem trivial at first description, but a few rounds of play are sufficient to uncover subtleties that might not otherwise be expected.

The game

Cards. 52, a standard pack, ranking normally (A K Q J T 9 8 7 6 5 4 3 2).

Game. Game is usually seven points up, lasts for several deals and typically takes 10 to 20 minutes to achieve. It is essentially a gambling game, settlement being made at the end of each game on the basis of scores.

Deal. Six cards to each player, in two batches of three; the others remain face down and out of play.

Object. There is a round of bidding to establish who is to be the pitcher. Pitcher determines the trump suit by leading from it. Tricks are played and the pitcher's object is to score as many points as he bid from amongst the following four features:

1. *High*   1 pt for holding (and therefore winning) the highest trump in play.
2. *Low*   1 pt for capturing, in a trick, the lowest trump in play.
3. *Jack*   1 pt for capturing the Jack of trumps (if in play).
4. *Game*   1 pt for taking in tricks the highest value of scoring cards reckoned on the following basis: any Ace 4, King 3, Queen 2, Jack 1, Ten 10.

(There are 28 cards out of play, so the highest trump in play will not necessarily be the Ace nor the lowest the Deuce. If there is only one trump in play it counts 2, for both highest and lowest, and if it is the Jack it counts 3 for Jack as well. If the Jack is not in play, which happens more often than not, then there are only three game points to be made. Note that although each Ten counts high when scoring for game, it still ranks in normal position between Jack and Nine.)

Bidding. Starting at left of dealer, each player in turn has one chance to bid or pass. The only possible bids are of one, two, three or four, according to the number of scoring features each thinks he can make using his own trump suit. Each succeeding bid must be higher than the previous one. Since four cannot be overbid, a player intending four needn't state it but simply pitches, i.e. leads to the first trick. If all players pass, cards are gathered and the deal moves on.

Tricks. Highest bidder becomes pitcher and leads to the first trick. The suit of the card he pitches, or leads, automatically becomes the trump suit for that round.

When trumps are led players must follow suit if they can. To a non-trump lead, however, each player may either follow suit or trump (even if able to follow), whichever he prefers, but he may not discard from a side-suit. If void in the suit led, a player may either trump or discard from a side-suit.

The trick is won by the highest card of the suit led or by the highest trump if any are played, and the winner of one trick leads to the next.

Score. At the end of play, tricks are examined and whoever has a scoring feature (high, low, Jack, game) scores 1 pt for it. If the Jack was out of play only three game points are available, and if two players tie for game – taking the same value of cards in tricks – then nobody scores the 1 pt for game.

If pitcher has made at least what he bid, he scores what he makes; if not, he is set back by the amount of his bid (hence the alternative name of the game, Setback). Thus, if he bid three and made only two, three is subtracted from his score. A minus score is therefore possible, and is usually indicated by being written with a circle around it.

The winner is the first player to reach or exceed seven points, or whatever total has previously been agreed. All hands are fully played out, and if more than one player including the pitcher goes out on the same hand then pitcher is declared the winner. If more than one goes out but not including the pitcher, then their points are reckoned in order high – low – Jack – game, and the first to have gone out on this basis wins.

Settlement. The winner pays nothing, but receives from the others. As a loser you pay one unit to the winner, plus one unit for each time you were set back during the game, plus one unit if you finished the game in the hole (i.e. with a minus score).

Variants

The point for low. Originally, the point for 'low' went to the player who was dealt the lowest trump in play, regardless of whether he subsequently made or lost it in a trick. It is now customary to score only for capturing the lowest trump in a trick. Players should agree beforehand which version to follow. (It is tempting, but misleading, to assume that more skill is required to capture it from someone else than to know you've got it in the first place.)

Smudge. 'Smudge' is a bid of four made on the understanding that if the bid is successful the bidder scores whatever he needs to win the game. It is therefore particularly useful to a player who is trailing when one or more of the others are close to seven. A player may not bid smudge, however, if he is in the hole; the best he can do from that position is to bid and make all four. There is no extra penalty for failing to make smudge. As a sort of 'double or quits' this variant may be recommended, though it hardly speeds the game up, as four is so rarely bid anyway.

Dealer's overcall. Although in the bidding each new bid must be higher than the preceding one, it may be accepted that dealer can 'relieve' an earlier player of his bid by bidding the same amount. This variant is to be recommended, as it injects a little more variety into the bidding. Note that when this rule is followed, a bid of four can be overtaken by dealer, so an earlier player should merely state 'four' and should not automatically pitch the first card until dealer has passed.

Joker fifth point. A recent development is the addition of a Joker as a fifth point, the usual rule being that it counts below the Two of the trump suit. Whoever captures the Joker in a trick scores 1 pt for it (it does not also count as the lowest trump in play for the purpose of scoring 'low'). If pitcher leads the Joker to the first trick, he states what suit it belongs to for the purpose of establishing trumps, which must of course be followed immediately. With Joker fifth, the highest bid is five, and smudge becomes a pitcher-takes-all bid of five.

Joker fifth is an elaboration that may be disregarded by players who prefer the game to the gambling. Yet further elaborations, such as scoring for the Nine of trumps ('sancho'), the Five of trumps ('pedro'), and others, give rise to virtually new games which are faster but more haphazard than straightforward Auction Pitch.

Hints on play

The play of Auction Pitch hinges almost entirely on trumps. High cards in side-suits are weaker than in most trick-taking games, where there is an obligation to follow suit. Here you may follow suit or trump ad lib. Hence only the pitcher can normally expect to clear out trumps and make with a top card of another colour, for of course pitcher only becomes pitcher by virtue of his strength in trumps. The strategy of his own game will be to clear trumps first – which he is virtually obliged to do in any case because of the requisite trump lead – and to keep forcing them until he is in a position to make good with some side cards. His opponents will correspondingly encourage him to trump tricks that are worth little.

In the bidding, then, the hand must be assessed by reference to its obvious trump suit – only rarely will there be more than one. Length in trumps is better than strength in side-suits. For example, three middling trumps will often produce the point for game, while a side Ace, even singleton, disappears to a trump. Remember that the deal of cards in batches of three instead of one at a time leads to unequal distributions that in any other game would be considered abnormal. In Auction Pitch, a void in the hand is the rule rather than the exception. Indeed, it would be less true to describe a void as a point of strength than to call the absence of a void a positive weakness. A typical hand contains three of one suit and two of another, and if the three includes Ace, King or Queen it is the obvious trump.

Ace of trumps is a certain point for high, Two of trumps only for low if you can be sure of trumping with it and not being over-trumped (assuming you do not play the version in which the point is scored for having been dealt it). To be confident of trumping in with the lowest you must have at least three trumps altogether and preferably four.

There is about a three-in-five chance that your King will be the highest in play or your Three of trumps the lowest; the chance of your Queen being high or your Four low is no better than one in three. If your highest trump is the Jack, you should have it guarded twice to be confident of not losing it to an upper trump. Remember that if you yourself do not hold the scoring Jack there is only a two-in-five chance that it will be in play, and if it is out of play there are only three game points to score. At the other extreme, however, it is theoretically possible to win high, low, Jack *and* game for all four on the strength of a singleton Jack. Possible, but unlikely!

Do not count on making a side Ace unless you have three strong trumps with which to draw the opposition.

It is easy to overreach yourself in the bidding, so do not bid more than you dare especially if you are first or second to call. If dealer is allowed to overcall (recommended) he has a strong position by bidding last, and should not fight shy of taking advantage.

As pitcher, regard the lead of a top trump (Ace, King or Queen) as a general rule to depart from if circumstances seem to warrant it – the strongest circumstance, of course, being the lack of any of those cards. You will obviously never lead the Jack if it is your top trump, and you should even think twice about leading it if you hold a higher card. What happens next depends largely on how players respond to the trump lead. If all show themselves void you are bound to make high, low, and Jack if you have it. An opponent who plays high to a high lead, or drops Jack, Ten or what may well be regarded as the lowest trump, has probably played his last. Anything from Four to Nine may be regarded with suspicion – there is probably another where that came from, and it may be high enough to be dangerous, especially if you hold the Jack. So far as you can without risking the loss of your Jack, Ten (which counts to game) or lowest, you should continue trumps in order to knock as many out as possible. But always be prepared to find three trumps in one opponent's hand, and do not lead Jack or low until you feel them safe.

The most frequent decision that has to be made in play is whether, upon the lead of a side in which you hold a top card, you should follow and take it or disgorge a trump instead. The answer depends on how you estimate the trump holding of the player or two players to follow you: you may be trumped if you follow suit high, or over-trumped if you trump. It is all a matter of judgment.

The extent to which the non-bidders play cooperatively depends much upon the score, for if (as an example) pitcher is trailing and one opponent needs only a single point to game, the latter is only going to be concerned about his single point. Assuming, however, that they are out to beat the pitcher, their best bet is to force him to play second as often as possible – in other words, try to give tricks to the player on pitcher's right. To obviate his point for game, it is also desirable to 'smear', that is, throw high-counting cards (especially Tens) onto one player consistently.

Having the lead, player on dealer's right will do well to lead out nondescript cards from side-suits, especially those in which he holds more rather than fewer cards.

Sample deals

The following deal is worth looking at in some detail. The cards fall thus:

Abel	♠J 7 6 ♣J ◇T 4 (*void in* ♡)
Baker	♠5 ♡T 4 2 ♣K 4 (*void in* ◇)
Charlie	♡Q 6 ♣7 5 ◇Q 5 (*void in* ♠)
Dealer	♡K 8 3 ♣Q ◇A K (*void in* ♠)

Only Dealer has a biddable hand, and after the others pass he bids a possibly cautious 'two', reckoning his King and Three as points for high and low respectively. He duly pitches the King:

A	B	C	D	
♠ 6	♡ 4	♡ 6	♡ K	D assumes there are more trumps about (correctly), and presses the suit in order to clear the way for his probable Three low ...
♠ 7	♡ T	♡ Q	♡ 8	Now C stands better to make the point for game, but D feels sure he has cleared the hearts.
◇ 4	♠ 5	◇ Q	♡ 3	One for low ?

◇ T	♡ 2!	◇ 5	◇ K	No! The Two *was* in play, and even more points have gone in counting cards towards game. Hardly worth the fussiness of playing King rather than Ace.
♣ J	♣ K	♣ 5	♣ Q	More bad news. The King's in it too.
♠ J	♣ 4	♣ 7	◇ A	
	low		*high*	
	game			

0	2	0	−2

Dealer has been dogged by bad luck. His Three was undercut, his ♣Q was overpowered, and his three trumps were matched by three in another's hand. As for the counting cards to game, it's as well he didn't reckon on it for a third point.

Or is it? For further examination shows that the game was more than tenable with a different lead – the Eight instead of the King. Like this:

A	B	C	D	
♠ 6	♡ T	♡ Q	♡ 8	
◇ 4	♡ 2	◇ Q	◇ K	Had C led ♡6, a reasonable possibility, D would still win. D avoids trumping here because he needs to conserve his trumps and hopes that someone else will have occasion to trump – as in fact happens, since B, playing last, can be assured of one for low.
♣ J	♣ K	♣ 5	♡ 3	D is safe to trump in low, since it is a well-known fact to all around the table that Abel is void in trumps.
			♡ K	... and D takes the rest.
	low		*high*	
			game	

0	1	0	2

Having now shown that Dealer did have a bid in hearts, the question on everybody's lips is 'Ought he to know that leading the Eight wins whereas leading the King loses?'.

It is a question that I propose to sidestep altogether by simply pointing out that if he bid on the strength of his two top *diamonds* instead of his trio of miscellaneous hearts, he plays (*a*) ◇A, (*b*) ◇K, (*c*) ♡K and goes on to win three for high, low *and* game!

On the whole, though, I am inclined to believe that his first pitch was proper, even though it lost.

Here is another interesting situation:

Abel   ♠A ♡3 ♣J 8 6 2 (*void in* ◇)
Baker   ♠6 ♡Q T 9 ♣9 ◇8
Charlie ♠9 8 ♡5 ♣A ◇9 2
Dealer ♠K T ♡3 ♣K T 5 (*void in* ◇)

Only the players with voids have biddable hands. Baker and Charlie pass (note how an absence of voids is a weakness), and Dealer bids two with an eye to his clubs. Abel thereupon bids three with an eye to *his* clubs, and pitches the Eight:

A	B	C	D	
♣8	♣9	♣A!	♣5	Dealer is surprised to find his suit pitched, and both he and Abel are even more surprised to see the Ace turned up.
♠A	♠6	♠9	♠K	Dealer might have trumped, but he doesn't wish to give ten away, and the King may be used to catch something valuable.
◇3	◇8	◇9	♣T	Now he trumps in order to lead through Abel.
♣2	♡9	♡5	♡3	A miscellaneous lead, and pointless in the event, though Abel was taking a chance on playing the lowest trump with two other players to follow. However, he is

now lulled into a false sense of
security, and decides that it must
now be safe to lead the Jack.

| ♣ J | ♡ Q | ◇ 2 | ♣ K! | Which it isn't. |
| ♣ 6 | ♡ T | ♠ 8 | ♠ T | The two Tens fail to compensate . . . |

| low | | high | Jack |
game			
−3		0	1	1

Abel ought to have acted on the assumption that someone else
could take the Jack, and ought, therefore, to have played his last
two cards the other way round. Had he done so, he would have
made his bid.

REVERSE GAMES
Domino Hearts—Slobberhannes—Bassadewitz

There is a large family of games in which, although tricks are played 'in the normal way' (see page 7), the object is not to win tricks but either to avoid winning them, or more usually, to avoid winning specific penalty cards which they may contain. One such ancestral game was called Reversis, since the object was regarded as being the reverse of normal trick-playing procedure, and it would be convenient and proper to group them together under the heading 'Reverse family'. Because the Reverse games best known to English and American card-players are those in which the penalty cards are always hearts, the term 'Hearts family' is more generally used.

Only one of the Reverse games grouped together in this chapter features hearts as the penalty to be avoided, though four players may also play Black Maria, which is described in the section on Card Games for Three. Domino Hearts starts off like the Block Game at dominoes, whence its name, but soon reaches a point at which the play is exactly like that at Black Maria. Slobberhannes, though little played, is a far more subtle game than its bald description might suggest, and is worthy of revival. Bassadewitz, for whose inclusion I make no apology, is (or was) an obscure nineteenth-century German game which will be of interest to players of Skat, Pinochle or versions of Jass.

They are grouped together partly because they follow much the same principles and call for similar skills, and partly because none of them merits in-depth treatment on its own.

Domino Hearts

Cards. A standard 52-card pack.

Deal. Deal six cards each, one at a time, and place the remainder of the pack face down to one side of the table to form a stock.

Object. The ultimate object of the game is to avoid taking any tricks containing hearts, though sometimes little may be done towards this end until the undealt stock of cards is exhausted.

Play: first half. There are no trumps. The player to the dealer's left leads to the first trick, and others must follow suit. The trick is won by the person who played the highest card of the suit led, and he then leads to the next trick. If you are unable to follow suit to the card led you may not play anything else, but must instead draw cards from the top of the stock and add them to your hand until you can follow suit. If you run out of cards before the stock is exhausted you stop playing for the rest of the deal while the others continue in the normal way. This continues until the stock is exhausted.

Play: second half. As soon as the last card of the stock has been drawn, the rules of play change. If now any player is unable to follow suit to the card led, he may discard anything from his hand. As soon as a player plays his last card, he drops out. (If he won a trick with it, the next lead is made by the player on his left.) When only one player has any cards left, he adds them to his won tricks and play ceases.

Score. Each player scores a penalty of 1 pt for every heart he has taken. The winner is the player with the lowest score after a previously agreed number of deals (which should be a multiple of four), or with the lowest score as soon as one player reaches a previously agreed penalty total, such as 30 for a game of reasonable length.

If a plus score is preferred, each player scores the total number of hearts taken by his three opponents (or, which comes to the same thing, thirteen minus the number he has taken himself). In this case the winner is the first player to reach or exceed a score of (say) 30.

Hints on play

The situation when the stock is exhausted is exactly like that of other Hearts games, except that players do not necessarily hold the same number of cards, and the same principles of play therefore apply.

Your chief concern is to avoid taking hearts – 'clean' tricks, containing none of them, are perfectly safe. With several low hearts (having regard to those that have been taken during the first half of the game), it is good practice to lead them out, as others will be forced to take, and there will be few if any left for tricks you may have to win later with high cards in other suits. With only high hearts, your only chance to avoid being forced to win with them is to have the opportunity of throwing them to leads of suits in which you are void; therefore, your chief concern will be to create voids in other suits. Do this by leading them if it appears safe to do so – that is, if there is little danger of others' throwing hearts to them, and by throwing them to other suit leads in which you may also be void. This point had better be illustrated. Suppose, for example, you hold

♡5　♣K　♢—　♠Q 4 2

and diamonds are led; here it would be safer to throw the ♣K than the ♡5, as you thereby create two voids and get rid of a dangerous card with which you might later be forced to take a trick containing penalty cards. It is unnecessary to throw the ♡5, as it is sufficiently low to be unlikely to take a heart trick. Nor need you worry about the ♠Q, for, holding the Four and the Two, you can expect to escape from taking a trick on two leads of spades, and by the time these have gone you will almost certainly have had an opportunity to discard the Queen to a lead in one of your voids.

Again, given the lead from the above hand, play ♡5. This can only be a liability in the unlikely event that the three lower cards are distributed one each amongst your opponents, even assuming they have not been played out during the first half of the game.

There is one feature in which the game differs from normal Hearts, and this is that players have hands of unequal lengths in the second part of the game. If, therefore, you hold the longest hand, you must avoid a situation in which others go out and leave you with unplayed hearts to add to your tricks at the end of the game. With a long hand, lose no opportunity to get rid of hearts.

What happens in the first half of the game is to a large extent a matter of chance, depending much upon what cards you have to draw before being able to follow suit. You therefore have little control over the holding of cards with which you enter the second half.

Having to draw cards from the stock when unable to follow suit can be advantageous, especially if your holding of hearts lacks low ranks with which to avoid being forced to take. If you do have low ones, hearts are very good to lead in the first half, as anyone who is void will have to draw until they can follow suit and is therefore unlikely to be able to leave you holding the baby (or, more precisely, holding the trick with a low card).

Generally, however, you would prefer not to draw – in fact, the objective of escaping play by getting rid of all your cards in the first half of the game would be a good one to aim for, if only the mechanics of the game enabled you to exert sufficient control over the process. Try to force others to draw as often as possible by leading from your longest suit (on the assumption that they are likely to be deficient in it), and – except in hearts, of course – play high to win as often as possible, in order to be able to dictate the suit of the next trick. But when the stock is near its end lead low, in case a player void in the suit exhausts the stock without finding any and starts throwing hearts.

Sample deal

South ♡5 4 ♣8 ◇T 5 ♠9
West ♡T ♣K ◇9 7 ♠K T
North ♡J 8 ♣9 4 ◇K 2 ♠—
East ♡Q 7 ♣2 ◇Q ♠J 8

S	W	N	E	
♡ 5	♡ T	♡ 8	♡ 7	South can afford to open aggressively.
♠ 9	♠ K	♠ Q	♠ J	North, void in spades, drew ♣A, ♡3, ♠Q before playing.
♠ 4	♠ T	♠ A	♠ 8	West drew ◇4, ♠4; South drew ♣ 7, ♠4.
♣ 8	♣ K	♣ A	♣ 2	
◇ 5	◇ 9	◇ K	◇ Q	
♣ 7	♣ Q	♣ 9	♣ 5	North drew ♡A, ♠6; East drew ♣5.
♠ 2	♠ 6	♠ 5	♠ 7	A profitable suit lead from West, the others having to draw cards with the following results: North ♣T, ◇A, ♣3, ♡6, ♠5; East ♡9, ♣6, ♣J, ◇J, ◇8, ♡2, ♠7; South ♠2.
◇ T	◇ 7	◇ A	◇ J	
◇ 6	♡ A	◇ 4	♡ 8	A bad lead from East – he should have watched the stock and led low. South drew ♡K, ♠3, ◇6; West drew the last card, which was ♡A, and thereby entitled himself to throw it to the trick. Now he is out of cards and play.
	out			

At the start of the second half, only three players are left in; their hands are as follows:

```
South   ♡K 4 ♠3
North   ♡J 6 3 ♣T 4 3 ◇3 2
East    ♡Q 9 2 ♣J 6
```

Although North appears to lie at a disadvantage in holding the most cards, they are comparatively safe ones – he is unlikely to be forced into taking a trick, and need concentrate only on throwing out the hearts before his opponents run out of cards altogether. And he will be more than happy with a heart lead. It is now East to lead:

S	W	N	E	
♡ K	—	♣ 4	♣ 6	Unlucky or ill-judged? East did not want to lead his only safe heart, preferring to retain the Two in order to escape from a heart lead; knowing the highest club in play to be the Ten, he hoped to have his Six overtaken.
♡ 4	—	♡ 3	♡ 2	Now the Two is his only hope.
♠ 3	—	♡ J	♡ Q	An unhappy last trick for South, who is now out of cards. The lead therefore passes to the next active player on his left, who is North.
—	—	♣ T	♣ J	
		♡ 6	♡ 9	
5	4	0	4	penalty cards (hearts) taken
8	9	13	9	score by plus-score system

It will be noted that West, in the event, gained nothing by going out first, and that North, though lumbered with the longest hand at the start of the second half, succeeded in avoiding all penalties.

Slobberhannes

This refined little game belies the grossness of its unexplained low-Germanic title – which indeed may have been responsible for its eclipse. It is similar to, but in my view finer than, the game of Polignac, which is blessed with a more civilised-sounding name.

Cards. A 32-card Piquet pack (i.e. lacking all Sixes and lower ranks).

Deal. Cut the pack to determine who is to lead to the first trick. This privilege goes to the player cutting the highest card (Ace counting high). The cards are then shuffled and dealt, one at a time, by the player to the leader's right, each player receiving eight.

Object. To avoid winning the first trick, the last trick, and the trick containing ♣Q.

Play. Cards rank in their usual order, from high to low: A K Q J T 9 8 7. There are no trumps, and the normal rules of trick-taking apply: follow suit to the card led if possible; if not, play any card. The trick is taken by the highest card of the suit led, and the winner of a trick leads to the next.

Score. There is a penalty of one point each for taking the first trick, the last trick and the ♣Q, and an additional penalty point if one player takes all three (he therefore counts four instead of three).

Revoke. It is customary to count one penalty point for revoking (failing to follow suit though able to do so).

Hints on play

The play revolves entirely around the three penalty features, and winning or losing tricks in itself is meaningless except in assisting you to avoid them. It is vital to observe how opponents are playing and to remember the cards that have gone, for although your play to many tricks may be forced, there are few games in which so much may hinge on making the correct choice of play when the occasion arises.

Unless you have exceptionally bad cards, or the cards are exceptionally badly distributed, it is easy to avoid winning the first trick when you have the lead. Anything lower than Ten will almost certainly lose: the lead of a Nine, for example, can only fail if one opponent is void in the suit and the Eight and Seven lie between the other two instead of in one hand. The lead of a Ten, if you hold nothing lower, will only lose if the Nine, Eight and Seven are evenly distributed amongst the other players: the chances are five to two in your favour.

In defensive play against the ♣Q penalty, the penalty card itself as well as ♣K and ♣A are dangerous to hold and must be got rid of unless adequately guarded. If you hold one of these cards and a lower club you are probably safe, and more certainly so if you hold two lower. If you hold low clubs only the suit may safely be led; in fact you should lead them, to avoid being left with possibly winning clubs towards the last trick after the dangerous cards have been thrown. If you hold high clubs only your sole chance of losing them is to tricks led in suits of which you have none, for which purpose, of course, it is desirable to create voids where you can.

Avoidance of the last trick is effected by playing high during the course of the game and retaining low cards for the end play. Much of the excitement of the game derives from the clash that may arise in pursuit of these objectives: the danger of playing high cards in mid-game to avoid taking the last trick with any of them lies in the possibility that opponents will void themselves in the suit you are leading and so spring the black Queen upon you. This is why so much depends on close observation of what the others are playing.

Sample game

South cuts highest and acquires the lead, and East deals, with the following result:

South	♣J T	♦T 9	♠K J	♡K T
West	♣K 8	♦J	♠Q T 9	♡9 8
North	♣A 9	♦K Q 7	♠8	♡A 7
East	♣Q 7	♦A 8	♠A 7	♡Q J

A very even distribution. South has middling cards and may have difficulty in losing the last trick, though he seems safe in clubs. Each of his opponents has a high club once guarded, and can therefore play with a view to avoiding the penalty.

1st trick

South	♦ T
West	♦ J
North	♦ 7
East	♦ 8

South leads the safest of his middling cards. He might, for fun, have led clubs and rendered the Queen penalty imminent; but although there is only a two-in-seven chance that the three lower clubs are evenly distributed in general theory, in actual practice his own holding is so evenly distributed (two of each suit) as to suggest that the two against might prove to be more probable than the five for. And, in the event, he is right.

West had no option but to take the trick, but as consolation for his singleton Jack he now has a void suit through which his ♣K may be led to safety.

2nd trick

West	♣ Q
North	♠ 8
East	♠ A
South	♠ K

West could lead a heart with a view to a second void, or the high spade with a view to retaining low cards for the end play; he chooses the latter.

3rd trick

East	◇ A
South	◇ 9
West	♣ K
North	◇ Q

East faces problems with his lead. Clubs are not on; diamonds have gone one round, and if he leads the Ace he could possibly draw both ♣A and ♣K, leaving his Queen high; and to lead his best card, ♠7, may leave him with the last trick.

He chooses the ◇A, which is good for West as it enables him to offload his dangerous King, and good for North, as the ◇K with which he is left is now the only diamond in play and hence is no liability for the last trick (unless, of course, he wins the penultimate trick and is forced to lead it).

4th trick

East	♡ Q
South	♡ K
West	♡ 9
North	♡ A

This lead suits everybody.

5th trick
North   ♡ 7
East   ♡ J
South   ♡ T
West   ♡ 8

All these cards, including the lead, are singletons and therefore forced. North would obviously not lead ◇K – it being the only diamond in play, the holder of ♣Q would throw it to him immediately. The same would happen on the lead of ♣A; and the lead of ♣9 would certainly give him the last trick.

6th trick
East   ♠ 7
South   ♠ J
West   ♠ T
North   ♣ A

East's lead is obvious. South and West have no choice; North is pleased to lose his Ace. But the only small consolation for East, whose Queen is now high, lies in the fact that he is playing last to the next trick and can therefore make his choice of play in full knowledge of the consequences.

7th trick
South   ♣ J
West   ♣ 8
North   ♣ 9
East   ♣ Q!

East is forced to take the trick with his own penalty card. Knowing the only other club in play to be the Ten, he can see that if it lies with South, and he throws the Seven, South's next lead of ♣T will give him (East) the Queen *and* the last trick for two penalties. By taking the Queen himself, East can lead ♣7 in the knowledge that it will be taken by Ten.

Why, it may be asked, does he act on the assumption that ♣T lies with South, and not with West or North, in which case East could have played the Seven and avoided both penalties? Is he not accepting a certain penalty point in exchange for a two-in-three chance of escaping the double penalty?

The answer is that East is either a brilliant player or has been taking notes surreptitiously under the table. The outstanding cards are ♣T, ♢K and ♠9, West has shown himself void in diamonds (*3rd trick*), and North in spades (*6th trick*). So the three possibilities of distribution are: South ♣, West ♠, North ♢ (the unfavourable distribution), or South ♠, West ♣, North ♢, or South ♢, West ♠, North ♣. Now, the third possibility is unlikely, as South would surely have played ♢K to the *3rd trick* instead of the Nine; and if West had held ♣T, he would in the present trick surely have played it in preference to the Eight, having seen the Jack but not the Nine (which came after him, from North).

East therefore takes the risk, and is justified by the result of the ...

7th trick

East	♣ 7
South	♣ T!
West	♠ 9
North	♢ K

Thus South, North and East score one penalty apiece for last, first and Queen respectively, and North emerges with a clean sheet.

Bassadewitz

There is a large group of games, of central European origin, in which tricks are of no value in themselves but only for the scoring cards, or 'counters', which they may contain. The counting cards are, typically, Ace 11, Ten 10, King 4, Queen 3, and Jack 2, making a total of 30 points to be won in each suit, or 120 in the whole pack. Many fine games, including Skat and Pinochle, belong to this family.

Bassadewitz is a 'reverse' member of it: the object is to score as few points as possible by the capture of counting cards – in other

words, to try to avoid taking them. The name is pronounced
with the stress on the second syllable, and the W like a V; an
alternative version of the name is Bassarowitz, and I have no
idea as to the origin of either. The game is taken from a book
published in 1888 called *German and French Games at Cards*, by
a man who wrote under the name Aquarius in order to hide his
real name, which was, in fact, Jackson – Louis d'Aguilar
Jackson, to do him justice.

The game

Cards. A 32-card Piquet pack (no Sixes or lower ranks).

Deal. Deal cards two at a time, face down, until each player has
eight.

Object. Tricks are played at no-trump and the object is to avoid
taking points in counting-cards, reckoning as follows:

Ace	11 each
King	4 each
Queen	3 each
Jack	2 each
Ten	10 each
9, 8, 7	0

An alternative object, if the hand of cards merits the attempt,
is to win all eight tricks. This need not be bid or announced
beforehand in order to be valid.

Play. Cards rank in their normal order (Ace high, Seven low),
with the Ten in its usual place between Nine and Jack – even
though it counts 10 points when captured. The player on dealer's
left leads to the first trick. Normal rules of trick-taking apply:
follow suit if possible; if not, play from any suit. The trick is
taken by the highest card of the suit led, and the winner of a trick
leads to the next.

Score. At the end of the game each player totals the value of
counting cards that he has taken in tricks (as a check, the four

totals should make 120 in aggregate). The player with the lowest total scores 5, second lowest 4, third lowest 3, and the player with the most scores 0. In the event of a tie, benefit is given to the 'elder' of the tying players (i.e. the player reached first when counted leftwards from the dealer, dealer himself being 'youngest'). If a player takes all eight tricks, he scores 12 and the others nought.

If the game is played for stakes, as the original was, the dealer puts up 12 units at the start of the game and they are split 5–4–3 as described above. A player who took all eight tricks is paid four units by each opponent, and the pool is carried forward to the next deal, payments from it being doubled.

Hints on play

The interest of Bassadewitz, as opposed to other trick-avoidance games, lies in the score that attaches to individual cards, and especially to the high score of the mid-ranking Ten. This is always a good card to throw to someone else's trick. From the other point of view, if in any suit you lack the Ten but hold higher ranks, you must watch the fall of cards carefully and not lead a face card until the Ten has gone. The Ten is a good card to lead if you hold at least one lower; if you do not, there is a two-to-five chance (as in Slobberhannes) that the three lower cards will fall to it and leave you with the penalty.

When void in a suit, discard the highest-scoring card you can; conversely, lead a low rank when embarking upon a suit for the second or third time round, for fear that a player void in it will force you to capture an Ace or Ten in the trick.

When you have sufficient experience of the game to be able to control your cards well, and the opportunity arises to do so, it is worth keeping track of which player or players have yet to take tricks and attempting to 'reserve' a spare Ace or Ten to throw to them when they start to do so, rather than dropping it at the first available opportunity.

If you must win a trick, play as high as you dare. For example, suppose you hold the Ace and Ten only of a suit, and a lead of the Nine is followed by the Eight and the Seven. Even for the extra point against you, you must take with the Ace (not the Ten), then lead the Ten out: whoever takes it will probably pick up at least 17 to your 11 points. Or again, suppose you hold Ace, Nine, and the player on your right leads the Jack on the first appearance of that suit. Take it with the Ace. Almost certainly the leader will have played from Jack, Ten and nothing lower – he certainly wouldn't lead the Jack if he didn't have the Ten, and if he had any rank lower than the Ten he would have led the Ten rather than the Jack. If now you play the Nine, you leave yourself with an Ace, which will probably be forced later to take the Ten as well for a penalty of at least 21, and possibly an additional 10 or 11 from a player void in the suit, as opposed to the 13 which your early Ace capture entails.

Sample game

South	♠Q 9	♡J T	♣A	♢T 9 8
West	♠A J	♡K	♣J T 7	♢K 7
North	♠8	♡Q 9 8	♣8	♢A Q J
East	♠K T 7	♡A 7	♣K Q 9	♢—

South leads, and his preoccupation lies with the ♣A, which he is unlikely to be able to lose safely.

Postscript. Since the account above was first published my attention has been drawn to the fact that Bassadewitz is not, in fact, a member of the 'Ace 11, Ten 10' family of card games, the correct value of the Ace being not 11 but 5 card points (making 96 in the whole pack instead of 120). There are other differences, too, but the game works perfectly well as here described.

	S	W	N	E
W17	♡ T	♡ K	♡ Q	♡ 7	A standard lead, giving West 17 points.
S 21	♣ A	♣ T	♣ 8	♣ 9	An equally standard return, giving his 21.
E 24	♡ J	♠ A	♡ 9	♡ A	West, void in hearts, throws his most dangerous card.
W12	♠ 9	♠ J	♠ 8	♠ T	
E 19	♠ Q	♣ J	♢ A	♣ Q	West has a safe lead, as only the King and Queen remain.
E 7	♢ 9	♢ K	♡ Q	♠ 7	East has no choice, and must take this and the final tricks.
E 6	♢ 8	♢ 7	♢ J	♠ K	South is holding his Ten back, hoping to throw it to
E 14	♢ T	♣ 7	♡ 8	♣ K	North, who has taken none.

120 = 21 + 29 + 0 + 70	*for points taken in tricks*
4 3 5 0	*score*

6. ROUND GAMES

The following games are not designed for any specific number of players, most of them being suitable for any small group from about four to seven players. Many will be recognised as relatives or even variants of games described in earlier sections.

Although some of these games are often played for 'small stakes', they are all capable of being scored conveniently in writing and are of sufficient interest in their own right to render that of monetary interest surplus to requirements. Round games which cannot be easily scored on paper, requiring counters or chips instead, are classed as gambling games and covered in the section following this one.

Most of these games are fast and fun, and suitable for mixed family groups of all ages.

Catch the Ten

Catch the Ten, also known as Scotch Whist, is a nice sociable round game calling for just enough calculation to make it interesting. It is interesting enough anyway as being one of the very few games of apparently British origin in which tricks are played with the object of capturing certain cards bearing a point value. Although most continental card games are of this type, the only other English one is All Fours (together with its derivatives).

Catch the Ten is suitable for any number of players from two to eight. A short pack is used for it, one of 36 cards of which the lowest is Six. This is produced by taking an ordinary pack and rejecting all the Twos, Threes, Fours and Fives. If five or seven players are taking part, also remove one of the Sixes; if eight, increase the size to 40 cards by adding in the Fives. This is to ensure that everyone receives the same number.

Deal all the cards round one at a time. (Four players will start with nine cards each, five with seven, six with six, seven or eight with five.) If two are playing, deal each of them three separate hands of six cards each; if three, two separate hands of six cards each. In these instances, the players play each of their hands separately as if they were different people, holding only one hand at a time.

Choose a trump suit at random, either by cutting the pack of undealt cards or by turning the last card of the deal face up.

The object of play is to win tricks, and especially to capture the top five trumps, which rank in the following order and have these point values:

Jack	11
Ace	4
King	3
Queen	2
Ten	10

The Jack, of course, cannot be captured but will be retained by the player to whom it is dealt.

Normal rules of trick taking apply. The player to the dealer's left leads to the first trick, and thereafter the winner of each trick leads to the left. Suit must be followed if possible, otherwise any card may be played. The trick is won by the highest card of the suit led or by the highest trump if any are played.

At the end of play each person scores the combined value of any scoring trumps won in tricks, plus one point for each card taken in excess of the number originally dealt. For example, in the four-player game, a player finishing with twelve cards in tricks scores an extra three points.

The game may be played for an agreed number of rounds or up to a predetermined target.

Several variants exist or suggest themselves. In a version called French Whist, for example, the ◇T counts 10 points to whoever captures it in tricks, even if it is not trumps. Players who are used to Skat or other Central European card games will find it easier to count Ace 11, King 4, Queen 3, Jack 2, Ten 10, which is a well known card game schedule, comes to the same thing as the one described above, and does not call for a re-ordering of cards in the trump suit. If the winning of 11 points by the player dealt the top trump is felt to be an unfair advantage, you could introduce a rule whereby the lowest trump (normally the Six) beats the highest trump if they fall to the same trick.

Compartment Full

This strange little relative of Rummy may have been invented by B. C. Westall, my only source for it being a book of card games compiled by that writer during the 1920s. (Which was still in the age of the train, as the title may suggest to readers old enough to remember what real trains were.) On the other hand, Westall does not claim authorship, and likens the game to Mah Jong rather than Rummy.

Compartment Full is playable by any number from four to eight, and requires two full packs shuffled together, 104 cards in all. Deal ten each and place the remainder face down at the centre of the table to form a stock.

The method of play is like that of Rummy but more exciting. The player at dealer's left starts by drawing the top card of stock, adding it to his hand, and discarding any one of his eleven cards face up on the table. After that, each player in turn either draws the top card of stock, or takes any one of the previous discards, and throws out one card in its place. Note that all discards are available to anyone who wants them, not just the top one of a pile as at ordinary Rummy.

Now the object of play. Basically it is to acquire scoring combinations of cards as indicated in the table below. At the same time, it is to be the first to get all ten of one's cards into scoring combinations: the player who achieves this ends the game by announcing 'Compartment full' and laying his hand face up on the table. There is a bonus for doing this.

All 8 Aces	.	.	.	.	.	.	50
7 Aces	.	.	.	.	.	.	40
6 Aces	.	.	.	.	.	.	30
5 Aces	.	.	.	.	.	.	20
4 Aces	.	.	.	.	.	.	10

All 8 of K, Q or J	25	
7 of K, Q or J	20	
6 of K, Q or J	15	
5 of K, Q or J	10	
4 of K, Q or J	5	
Suit sequence of 10 cards . . .	50	⎫
. . . . . . 9 . . .	25	⎬ not including
. . . . . . 8 . . .	20	⎭ K, Q or J.
. . . . . . 7 . . .	15	⎱ Ace counts as
. . . . . . 6 . . .	10	⎰ '1'
. . . . . . 5 . . .	5	⎭
Bonus for Compartment Full	50	

Notice that certain high scoring combinations, though worth aiming for if the chances are good, do not allow a player to go out. It is possible to go out with six Aces and four of a kind, but not with seven or more Aces, as there are no valid combinations involving only three or two cards to account for the remainder. Note also that suit sequences may be of numeral cards only, Ace counting low (A, 2, 3, 4, 5 being the lowest sequence).

Several rounds are played, the winner being the first to reach 500 points.

Fifty One and One Hundred

A distinctive family of arithmetical card games are played in Central Europe. They are quick and easy to play, and open to as many variations as you care to invent. Here are two to be getting on with. Both are played with a 32-card pack (nothing lower than Seven), and from two to six players can be accommodated.

Fifty One

Each player receives five cards. The next is turned face up to start a waste pile and the rest are left out of play. Each rank has a point value as follows:

A	K	Q	J	T	9	8	7
1	4	3	2	-1	0	8	1

The value of the turn-up is announced by the dealer. Starting at his left, each in turn plays a card face up to the waste pile, adding its value to the previous total and announcing the new total. For example, if the turn-up is a King the dealer says 'Four'. Abel plays an Eight and says 'Twelve', Baker a Ten and says 'Eleven', and so on.

Whoever makes the total exceed 50 loses the game. (I have no authority for saying so, but suppose that he loses a number of points equivalent to the amount he makes over 50, or pays everybody that number of chips.)

One Hundred

In this game, as many cards are dealt as will give everyone an equal number. The remainder are formed into the start of a waste pile whose initial value is their combined total. The point value of individual cards is now:

A	K	Q	J	T	9	8	7
11	4	3	2	10	9	8	7

. . . and the loser is the player who makes the total go above 100. However – and this is more fun – if a player makes the total 100 exactly, he wins. (Though I'm afraid my source does not state *what* he wins. You will have to use your imagination.)

Hearts

The title 'Hearts' is applied to a family of trick taking games in which the object is either to avoid taking tricks altogether, or at least to avoid winning tricks containing certain specified penalty cards – typically any belonging to the suit of hearts. We have already described Black Maria as a Hearts game particularly suitable for three, and several other relatives in the section for four players. Any of those games may be played by any number of players from three to eight, by changing the number of cards dealt to each after, if necessary, removing the lowest ranking cards so as to make them divide evenly.

Here are some more variations on a theme. Why not play a

form of Dealer's Choice, in which each new dealer announces what form of Hearts is to be played, and may invent new ones for the purpose?

Widow Hearts

This is the most basic form of Hearts for any number of players. 'Widow' is a technical term denoting a small number of undealt cards, which in this case will be the ones left over after the pack has been dealt round as far as it will go so that every player has the same number of cards. The widow is left face down on the table and is awarded to the player winning the last trick – together with any penalty points it may contain. (As a variation, it may be dealt face up to enable players to calculate their hands better.)

The player at dealer's left leads to the first trick, after which the winner of each trick leads to the next. Suit must be followed if possible, otherwise any card may be played. There are no trumps, and the trick is always won by the highest card of the suit led. The cards of the widow are added to those captured by the winner of the last trick.

Each player scores one penalty point for each heart captured in his tricks, and the game ends when one player has reached a predetermined losing target. (E.g. 31 in this version, but raise it according to the total value of penalties in each variation. A good way of agreeing a target is to roughly divide the total number of penalties by the number of players, multiply by ten and round it off, so that an average game lasts ten deals.)

In most Hearts games, a player who captures *all* the penalty cards scores their total value in his favour. This turns a really bad hand into a good one, and may be recommended.

There are several variations in the scoring of penalty points.

In *Spot Hearts*, each heart counts as its face value in penalties, the lowest being Two, worth 2, and with Jack 11, Queen 12, King 13 and Ace 14 against. Total penalties: 104.

In *Black Maria*, each heart counts 1 against and the ♠Q counts 13 against, for a total of 26 penalties. Or ♠Q counts 13,

♠K 10 and ♠A 7, for a total of 43. In *Pink Lady*, ♡Q also counts 13 against.

In *Greek Hearts*, numeral hearts count 1 each, court hearts 10 each, ♡A 15 and ♠Q 50 – total 104.

In *Omnibus Hearts*, ♢T (or some say ♢J) counts 10 points in favour of the player winning it in tricks, thus reducing the total number of penalties by ten.

In *Trump Hearts*, hearts are not only penalties but also trumps, and a rule may be introduced making it obligatory to trump if unable to follow suit.

In *Hearts and Flowers*, hearts count against and clubs count the same amount in favour of their winners, so the total number of penalties is zero (in which case, find some other way of determining the target score!)

In *Hearts, Flowers and Trumps*, which I have just invented, hearts count against, clubs count in favour, and spades are trumps (but it is not obligatory to trump when void). Since diamonds have no part to play in this scheme of things, one might suggest *Hearts, Flowers, Trumps and Diamonds*, which is the same, except that spades can only trump tricks which do not contain diamonds – the appearance of a diamond in a trick leaves it won by the highest card of the suit led.

Minimisère

A simple but ingenious game of my invention, Minimisère was originally intended as a five-player game, which is the version described first. Social necessity has resulted in adaptations for four or six players, which follow the main description.

Five players use a 25-card pack consisting of A, K, Q, J, T, 9 in each suit, plus a Joker. Deal five cards each. Tricks are played in the usual way, but without trumps, so that each trick is won by the highest card of the suit led. The Joker may be played at any time: it wins if led to a trick (other players may throw any card on it), otherwise it loses.

The object of play is to take either no tricks, or the majority of them – but not all five. Each player scores according to the number of tricks he wins as follows:

0 tricks	5 points
1 trick	1
2 tricks	2
3 tricks	6
4 tricks	8
5 tricks	0

This scoring system may look arbitrary but in fact it is quite cunningly worked out to give the best reward for achieving the most difficult object. Once you start taking tricks you are forced to go on, but as soon as this becomes plain the other players will deliberately lead you into taking all five.

Before play, however, you may bid 'The Lot'. This means you undertake to win all five tricks. If successful you score 10 to the others' 0 each; otherwise you score 0 and they all score 5 regardless of how many tricks they win. (If you wish to bid The Lot, the one nearest the dealer's left has priority. Dealer counts as being furthest away from his own left.)

The winner is the first to reach a target of 25 points.

Four players use 28 cards, consisting of A, K, Q, J, T, 9 and 2 of each suit. There are no trumps and it is obligatory to follow suit if possible. A Two wins the trick if led to it, otherwise it loses. The scoring is: 7 tricks 0, 6 tricks 12, 5 tricks 10, 4 tricks 8, 3 tricks 3, 2 tricks 2, 1 trick 1, 0 tricks 7. 'The Lot' wins 14 to 0 or loses 0 to 7 each. The target score is 31.

Six players use a 42-card pack consisting of two Jokers and A, K, Q, J, T, 9, 8, 7, 6, 2 in each suit. Scoring for tricks is the same as in the four hand game. Jokers (which may be played at any time) and Twos win the tricks to which they are led, otherwise they lose. If a Joker is led, its player announces what suit is to follow it, to which others must hold if possible.

Nap

Nap is short for Napoleon, but the abbreviation is so common that I doubt if many players are aware of its origin. It is the chief English representative of the Five-card or Triumph family of card games, of which the most classic instances are Ecarté for two players (p. 160) and Euchre, best for four (p. 407). It is said to have been introduced into Britain from America in about 1865. I am not aware of any Nap-playing tradition in that country, though Euchre was certainly a popular American family card game throughout the 19th century. As with any living game, details of play may vary from region to region and are constantly evolving. The following version may be regarded as a description of the basic idea rather than as a standard set of 'official rules'.

The game is played with a full pack of 52 cards by any number of participants from two to seven, five being an ideal number. It may be played for counters or pennies, or else scores recorded on paper, and last for any agreed period.

Shuffle the cards thoroughly and deal five each in batches of three then two (or singly, if agreed). The remainder have no part to play and are left face down. At each deal, the player making the highest bid chooses the trump suit, if any, and leads to the first trick with the object of taking at least as many tricks as he bid. Starting at dealer's left, each in turn may pass or announce any bid higher than the previous one. A player who has passed may not bid in the same deal.

The bids and their values are:

One trick	1
Two tricks	2
Three tricks	3
Mis	3 (no tricks, no trumps)
Four	4
Nap (five)	10 if won, 5 if lost
Wellington	10 (20) won, 10 lost
Blücher	10 (40) won, 20 lost

The amounts referred to are paid by each player to the bidder if he wins, or by the bidder to each opponent if he loses, or else are simply recorded as scores on paper. A bid of Wellington may only be made when an opponent has already bid Nap. It is also a bid to win five tricks, but for extra game value. Similarly, Blücher may only be used to overcall a bid of Wellington – either by the player who originally bid Nap and was overcalled, or, less probably, by someone else. Not all players recognise either or both of the bids above Napoleon, named after other notable leaders at the Battle of Waterloo.

The highest bidder leads to the first trick, and whatever suit he plays becomes trump for his game, unless he is playing Mis. Normal rules of trick taking apply: follow suit if possible, otherwise play any card. The trick is won by the highest card of the suit led or by the highest trump if any are played, and the winner of one trick leads to the next. The bidder wins or loses according to the above schedule, with no credit for taking more than he bid.

Some players add a Joker to the pack. In this case it counts as the highest trump. Some players do not recognise the bid of Mis – probably the same ones as play with a Joker, as this overcomes the problem of inventing special rules for the Joker in a non-trump game.

A worthier variation on the game involves stripping the pack according to the number taking part, so that only about one third of the cards remain unused. This increases the skill factor somewhat. Three may play with a 24-card pack, four with 32, five with 40, six with 44 or 48. Stripping is done by removing as many low cards as necessary, from the Two upwards.

Also recorded is a version in which each player is dealt seven cards from a full pack, but discards two before bidding takes place.

Amongst equally matched players Nap is to some extent a game of luck, but it is remarkable how consistently well experienced players win over comparative novices with equal or even worse cards. Skill seems to be equally compounded of calculation and intuition. It is a matter of calculation, for example, that a bid if three (regarded by some circles as the minimum permissible bid) requires at least three trumps and at least Queens in the side suits, and that this requirement increases with more players round the table, but decreases with the number who have already passed before you come to bid. It is also calculable that you should rarely bid high without the Ace of trumps, that one loser is acceptable in side suits (unless bidding five, of course), and that probable losing cards should be lost earlier rather than later in the play. Intuition or judgment is relevant to the extent that good players learn to observe their opponents' patterns of play, even their behaviour and mannerisms, and adjust their game accordingly – rather as in Brag or Poker. They also have a knack of divining a bidder's weak suit and holding back their superior cards in it instead of discarding them when unable to follow suit.

Variants

Peep Nap. An extra card is dealt face down. As each player bids, he may – but need not – privily peep at it on payment of one counter to a pool (which goes to the next player to win a bid of five tricks). The highest bidder may then take the peep card in exchange for an unwanted card from his hand immediately before leading to the first trick, provided that he has previously peeped and paid for the privilege.

Alternatively, each player before making a bid may (on payment) take the peep card or 'floater' and discard one face down in its place, which in turn may be exchanged by the next bidder, and so on.

Widow Nap. (Also known as Sir Garnet in the books, though I dare say renamed Alf Garnet by anyone who has heard of it in practice.) An extra hand or 'widow' of five cards is dealt, face down. If the highest bidder is playing for five tricks (Nap or higher), he may, immediately before leading, take the widow and discard any five cards face down in their place. This makes high bids more frequent. It also makes them easier, and a bidder who takes advantage of this option must pay double if he loses.

Purchase Nap might almost be regarded as a cross between Nap and Poker. After the deal but before the bidding, the dealer addresses himself to each player in turn and asks how many cards, if any, he wishes to purchase. A player wishing to buy discards any number from his hand and receives the same number of replacements from the top of the stock at the rate of one counter each. Payments are made to a pool, which goes to the first player to win a bid of five.

Seven-card Nap is played like basic five-card Nap, except, of course, that seven cards are dealt and seven tricks played. The bids and their values are:

bid:	3	4	5	*mis*	6	7
win:	3	4	10	10	20	30
lose:	3	4	5	5	10	15

Oh Hell!

. . . is a title that may be left to speak for itself at the end of a deal. Others have been suggested by a process of bowdlerisation (Oh Well!, Oh Pshaw! (Have you ever heard anyone actually say 'pshaw'?), Blackout, Jungle Bridge, etc.), but Oh Hell! is traditional and therefore best. It seems to have sprung up during the 1930s and has been credited to Geoffrey Mott-Smith, though he speaks of it as of one not his own, and resemblances will be noted to the probably more popular – because less skilful – game of Knockout Whist (p. 572).

It makes a good game for any number of players from three to seven and uses a full 52-card pack. Play consists of a number of deals, with each player dealing in turn.

In the first deal, everybody receives one card, and the next is turned face up to determine trumps for the deal. Each player in turn announces how many of the one trick he thinks he will win – i.e. either none or one – and this is noted by his name on the scoresheet by the dealer (or whoever is appointed as the One Great Scorer). The player at dealer's left leads his card, and the trick is won by the highest card of that suit, or the highest trump if any is played. A player whose bid was correct scores 10 plus the number of tricks he took, i.e. 10 or 11 points as the case may be.

All is not as daft as it sounds. In the second deal two cards each are dealt and two tricks played, followed by three in the third deal, four in the fourth deal, and so on for as long as it is possible for everyone around the table to receive the same number of cards. At each deal the first undealt card is turned for trump, and if none remain the round is played at no trump. Each player announces how many tricks he thinks he will win, and scores 10 plus that number if he takes the said number *exactly* – nothing if he takes more or fewer tricks.

There are several variations in the scoring and some interesting additional rules. One of the best is that the total number of tricks bid at each round must not equal the number to be played, so that at least one player is bound not to make his bid. This is achieved by adding the bids and preventing the dealer (who bids last) from announcing the number which brings the total to the number of tricks played. A good scoring variation is to award for a successful misère bid (which is easy to make) the same number of points as cards dealt and tricks played for that round, instead of a flat ten.

Pip-Pip!

A great game of fun for almost any number of players, though four to seven is best, Pip-Pip appears to be dimly related to games of the Bézique and Skat families and especially to Tyzicha (p. 323). It dates from the 1920s, so far as can be ascertained.

The game requires two full packs shuffled together to make 104 cards in all. Seven are dealt to each player, the rest placed face down as a stockpile, and the top card of stock is laid face up beside or underneath it to show the initial trump suit. Changing the trump suit is one of the objects of play. The other is to capture scoring cards in tricks. For this purpose the Deuce (Two) is the highest card of each suit, followed by the Ace, and so downwards to the Three, with the five highest cards in each suit having point values as follows:

each Deuce	11
Ace	10
King	5
Queen	4
Jack	3

(Players accustomed to Skat and other such games may prefer to substitute the better known schedule of Ace 11, Ten, King 4, Queen 3, Jack 2, and demote the Two to its usual status at the bottom of each suit.)

The player at dealer's left leads to the first trick, and the winner of each trick to the next. Normal rules apply – follow suit if possible, otherwise play any card, and the trick is won by the highest card of the suit led or the highest trump if any are played. If two identical highest cards fall to a trick, the second beats the first.

At the end of each trick its winner draws the top card of the stock, adds it to his hand, and waits for everyone else to do so in turn before leading to the next. When not enough cards remain to go around, the original trump card not being available for drawing, the remaining cards are turned face up and play continues without drawing until all hands are exhausted.

Now for the point of the game. If at any time during play a player manages to get a King and a Queen of the same suit into his hand, he may change the trump suit by laying them face up on the table and announcing 'Pip-Pip!', together with the name of the suit to which the pair belong. This scores a bonus of 50 points. However, pipping may not take place during the course of a trick: the announcement must be made at some time after the end of one trick and before the first card is led to the next – usually (but not necessarily) immediately upon drawing a marriage partner from the stockpile. Pipping need not take place immediately, in fact it is sometimes advantageous to wait a while, especially after the stock has been closed if it is known that some high scoring cards are still to come.

If two players pip in the same round, both score 50 and the trump is changed to that of the player who called second. If no agreement can be reached in the case of a simultaneous call, it goes to that of the player farthest away from the left of the leader to the next trick (he counting as furthest away from his own left for this purpose).

When a trump is made, the holder of the King and Queen leaves them face up on the table before him, though they still count as part of his hand. Neither of them may subsequently be used to pip again if the second partner is drawn from the pack: to entrump the same suit the player must get both of the outstanding partners and use them together. It is not permissible to pip in the same suit as the current trump. The purpose of pipping is to change the trump, not confirm it.

Poker Squares

Another popular game of the 1920s, Poker Squares is the competitive version of Poker Patience described on page 39.

Each player needs a pack of cards and a private play area large enough to accommodate a square of $5 \times 5 = 25$ cards laid out without overlapping. All except one player – the Caller – arrange their cards in suit and rank order so as to be able to pick out any specified card immediately. The Caller shuffles his pack, and plays a game of Poker Patience. As he turns each card, he announces what it is. Everybody else takes the same card and uses it to build up his own Poker square. When 25 have been played, each player adds the value of the Poker hands made by his five rows and five columns and the player with the highest score is the winner.

Rolling Stone

A good off-the-cuff game for any group of players of any age, Rolling Stone is also known as Enflé under its French hat and Schwellen under its German. As the foreign titles refer to the way in which players' hands tend to increase in size – hands of cards, that is – an equivalent English title might be 'Inflation'.

The method of play is more or less standard but the number of cards is variable. Ideally, each player should receive eight cards and there should be none left over. Four should therefore use a 32-card pack with no rank lower than Seven, five a 40-card pack with nothing lower than Five, six a full pack with the Twos omitted, and seven or more two appropriately shortened packs shuffled together. Alternatively, use one full pack if there are fewer than seven players and two shuffled together if more. In this case deal any suitable number from eight to ten cards each, leaving (if necessary) the rest of cards out of play: they should not exceed the number received by each player.

The object is to get rid of all one's cards. The player at dealer's left leads any card. The others in turn must follow by playing a card of the same suit if possible. If everyone follows suit, those cards are thrown out of the game and whoever played the highest of them leads to the next round. (If two packs are used and identical cards are highest, the first played beats the second.)

If anyone cannot follow suit, he may not play but must instead pick up all the cards so far played and add them to his hand. He then leads any card he likes to the next round.

As soon as one player plays his last card the game ends. He scores 1 point or wins 1 chip in respect of each card remaining in every other player's hand.

Rummy

Rummy properly denotes a whole family of games based on the same basic idea, all of which were virtually unknown a hundred years ago but during the course of this century have achieved widespread popularity as a rival group of games to those of the trick taking type.

The best Rummy games are those for specific numbers of players. Covered elsewhere in this volume are Gin Rummy for two, Oklahoma and Michigan Rum for three, Canasta and the hybrid Calypso for four.

The simplest game for any number of players is Seven-card Rummy, which may be played as follows.

After thorough shuffling, the dealer gives everybody seven cards and turns the rest face down to form a stockpile. The top of the stock is turned face up beside it to start a waste pile, to which players contribute during the course of the game.

The object of play is to be the first to 'go out' by getting rid of all your cards. Cards may only be disposed of in matched sets of three or four of a kind, or suit sequences of three or more cards, for which purpose Ace may count low (as in A–2–3–, etc.) or high (as in A–K–Q–, etc.).

The method by which cards are exchanged in order to achieve matched sets is as follows. Starting at dealer's left, each in turn draws either the top card of stock or the top card of the waste pile, adds it to his hand, makes or extends a meld if possible, and finishes by discarding one card face up to the waste pile. A meld is a group or suit sequence as defined above. Extending a meld, or 'laying off', means adding a card which matches an existing meld, whether one's own or somebody else's – for example, adding the fourth Jack to a meld of the other three, or the ♡4 and ♡9 to a heart sequence consisting already of 5–6–7–8.

If no one goes out before the stock is exhausted, the player confronted only with a waste pile may either draw its top card in the usual way, or turn the whole pile upside down to start a new stock, taking the top card of it instead.

Play ceases as soon as one player goes out. He wins, or each other player loses, the combined face value of all cards left in his opponents' hands. (Ace = 1, others face value, courts 10 each.) A player 'goes rummy' by melding all his cards in one go, for which feat he scores double.

Swedish Rummy

. . . is not really a Rummy game, rather more related to such Stops games as Newmarket and Pope Joan. It is in fact one of a number of minor variations on a basic theme, of which the simplest is given below. Others are suggested and can easily be invented – they include such titles as Crazy Eights, Switch, Black Jack, Rockaway, Mau Mau, and have even given rise to a proprietary card game, with some interesting novel features, under the name of Uno.

Use a single pack for two to five players, or two shuffled together for six or more. Deal five cards each, or seven if only two are playing. Place the rest face down as a stockpile and turn the top one face up beside it to act as a starter. If the starter is an Ace, bury it in the stockpile and turn the next one.

The object is to be the first to get rid of all your cards. Each in turn plays (if possible) a card from his hand to the waste pile built up on the starter. The card played must match the previous one by rank or suit. Aces, however, are wild. An Ace may be played at any time, and its player specifies what suit is required to follow it. Anyone who is unable to play a card, or thinks it advisable not to, must draw cards from the stock until he can or will play, or gets stuck because the stock runs out, in which case play passes to his left.

Play ends when one Player runs out of cards or when the game blocks. If it blocks, the winner is the player with the lowest value of cards left in hand, counting Ace 50, courts 10 each, numerals at face value. The winner scores from each other player the difference in value between his hand and theirs.

In a variation called *Switch*, there are additional penalty cards: Twos, Fours and Jacks. If a Two is played, the next in turn may not play but must draw two cards from stock. Similarly, the play of a Four forces the next to draw Four. However, the next in turn may himself play one of the same rank, thereby doubling the number of cards which must be drawn by the next. The play of a Jack reverses the direction of play until the next Jack appears – i.e. from clockwise to anti-clockwise, or vice versa.

Any of these games may be played in partnerships of two against two. Both must go out to win.

7. GAMBLING GAMES

Argument over what exactly is meant by 'gambling', and whether it is to be regarded as morally defensible, objectionable or neutral, seems unlikely to end in the conversion of anyone from one viewpoint to another. Most dictionaries include the definition 'playing for money', by which yardstick Bridge is a gambling game if you settle up afterwards and not if you don't. There are those who argue that it is only gambling if you wager money on some outcome over which you have no control, like football pools, but not if you are playing a game of high skill such as Poker. The plain fact is that some people will only play cards for money, and some will not do so in any circumstances. It may be, as so often happens, that acceptable behaviour lies between two extremes; that it is, for example, as artificial to play Bridge for money as it is to play Poker for bits of plastic.

The games in this section are round games, like those of the previous pages, to the extent that they are playable by virtually any number from four to seven or eight. What makes them gambling games, for the purpose of classification into one group or the other, is the purely technical question as to whether or not the outcome can be satisfactorily represented as a written score (on which settlements can always be made if desired). Games in the preceding section *can* be so played, even if some are usually not. Common to the following games is the fact that written scores are impossible or at least inconvenient to keep. They must, therefore, be played for real objects, be they coin of the realm, coloured counters, matchsticks, chocolate drops or cowrie shells.

This feature does mean that such games are gambling games by nature, which in turn suggests that monetary interest may be a substitute for mental interest, or skill. The skill content of Knockout Whist and Newmarket, true enough, is nugatory. But it would be a mistake to be carried away by this assumption. Pontoon calls for a fair degree of skill, and the skill content of Poker, though of a different kind (intuitive rather than analytic) is at least as high as that of Bridge.

POKER

Poker is the modern and world-wide representative of a family of card games which can be traced back in continuous tradition as far as the 15th century – something of a record. Henry VIII and his daughter Elizabeth I played Primero, a Poker ancestor still popular in Italy under the name Primiera. Samuel Pepys was well acquainted with the related game of Post and Pair, and Hoyle himself (died 1769) wrote a treatise on Brag.

The earliest record of Poker itself suggests that the game evolved in New Orleans and up and down the Mississippi in the steamboats associated with that town at some time during the 1820s. Though essentially American, it could be described as of French origin, for the purchase of Louisiana from France was made but a few years previously, and Poker bears distinct resemblances to the 18th-century French gambling game of Poque (the word itself, appropriately enough, being related to 'pocket', wherein a great deal of associated activity takes place).

Poker remained very much a roughneck's game as it underwent its major developments during the 19th century and was long denied acceptance in 'polite society'. During the present century it has acquired popular status not merely throughout the world but in further levels of society, to the extent that it can be satisfactorily played as a family game largely for fun. This concept is greeted with contempt by the last bastions of male chauvinist piggery, most of the literature on the subject being addressed by professional illiterates to a readership of thugs.

It is probably for this reason that Poker is a greatly misunderstood game to those people who have never tried it, and I dare say that the misunderstandings to which it is most prone are the very ones which put the non-players off to start with. Here, then, are three fundamental facts of Poker life which must be grasped by anyone wishing to embark for the first time on one of the world's greatest games.

First: *Poker is not so much a card game as a gambling game played with cards.* In Poker, unlike nearly all other card games, you do not manipulate the cards themselves – indeed, in most forms of Poker you need hardly touch them for most of the time. All the actual play takes place with money, or (preferably) counters or chips representing something of value, which may be as substantial as money or as abstract as esteem, depending on what your personal scale of values is. If Poker is not a card game, it *is* two other games in one: a game of economic management and a game of psychology. You are playing not against the cards but almost entirely against the other players. It is for this reason that, of all games, Poker is the least successful when played with computers. You cannot out-psych something that does not have a psyche. Yet another measure of the relative unimportance of cards is that you can play exactly the same game of money management and psychology with combinable things other than cards – dominoes, for instance, or dice, or even scrabble tiles.

Second: *Poker is not a gamble but a game of skill.* 'Gambling' is an ambiguous word. It is used for the pointless activity of wagering on the outcome of things over which you have no control, such as the numbers that come up in Bingo, the draws that come up in football matches or the fruit symbols in a one-armed bandit. By dictionary definition, however, it also applies to any contest of skill in which it is agreed that the loser will pay or otherwise benefit the winner. Poker is not a mindless wager – it is quite definitely a game of skill. The skill involved is not the intellectual, analytic stuff of Chess, say; rather, it is the skill of psychology, intuition and fine judgment. If you want to test this assertion the hard way, just play for an hour or so with an experienced player. Otherwise, take my word for it.

Third: *Poker is not a single, standardised game but a collection of private variations on a theme.* In this respect, Poker differs most markedly from highly organised games subject to international control such as Bridge and Chess, and indeed from most other games anyway. In theory there is a more or less 'standard' game known as Draw Poker, which, by venerable tradition, is taught to beginners to bring them to grips with the nature of the game. (We will follow this path shortly.) In practice, however, there are hundreds of variations on a Poker theme. New ones are invented every day (they must be, somewhere in the world), while old ones drop out to be revived or forgotten according to merit and changes in fashion.

Only two distinct 'rules' of play are common to virtually all forms of the game, namely those relating to the definition of *Poker hands* and to the basic mechanics of *betting*. It is with these, then, that we shall make our start.

Poker hands

A Poker hand is a hand of five cards – any five, dealt at random. All possible hands – and there are 2,598,960 of them in total – rank in order of priority according to how rare or common is the pattern of related cards in each one. From rarest to commonest, which is to say from highest to lowest in terms of beating one another, the various recognised Poker hands are:

Straight Flush. Five cards of the same suit and in numerical sequence, for which purpose Ace may count high or low. Thus the highest possible SF is A–K–Q–J–T in any one suit, the lowest 5–4–3–2–A. If two SFs are competing against each other, the one with the higher top card wins. If both have the same top card, it is a tie, since no suit is better than another. (A–K–Q–J–T of a suit is known as a Royal Flush, for obvious reasons.)

Four of a Kind, or Fours (4s). Next below the SF is a hand containing all four cards of the same rank – the fifth card can be anything. As between competing 4s, the one with the higher-ranking set of four wins. Thus the highest 4s is A–A–A–A–*x*, the lowest 2–2–2–2–*x*.

Full House. Next down comes a hand containing three of one rank and two of another, the highest possible being A–A–A–K–K and the lowest 2–2–2–3–3. Between competing

FHs, the one with the higher-ranking set of three wins, e.g. 3-3-3-2-2 beats 2-2-2-A-A.

Flush. Five of the same suit but not forming a perfect sequence (otherwise it would be a Straight Flush). Between competing FLs the one with the higher top card wins, regardless of suit, e.g. T-9-8-7-5 would be beaten by Q-7-5-4-2. If both have the same top card, go by the second highest, and so on (e.g. J-8-7-3-2 beats J-8-6-5-4). Only if all five are the same (an extremely unlikely occurrence) do the two flushes tie.

Straight. Five cards in numerical sequence but not all of the same suit (otherwise it would be a Straight Flush). Ace may count high or low, as with the SF, and if two STs are competing against each other the one with the higher ranking top card wins – if equal, they tie.

Three of a Kind, Threes or Triplets (Trips) – which we will here abbreviate to 3s, pronounced 'threes'. A hand with three cards of the same rank, accompanied by two cards of different ranks – for example, A-A-A-K-9, or 2-2-2-Q-J etc. Between two of them, the one with the higher ranking triplet wins.

Two Pair (2P). Two cards of one rank, two of another, accompanied by a fifth entirely unrelated card. The one containing the best pair wins, or second best if equal. If both contain the same two pairs, it is decided on the fifth card. For example, A-A-9-9-2 beats K-K-Q-Q J, which in turn beats K-K-Q-Q-9. It is possible, but highly unlikely, for two 2Ps to tie.

One Pair (1P). Two cards of the same rank, with three unrelated cards – e.g. K-K-9-6-5. Obviously, a higher pair beats a hand with a lower pair. If both pairs are equal, it is decided on the highest ranking odd card, or second or third highest if necessary.

Nothing, No Hand or Nix. Five unrelated cards, no two of the same rank and forming neither a sequence nor a flush. As between two such hands, the one with the highest top card wins, or second highest if equal, and so on.

In this and all previous examples, the highest rank is Ace, followed by K, Q, J, T, and so on down to 2. Ace only counts low when needed to form a Straight or Straight Flush.

These are all the orthodox Poker hands recognised in all forms of Poker. Sometimes, for fun, other types of hand may be granted recognition, such as the Blaze, which is all five being court cards, or the self-explanatory Fourflush. 'Freak hand Poker' based on this and other ideas has its aficionados, but is not all that common.

Poker cannot be successfully played without instant recognition of each type of hand for its true worth. The following table indicates their relative value by showing how rare or common they are. The first column of figures shows how many different hands there are of each type. The second expresses the same thing as a percentage of the total number of possible hands. The third shows the odds-to-one against being dealt such a hand straight from the pack (higher figures rounded to nearest 50):

Hand		Number	Per cent	Odds-to-1 against
SF	Straight flush	40	0·0015	65,000
4S	Four of a kind	624	0·024	4,150
FH	Full house	3,744	0·144	700
FL	Flush	5,108	0·196	500
ST	Straight	10,200	0·392	250
3S	Three of a kind	54,912	2·13	46
2P	Two pair	123,552	4·75	20
1P	One pair	1,098,240	42·25	1½
NX	Nothing	1,302,540	50·12	1
	Total	2,598,960	(100%)	

From this it will be seen that about half the hands dealt are nothing in particular, and most of the rest are one pair. At an evening of ordinary Draw Poker, most of the pots will be won on two pair or threes, while anything higher than a Full House would be something of an event. In case this sounds unexciting, it may be worth noting that different types of Poker game increase the frequency of winning on higher hands – for example, by dealing seven or more cards and allowing the player to choose the best five from them.

Method of betting

Poker differs from many gambling games in that all players are equal. There is no banker, and therefore nobody has a built-in advantage (except to the extent that skill gives one an edge). Players have complete control over their resources and may plunge or draw back as they see fit. If they get bad hands they are not obliged to play them but can drop out without penalty, unlike most other card games.

The basic method of betting common to all varieties of Poker, except where variations may be deliberately introduced for particular effect, is based on the building up of a 'pot' by a process which used to be known as 'vying' – an apt word now sadly out of fashion. The pot or kitty is the amount which is won by the winner of each deal, and is gradually built up during the course of the deal as players contribute their bets to it.

The pot usually starts, or is seeded, as it were, with a small, compulsory contribution from each player known as the 'ante', so called because it is made before any cards are dealt. It has the psychological function of giving everyone an interest in the pot. It is only a small amount, so that if you do get bad cards you can drop out and will not have lost much on one deal, but if you keep dropping out throughout the game through lack of confidence or laziness your lost antes will build up and you will finish up out of pocket for nothing.

Once the cards have been dealt and each hand is under way, each player in turn may either drop out for nothing or pay to stay in. The first better's payment (though subject to certain agreed rules) may be any amount. Thereafter, each player must

pay at least the same amount as the preceding player in order
to stay in the pot. If all those who stay in do so by paying the
same amount, then, as soon as the turn comes round again to
the first better, the betting period is at an end since all bets
have been equalised. Whoever then has the best hand wins the
pot.

However, during the round of bets following that of the first
better, a subsequent player may 'raise' – that is, pay the amount
it costs to stay in plus a bit extra. In this case the betting round
does not end when it reaches the first better, because the player
who raised and those who followed him by paying the same
amount will have paid more than those who preceded the
raiser. Therefore the bets are not equalised until the turn comes
round to the raiser. Of course, if someone else makes another
raise, the turn is pushed further round the table.

This process continues until the person who made the last
raise has not been re-raised, and all other players have either
paid the new amount it costs to stay or have dropped out.
(Those who drop out leave in the pot what they have paid to
date – they don't get it back.) Then the hands are revealed and
the winner takes the pot.

It sometimes happens that one player raises and none of the
others dare meet him but all drop out instead. In this event,
when there is only one player left in the pot, he wins it automatically, without having to show his hand. This is because an
agreed fiction of the game is that what you are paying for at
each betting turn is the right to 'see' the best hand. If all have
dropped out except one then no one has paid to 'see' him, which
is why he need not show his hand. It may not even be the best
hand at the table – but there is no redress if he shows it and
anyone who has dropped finds he has a better one.

Thus you can see that the game is not necessarily won by the
player who has the best hand, but only by the best hand who
continues to back it until the betting period is over. It is
theoretically possible for a good player to frighten everyone
else out of the pot and win it on a quite feeble hand, possibly
the worst one at the table. This is what is generally known as
'bluff', but is better termed 'psychology'. In turn, you can see

where the skill of the game lies. Partly, it is mathematical. At the start of play you have to be able to assess the strength of your hand by reference to the probability of its being the best one round the table. As play progresses, however, the mathematical is replaced by the psychological, as you seek to infer the hands actually held by your opponents by reference to their betting patterns and their general behaviour: the better you know them, as individuals, the more effectively you can do this. Psychology is of considerably greater value than mathematical skill at Poker – which may be one reason why so many men go to any lengths to keep women out of it.

Poker chips

It is much more convenient, not to say hygienic, to play with proper Poker chips or similar coloured counters than with 'filthy lucre' itself. Poker chips are available in a variety of shapes and colours, but round is sufficient and three colours adequate for the purpose. By custom, the white chip represents the basic unit of value, which may be set beforehand at any agreed monetary amount from a halfpenny to a hundred pounds. The next value up is represented by red chips, each of which counts as so many whites, then blue, representing a greater number of whites. Yellow and black are the official continuation colours. Green is avoided because the commonest form of colour blindness confuses red with green (and men are considerably more prone to it than women!). The actual number of whites represented by each higher colour may follow any agreed schedule – for example:

white	1	1	1	1
red	2	2	5	5
blue	5	10	20	25
yellow	25	25	50	100
black	100	100	200	250

Which schedule is followed depends on the strength of betting likely to be encountered, which in turn depends on the variety of Poker played and the nature of the players round the table. Draw Poker for beginners works well enough on the white–1, red–2, blue–5 schedule. Extra colours and steeper schedules become more appropriate with greater experience and more outrageous perversions of the basic game.

Varieties of Poker

The various types of Poker may be broadly grouped into three according to the structure or mechanics of the game. Each of these three in turn may be played 'high', 'low' or both, and even the nine basic types thus produced can be jazzed up with a number of features applicable to all of them.

The three structural types are:

Draw Poker. Each player is dealt five cards. There is a round of betting. When bets are equalised each player may reject unwanted cards from his hand and be dealt replacements from the pack, with a view to finishing with a better hand than originally dealt. This is known as the draw. After the draw there is a new period of betting on the final hands. When bets are equalised this time, there is a showdown, and the player with the best hand wins the pot.

Stud Poker. Each player is dealt five or more cards according to the variety being played. Some are dealt face down, some face up. Players may see their own down-cards but not anybody else's. Their up-cards are visible to all. The cards are dealt one at a time (up or down in a predetermined pattern according to the variety being played), and a round of betting follows each card dealt. When a showdown is reached, each player left in the pot chooses the best five of his cards as his final hand, and the best such hand wins the pot. (There is no draw.) Stud is almost entirely a game of psychology, by comparison with the more mathematical Draw.

Spit Poker. This is not a widely recognised term, most Poker players classing these games as forms of Stud simply because there is no draw (though there is in some varieties!). Each player is dealt a number of cards face down, which only he may see. A number of other cards are dealt face up to the table, or they may be dealt face down and be turned up in course of play. The cards dealt to the table are known as communal cards, or spits, and 'belong' to all players. When a showdown is reached, each player chooses as his final hand whichever five cards suit him best, which may come entirely from his own hand, or include one or more of the spits. The spits are left on the table and may count as part of anyone's hand, so, in effect, different players may finish with some of the same cards in their hands. Spit Poker games are more mathematical than Stud and more psychological than Draw, and probably for this reason have become especially popular in recent years.

Each of these may be played on any of the following bases:

High. In the event of a showdown, the pot is won by the holder of the highest ranking Poker hand in accordance with the table on p. 540, or shared between them in case of a tie.

High–Low or *Hilo.* In this case the pot is evenly divided between the holder of the highest ranking Poker hand and the holder of the lowest. For the latter purpose a hand lacking any combination is lower than, and therefore beats, a hand with a pair or higher. As between two competing combinationless hands, find out in the normal way which one is higher, and the other by definition is lower and therefore better. For example, in the contest for low, J–9–8–7–6 beats Q–5–4–3–2 because a Queen-high hand is higher than a Jack-high hand. Ace normally counts high for this purpose, so that the lowest possible hand is a 'seventy-five', i.e. 7–5–4–3–2. (If the Seven were replaced by a Six the hand would be a straight and therefore useless for the low half of the pot.) Some players, however, permit Ace to count low, in which case the lowest possible hand is a 'sixty-four', i.e. 6–4–3–2–A.

Low or *Lowball.* The pot is won by the holder of the lowest ranking Poker hand, or shared between two equal lowest, with nothing for the highest hand. Since lowball games are invariably won on combinationless hands, the normal Poker combinations of straight and flush are ignored, with the result that the lowest possible hand is 5–4–3–2–A, even if of the same suit. A pair, however, or threes, is useless for a low pot.

Other ways of varying the play, such as with the introduction of wild cards etc., will be described later.

Basic Draw Poker

With slight regional variations, this is the original form of the game and the most widely played throughout the world. It differs in some respects from the form described in many English books, which I refer to (in *Teach Yourself Poker and Brag*) as English Club Poker. It is also, but not quite accurately, sometimes known as Jackpots.

Preliminaries. From five to seven is a good number of players. With fewer, the game is dull; with more, there are not enough cards to go round in comfort. Each player should start with the equivalent of 200 chips in whites, reds and blues. Set a time limit on play and stop play at the end of the deal in which the limit expires. Agree on the value of the chips, the amount of the ante (ideally, one white chip), the maximum permitted raise in the first betting round (e.g. five whites or equivalent) and the maximum permitted in the second round (e.g. ten whites or equivalent). Alternatively, agree to play 'pot limits' – i.e. the maximum permitted raise is the size of the pot at the time it is made.

Shuffling the cards. Theoretically each new deal should be made from a thoroughly shuffled pack, and it is permissible to alternate between two packs so that one can be shuffled while the other is being dealt. In practice one pack is used continuously until a new one is called for – which anyone may do if he feels (rightly or wrongly) that the cards are 'running against him'. Also, in practice, there are people who prefer to play without shuffling the cards between deals, in order to produce 'more exciting hands'. There are such people who do this in all card games as a matter of course. It is a childish habit and has nothing to commend it.

Anybody who wishes has a right to shuffle, but the dealer has

the right to shuffle last. Before dealing, he should have the cards
cut by the player on his right. The purpose of this is to prevent
the bottom card of the pack from being seen by anyone, as may
sometimes happen at the end of a shuffle. For similar but less
tenable reasons, some players insist that the top card of the
pack be 'burned' immediately before dealing – that is, transferred from the top to the bottom of the pack.

Ante. Before the deal, each player contributes to the pot by
paying an ante of one white chip, placing it in the centre of the
table.

Deal. Deal cards one at a time, face down, in rotation, starting
at dealer's left, until each player has received five cards.

Opening. Each player in turn, starting at dealer's left, may drop,
check, or bet. A player *drops* if he has bad cards and does not
wish to stay in the deal, by laying his cards face down on the
table and announcing that he is out of the present pot. He
checks, by announcing 'I check' or knocking on the table, if he
wishes to stay in and play the hand but is either unwilling or
unqualified to make the first or opening bet. The opening bet
may only be made by a player whose hand contains a pair of
Jacks or better (unless previous agreement has been made to
'open on anything'). He does so by announcing 'Open for two',
or however many chips it may be, and pushes that number
forwards towards the middle of the table – though not actually
in it with the antes, as it is necessary during the course of the
game to be able to see exactly how much each player has so far
bet, and so determine whether or not the bets have been
equalised.

  If no player has opened the betting before the turn comes
round again to the first to speak, the cards are thrown in and the
next deal ensues. The antes stay in the middle of the table as
part of the next pot, to which a fresh ante is made by each
player.

Continuation of first betting period. Once somebody has opened, each player thereafter must do one of the following: drop out of play, stay in or 'stay' by increasing his stake so that it equals that of the previous player still in the game, or equal the last bet and 'raise'.

Example: Player A says 'Open for two'. Player B says 'Drop' and throws in his cards. Player C says 'Stay for two', staking two chips to equal the stake of the opener. Player D says 'Stay for two and raise two', pushing four chips towards the pot. Player E says 'Stay for four', since D has increased the amount necessary to stay in the pot and E does not wish to raise further. Back round to player A again, and he must pay two if he wishes to stay, since he is two short of the amount so far staked by E and D.

This continues until one of two things happens:

1. Somebody raises and everybody else drops. The last raiser wins the pot without showing his hand and the deal is at an end.

2. More usually, all bets are equalised between the two or more players who have stayed in the pot. Note: if one person raises and the others either drop or stay but do not re-raise, the betting period is at an end: a player may not re-raise himself.

When all bets are equalised it is time for the draw.

The draw. The dealer now addresses everybody in turn who is still in the game, starting at his left, and asks whether they want to 'stand pat' (keep the cards they were dealt) or exchange any. If not standing pat, each player discards from one to three cards, face down, and receives the same number dealt face down one at a time from the top of the pack. When the dealer gets round to himself he must announce clearly how many he is discarding and drawing.

Because it is nonsensical to exchange more than three cards in the draw, some players insist on a rule prohibiting the exchange of more, as implied in the paragraph above. Players should agree beforehand whether or not this rule applies. Serious players rarely, if ever, draw more than two.

If the player who opened the betting did so on a high pair – Jacks or better – it is quite possible that he may want to discard one of them in the draw. This is known as 'splitting openers'.

He need not announce that he is doing so, but must keep track of his discards in case he wins the pot, for he may then be required to show that he was qualified to make the opening bet.

Second betting period. This time the first person to speak is not necessarily the player at dealer's left but the one who opened the first betting period. He may drop, bet, or check. Checking means that he wishes to stay in the pot but does not wish to open the betting this time round. If he checks, each player in turn after him has the same options. If everybody checks, then the original opener may not check again but must either drop or open the second period of betting.

Once the betting period has been opened, each player in turn after the opener may drop, meet the amount of the last bet, or meet it and raise again. This continues in exactly the same way as the first betting period. If all but one player drop out, the one left in wins the pot. Otherwise, betting continues until all bets have been equalised, at which point there is a showdown. All those still in the pot reveal their hands – they must do so, and must reveal them entirely – and the pot goes to the player with the best hand, or is divided equally if two have identical best hands. If the pot is won by the original opener and he cannot prove that he was qualified to open, it goes to the second best hand. If there is no second best (all but the opener having dropped), the pot is carried forward to the next deal.

Irregularities. In the event of a misdeal, such as exposing a card, dealing in the wrong order or with an imperfect or unshuffled pack, the cards are gathered in and the same dealer deals again after shuffling and cutting. If he misdeals twice in succession he forfeits the deal, which passes to the left.

If a player bet out of order, he must do whatever he said he was going to do (drop, bet or raise) when his proper turn comes round – he may not say one thing at the wrong time and do something different at the right.

If too many players exchange too many cards there may not be enough left in the pack to meet everyone's draw requirements.

In this case the dealer deals cards from the pack as far as they will go short of the last card. This he keeps, and adds it to all the dropped hands and discards of the other players, except the discards of the original opener in case he split openers and has to prove it later. The new pack must be shuffled and cut, after which the draw can be continued from it.

If a player runs out of chips during the course of a hand he may (by previous agreement) be permitted to 'tap out'. This means that he may stay in the pot free of charge, provided that he does not raise but only notionally meets existing bets, and may even take part in the draw. All bets made after a player has tapped out are kept slightly apart from those made previously. If the tapper-out emerges the winner, he takes only the main pot: all the bets made after he tapped out constitute a second prize which goes to the second best hand. If not, he is out of the game, unless permitted to buy himself back in.

Draw Poker strategy

Whole books can be written about strategy at Draw Poker, and have been, and pretty boring they are too. There is no substitute for experience, and in these pages no space to do more than outline the broadest of hints.

Character of game. How you play depends largely on how everyone else is playing. A 'loose' game is one in which players fool around, take reckless chances and reach bankruptcy at great speed. A 'tight' game is one in which the participants are either mathematicians or money grubbers or both: the game is played in expressionless silence, the draws are all of one card if any, and the action is only enlivened by long periods of rumination before each player makes a move. Needless to say, a sensible game steers a middle course between two extremes. A game is a social activity and players should be sociable without being silly, otherwise it will not serve its primary purpose of generating enjoyment at the exercise of skill. To any well balanced person the monetary aspect of the game is a secondary consideration, if it exists at all.

As a game progresses, it usually tends to get looser. It also gets looser if the table is a mixture of loose and tight players. In order to counterbalance this, I would recommend that you tend to err on the side of tightness, without going so far as to become a po-faced skinflint.

Position. Be conscious of your position during every deal. In the first betting period, the player at dealer's left may have a hand qualified to open, but if it is only a pair of Jacks (say), the bare minimum, he has as yet no way of knowing what the opposition is likely to hold. He may open and find himself raised all around the table, or he may check and find the deal passed up by everybody. The dealer, on the other hand, is in the best position to make a positive decision, because he will have heard all his opponents' initial reactions to their hands before he comes to speak. It is therefore sensible for a player in an early position to open with not less than a pair of Queens, Kings or even Aces, depending on how many there are at the table.

Throughout the game, it is useful to erase from your consciousness, from your vision if possible, those players who have dropped, and see only yourself in relation to those left in the pot. Your actions may then be guided by whether the players on your immediate right and left are tight or loose players, whether they are winning or losing, and so on.

First betting period. The first betting period is rather more mathematical than the second. First, you must assess the strength of your hand by whether it is probably the best, or the worst, or about middling. Since about half the hands dealt are nothing and most of the others are a pair, you can immediately assess a low or non-pair hand as worthless. On average, about half the people round the table should get a pair, which is why the minimum worth while opening hand is a pair of Jacks. Remember that the more players there are taking part, the greater likelihood there is of at least one opponent being dealt a strong hand, say two pair or three of a kind. Mathematics also enter into it because in the first period you are only partly betting on what your hand *is* – a greater consideration is what

it may *become* after the draw. For this purpose the table on p.
553 is worth being acquainted with. The first column shows
the type of hand you may be dealt and the amount of it you
would keep when discarding. (A 'kicker' is an Ace accompany-
ing the main combination, which you may keep hold of in hope
of pairing it. With three of a kind, the kicker may be any rank.)
The next shows how many cards you might exchange from it,
followed by the type of hand you hope to get as a result. For
each type of desired result, the final column shows the odds
against actually getting it.

A word about odds and probabilities. It is not worth
attempting to commit them to memory if you haven't got that
sort of mind, but sufficient to know which combinations are
worth going for and which are very long shots. If you do
remember any of the figures, one way of using them is this:
if the odds offered you by the pot are greater than those offered
by the draw, make the draw; if not, don't. For example, suppose there are 25 chips in the pot (including the ones you have
so far staked) and it costs you five to stay in. Then the pot is
offering odds of 25 to 5 or 5 : 1. It is therefore worth staying in
on a high pair, since the odds of improving after discarding
three are 3 : 1 against, which is shorter than the odds offered
by the pot. But it is less worth while pursuing a two pair hand,
as the odds against improvement are 11 : 1. Of course, the odds
are not everything – they are only a guide. Poker is primarily an
intuitive game; but, just as there is no reason why intuition
should not enter your calculations, so there is no reason why
calculations should not form part of your intuition.

Playing the dealt hand. If you are dealt a high five-card combination (straight, flush, full house or straight flush), you have
no discarding problems and will stand pat. Mathematics hardly
enter into it: your objective is the psychological one of betting
hard enough to build up a good pot but not so hard as to frighten
everybody out of it.

Four of a kind is similar, except that you have the option of
standing pat or discarding the odd card just for fun – but make
sure you don't discard the wrong one or the joke will misfire

badly. Some people deem it immoral to discard one from four of a kind, but how often are you likely to be in the happy position of so tussling with your conscience?

Table 3 *Chances of improving the hand at 5-card Draw*

Hand dealt	Cards drawn	Possible improvement	Odds-to-1 against*
Ace high	4	1P Aces	3
		2P Aces up	14
One pair	3	any	$2\frac{1}{2}$
		2P	5
		3S	7†
		FH	97
		4S	360
One pair + Ace kicker	2	any	3
		2P Aces up	$7\frac{1}{2}$
		2P other	17
		3S	12
		FH	120
		4S	1,080
Two pair	1	FH only	11
Threes	2	any	$8\frac{1}{2}$
		FH	$15\frac{1}{2}$
		4S	$22\frac{1}{2}$
Threes + kicker	1	any	11
		FH	$14\frac{1}{2}$
		4S	46
Fourstraight, double-ended	1	ST	5
Fourstraight, one place open	1	ST	11
Fourflush	1	FL	4
Four-card SF, double ended	1	ST or FL	2
		SF	$22\frac{1}{2}$
Four-card SF, one place open	1	ST or FL	3
		SF	46

* Odds over 100 are rounded.

† Often quoted as 8:1 against, but in fact 1 in 8 or 7:1 against (ignoring fractions).

Any of these combinations are likely to be winners in the first round. But what counts is not the first but the second round. Bear in mind that players with worse hands may nevertheless convert them into better as the result of the draw. You don't want to bet so hard as to drive out such speculators, but you must remember that a pat hand, though probably the best going in, is not necessarily the best coming out.

Three of a kind is a good hand. It is usually the best going in and quite often the best even after the draw. It also gives you the greatest variety of options. You may discard two, giving yourself the best chances of making any improvement, or one, which gives fair chances and has the advantage of revealing no information about the shape of your hand, since one card is the commonest and least tell tale draw in sensible Poker. Or, if not too many remain in the pot, you may even take a chance and stand pat on it.

Two pair, by contrast, is the most awkward dealt hand to cope with, in many ways worse than a pair. The only sensible discard from two pair is one card, and the odds against improving (a full house being the only possible improvement) are 11 : 1. The only advantage is that the one-card discard at least gives nothing away. The problem, of course, is that two pair is usually the best hand going in, but rarely the best coming out. This applies especially if the pairs are low, since an opponent who went in with a high pair may well convert to a winning two pair. Hence the best thing to do with two pair is to bet hard in the first round if you bet at all, in order to drive out as much opposition as possible, and be prepared to relinquish it in the second period if it then seems unlikely to be the best round the table.

If you have a pair, discarding three is a dead give-away. However, you have the consolation of the best chances of making any improvement – $2\frac{1}{2}$ to 1 according to the table, with a number of different hands as your ultimate prize. To give less away about your hand, you may keep the pair and a 'kicker' and merely exchange two. The higher the kicker, the better. With a pair and an Ace, few players would discard the Ace. If in the sort of company that invariably draws no cards or one, you could be ridiculously cheeky and discard one, keeping two kickers. The odds of making any improvement at all are about 5 : 1, specifically 7 : 1 against getting two pair and $22\frac{1}{2}$: 1 against threes. But don't make a habit of it.

The only combinationless hands worth taking seriously are fourflushes and open ended fourstraights, each of which is worthless in the first period and remains worthless in the second unless improved by the draw of one card, in which case they become very probable winners. If you have four cards of a suit the chances of drawing a fifth are about four to one against. If it fails you will either have to disown it in the second period or try to bluff it out, but at least it has the advantage of requiring the draw of only one card.

A hand containing four cards to a straight is only worth playing if they form an open ended sequence fillable by either of two cards, such as 7–8–9–T, which can be filled by a Six or a Jack. The odds are only 5 : 1 in this case, but are less worth playing in the case of an inside straight (e.g. 6–7–rubbish–8–9) or a closed straight (i.e. A–2–3–4–rubbish or A–K–Q–J–rubbish). Here only one rank will do, and the odds against are 11 : 1.

Related hands are the pair-bobtail and four to a straight flush. If you have a four-card straight flush the odds against improvement are considerably shorter – 2 : 1 in the case of an open ended fourstraight and 3 : 1 if only one rank will fill the straight. In the former case, say 6–7–8–9 of spades, either of two cards will make a straight flush, any of six others will make a straight, and any of seven others a flush.

A pair-bobtail is a four-card straight or flush and a fifth card of the same rank as one of the others – for example, J–J–T–9–8 is a pair and an open ended straight, while ♠J–♡J–7–4–2 is a pair combined with a fourflush. The question in these cases is whether to keep the pair and discard the other three, or to go for the higher combination by breaking the pair up. In the first case you finish up with a pair, which is not a strong hand, but better than nothing and quite capable of winning a pot. In the second, you may finish up with a probably unbeatable hand, but only if you make it – if not, the loss of the pair leaves you worse off than when you started. The odds favour keeping the pair in most cases, and forgoing the chance of the higher hand, especially if the pair is as high as Aces or Kings.

General. The second betting period is less mathematical and more psychological. You will have seen how many cards are being drawn by your opponents, they will have seen how many are being drawn by you, and everyone will be trying to relate this to their knowledge of how everybody else thinks and behaves over the Poker table.

The two most useful generalisations that can be made for this period and for all other forms of Poker generally are as follows. First, if at any stage in the proceedings you really believe your hand is not the best round the table, drop it. You may be able to bluff your opponents into thinking your hand is better or worse than it really is, but you can't bluff the hand itself. The other side of the coin is that, having once decided that you are going to follow a hand through, do so with inner confidence. Never just string along in the hope that everyone else will drop out first and leave you to sweep the pot without showing your hand.

Second, the most dangerous property of a poor Poker player (in both senses of the word!) is predictability. Poker gives you plenty of opportunities for varying the way in which you draw cards and play the hands. If it becomes known that you always do the same thing – such as standing pat on two pair or betting too hard on a low straight, or holding your cards tight and close to the chest when you are sure you have a winner – then more observant players will note and remember it. I would say that the true meaning of the much misunderstood word 'bluff' lies in avoiding any sort of predictability in the way you play.

Stud Poker

There is no draw in Stud Poker. Instead, some of your cards are dealt and kept face up, so that everyone can see part of everyone else's hand. For this reason Stud is more suitable than Draw for larger groups of players, eight being a good table. There are endless variations on the basic theme, but we will start with the simplest.

Five-card or Short Stud

Everyone antes the minimum amount before the deal, or else (and preferably) the dealer *edges* by putting up as many chips as there are players.

After the shuffle and cut, deal a round of one card face down to each player followed by one card face up. Each player looks at his down-card and places it face down on the table before him as his hole card, partly covering it with his up-card.

The first betting interval follows, opened by the player showing the highest ranking up-card, or, in the case of a tie, by the tied player nearest to the dealer's left (dealer himself, if tied, counting as furthest from his own left). At this and each subsequent betting interval it is the dealer's responsibility to announce who is to bet first. The first to speak must either bet or *fold* (drop): at this stage it is not permitted to check or pass. Each subsequent player then folds, pays an equal amount to stay in, or raises by increasing that amount. After any raise there must be another complete round of announcements to enable each active player to fold, equalise or re-raise. This continues until all bets are equalised, or all but one player fold, in which case the one remaining wins the pot without exposing his hole card.

If two or more remain in the pot, deal each active player another up-card. Cards should be dealt with one hand from the top of the squared-up pack, which remains face down on the table. In some circles it is customary for the dealer to announce, as he deals each card, the best hand that could be held on the evidence of the player's up-cards at that moment, e.g. 'One pair', 'Ace high', 'Possible flush', etc.

The first to speak in this and subsequent betting intervals is the player showing the greatest number or highest value of paired cards if any, or the highest ranking individual card if not, followed by the second highest in the event of a tie and so on. First-to-speak may now check instead of folding or betting if he wishes, and if he checks each subsequent player has the same three options until someone bets, after which the others must fold, call or raise. If everyone checks the betting interval ends and the next card is dealt. A third and fourth upcard are dealt in this way, each followed by a betting interval.

A showdown is reached when the last person to raise has been called. All those in the pot must reveal their hole cards and the best hand wins the pot. If everyone checks there is an automatic showdown. If one player raises and everyone else folds he wins the pot without revealing his hole card.

Because there is no draw the winning hand is on average lower than in Draw Poker – often as low as a pair, sometimes merely a high card. Most of the action centres on paired combinations rather than straights and flushes. In practice this means you should not normally aim for, or bluff on, a possible straight or flush until you have your third up-card, unless your up-cards reveal a substantial threat – for instance, the possibility of a straight flush or at least a winning high pair.

American Seven-card or Long Stud

Long Stud is played like Short Stud except that there are five betting intervals, which follow these deals:

1 Two cards down followed by one up
2 A second up-card
3 A third up-card
4 A fourth up-card
5 A third down-card.

By the last round, then, each player has four cards visible and three hole cards. When it comes to a showdown he selects any five cards from his seven to act as his final hand.

Strategy is the least of your worries. The first thing you have to do is recognise potential hands when you see them. Not for nothing is Long Stud known as *Down the River*, as you may gather when you note that a player showing four rubbish cards may actually be sitting on four of a kind. A useful exercise is to deal out seven hands without looking at the down-cards and then make a note of what is the best hand that each player could possibly be nursing.

English Long Stud

Either everyone antes one chip, or (preferably) dealer edges as many chips as there are players. Assuming an ante and minimum bet of one chip, it may be agreed to limit raises to one chip in all betting intervals except the last, or to increase them gradually – say by one additional chip per interval until the last is reached, for which a maximum may be specified.

The difference between English and American Long Stud is that, in English, the sixth and seventh are not dealt in addition to the first five but as replacements for two discards from the first five. In effect, it is a cross between Stud and Draw, with a maximum buy of two cards.

A betting interval follows each of the following events:

1 Deal a first down-card to each player, then a second. When they have looked at their hole cards and placed them face down on the table, deal a third card face up to each player. Highest up-card speaks first. He may not check in this round.

2 Deal a second up-card. Highest visible pair speaks first, or best individual card if none. From now on first-to-speak may check, and if all players check the betting interval ends.

3 Deal a third up-card. At this and each subsequent deal first-to-speak is the player showing the highest number of paired cards, or highest ranking if tied.

4 Each player in rotation from the dealer's left now discards any one of his cards and receives a replacement from the top of the pack. The replacement is dealt face up if an up-card was thrown, down if a down-card was rejected. A player may stand pat if he wishes, but must then also stand pat on the next round.

5 A second discard is made and replaced, the replacement again being dealt up or down to match the discard. A player may stand pat if he wishes, and must do so if he stood pat before. This inaugurates the last interval.

As to strategy, the addition of what amounts to a two-card

draw increases the mathematical skill factor of the game (not necessarily the psychological skill factor) and has an effect on the average final hands. The incidence of 2P and 3S is reduced because only two can be drawn to 1P instead of the three at Draw Poker, but that of ST and FL increased because two can be drawn to a bobtail instead of only one at Draw.

Common card or Spit Poker

The varieties of Poker characterised under this heading are those in which one or more cards are dealt face up and may be used by any or all players as if they were part of their own hands. The original and simplest form was a variety of Draw known as Spit in the Ocean. One of countless modern developments of the theme is known as Hold 'em. And these two are all we have space for. For more, see *Teach Yourself Poker and Brag*.

Spit in the Ocean

This is basically five-card Draw except that the fifth card is a spit. Deal four cards to each player and one face up to the table. There is no minimum opening requirement, in fact the player at dealer's left may be required by previous agreement to open the betting regardless. When bets are equal in the first round, each player may discard and draw up to four replacements. In the event of a showdown the pot is won by the best five-card hand, counting the central spit as the fifth card. The average winning hand is lower than at ordinary Draw Poker, since everybody has the same fifth card and nobody can change it.

Hold 'em

Deal two cards face down to each player, followed by a round of betting. Deal three cards face up to the centre of the table, and bet again. Then deal two more spits face up, one at a time, with a betting period after each one. When all bets are equalised, the pot is won by the player who can make the best five-card hand, counting for this purpose any five out of seven – i.e. his own two and the five spits. The average winning hand is in the straight-to-flush region, usually a full house if the spits include a pair.

Wild cards

All forms of Poker may be played with one or more cards 'wild'. The original and dullest version involves adding a Joker to the pack and allowing it to count as any desired card. Any card or cards may be specified as wild, ranging from 'one-eyed Jacks' (i.e. those Jacks depicted in profile, with only one eye visible, which is interesting because of the wide variety of different designs now encountered in standard packs), to 'all the spades'.

Perhaps the most popular, and certainly the most sensible, is 'Deuces wild', in which all four Twos may count as anything specified by the holder(s). Fun and complication is introduced by making the wild card variable. For example, in Stud Poker it may be agreed that each player's first hole card is wild for his hand only, so that he may count this and any others he receives of the same rank as wild. In forms of Spit Poker it may be stated that the first spit is wild, together with all others of the same rank. And so on.

The more wild cards there are in a game, the higher the average winning hand. It should also be pointed out that the highest hand is five of a kind, the best possible being four Aces and a wild card, counting as five Aces. Between equal hands containing wild cards, the one with fewest wild cards wins – unless agreed otherwise.

Dealer's Choice

If it's variety you're after in the game of Poker, the best way of introducing it is to play Dealer's Choice. This means that each player in turn, as he becomes the dealer, chooses the variety of Poker to be played, which may be a standard one or one invented by himself. He must, of course, explain the rules fully and carefully, and anyone who does not wish to take part may drop out while that variety is in progress. For each game a complete round is played – that is, as many deals as there are players, with each player dealing once.

BRAG

Technically, Brag is a simple forerunner and possible ancestor of Poker. Winning combinations consist of only three cards instead of five, and there is no draw. Like Solo, Nap and Cribbage it may be represented as one of Britain's national card games, just as Primiera is specifically Italian and Belote peculiarly French, thus contrasting with such sophisticated games as Poker and Bridge, which are international in appeal albeit restricted to certain social classes. As such, Brag tends to be ignored, if not actually looked down on, by the sort of people who play Bridge and Poker. Lest this be thought an exaggeration, let two pieces of evidence speak for themselves. First: if you take the form of Brag described in most card-game books you will find that it bears little relation to the form actually played in Britain today. Most writers content themselves with perpetuating a standard account which seems to go back to the days of Edmond Hoyle, nearly 250 years ago. This is the form which I describe later (for completeness) under the name 'Classical' Brag.

Modern Brag has undergone some changes of its own as well as having absorbed some elements from its close relative Poker. There is considerable scope for further research on exactly how the game is played in perhaps different ways from region to region. It is to be regretted that Arthur Taylor in his study of English pub games avoids describing it because he feels it to be too well known and adequately covered in the text-books. If only he had read them first and then compared them with what he had seen in practice!

The following account of what I call Modern Brag is based on my own local knowledge of the game, supplemented by notes communicated by various correspondents throughout the country. If you disagree with it, or know of any local variants, I shall be glad to be informed via the publishers.

Modern Brag

The hands

A Brag hand consists of three cards. More may be dealt, but only three selected when it comes to a showdown. From highest to lowest, the competing hands are:

Prial (= *Pair Royal*). Three cards of the same rank. A prial of Aces beats a prial of Kings, and so on down to the lowest prial (Twos). A prial of Aces, however, is not the best hand but is beaten by a prial of Threes, although in most other respects Three ranks in its normal position between Two and Four.

Flush Run (*or Running Flush*). Three cards in suit and sequence, such as 2–3–4 or Q–K–A. As between flush runs, the one with the highest-ranking top card wins. The Q–K–A hand, however, is not highest but is beaten by A–2–3, which can be beaten only by a prial.

Run. Three cards in numerical sequence but not all of the same suit. The highest is A–2–3, followed by A–K–Q, and the lowest is 4–3–2.

Flush. Any three cards of the same suit. As between competing flushes, the one with the highest top card wins, or second highest if tied, or third if tied again. Ace is highest, Two lowest, Three second lowest.

Pair. Two cards of the same rank, the third one odd. A pair of Aces beats Kings, and so on down to Threes and then Twos (lowest). If tied, the rank of the odd card decides.

High card. As between competing hands containing none of these combinations, the best is the one with the highest ranking top card, or second if tied, and so on. Ace is high, Three and Two are low.

Wild cards (Braggers)

One or more cards may be designated wild, standing for any card nominated by its holder. The Jack of clubs and/or any other

Jack or Ace is traditional. Alternatively a Joker may be added to the pack as a wild card. Traditionally, a hand containing wild cards beats an equal hand containing none or fewer, but this seems now to have been reversed under the influence of Poker.

Play

Decide first dealer by any agreed means. A game consists of any number of deals so long as all players deal the same number of times. Cards are shuffled at the start of play and immediately after any deal won with a prial, but not otherwise. Dealer antes an agreed amount and deals cards face down one at a time clockwise around the table until everyone has three. Place the remainder face *up* to the left to show the position of the deal.

Players now look at their cards (unless playing blind, as explained below). The first player to dealer's left must either bet any amount not less than the ante, or *stack*, i.e. throw his cards in, which he does by squaring them up and placing them face *up* on the top of the undealt portion of the pack.

Thereafter each player must do one of the following:

Stack his cards if he does not wish to continue play;
Stay by increasing his stake to equalise that of the previous active player on his right; or
Raise by equalising (as above) and adding a further amount which subsequent players must meet if they wish to stay.

This continues until only two players are left in. Either of them may then stack (in which case the other wins without showing his cards), or raise, or *see* his opponent by equalising the stakes. The better hand then wins the pot, pool or kitty. If the caller admits defeat, he need not show his hand.

It should be noted that there is no 'showdown' with more than two players as there is at Poker. If all stakes are equalised when there are three or more players still in, the next to speak must either stack or raise.

Betting Blind

Some schools permit players to bet *blind*, that is, without looking at their hand but leaving their cards face down on the table. A blind player may stack, stay or raise in the usual way, and may cease to play blind at any time by taking up his cards. So long as he does play blind, however, he need only bet half the appropriate stakes, while non-blind or 'open' players must bet double the amount by which he raises. In this game there is a rule that 'you cannot see a blind man'. Consequently, if one of the last two left in is playing blind the other must either keep equalising the amount he bets, or raise it, until either of them stacks or the blind man takes up his cards. If both continue to play blind the situation is even more amusing, though in some schools it is permitted for a blind man to 'see' a blind man. If everybody stacks, leaving a blind man to win the kitty with his unseen hand, he is permitted (if he wishes) to keep the same hand for his next deal, provided that he does not look at it until the betting is under way. In this case it is customary to deal him three cards in the usual way, but face up, in order to 'preserve the order of the cards'. These are then stacked before play begins.

Other Forms of Brag

American Brag

This is played like Poker but with three cards and Brag hands. All Jacks and Nines are wild cards (braggers). The highest hand is three braggers, since wild hands beat natural hands of the same degree.

Bastard

Everyone antes an agreed amount. Three cards are dealt to each player and three face up to the middle of the table as a spare hand. Each player in turn may exchange any or all of his cards for the spare hand, and the process of exchanging with the cards in the middle continues until one player, satisfied with his hand, ends the game by knocking. The others may then stick or make one more exchange before the showdown, at which the best hand wins. In an improved version of the game, a player may exchange either one or all three cards, but not two, and/or each player following a knock *must* exchange one last time. This version renders the name of the game even more appropriate.

Classical Brag

This is the old version of the game still described in the textbooks. There are no runs or flushes. The highest hand is a prial of Aces, followed by successively lower-ranking prials down to the Twos (nothing special about Threes). The next best hand is a pair, again ranking from Aces down to Twos, and with the odd card deciding in the event of a tie. Hands containing neither combination are decided on the highest cards as usual. There are three wild cards or braggers: ♣J, ◇A and ◇9. A hand with braggers beats an equal hand with none or fewer. Betting proceeds as at Poker rather than modern Brag, i.e. whenever all bets are equalised there is a showdown, regardless of how many are left in.

Crash

A logical extension of Nine-card Brag, which became popular around Norwich some years ago. Four players receive thirteen cards each and form them into four Brag hands, which they place face down in a row, rejecting the odd card. Each hand is then revealed in turn, in order from left to right or right to left but not at random, and the winner marks one point on a special scoring board. In some circles the last hand only scores if it is a pair or better. The game is won – after as many deals as it takes – by the first player to mark seven points, but if one player wins all four hands in a deal it is a *crash* and he wins outright. Anyone who has made no score at the end of a game may be required to pay extra to the winner, or to ante double stakes to the next pool. (A Crash board for marking the points consists of a square of wood about five inches each side, with two lines of thirteen holes drilled from corner to corner like a St Andrew's cross, the middle hole being common to both. Each player starts with his peg or matchstick at one corner and advances it one hole per point towards the centre, which, of course, it takes seven steps to reach. Arthur Taylor, the pub-game researcher, states that Crash boards are usually made by a little man round the corner.)

Five-card Brag

Five cards are dealt to each player, who rejects any two and plays the rest in the usual way. In this version there is nothing special about Threes, but the highest hand may be agreed to be a prial of Fives.

Seven- and Nine-card Brag

In Seven-card, as the name implies, seven cards are dealt to each player. He forms six of these into two Brag hands, placing the higher of them to his left and the lower to his right, and rejecting the odd card. When ready, the player at dealer's left turns up his left (higher) hand. Each in turn after him either passes, if he cannot beat it, or turns his left hand face up if he can. When this round is complete, the player showing the highest hand then turns up his right hand, and the others then likewise if they can beat it. A player whose two hands are each highest in their turn wins the pool, to which everyone will have anted an agreed amount at the start of play. A player who wins on one hand and ties for best on the other also takes the pool, and in the unlikely event of two ties the pool is split, but if two different players each win one hand the pool is carried forward to the next deal. Refinements: (a) there is nothing special about Threes, but a prial of Sevens is the top hand, beating a prial of Aces; (b) if anyone is dealt four of a kind amongst his seven cards he exposes them immediately, and the highest ranking four of a kind wins the pool. Four Aces may be beaten, in some circles, by four Fours or four Sevens (as agreed).

Nine-card Brag works on the same principle. Each player receives nine cards and arranges them into three Brag hands, which are revealed in order from highest to lowest as described above. A player must win all three hands to take the pool, or at least tie best on any he does not win outright, otherwise the pool is carried forward. The highest hand is four of a kind, which wins outright if dealt originally. Four Nines (or Fours, as agreed) beat any other four, and a prial of Nines (or Threes) beats any other prial.

Three-stake Brag

This is Classical Brag (see above) played in the following way: each player puts up three separate stakes before the deal, and receives two cards face down and one face up. The player with the highest-ranking upcard wins the first stake, or, if there is a tie for best, it goes to the first tied player to the dealer's left. Next, the hands are taken up and bet on in the normal way. The additional amounts go to augment the second stake, which is won by the player with the best hand or by the last remaining player if the others all drop. Finally, each player reveals his three cards and the third stake goes to the player whose cards total the nearest to 31 (counting Ace 11, courts 10, others face value). A player whose cards total under 31 may draw one or more cards in order to approach this total more nearly, but if he exceeds 31 he is bust and cannot win the stake. But it is not a bust if the original three cards exceed 31 – e.g. a hand worth 33 would win over a hand worth 28 and tie with a hand worth 29. In the event of a tie the stake is shared. This game is of some historic interest, being substantially the same as *Post and Pair* described in Cotton's *Compleat Gamester*, 1674.

COMMERCE

A venerable old gambling game still played in some domestic circles, Commerce is suitable for any number of players from three to twelve. In order of priority, the winning hands are:

Tricon (*Triplets*). Three cards of the same rank, Ace highest, Two lowest.

Sequence (*Straight Flush*). Three cards of the same suit in numerical sequence, the highest being AKQ, the lowest 32A.

Point. The greatest pip-value of cards in any one suit, counting Ace 11, courts 10 each and others at face value. (Thus a three-card flush worth 14 would be beaten by a two-card flush worth 15, or a two-card flush worth only 9 by a hand of three cards of different suits if at least one was worth 10 or more.)

In the event of a tie for highest, the dealer wins if he is one of the tied players, or, if not, the tied player nearest his left.

Original Commerce

Players ante a fixed amount and receive three cards each, face down. In dealing, three cards are dealt face up to the middle of the table. Before looking at his cards, the dealer may, if he wishes, take the spare hand and replace it with the cards he dealt himself, turning them face up. When everyone has taken up his cards, each in turn takes any number of cards from the spare hand, replacing them with an equal number of discards. When a player is satisfied with his hand he stops exchanging, and may not thereafter come back in again. When everyone has stopped exchanging the hands are compared and the highest wins the pot.

Trade or Barter

In this version there is no spare hand. Starting with the player at the dealer's left, each in turn may trade or barter. To trade, he pays one chip to the dealer and is dealt another card face down from the top of the pack in exchange for a reject. Payments made in this way do not go into the pot but are profit for the dealer. To barter, he takes an unwanted card and offers it face down to the player next in turn. Without seeing it first, this player may either take it in exchange for a card of his own, in which case it then becomes his turn to trade or barter, or else knocks to show that he is satisfied with his hand. As soon as a player knocks the play is at an end and the best hand wins the pot. If the dealer fails to win he pays one chip to the winner, and if he fails though holding a tricon, sequence or flush (of two or three cards) he pays one chip to each other player. If any player is satisfied with his hand as dealt he may knock before his turn and so prevent any trading.

KNOCKOUT WHIST

Knockout (as I prefer to call it) is a childishly simple gambling game which seems to have been gaining in popularity in recent years, though it is no novelty. Many young players refer to it simply as 'Whist', which is rather an insult to the classic game of that name described on p. 381.

From four to seven may take part, or even more except that the game then becomes shorter and somewhat unbalanced. A full pack of 52 cards is used. Everyone contributes an equal amount to a pool, which will be taken by the eventual winner.

A game consists of a number of deals. After each deal, anyone who has failed to win a trick drops out of play until there is only one player left – namely, the winner.

On the first deal, seven cards are dealt to each player; six are dealt on the second deal, five on the third, and so on, so that if no winner emerges by the time the last round is reached there will be a final deal of one card and only one person can take a trick at all. If more than seven are playing the first deal must be of six cards, or as many as will enable all players to receive the same number.

On the first round the top card of the undealt stock is turned for trumps. The dealer leads to the first trick, and usual trick taking rules apply – follow suit if possible, otherwise play anything; the trick is won by the highest card of the suit led or by the highest trump if they are played, and the winner of each trick leads to the next.

Anyone who fails to take a trick drops out before the second round. (In some circles, however, everyone may stay in to the second round, and only after that must drop out at the end of each round on failing to take a trick.)

On the second and subsequent rounds the trump suit is chosen by the player who took most tricks on the previous round, who also shuffles, deals and leads. In the event of a tie, this privilege goes to the player drawing the highest card from the shuffled pack (Ace high or low as previously agreed).

NEWMARKET

A simple and popular game, ideal for all ages from children to grannies, Newmarket is the chief representative of a family of games going back to one called Comet, popular in 18th century France, and Nain Jaune, or Yellow Dwarf, still played in that country. It has replaced Pope Joan, much played in the earlier part of the last century, and Spin or Spinado, which enjoyed a brief success thereafter. Games of this type – generically known as 'Stops' games for reasons that will become obvious – seem to have enjoyed an upsurge in recent years, with many new variations appearing amongst pub players throughout the country.

Newmarket is a gambling game that needs to be played with coins or counters. Any number from three to eight can be accommodated. A full 52-card pack is used. In addition, four more cards from an old pack are needed to make a layout in the centre of the table, the required cards being ♠A, ♡K, ♣Q, ◇J and known as the 'boodle' cards.

The boodle cards are arranged in a square at the centre of the table. Each player bets by distributing four counters (or any other agreed number) amongst the boodle cards – e.g. by placing all four on one card, or one each on all four, or any other such combination. The cards are then dealt out in the following way: one to each player, one to a dead hand (face down on the table), then one to each again including the dead hand, and so on until the cards run out. Unlike most games, it does not matter if some receive more cards than others. The cards of the dead hand are left face down and take no part in the proceedings.

There is a twofold object: to play a card corresponding to one of the boodle cards if you have it, in which case you win all the chips staked on it, and to be the first to get rid of all your cards, which ends the game and earns you chips from other players.

The player at dealer's left starts by playing one of his cards face up to the table. It may be of any suit, but must be the lowest he has of that suit (Ace being low, King high). Whoever holds the next higher card of the same suit then plays it, and this continues throughout play (in theory), the next higher card of the same suit always being played by whoever holds it. In practice, of course, the sequence will come to an end for one of two reasons. All Kings are stops, and will end the sequence, because there is no higher card. Similarly, if the next required card is in the dead hand then the last card played is itself a stop and ends the sequence. Whoever plays a stop is then entitled to start a new sequence, for which purpose he may play any card provided that it is the lowest one he has of its suit. (Some players introduce a rule stating that he must change suits if possible, a point that should be agreed beforehand.) As stated, whoever plays a card identical to one of the boodle cards immediately wins all the chips staked on it. If such a card happens to lie in the dead hand, the amount on that card is carried forward to the next deal.

The play ends as soon as one person plays his last card. Each other player then pays him one chip for each card remaining in his hand. If any of the boodle cards has failed to pay out at the end of the evening, cards may be dealt face up around the table, and whoever gets the appropriate card wins the outstanding amount.

PONTOON

Pontoon is the only name by which I have ever heard the game called in actual play, though all the books call it Vingt-un, which is not-quite-French for the magic number twenty-one on which all the excitement hinges. American writers have stated that the British call it Van John, which I have never heard, and that Pontoon is the Australian name, for which I cannot vouch. The American equivalent is Blackjack – but it is only an equivalent, and far from being the same game. Although the mathematics is much the same, any strategy applicable to one is likely to prove unworkable for the other. In any case, Blackjack is played almost exclusively in casinos – British as well as American – whereas Pontoon is essentially a game of pub and home. And long may it remain so.

As befits a game of pub, home and World War, there are neither standard rules nor standard terminology. All that can be claimed for the following account is that it is the South London version on which I was brought up.

The game

Cards. A standard 52-card pack.

Preliminaries. Pontoon is played for chips, counters or other manageable objects. Agree first on minimum and maximum permitted stakes (say, one to five), then each player should start with at least ten times the maximum stake (say fifty). Each deal is a separate event and is settled individually. The game ends when one player goes broke, or after an agreed time-limit. Choose first banker by drawing a card from the pack: Ace counts high, and highest banks first. The bankership subsequently passes to the first punter (player against the bank) to make a winning pontoon.

Shuffling. The cards are shuffled before the game starts, and by each player when he takes over the bank. After each deal the banker returns all played cards to the bottom of the pack and cuts, but does not shuffle, before dealing. (Players may agree beforehand to dispense with the cutting rule.)

Value of cards. Cards are only of interest for their numerical values, suit being completely irrelevant. Court cards count ten each, others their face value, and Ace either one or eleven at the discretion of the holder (and he may change his mind about it as often as he likes). Cards worth ten (T J Q K) are called tenths.

Object of the game. At each round of play each punter's object is to acquire a better hand of cards than the banker's. In the event of equality, the banker always wins. The value of a hand is the total value of the cards it comprises. The possible hands rank as follows:

> Bust (over 21) – always loses, but banker wins equality.
> A count of 16 to 21 – the higher, the better.
> Pontoon – a count of 21 consisting of two cards, an Ace and a tenth.
> Five-card trick – five cards not exceeding 21 in sum.
> Royal pontoon – 21 made on three Sevens (only valid when held by a punter: in the banker's hand it is an ordinary '21').

The deal and stake. The banker deals one card face down to each player, in clockwise rotation ending with himself. Each punter (but not the banker) looks at his card and places a stake beside it, leaving the card face down on the table before him. The banker then deals everyone a second card face down.

Pontoons? The banker now looks at his cards, without revealing them, to see if he has a pontoon (an Ace and a tenth). If so he shows it, and each punter pays him twice his stake, unless he also has a pontoon, in which case he shows it and only loses his single stake. If the banker does not have a pontoon he leaves his cards face down and indicates his readiness to play further. In this event, any player holding a pontoon must face his Ace to show that he cannot lose and will be taking over the bankership.

Pairs ? Any punter who has two cards of the same rank may split them, and play them as two separate hands. For this purpose they must be of the same rank: different tenths, such as a Queen and a Jack, will not do. The player indicates that he is splitting by separating the two cards, laying the whole of his stake against one of them and placing exactly the same amount as his stake against the other. The banker than deals him two more cards, one for each hand. Again, the punter looks at his second cards, and may split again if he has another pair. In all subsequent play, a punter who has split pairs must count himself as two (or more) separate people, and concern himself with each hand individually.

Stick, buy, twist or bust. The banker now addresses himself to each player in turn, dealing him as many more cards as requested, until the punter either sticks or announces himself bust. So long as the punter's count is less than 16 he must either buy or twist another card. At a count of 16 or more he may buy or twist, or else stick, thus indicating satisfaction with his hand and his intention to compete against the bank. At a count of 22 or more he must announce himself bust and hand his cards to the banker, who returns them to the bottom of the pack and appropriates the loser's stake.

If the punter says 'buy' the banker deals him a card face down; if he says 'twist', the card is dealt face up. In order to buy a card the punter must first increase his stake, but he must not pay less than he did for the previous card, nor more than the total already staked. As soon as he has twisted a card, he may only acquire more by twisting and may not revert to buying. If he gets a total of four cards with a combined count of 11 or less, so that he is bound to make a five-card trick, he may not buy but only twist a fifth. In any case, even when he (legally) buys a fifth card it is dealt face up instead of down. No player may have more than five cards in any one hand.

The banker's play. If everybody busts, the bank wins all stakes and there is no further play. If any punter is left in, however, the banker now reveals his two cards and continues to deal himself more cards, face up, until he either sticks or busts. (He may not split pairs.)

If the banker busts, each punter left in the game reveals his own cards and collects from the banker an amount equivalent to his stake if he has a count of 16 to 21, or twice his stake if he has a pontoon or a five-card trick, or three times his stake if he has a royal pontoon (three Sevens).

If the banker sticks at a count of 21 he wins the single stake of any punter with 21 or less, but is beaten by and pays out a single stake to a punter's pontoon, double stake to a five-card trick, treble stake to a royal pontoon. If his count is less than 21 he pays anyone with a higher count. (With a count of 17, for example, he says 'Pay 18', and anyone with 18 or more turns his cards face up to claim payment.)

If the banker has a five-card trick he beats anything except pontoon and royal pontoon. Banker's royal pontoon (three Sevens) counts only as an ordinary 21, and loses to pontoons and five-card tricks.

See Table for greater clarity.

Bank take-over. The bank is taken over by any punter who wins a pontoon (not a royal pontoon or a five-card trick), but not if he does so on a split hand. If more than one has a pontoon, it goes to the first of them to the present banker's left.

Table of eventualities at Pontoon

Punter's hand	is beaten by banker's:	is paid if unbeaten:
bust (over 21)	anything	—
count of 16–21	equal or higher count	single stake
pontoon (A+tenth)	pontoon only	double stake
five-card trick	five-card trick*	double stake
royal pontoon	—(unbeatable)	treble stake

*Not pontoon, since if the banker had one nobody could have drawn five cards! In some circles, incidentally, a banker's five-card trick beats a pontoon. This marginally increases the excitement on some hands, but it contravenes the spirit of the game, and anything which further increases the banker's advantage (as this does) is to be deprecated.

Hints on play

Skill at gambling consists in playing systematically, though not necessarily to a 'system'; adjusting the amount of your stake to the probability of winning; and resisting the temptation to stake wildly when low on resources. My recommended one-to-five minimum/maximum stake enables you to (a) distinguish between a low, a middling and a high stake, in accordance with the probabilities, and (b) adjust this scale to your current resources. For example, when low on funds you should play cheese-paringly and fix your stakes at, say, 1, 2 or 3; when well off you may fix them at 2, 3, 4 or 3, 4, 5; or at any other time work to a 1, 3, 5 series of gradations.

Do not underestimate the bank's advantage. Most of the banker's income derives from punters who bust, for they still pay him whether or not the banker himself busts. Another large proportion comes from the fact that he wins from equals. And, in his own play, he has an advantage in knowing how many punters are standing against him. As a player, your safest course is to stick when you can – even at 16, since the mean value of a card is seven, and the chances of your not busting are 2–1 against. The banker may conceivably stick at 16 if there is only one punter against him, but with three against him (or up to six, counting split hands) the draw of another card is more likely to win than an agreement to 'pay seventeens'.

The probability that the banker has a pontoon, or that you will be dealt one from scratch, is about 0.024, equivalent to less than $2\frac{1}{2}$ per cent, or one in every 41 hands. (Hence, in a four-player game expect to see a pontoon once in every ten deals.) The probability of being dealt a five-card trick from scratch, according to my calculations, is twice as high – amounting to about 0.045, or $4\frac{1}{2}$ per cent, or one in every 22–23 hands. If fewer actually appear than this figure suggests, it is clearly because many potential five-card tricks are not filled out, but abandoned at the fourth or even third card. The probability that the banker will bust after you have stuck is about 0.3, or three in ten. This figure assumes that he follows the policy of always sticking when he can; if not, your chances improve.

The fact that an Ace may count 1 or 11 introduces some fascinating complications. In Blackjack terminology a hand containing an Ace and not exceeding 21 is described as 'soft'; if it exceeds 21 by counting the Ace as 11 it is 'hard'. It is pretty obvious that you should always stick at, say, 18 – but what about a 'soft' 18, which alternatively counts 8? Here the answer depends in part on how many cards you have – with four, for example, a count of 8 guarantees you a five-card trick; with three, you must consider the possibility of drawing an Eight or Nine, which gives you a lower stickable number, an Ace, Two or Three, which gives you a 21 or a five-card trick, a tenth, which leaves you back where you started (with 18), or one of the other four ranks, which complicate matters further.

Whether or not to split pairs is not a difficult question provided that you follow a policy in deciding which counts are good and which bad. If the individual count of each card is better than the total count of both, split them; otherwise, don't. All you need then is a good policy.

In view of the possibility of a five-card trick, the number of cards on which you reach a given count is of considerable significance. The following suggestions for strategy are therefore subdivided into the numbers of cards held.

First card. Stake high on an Ace, for obvious reasons. The probability of being dealt a tenth next is about 0.38, giving two chances in five of making a pontoon. On a tenth, stake high, but with reservations. The probability of a pontoon is less than 0.08 (12–1 against). You have a three-in-ten chance of getting a second tenth, and must weigh that against the possibility that banker will make 20 or 21. In straitened circumstances, make it a middling stake. On anything else, prefer to stake low.

Second card (no pair). Stick on 16–20 (hard): your chances of *not* busting if you twist at 16 are barely two in five, and naturally worse on higher numbers. The banker will certainly beat your 16 if he sticks, but it is safer to bank on his busting than to try it yourself. On a soft 18–20, stick if you want to play it safe. Soft 16/17 is better counted as 6/7.

A hard count of 12–15 is the worst range of all, and the safest procedure is to twist. The fact that the mean value of a card is seven should not be taken to imply that 14 is the most promising count: 12 is clearly better, as it gives you the smallest chance of busting. A soft count of 12–15 should, of course, be regarded as 2–5.

A count of 10 or 11 is highly favourable – see *First card* for the probabilities. Buy, rather than twist.

On a count of less than 10, buy, for a modest amount. Do not start splashing out yet against the possibility of a five-card trick.

Splitting pairs. Aces: you will do better to split than to regard them as the foundation of a five card trick.

Tenths: the question here is whether a count of 20 in the hand is better than two chances of a pontoon in the bush. It surely is. Don't split.

Nines: your choice is to stick at 18, or to try for two slightly-better-than-even chances of not doing worse. Don't split unless you can afford to indulge a delight in gambling for the sake of it.

Eights: your choice is to stick at 16, twist to a 5-in-13 chance of improving, or split on two 9-in-13 chances of improving a count of eight. Splitting is best; sticking worst.

Sevens, Sixes: neither rank allows you to stick, and both put you in the dreaded 12–15 range. Always split. (The odds of a royal pontoon from a pair of Sevens are 24–1 against.)

Don't split Fives, as 10 is a good count to buy to. Split Fours: it's true that they are of a favourable average value for a five-card trick, but the chances are not good, and 8 is a bad count to buy to. Don't split Threes or Twos: both 6 and 4 are acceptable counts to buy to, and you may be permitted the thought of a five-card trick.

Third card. Stick on hard 16–21. If you must gamble on soft 20, twist, don't buy: you have one chance of improving, four of equalising, eight of doing worse. Whether you count this as only a five-in-thirteen chance of not doing worse, or an eight-in-thirteen chance of not doing better, the odds are still not in your favour. Soft 18 or 19 is best left alone, but you may twist (or even buy, if you can afford it) to soft 16 or 17, either of which is at least in the running for a five-card trick.

With 12–15 (hard), twist, as for the same total on two cards. Count soft 14–15 as 4–5 and buy with a view to a five-card trick. If you have soft 13, you have been playing it all wrong, and soft 12 on three cards is only obtainable with a card counting zero, which Pontoon has not yet invented.

Buy gladly with 10 or 11, and with a view to a five-card trick on a count of 4-7. Buy cheaply or twist, on a count of 8-9.

Fourth card. If you have from 5 to 11, you are obliged to twist, as the five-card trick is beyond question. From 12 to 20, of course, your only concern is not to bust, and the probability of doing so gradually increases as follows:

> *Count of* 12 : 0.31 *probability* (3 *in* 10 *chances of busting*)
> 13 : 0.38
> 14 : 0.46
> 15 : 0.54
> 16 : 0.62
> 17 : 0.69
> 18 : 0.77
> 19 : 0.85
> 20 : 0.92

In general, then, you may consider buying so long as your chances of not busting are better than even, i.e. up to a count of 14. You can't stick at 15, so whether you buy or twist is a question that must be answered by balancing the slightly-worse-than-even chance of improving against how much you can afford to gamble.

From 16 upwards the probability of making a five-card trick is exactly the same as that of improving a similar count on a smaller number of cards. However, the difference is that you now stand to win twice your stake if successful as against losing only your single stake if you bust. At 16, then, you have 62 chances in 100 of losing one stake (*total:* minus 62), but 38 chances of gaining two stakes (*total:* plus 76). This produces a balance of +8 in your favour, so at 16 it is worth buying if you can afford it, or twisting if not. At a count of 17, a similar calculation of the balance turns out to be almost the same amount against you, so it would be slightly better to stick. At 18 or more, you should stick.

Banker's play. The same suggestions as those made above for punters apply also when you are the banker, only more so, since you have a natural advantage. If you always stick when you can, you are bound to win in the long run. But, since you don't know how long a run you are going to get, you may be influenced in some of your decisions by the number of punters standing against you. For example, with three against you it is hardly worth sticking at 16; with only one against you, you will already have gained two stakes and can well afford to take another card to a count of 16.

Sample round

The players are Abel, Baker, Charlie and Dealer (banker), who distributes cards as follows:

First two cards
A is dealt ♣3, stakes 3, dealt ♣2 for a count of 5.
B is dealt ♡K, stakes 4, dealt ♠2 for a count of 12.
C is dealt ♡8, stakes 2, dealt ♠8, splits, staking 2 on each count of 8.
C-right is dealt ◇6, counts 14.
C-left is dealt ♠3, counts 11.
D deals himself ♠A ◇2, counts 3 or 13.

Further transactions
A (staking 3 on 5) buys ♣T for 2, counts 15
(staking 5 on 15) twists ♡5, sticks at 20.

B (staking 4 on 12) twists ♣9, sticks at 21.

C-right (staking 2 on 14) twists ♠K, busts.

C-left (staking 2 on 11) buys ♡A for 2, counts 12
(now staking 4 on 13) twists ◇A, counts 14, twists ♣4 for 18 on
a five-card trick.

Dealer is now facing three hands (out of four) on a count of 3 or
13. Draws ♠Q for 13, ♡7 for 20, announces 'Pay twenty-ones'.

Result

Abel (20) pays 5 to Dealer ...	−5 for A
Baker (21) receives 4 from Dealer ...	+4 for B
Charlie Right (bust) pays 2 to Dealer ...	+6 for C
Charlie Left (five cards) receives 2 × 4 from Dealer ...	
	−5 for D

Variants

Gambling games vary more widely and change faster than any
other type of game, which is why book descriptions of Vingt-un
tend to sound archaic (it should be regarded as a forerunner of
Pontoon rather than the same game).

In some circles, a pontoon is strictly defined as an Ace and a
'royal', Ace and Ten being only an ordinary 21. The objection to
this is that it increases the banker's advantage by reducing a
punter's chance to take over by 25 per cent.

Some permit the banker to look at his first card before dealing
out any seconds, and, if he likes what he sees, to announce
'Double'. In this case all players must double the stake they have
placed on their first card before the seconds are dealt. Again, it
may be objected that this works to the banker's advantage.

There are various ways of changing the bankership. The least
satisfactory, though clearly the fairest, is for each player to deal
in turn. Or the banker may offer to sell the bankership, or enter-
tain an offer to buy it, at any time, so long as the price is acceptable. This is usually followed when the banker has been playing
so badly that he cannot afford to lose too heavily on the following
round.

A Joker may be conveniently put to use as a marker card. Place it at the bottom of the pack before the first deal. When it appears at the top, shuffle the cards, or allow the bankership to pass to the left or be sold by auction.

GLOSSARY OF CARD PLAYING TERMS

ANTE A fixed amount staked by the dealer, or by every player before cards are dealt.

AUCTION Procedure by which players bid for the right to specify certain conditions of the game (such as the trump suit) in return for an undertaking to achieve a higher valued objective than anyone else.

AVAILABLE (Patience) Describes a card which, by the particular rules of the game, may be taken and used for building, packing, etc.

BID Offer to achieve a higher valued objective than anyone else in return for the right to specify certain conditions of play, such as the trump suit.

BUILD (Patience) To add a card to a pile (see *Suite*) in such a way as to continue the sequence.

COMBINATION A set of matching cards for which a score or payment may be due by the rules of the particular game.

CONTRACT An irrevocable undertaking to achieve a certain objective after bidding higher than anyone else and specifying conditions of play.

COURT (CARD) A King, Queen or Jack (originally *coat* card). In America it is called *face card*.

DECLARE Various meanings according to context, but generally either (a) to announce the conditions of the game or the objective to be achieved, or (b) to show and score for a scoring combination of cards.

DISCARD To reject an unwanted card from the hand. Often used in the sense of RENOUNCE (see below).

ELDEST The player sitting immediately next the dealer (on his left if the game is played clockwise round the table, his right otherwise), who normally has the privilege of bidding or playing first. In two-player games the non-dealer is elder.

EXCHANGE To discard unwanted cards and replace them with fresh ones. In some games the discard is made before replacements are seen: in others, replacements are taken first and may form part of the discard.

EXPOSED (Patience) Describes a card whose face is uncovered, i.e. not overlapped by another card, and which is therefore *available*.

FLUSH Cards of the same suit.

FOLLOW (SUIT) Whoever plays first (e.g. to a trick) is said to lead, the others to follow. To play a card of the same suit as the leader is to follow suit.

FOREHAND Same as ELDEST.

GAME Several related meanings. (a) Complete period of play at the end of which all scores are settled – may be anything from one deal to a whole session. (b) The target score which, when reached by at least one player, terminates the period of play and settlement, e.g. a game may be described as '500 up' – i.e., played up to a score of 500. (c) The stated objective and conditions of play for one particular deal – e.g. 'game in diamonds' means diamonds are trumps. (d) In Bridge, the number of points still needed to win a game by a side that may already have a part-score. (e) In contradiction of (a) above, several 'games' may constitute a larger self-contained period of play – see RUBBER below.

GUARD(ED) In trick play a card in the hand is guarded by at least as many lower cards (guards) as there are cards above it lacking from the hand, e.g., if one's highest spade is the Queen it must be guarded by two lower cards to throw to leads of ♠A and ♠K in order to promote the Queen to top position.

HAND (a) The cards held in a player's hand. (b) A player (as in 'eldest hand'). (c) Period of play between the point at which all cards have been dealt and the point at which all have been played, none remaining in the hand.

HEAD In tricks, to play a higher ranking card of the suit led than any that have so far been played to the trick. In some games it is obligatory to head the trick if possible.

HONOURS Certain cards for which the rules of the game may prescribe a score of payment to their holder.

LEAD To play the first card of a deal or to a trick.

LONG Describes the holding of more than the average number

of cards of a given suit, 'average' being the total number of that suit divided by the number of players.

MELD A winning or scoring set of cards that match one another by rank and/or suit (see p. 9). To show or declare such a set.

MISÈRE An undertaking to lose every trick.

NUMERALS Cards other than court cards. (There is no general English term, but the American is *spot cards*.)

OPPONENT Sometimes has also the specialised meaning of one who is playing against a solo player or declarer. Thus the opponents of the soloist are not necessarily opponents of one another.

OUVERT A game played *ouvert* is one in which the principal player's hand of cards is exposed to the view of his opponents.

OVERCALL To make a higher bid than the preceding bidder.

OVERTRICK A trick in excess of the number required to win.

PACK (Patience) To place one card on top of another which lies in sequence with it. Usually packing is carried out in reverse order from building – e.g. if you build in ascending sequence (A, 2, 3 etc), you pack in descending sequence (K, Q, J etc).

PASS To refrain from bidding.

PIP (–VALUE) Literally, a pip is a suit symbol printed on a card. The pip value of a card is its value when captured, for example in a trick. The term avoids confusion with 'points' in the scoring sense.

PLAIN SUIT One that is not trumps.

RANK The denomination of a card – e.g. Ace, King, Two Three and so on.

RENEGE Sometimes used in the senses of ruff or revoke or renounce, but perhaps best used in the sense of failing to follow suit in games or circumstances in which there is no legal requirement to do so.

RENOUNCE Loosely, to fail to follow suit; strictly, to play a card other than a trump when unable to follow suit.

REVOKE To fail to follow suit, even though able and required to do so, for which a penalty may be exacted.

ROUND Circumstance in which everybody around the table has had one, or an equal number, of opportunities to bid, play, receive cards etc. Also, for example, 'third round of trumps' means 'third occasion on which a trump has been led to a trick'.

RUBBER Equivalent to a match or tournament, the winner of a rubber being the first to win a certain number of games.

RUFF A trump. To play a trump to a non-trump lead.

SEQUENCE A set of cards in numerical or ranking sequence, such as A–2–3 or T–J–Q–K–A. In some games a sequence only counts if the constituent cards are also of the same suit.

SINGLETON The holding of only one card in a given suit.

SOLO(IST) A solo game is one in which one player (not usually called the soloist, though it seems the best word) undertakes to achieve his stated objective, without a partner, by playing against the combined efforts of everyone else to beat him.

STOCK The undealt portion of the pack if not all cards are dealt.

SUITE (Patience) A pile of cards, usually but not necessarily of the same suit, running in numerical order or *sequence*.

TABLEAU (Patience) An arrangement of rows, columns or other patterns of cards, in which cards are *packed* in sequence and from which they may be taken for *building*.

TRICK See Introduction p. 7.

TRUMP See Introduction p. 7.

VOID The holding of no cards in a given suit.

WIDOW A hand of cards dealt face down to the table (also called the *blind, skat, talon* or *kitty*), usually for the benefit of the highest bidder, who may exchange cards with them.

WILD CARD One that may represent any card its holder wishes.